The Development and Applications of Social Learning Theory

Centennial Psychology Series

Charles D. Spielberger, *General Editor*

The Development and Applications of Social Learning Theory

Selected Papers

Julian B. Rotter

PRAEGER

PRAEGER SPECIAL STUDIES • PRAEGER SCIENTIFIC

Library of Congress Cataloging in Publication Data

Rotter, Julian B.
  The development and applications of social
learning theory.

  (Centennial psychology series)
  Bibliography: p.
  Includes indexes.
  1. Social learning. 2. Personality. I. Title.
II. Series.
HQ783.R67 1982   155   82–16710
ISBN 0–03–059004–3

Published in 1982 by Praeger Publishers
CBS Educational and Professional Publishing
a Division of CBS Inc.
521 Fifth Avenue, New York, New York 10175, U.S.A.

© 1982 by Praeger Publishers

23456789 052 987654321

Printed in the United States of America

To My Students

Contents

Editor's Introduction

The founding of Wilhelm Wundt's laboratory at Leipzig in 1879 is widely acclaimed as the landmark event that provided the initial impetus for the development of psychology as an experimental science. To commemorate scientific psychology's one hundredth anniversary, Praeger Publishers commissioned the Centennial Psychology Series. The general goals of the Series are to present, in both historical and contemporary perspective, the most important papers of distinguished contributors to psychological theory and research.

As psychology begins its second century, the Centennial Series proposes to examine the foundation on which scientific psychology is built. Each volume provides a unique opportunity for the reader to witness the emerging theoretical insights of eminent psychologists whose seminal work has served to define and shape their respective fields, and to share with them the excitement associated with the discovery of new scientific knowledge.

The selection of the Series authors was an extremely difficult task. Indexes of scientific citations and rosters of the recipients of prestigious awards for research contributions were examined. Nominations were invited from leading authorities in various fields of psychology. The opinions of experienced teachers of psychology and recent graduates of doctoral programs were solicited. There was, in addition, a self-selection factor: a few of the distinguished senior psychologists invited to participate in the Series were not able to do so, most often because of demanding commitments or ill health.

Each Series author was invited to develop a volume comprising five major parts: (1) an original introductory chapter; (2) previously published articles and original papers selected by the author; (3) a concluding chapter; (4) a brief autobiography; and (5) a complete bibliography of the author's publications. The main content of each volume consists of articles and papers especially selected for this Series by the author. These papers trace the historical development of the author's work over a period of forty to fifty years. Each volume also provides a cogent presentation of the author's current research and theoretical viewpoints.

In their introductory chapters, Series authors were asked to describe the intellectual climate that prevailed at the beginning of their scientific careers, and to examine the evolution of the ideas that led them from one study to another. They were also invited to comment on significant factors—both scientific and personal— that stimulated and motivated them to embark on their research programs and to consider special opportunities or constraints that influenced their work, including experimental failures and blind alleys only rarely reported in the literature.

In order to preserve the historical record, most of the articles that are reprinted in the Series volumes have been reproduced exactly as they appeared when they were first published. In some cases, however, the authors have abridged their original papers (but not altered the content), so that redundant materials could be eliminated and more papers could be included.

In the concluding chapters, the Series authors were asked to comment on their selected papers, to describe representative studies on which they are currently working, and to evaluate the status of their research. They were also asked to discuss major methodological issues encountered in their respective fields of interest and to identify contemporary trends that are considered most promising for future scientific investigation.

The biographical sketch that is included in each Series volume supplements the autobiographical information contained in the original and concluding chapters. Perhaps the most difficult task faced by the Series authors was selecting a limited number of papers that they considered most representative from the complete bibliography of the author's life work that appears at the end of each volume.

The Centennial Psychology Series is especially designed for courses on the history of psychology. Individual volumes are also well suited for use as supplementary texts in those areas to which the authors have been major contributors. Students of psychology and related disciplines, as well as authorities in specialized fields, will find that each Series volume provides penetrating insight into the work of a significant contributor to the behavioral sciences. The Series also affords a unique perspective on psychological research as a living process.

Rotter's Contributions

Although general guidelines were suggested for each Series volume, the authors were encouraged to adapt the Series format to meet their individual needs. For this book, Professor Rotter has selected ten papers that reflect his highly original and creative contributions to the development of social learning theory, to methodology and empirical research on personality measurement, and to applications of social learning theory to problems of social importance.

Since the publication in 1954 of his classic book, *Social Learning and Clinical Psychology,* Rotter's work has reflected a unique integration of comprehensive theory; the assessment of theoretically relevant measures of individual differences; and empirical research on personality, psychopathology, and behavior change. The pervasive impact of social learning theory can be seen in the extensive research it has generated on personality change and, especially, in research on internal-external locus of control of reinforcement.

In the introductory chapter to this book and the brief biography of the author, Professor Rotter discusses some of the personal and professional experiences that have stimulated and guided his life work. Acknowledging his debt to early teachers, notably Alfred Adler, Kurt Lewin, and J. R. Kantor, Rotter recognizes the influence of Hull, Thorndyke, Tolman, and Krech in determining the starting point and influencing some of the directions taken in developing social learning theory. The basic assumptions and principles of social learning theory, as well as important ideas that preceded the theory and contributed to its development, are also described in the introductory chapter.

The reader will find the author's comments that precede each selected paper to be extremely helpful for understanding social learning theory. These comments serve to clarify the evolution and refinement of the theory and its applications to important social problems. The selected papers are organized according to the date the work described in each paper was conceived or initiated. Thus, reading the introductory comments and the papers in the order they appear in this book gives a unique perspective of the evolution and development of social learning theory.

In the final chapter, Professor Rotter provides succinct summaries of his distinguished contributions to three major areas of psychological science, and describes the general strategy for theory development that has guided his work. The discussion of important trends in social learning theory and his unique approach to the measurement of personality constructs provides valuable insights into the relationships between test-taking behavior and the nature of personality constructs. The importance of the psychological situation for understanding the significance of test responses and the role of a comprehensive theory for relating personality constructs to psychological tests represents an area in which Professor Rotter's contributions have been expecially important.

Acknowledgments

The interest and enthusiasm of all whom we have consulted concerning the establishment of the Series have been most gratifying, but I am especially grateful to Professors Anne Anastasi, Hans J. Eysenck, and Irving L. Janis for their many helpful comments and suggestions and for their early agreement to contribute to the Series. For his invaluable advice and consultation in the conception and planning of the Series, and for his dedicated and effective work in making it a reality, I am deeply indebted to Dr. George Zimmar, psychology editor for Praeger Publishers.

The Series was initiated while I was a Fellow-In-Residence at the Netherlands Institute for Advanced Study. I would like to express my appreciation to the director and staff of the Institute and to my NIAS colleagues for their stimulation, encouragement, and strong support of this endeavor.

Charles D. Spielberger

The Development and Applications of Social Learning Theory

1
Introduction

In selecting the papers to be included in this book, I have tried to keep in mind as a central theme the development, change, and applications of social learning theory. Social learning theory was developed in the years immediately following World War II and was presented originally in a series of mimeographed "tentative formulations," which were critically discussed with an extraordinary group of graduate students. The masters theses and doctoral dissertations of these students provided much of the empirical evidence testing the utility of the basic hypotheses of the theory. The culmination of this work, begun in 1946, was published in 1954 in a book titled *Social Learning and Clinical Psychology*. Although additions and refinements of the basic theory have continued, much of my work since that time has focused on applying the theory to problems in clinical, personality, and social psychology.

HISTORY OF SOCIAL LEARNING THEORY

Before I review the papers to follow and comment on their significance, some things need to be said about the theory itself. This theory did not, of course, spring full-blown from my head. It was, and remains, an attempt to synthesize the available knowledge and theorizing that preceded it. Alfred Adler was a strong early influence on my thinking. I was and continue to be impressed by his insights into human nature. He was neither a systematist in the modern sense

I would like to thank Dr. Dorothy J. Hochreich for her critical reading of this manuscript and her many helpful suggestions, and Ilene Whitacre for her valuable help in the preparation of this manuscript.

1

nor concerned with controlled studies of hypotheses, but his contributions were indeed great.

Kurt Lewin's first-hand influence and Clark Hull's books impressed me with the importance and potential value of carefully
articulated theory. Although the approaches of Adler and Lewin
contained many valuable insights, I felt that their theories lacked the
necessary ingredients to conceptualize the effects of past experience
in a way that would both explain and predict all behavior. For that
I had to turn to the learning theorists, not to discover who was right,
but to learn what each had to contribute to a reasonable theory that
would describe the behavior of *human beings* in complex environments. Some of the formulations of Clark Hull, E. L. Thorndike,
and E. C. Tolman, along with those of David Krech, found a place
in social learning theory. Finally, J. R. Kantor was influential in
setting out the broad assumptions of the theory, such as the rejection
of reductionism and the assumption that a truly psychological theory
was both possible and potentially useful.

The willingness to take concepts from many sources was not surprising at a time characterized by theoretical imperialism and the
practice of setting up straw men. Is a holistic view of psychology
better than an atomistic view? Is a perceptual explanation better
than a learning approach? Is a cognitive explanation better than a
behavioral one? I have learned to regard such questions as silly.
Theorists arguing one point of view often disregard or derogate data
and conclusions supporting the alternative view. It seemed clear to
me early in the game that these problems could be discussed intel-
ligently only when it was clear what aspects of behavior were the
focus of the prediction. Cognitive approaches were of little value in
predicting the behavior of rats; and approaches that did not take into
account the fact that human beings think, generalize along semantic
lines, and are motivated by social goals and reinforced by social reinforcements were extremely limited in their explanatory or predictive power. On the other hand, advocates of cognitive approaches
had had serious, though not insurmountable, problems in operation-
alizing their constructs. Thus every theory has its range of convenience—that is to say, its limitations. It follows that the utility of
any theory must be tested against the criterion of what exactly the
theory is designed to explain or predict.

Social learning theory in its earliest formulations was an attempt to integrate the two modern trends in American psychology—
the stimulus-response or reinforcement theories on the one hand,
and the cognitive or field theories on the other. Social learning
theory included both behavioral constructs and internal or subjective
constructs; but it required the performance of objective, indirect

operations to measure the subjective constructs. Consequently, the development of social learning theory has been concerned from the beginning with problems of measurement.

This social learning theory of personality involves both a *process theory* (that is, a theory of acquisition and change of learned, relatively stable, personal characteristics) and a *content theory*—a descriptive schema of individual differences. The process theory is necessary in order to study the effects of new experience and to apply general laws to individuals. The content, or descriptive, theory is necessary to achieve some efficiency in relating experience with one individual to the case of another who is similar in some important respect, and to describe in broader terms the effects of experience. However, a content theory is useful only if it is tied to useful methods of measurement and is consistent with the process theory. Consequently, several of the papers that follow are concerned with both methods of measurement and theoretical problems of measurement.

Social learning theory is a psychological theory: it begins with unlearned responses but does not attempt to delineate the antecedents of such unlearned responses. Although it is concerned with acquisition of new behaviors or modified unlearned responses, it explains such behavior at a molar level. New responses occur as unlearned or previously learned responses and are modified or combined into more refined or more complex behavior, a process speeded up by direct reinforcement or expected reinforcement through imitation.

The nature of unlearned reinforcements is similarly dealt with in social learning theory (SLT). In other words, we use an empirical law of effect and accept that certain stimulus conditions will result in an unlearned positive or negative state of the organism (reinforcement). Previously neutral stimulus conditions obtain value through their association with other already valued stimuli. However, the molecular conditions determining that association (that is, time, distances, objective similarity) are not of central concern to the theory. Data or theories that are directly concerned with these issues could, nevertheless, be entirely consistent with SLT and extend its predictive range.

Although physiological-stimulus drive reduction may be an antecedent of *some* unlearned reinforcements, we can dispense with the unnecessary and probably erroneous assumption that *all* unlearned reinforcements are the result of drive reduction or that secondary reinforcements are maintained because they lead to reduction of primal drives.

The name *social learning theory* derives from the principles that

(1) reinforcement is not tied to physiological drives or drive stimulus reduction, and (2) in complex postinfancy human behavior, it is the behavior of other humans—that is, social reinforcement—that becomes the more important determinant of behavior.

The term *social learning* was later used by Bandura and Walters (1963) to describe an approach to personality with a strong emphasis on learning by imitation, with a theoretical justification derived from Spence. Later, Bandura changed his view (Bandura, 1977) to de-emphasize drive reduction and to give a central place to expectancies and other cognitive variables. However, Bandura's approach still differs from this social learning theory in many ways; most important, it does not offer a systematic way to describe or explain relatively stable, generalized aspects of personality. In other words, it does not provide a comprehensive and systematic basis for de-scribing individual differences in generalized terms and the relation-ships among these relatively stable, generalized characteristics.

In the papers that follow, SLT will be explicated and brought up to date. It is important to bear in mind that the theory is focused on personality and personality change. It is helpful in under-standing this theory to recognize that it was devised with practical ends in mind. The motive for developing the theory was not abstract curiosity but, ultimately, the desire to be able to predict and change the behavior of individuals more efficiently. Although the theory can be and has been applied to other problems, its main emphasis has been to (1) develop an adequate process theory to explain how people learn or acquire their characteristic behaviors and attitudes; (2) pre-dict behavioral choice by the individual in a given situation; (3) develop a reliable, efficient discriptive language, integrated with the process theory, to delineate individual differences in behavior in the same or similar situations; and (4) understand how and under what conditions such attitudes and behaviors change.

The basic assumptions of SLT were described in considerable detail in 1954 in *Social Learning and Clinical Psychology*. They will be described here briefly, as they will serve to orient the reader to the papers that follow and will allow me to acknowledge some of my debts to others whose ideas preceded the development of this theory.

BASIC ASSUMPTIONS OF SOCIAL LEARNING THEORY

Above all else, SLT adopts a construct point of view. That is, we re-gard scientific terms as constructs—abstractions of some aspect or aspects of events. The ultimate test of their validity is their utility in prediction. One does not ask of an event, "What is it really?" but, rather, "How do I abstract some aspect of the event in order to obtain my purpose most efficiently?" One does not ask, "What is intelligence or schizophrenia really?" but, rather, "Are these good constructs for the purpose of predicting behavior or understanding how to change behavior from a particular point of view or interest?"

The first principle of SLT states:

1. *The unit of investigation for the study of personality is the interaction of the individual and his or her meaningful environment.* This statement essentially provides the basis for a field-theory approach to personality. Other approaches—such as Freud's (1938) instincts or mind entities, Kraepelin's (1913) disease entities, or Sheldon's (1942) constitutional types—seem to attempt to predict without systematic recourse to the environment or the situation. SLT takes the position that most predictive instances require an adequate description of the situation before useful predictions can be made. Reliance solely on internal determinants or states results in either highly general predictions or else inaccurate ones. The importance of a situational point of view is reflected throughout this book, and we shall have many occasions to illustrate it and comment on it.

This is clearly an interactionist approach to personality and behavior—a position recently regaining some popularity (Magnusson, 1981). J. R. Kantor (1924) and Kurt Lewin (1935), both former teachers of mine, systematically pressed this point of view, as did H. A. Murray (1938) and W. Coutu (1949). Many others writing in fields other than personality have also espoused this principle. It is easier to advocate than to put into practice, however, because it requires *both* a language of description for psychological situations or meaningful environments *and* a language of description for the relevant individual differences, if one is to be able to accumulate knowledge and make predictions.

Since the theory deals with human social behavior, the learning emphasis should be apparent. We accept the notion that the major portion of human social behavior is learned or modifiable behavior. This does not rule out the possibility that there may be other ways of describing human behavior. Likewise, there are important aspects of human behavior that cannot be described from a learning point of view—particularly the antecedents of early learned behavior, which may require other kinds of descriptions.

As a corollary of the previous postulate, SLT uses a historical approach to the study of personality. That is, in order to understand adequately, explain, or in some instances even describe personality, it is necessary to investigate antecedent events in the life of the individual. Obviously, the past does not cause the present; the past no longer exists except in its current residual effects. Nonetheless, it is our thesis that recourse to the past is necessary because our descriptive and diagnostic technology currently are not nearly adequate enough to allow us to depend solely on an ahistorical approach. It should be recognized, however, that the degree of reconstruction of the past that is necessary must always be gauged in terms of one's predictive purposes.

2. *Personality constructs are not dependent for explanation on constructs in any other field* (including physiology, biology, or neurology). Scientific constructs for one mode of description should be consistent with constructs in any other field of science, but no hierarchy of dependency exists among them.

3. *Behavior as described by personality constructs takes place in space and time.* Although all such events may be described by psychological constructs, it is presumed that they may also be described by physical constructs, as they are in such fields as physics, chemistry, and neurology. *Any conception that regards the events themselves (rather than the descriptions of the events) as different is rejected as dualistic.*

In effect, the two preceding principles reject notions of both reductionism and dualism. It is certainly true that descriptions of events are often correlated. For example, we may describe a child afflicted with Down's syndrome in terms of chromosomal anomalies, epicanthic folds, and so forth. These are primarily *physical* descriptions. At the same time, we may discuss the child in terms of IQ points, frustration tolerance, affectional needs, and the like. These are essentially *psychological* constructs. Although a correlation between descriptive levels often exists, it does not follow that it is better science to reduce psychological descriptions to a physical level of abstraction. As Cantor and Cromwell (1957) and Jessor (1958) point out, there are some basic difficulties with a reductionistic point of view. First, the implication often exists that by moving from molar levels to more molecular ones (from sociology to psychology or from psychology to biochemistry, for example), we get closer to truth or reality. As noted earlier, however, no description of behavior is "*true.*" At best, one description is more useful *for a particular purpose* than for another. No theory or description is anything more than a construction of reality imposed by the scientist for predictive purposes.

Second, it is often claimed that reduction to smaller units located within the organism necessarily improves prediction. Such a contention is not borne out, however. Each theory or description has a range of convenience. Although one might consult a neurologist concerning an abnormal reflex, one typically would not consult him to predict the outcome of a presidential election. The level of description employed is a function of the questions that need to be answered.

The second of the two immediately preceding postulates deals with *dualism.* Any conception that regards physiological events as causing psychological events is considered dualistic. Such terms as *physiological, psychological, biochemical,* and so forth refer to descriptive levels, not to reality. Therefore, to say that something physiological causes something psychological (or the reverse) is to say that one description causes another. J. R. Kantor (1947) has shown in great detail how the rejection of psychological constructs is in itself not monism, but an implied dualism that does not differentiate between events and descriptions of events.

4. *Not all behavior of an organism may be usefully described with personality constructs. Behavior that may usefully be described by personality constructs appears in organisms at a particular level or stage of complexity and a particular level or stage of development.* This postulate simply recognizes that each construction system has a particular range of convenience. Not all events can be usefully described in personality terms. Just as some events are not amenable to description in chemical terms, so too do some events resist psychological conceptualization. Indeed, currently it is uncertain at what species level or at what point in the development of the human individual psychological constructs begin usefully to apply. Undoubtedly, these are empirical questions. Physiological or other constructs may be useful for describing some of the conditions present when personality characteristics are first acquired.

Likewise, physiological or other constructs may be used by psychologists for any practical purpose. This is especially true when stable correlations between physiological and psychological descriptions have been found and when, practically, it is difficult to make both kinds of observations. Physiological descriptions alone are often valuable in indicating what the individuals *cannot* do but are rarely useful in predicting what they *will* do.

An individual may interact with him- or herself in the sense of using learned meanings (or symbols) that describe in physiological terms or terms characteristic of other modes of description. For example, the person may learn to describe him- or herself as "hungry," or "sexually aroused." Such reactions may usefully be described in psychological terms. These reactions, although they use physiological language, may correlate very poorly with actual organic states as described by the physiologist. This disparity is illustrated in work on emotions (Schacter, 1966) wherein two individuals, reacting to exactly the same chemical stimulation, nonetheless reported widely varying descriptions of their emotional states, depending on the environmental cues present.

5. *A person's experiences (or a person's interactions with his or her meaningful environment) influence each other. In other words, personality has unity.*

Typically, the concept of *unity* has had at least two meanings. In the first, unity is defined essentially in terms of a core personality; that is, each individual is thought of as possessing a core unity that largely determines all of his or her behavior. A second meaning of the term *unity* is the one intended here, however. That is, unity is defined in terms of relative stability and interdependence. As the individual becomes more experienced, personality becomes increasingly stable. The process of mediated stimulus generalization accounts in large part for this increasing stability and generality of responses to a class of situations. Individuals tend to select new experiences and interpretations of reality on the basis of previous experiences and conceptualizations. However, the presence of relative stability and generality does not mean that specificity of response and change with new experience are not also important principles of behavior.

SLT also attempts to discard the term *cause* in favor of a view that holds that adequate description in terms of relevant past and present conditions is a more useful approach to explanation. What actually is required is a specification of antecedent conditions adequate for prediction. How far back in time to go in terms of these antecedent conditions depends on the degree of predictive accuracy desired and the use to be made of the information.

6. *Behavior as described by personality constructs has a directional aspect. It may be said to be goal-directed. The directional aspect of behavior is inferred from the effect of reinforcing conditions.* This directional nature of behavior, accounting for selective response to cues and for choice behavior, is the motivational focus of SLT. The individual seeks to maximize his or her positive reinforcements in any situation. *Directionality* does not imply teleology, nor does *maximization of rewards* imply that the individual is incapable of planning or thinking in such a way that he or she chooses lesser rewards now in order to obtain greater rewards later.

The preceding principle is based on an *empirical law of effect.* Historically, a great deal of theoretical difficulty has arisen when reinforcement has been defined in drive-reduction terms. When one is dealing with simple organisms or behaviors, it is relatively easy to define a reinforcement as anything that reduces a drive. When one deals with human social behavior, however, the problem is different. For example, how can one show that a person who is very high in need achievement has experienced drive or need reduction through receiving an A in a college course? In short, the reinforcement of an enduring psychological need does not appear to reduce the individual's need, even temporarily.

Many object to an empirical law of effect because it appears circular; that is, there is no definition of a reinforcer independent of behavior. One cannot know whether something is reinforcing until the behavior has occurred. In practical terms, this is true if one is dealing with an individual from an unfamiliar culture. It also may be true to a degree in more familiar circumstances, inasmuch as most of us are sometimes motivated by relatively idiosyncratic goals. In some psychopathological cases, such idiosyncrasies pose particular problems. Individuals may occasionally show behavior that seems to resist explanation largely because the goals involved are dramatically different from those expected by most people. (Indeed, perhaps the sensitivity of some clinicians can be ascribed in part to the fact that they are very astute in ferreting out these extraordinary goals.)

Were it true that reinforcements or potential reinforcements could be identified *only* after they had occurred, then the concept truly would be circular. However, it *is* practically possible to identify specific events that have a known effect either for groups or for individuals. In such instances *predictions*—not just *postdictions*—can be made successfully. Pragmatically, as long as we can describe and identify objectively potential reinforcers in the majority of situations, there is no serious problem of circularity. Meehl (1950) has discussed this issue in great detail; the current emphasis on operant approaches also testifies to the efficacy of this view.

Drive reduction as an alternative view of reinforcement ceases to be useful in the study of complex social behavior. Needs—striving for recognition, love, social acceptance, dominance, and so forth—are not cyclical, so that hours of deprivation cannot be used as the operational measure for drive state. Nor can it be demonstrated that, following reinforcement, the social need is reduced or some presumed primary drive is reduced.

This SLT view of reinforcement is also consistent with studies of direct brain stimulation (Grossman, 1967; Olds & Olds, 1965) that indicate different brain centers for positive and negative reinforcement, as well as different patterns of response to such stimulation. Neurophysiologically, it seems well established that positive and negative reinforcements are two different processes that depend, at least originally, on built-in characteristics of the organism. Further,

they do not require the innervation of noncentral nerve centers involved in drive reduction.

In discussing motivation it is appropriate at this point to indicate
that when we focus on the environmental conditions that determine
the direction of behavior, we speak of *goals* or reinforcements. On
the other hand, when we focus on the person determining the direction, then we speak of *needs*. Both needs and goals are inferred from
the same referents—the interaction of the person with his or her
meaningful environment. Thus the distinction between goals and
needs is a semantic convenience.

Several additional points should be made about the nature of
needs. The needs of a person as described by personality constructs
are learned or acquired. Early goals or needs, and perhaps some later
ones, may be regarded as arising from association of new experiences
with reinforcement of reflex or unlearned behavior. Most later goals
or needs are acquired as a means of satisfying earlier, learned goals.
Learned behavior is goal-directed, and new goals derive their importance for the individual from their associations with earlier goals.

A person's behaviors, needs, and goals are not independent but
exist within functionally related systems. The nature of these relationships also is determined by previous experience. Although this
point will be discussed in greater detail subsequently, it is important
to point out here that many behaviors can lead to the same goal and
that many subgoals derive their reinforcing properties because they
lead in turn to the same, more comprehensive goal. Thus a group of
behaviors all culminating in the same effect will develop a greater degree of intergroup similarity than will a group of randomly selected
behaviors. Similarly, the values of a group of reinforcers that have
been associated with the same past satisfaction will have greater intergroup similarity than a random group of reinforcers. In other words,
prediction need not involve just specific behavior-reinforcement sequences, but may also involve groups of functionally related behaviors or reinforcements.

7. *The occurrence of a behavior of a person is determined not
only by the nature or importance of goals or reinforcements, but also
by the person's anticipation or expectancy that these goals will
occur. Such expectations are determined by previous experience and
can be quantified.* This principle is an attempt to handle the question
of how the individual in a given situation behaves in terms of potential reinforcers. The assumption is that a concept dealing with anticipation of reinforcement is necessary in order to account for behavior
directed at specific goals. In short, one needs a concept other than
simple value of reinforcement to account for human behavior.

Inclusion of an *expectancy* construct is now a growing trend in human psychological theory. Earlier theorists such as Tolman (1934), Brunswik (1951), and Postman (1951) expressed an expectancy point of view. The seminal views of Lewin (1951) in this area were also important to me.

The following papers will be preceded by commentary designed to show how they fit into the sequence of development, refinement, and application of SLT. The order is chronological, according to when the work was begun or conceived. This order will be close to, but not always identical with, the dates of publication.

REFERENCES

Bandura, A. Self-efficacy: Toward a unifying theory of behavior change. *Psychological Review*, 1977, *84*, 121–125.

Bandura, A., & Walters, R. H. *Social learning and personality.* New York: Holt, Rinehart and Winston, 1963.

Brunswik, E. The probability point of view. In M. H. Marx (Ed.), *Psychological theory.* New York: Macmillan, 1951.

Cantor, G. N., & Cromwell, R. L. The principle of reductionism and mental deficiency. *American Journal of Mental Deficiency*, 1957, *61*, 461–466.

Coutu, W. *Emergent human nature.* New York: Knopf, 1949.

Freud, S. *The basic writings of Sigmund Freud.* New York: Random House, 1938. (First German edition, 1904.)

Grossman, S. P. *A textbook of physiological psychology.* New York: Wiley, 1967.

Jessor, R. The problem of reductionism in psychology. *Psychological Review*, 1958, *65*, 170–178.

Kantor, J. R. *Principles of psychology* (Vols. 1, 2). New York: Knopf, 1924.

Kantor, J. R. *Problems of physiological psychology.* Bloomington, Ind.: Principia Press, 1947.

Kraepelin, E. *Lectures on clinical psychiatry.* London: Bailliere, Tindall, and Cox, 1913.

Lewin, K. *A dynamic theory of personality.* New York: McGraw-Hill, 1935.

Lewin, K. The nature of field theory. In M. H. Marx (Ed.) *Psychological theory.* New York: Macmillan, 1951.

Magnusson, D. (Ed.). *Toward a psychology of situations: An interactional perspective.* Hillsdale, N.J.: Lawrence Erlbaum Associates, 1981.

Meehl, P. E. On the circularity of the law of effect. *Psychological Bulletin,* 1950, *47*, 52–75.

Murray, H. A. *Explorations in Personality.* New York: Oxford University Press, 1938.

Olds, J., & Olds, M. Drives, rewards and the brain. In *New directions in psychology II.* New York: Holt, Rinehart and Winston, 1965.

Postman, L. Toward a general theory of cognition. In J. H. Rohrer & M. Sherif

(Eds.), *Social psychology at the crossroads*. New York: Harper, 1951. Pp. 242–272.

Rotter, J. B. *Social learning and clinical psychology*. New York: Johnson Reprint Company, 1973, 1980. (Originally published, 1954.)

Rotter, J. B. The role of the psychological situation in determining the direction of human behavior. In M. R. Jones (Ed.), *Nebraska Symposium on Motivation*, vol. 3. Lincoln: University of Nebraska Press, 1955. Pp. 245–269.

Rotter, J. B. The psychological situation in social learning theory. In D. Magnusson (Ed.), *Toward a psychology of situations: An interactional perspective*. Hillsdale, N.J.: Lawrence Erlbaum Associates, 1981.

Schacter, S. The interaction of cognitive and physiological determinants of emotional state. In C. D. Spielberger (Ed.), *Anxiety and behavior*. New York: Academic Press, 1966. Pp. 193–224.

Sheldon, W. H. *The varieties of temperament: A psychology of constitutional differences*. New York: Harper, 1942.

Tolman, E. C. Theories of learning. In F. A. Moss (Ed.), *Comparative psychology*. Englewood Cliffs, N.J.: Prentice-Hall, 1934.

Commentary to Chapter 2

Although this paper was published in 1944, an earlier version of it, written in 1939, in my second year of graduate work, represents the first theoretical article I attempted. It also shows very clearly the influence of Alfred Adler, with whom I had worked in my last two years as an undergraduate at Brooklyn College; at that time Adler was professor of medical psychology at the Long Island College of Medicine.

The paper also represents my earliest anticipatory formulation of the basic formula of SLT: B.P. = f(E & RV). In the case of stuttering, the proposition in this paper would read, "The behavior of stuttering is dependent on the availability of stuttering as a symptom based on past experience and the strength of the purpose or need that it would satisfy." The emphasis on the purposefulness of symptoms comes clearly from Adler. The analysis of the eight cases and their treatment was also heavily influenced by Adler.

In Adler's studies of patients, he always tried to discover the specific circumstances in which the symptom was learned; for example, the child who became enuretic after a displacing child was brought home from the hospital and the mother ignored him in order to change the infant's diapers. He did not use the term avail-ability, but he clearly implied something similar. The concept of the availability of the behavior, defense, or symptom was later replaced by expectancy—*a more measurable and all-inclusive term.*

Another influence involved here was that of Wendell Johnson, a general semanticist from whom I learned, among other things, to be careful in the use of words. Consequently, there was an attempt in this early paper to define terms explicitly, so that their referents were clear. At the time stuttering was usually regarded, at least in speech-correction circles, as the result of some organic dysfunction. It was the work of Johnson and his students that convinced me that stuttering might be better viewed as a psychological or attitudinal disorder. Many people had frequent speech interruptions but were not considered stutterers. Others had normal speech for their age but became stutterers without any obvious change in their organic functioning. Attitudes of parents and other significant adults seemed to be more important antecedents of stuttering than was simple frequency of speech interruption.

2

The Nature and Treatment of Stuttering: A Clinical Approach

From a previous experimental study (6), the author inferred a relationship between those environmental factors which are commonly called "pampering" and the occurrence of stuttering. If such factors play any etiological role in stuttering, this earlier study did not demonstrate in what manner they operate. In order to discover this, the history prior to stuttering and the development of the stuttering reaction were examined extensively in eight adults. An hypothesis became sufficiently well formulated that a therapeutic approach which it indicated was undertaken on five of the cases as a partial test of its validity. The history-taking and the therapy were carried out under somewhat controlled conditions as described below.

SUBJECTS AND PROCEDURE

The main criterion used in selecting the cases was the possibility of finding sufficient time when both the investigator and the case could meet conveniently. The general personality adjustment of the cases, as externally observed, and the severity of their stuttering covered a wide range. They were all of average or superior intelligence, in terms of Otis mental test scores. All but one (Case 2) had been subject to some previous form of therapy.

Rotter, Julian B. The nature and treatment of stuttering: A clinical approach. *Journal of Abnormal and Social Psychology*, 1944, *39*, 150–173. Copyright 1944 by the American Psychological Association. Reprinted by permission of the publisher and author.

The case work on which this article is partially based was done at The State University of Iowa under the general direction of Professor Wendell Johnson.

In the recording of histories, until a fairly complete and coherent picture was obtained the investigator refrained from any active interpretation or suggestion that might color the information given. However, it should be admitted that the nature of the questions tended to bring out certain kinds of information, although the material obtained must be regarded as factual.

Although an attempt was made to avoid bias in selecting subjects, the conclusions based on the study of cases do not rest on an assumption of random sampling or the number of cases studied. However, the author firmly believes that any general laws which hold for individuals who stutter operate in *every* individual case and are discoverable if the case is studied intensely enough. In fact the study of single factors in large numbers of subjects often acts to obscure the general laws which may be present. At least in the early stages of the investigation of a field, the thorough study of individual cases may well be more efficient for arriving at hypotheses.

The sources of information were as follows: (1) Direct questioning in regard to past events and attitudes; that is, with emphasis placed on actual events and on daily situational variations as well as variations over the entire ontogenetic development. (2) The subjects, parents, and in some cases teachers, were asked to describe their version of the circumstances preceding and during the onset of stuttering. (3) Before the subject could possibly discover any theoretical bias on the part of the investigator he was asked to write out in detail all of his earliest memories.[1] (4) The subject was asked to list in detail situations, goals, etc. (*a*) where he felt stuttering was a handicap; (*b*) where it made little or no difference; and (*c*) where it actually was of some help. He was also asked to list the situations which he feared most from the speech viewpoint. (5) After the subject was well along in therapy he was asked to write an autobiography, which in some cases produced additional facts.

The eight case histories given below are obviously not complete and are concerned almost wholly with psychological conditions. Information concerning organic states and ordinary civil facts was obtained but was not included here unless it seemed to have some important bearing on the development and course of the stuttering. At the conclusion of each history the interpretations of the author, based on his own evaluation of the case material, are presented. Once treatment was begun the subjects dropped all other therapeutic

---

[1] A discussion of the significance and interpretation of such earliest memories is given by Adler (1).

approaches. A detailed description of the therapeutic procedure will be given later. . . . [Seven additional case histories have been deleted.]

CASE 8, HELEN

Age 26, female, awkward in appearance. At least average intelligence. Attending first-year high school. Acts and dresses like a girl at least ten years younger. Background is marginal rural, parents poorly educated.

The youngest of ten children, she states that she was the favorite of the father until she was about twelve. From then on he no longer favored her. She stated that after this time he began to be rough to her. Her earliest memories, of which she reports a considerable number going back as far as two and a half years, are almost all concerned with her sisters, particularly the two nearest her age with whom intense feelings of rivalry were still evident. Although it was difficult to get any precise notion of the home background, we know the family was Catholic and quite religious and that two of her sisters have become nuns. She states that the sister nearest her in age dominated her as a child and made her feel inferior. In school she was always conscious of being awkward. She left school after finishing grammar grades and worked on the farm. When about sixteen she exhibited a great deal of jealousy and aggression towards her next oldest sister and a niece of her own age who were being "taken out" by two brothers. When questioned about her sexual attitudes she replied that if she stayed close to religion she would not be tempted sexually or in other forms of sin. She had never gone out with a young man and stated that kissing was sinful. Around the home she had to work hard as all the older brothers and sisters were leaving. Helen claimed that she could not go to business school, or get married, because she had to take care of her parents, who were not very appreciative of her efforts.

Speech History

Helen states that she began to have trouble with her speech around the age of ten. However, this must be something of an afterthought as nobody paid any attention to her speech as being different at this time, and she says that is was not at all prominent. About the age of fourteen it suddenly became more evident. This was at the same time that her sister and niece began to go out with the two brothers. At the end of that year she decided that the young man going out with her sister really loved her and not her sister and that she could marry him except for the fact that she was a stutterer. At sixteen she noticed an advertisement for curing stuttering by correspondence. She took this course, spending large amounts of time "doing her lessons aloud," and at the same time her stuttering became much more severe. It continued to be severe until the age of twenty-five when all of the brothers and sisters had left home and the parents were much too old to care whether Helen stuttered or not.

At this time she came to the Iowa Speech Clinic to be cured of the stuttering that had practically disappeared before she came. She decided to go back to school and entered the first year of high school. At first her contact with other stutterers and the clinic as a whole exaggerated her own stuttering but after a short period she cleared up rapidly except for occasional blocks which, when they did occur, were very long and severe. She tried shifting handedness and later the bounce technique. When beginning conferences her only blocks were rare, long, easy "bounces" which were accompanied by a smile and seeming enjoyment. When she thought that she was alone she usually talked to herself aloud. She stated that she had been doing this for the last few years and that she also spent a great deal of time daydreaming. Her voice was high-pitched and sounded like that of a child of thirteen. She appeared to receive a great deal of satisfaction from working on her stuttering and followed all instructions and assignments slavishly. When asked to list the situations where stuttering was a handicap she listed a series of words on which she "always" stuttered. She was asked to read them and did so without blocking on any of them. For ways that stuttering was of some help she gave a list of easy situations. When corrected as to the assignment she finally stated that, "It has given me a deeper insight into how other people feel when they are humiliated; also a deeper and kinder understanding of their sorrows and difficulties." After a few weeks of conferences she was told casually that someone who had heard her talk did not think that she was a stutterer. The following day when in "stutterers' class" she was called on to speak and said quite angrily and fluently, "I hear that there is a rumor that I have stopped stuttering and am no longer a stutterer and I would like to find out who the person is who started it because it certainly is not so." This fluent outburst was then followed by a very long bounce accompanied with an expression of great pain.

Interpretation

This girl shows many neurotic signs entirely apart from any stuttering. Her complete isolation at the time of coming to Iowa, the excessive phantasies, the desire still to be a child and her consequent childlike behavior, her strong feelings of inferiority and her sexual inhibitions, are some of them. The stuttering arose just about the same time that her father no longer favored her but began to be rough towards her. It increased when competition with her sister and niece began to enter the heterosexual field and immediately became an excuse for her own lack of success in that field. The advertisement in the magazine convinced her even further that this was a good way to protect herself against a feeling of being a failure and she spent much time with her lessons bringing the stuttering to everybody's attention as much as possible. When there was no longer anyone at home to impress with her handicap the stuttering became less severe and she first decided to come to Iowa. Once at Iowa her speech became worse as she found a new group whom she could impress with her handicap, but improved rapidly as such behavior brought social approval. However, she would improve only so far and no further, possibly having no intention of ever giving up this mechanism unless an equally good one be substituted for it.

DISCUSSION OF CASE HISTORIES

In reviewing these case histories certain common points present themselves. Perhaps the most striking of these is the wide variations in speech from severe stuttering to none at all. This is evident in both the ontogenetic and cross-sectional history of the individual. One stutterer may have blocks with one individual and not with another; one may always stutter when speaking over a phone, another never; one more at school and one more at home; and for all of them there are periods when they did not stutter at all or only very slightly and periods when their stuttering was very severe. In fact we might almost say that this variability is one of the most characteristic behavior reactions of stuttering and that the key to understanding stuttering as a whole, or the stuttering of any single stutterer, lies in understanding the nature and reasons for these variations. It is immediately apparent in all these cases that no physiological, "habitual," or heredity theory can account for these variations. However, they did follow in every case clear-cut psychological lines which could account for both the long-term and immediate, daily variations. Such a psychological explanation was always in terms of the stutterers' goals and their feelings of adequacy or inadequacy.

A second outstanding similarity in these cases is that at the onset the stuttering always seemed to come from "without" rather than from "within." That is, the child never seemed merely to have something happen to his speech either gradually or suddenly due to some inner physiological condition, but what did occur was that some event or series of events changed his own attitude to the speech he had always had. None of these cases started to stutter without first discovering that interruptions in speech had some very definite effect on the people around him. It may be that in several of these instances the teacher and parents were simply reacting to the child's general state of upset rather than to the speech alone. However, in these cases the child felt they were reacting to his speech as that was the most dramatic manifestation of the emotional disturbance. Many children, however, go through similar experiences and do not become stutterers. Any theory of stuttering must also allow for other factors which will account for the continuance of these interruptions in some cases and not in others.

The manner in which "pampering" operated in the development of stuttering seemed also to be clearly indicated in all these cases.[2] It appears that the pampering has an indirect effect by giving rise to fears and feelings of inadequacy or inferiority which result in emotional breakdown, under certain conditions, and the consequent inability to control speech. The child pampered at home meets situations outside of the home in which he is treated differently. These act as traumata and the feelings of inadequacy center about the very thing the child has always received the most of but suddenly feels he is no longer receiving.

In the case of all these stutterers some such need was served in the beginning and during the course of the stuttering. That is to say, after the stuttering reaction became available to the child and took on some special meaning, such as, "this will excuse me from recitation," or "this will bring me a great deal of attention," or "this will make my mother concerned over me so that she has to protect me even more," or any other, the speech reaction persisted if it fitted in with the particular needs of the child at that time.

A fourth striking element in all these histories lies in the generality of the attitude towards stuttering. The subject who used stuttering as a rationalization for failure had many other mechanisms by which he rationalized failure. The subject who developed stuttering following displacement by a younger sister also developed many other mechanisms unconsciously designed to retain control of the parents. To use an expression of Adler's, we can say that the stuttering and the attitude towards it were always characteristic of the subject's whole "style of life."

UNDERSTANDING STUTTERING

An examination of the experimental literature as well as clinical evidence points to the impossibility of defining stuttering simply in terms of speech alone. Many so-called normal speakers have more frequent and longer speech blocks or interruptions than some stut-

---

[2] Pampering was defined in the earlier article already cited as including ". . . those types of behavior that are sometimes called babying, spoiling, over-protecting, etc. It can be described as that type of training which affects the child so that he becomes dependent on others to do things for him and to solve his problems, so that the child feels inadequate to solve his own problems successfully."

terers. Cases have even been reported of people coming to a speech clinic because they were afraid that they would "stutter" but who actually had quite fluent speech.

Of the eight cases included in this study seven could talk to themselves when absolutely alone without any speech interruptions, the eighth had occasional interruptions, however much less than usual. This finding has been duplicated in other clinics. This is only one of a whole wealth of facts that point to the inadequacy of either defining or understanding stuttering merely in terms of speech mechanisms. The definition to be given here is in part suggested by the work of Wendell Johnson. *Stuttering is defined as a rhythmic disorder in speech in a person who is aware of his speech as being different from that of other people and who reacts to it as if it were a handicap.*

It is also necessary to define the word "need" which has already been used frequently. As used here "need" is not to be confused with the term as applied to connote a relatively undifferentiated physiological state. It seems sufficient for present purposes to define a need as *a behavioral tendency to attain a particular goal or complex of goals of which the individual may or may not be aware.* That is, a need is the behavioral coordinate of a goal.

This theory states that in order for a child to begin stuttering two simultaneous conditions must exist. These are the availability of stuttering and the need for it. By availability is meant some meaningful contact with the phenomena of stuttering so that a definite attitude is taken towards interruptions in speech through the behavior of the people in the immediate environment. So, the child who has a relative or close friend who stutters, and who is treated in some characteristic fashion by the people around him, has stuttering available to him. The child who has never heard the word "stutterer" but is causing concern and comment from his parents or teachers because "he is speaking too rapidly" or "stumbling over his words" has stuttering available to him. The child who finds people reacting to his own emotional states with their consequent loss of speech control and the child whose speech pattern is hesitant either through training or organic causes, and sooner or later finds that he may belong in a special class of people due to his speech, have stuttering available.

The need is not for stuttering as such but for a mechanism which will serve some definite purpose. So, the need exists with the child who wishes to avoid the painful situation of reciting, for the child who wishes to gain attention, for the one who wishes to wrest back control of the parents from a sibling, for someone who finds it necessary to find an excuse for a particular failure, and then for all future imagined failures; it is present in the child who wants to convince his parents that he requires more protection than he is getting. It might be argued that such needs are present with almost all children, but in order for them to result in some such behavior as stuttering it must be so great that other goals such as direct achievement and the admiration of other school children are willingly sacrificed for this more important one.

For stuttering to persist it must serve some important purpose— one that is in keeping with the whole experiential history and with the whole organization of the personality. This purpose may change with time; it may remain and others be added; it may remain constant; or it is possible that the need may disappear in the adult and the stuttering remain. In the latter case the habitual speech pattern persists but this may change slowly to become less and less unusual or will be cleared up entirely by almost any kind of therapy. The fact that almost any treatment, no matter how weird, will result in some permanent cures is accounted for here by the cases we consider as those where the need has disappeared.[3] In these cases the environment, so to speak, forces the individual into a situation where the defense is no longer necessary. Some good man or woman, for example, shows them that they need not defend themselves against the thesis that "no one loves me"; or, as in the case of the stutterer who received a job teaching because of the shortage of commercial teachers, they no longer need to defend themselves against the feeling that they cannot cope with the world themselves, and, as he did, they may give up stuttering completely. In most cases the actual purpose changes or at least takes on additional meanings. What may start as a method of gaining attention may become a means of protecting oneself against the feared failures in the realms of sexual and occupational achievement.[4]

It is apparent that this theory did not arise solely out of an examination of these eight cases and the experiment that motivated this study, but from clinical experience with many cases of stutterers and nonstutterers and contact with the literature in the field of psy-

---

[3] Sometimes, however, it is also possible, under conditions of strong suggestion, for the subject to give up one mechanism and to substitute another.

[4] It has been stated at times that the stutterer does not stutter because he is insecure but is insecure because he stutters. Although in this paper we have tried to relate insecurity to the etiology of stuttering we must admit that there is some circularity in this relationship. The individual who has already begun to stutter (in other terms, one who has already developed secondary reactions) finds, particularly as he approaches adulthood, that the stuttering brings considerable punishment. Under these circumstances he may stop stuttering, as many do, or, becoming more insecure, he may lean even more heavily on his "handicap" as a defense mechanism.

chology and stuttering. It is impossible to discuss all or even a large part of the theoretical and research literature on stuttering in relation to this theory; however, it is necessary to examine certain main lines of evidence.

Other extensive, published case histories seem to fall as easily into this framework as the eight given here. For example Johnson's (4) autobiographical history and the cases published by Brown (2) contain all the necessary elements outlined above.

The evidence from the many physiological lines of work at first seems to oppose such a formulation. However, there are two important characteristics of these studies to be considered. The neurophysiological disturbances are not consistent from stutterer to stutterer nor are they consistent within the individual. Just as a hand functions differently when it is lifting a ten-pound weight than when lifting a one-ounce weight, so does the neurophysiological mechanism function differently when the individual is stuttering than when he is speaking normally. The mistake lies in believing that the physiological difference is the cause of a psychological act.[5] The individual may learn to perform the motor acts which produce blocking or repetition just as well as he learns those which lead to "normal" speech and probably is just as much unaware of how he has learned to hesitate as he is unaware of how he has learned to speak fluently. It is obvious that an unlimited number of possible acts can cause speech interruptions, and in studying stuttering we find just such an endless variety. It has been clinically demonstrated many times that one can easily change the way in which a particular case stutters. *The studies on physiological dysfunctions give part of the description of how the individual stutters but do not relate to why the individual stutters.*

Concerning the alleged number of stutterers whose handedness had been shifted it should be pointed out that for every stutterer who has been shifted there are anywhere from ten to sixty people (estimates of the number of people born left-handed vary widely) who have been shifted and who do not stutter. It is clear, however, that the emotional upset of such a shift might in some cases provide a basis for the frequent affective breakdowns of which we have spoken.

The evidence from studies on the importance of psychological

---

[5] It must be remembered that the hysterically blind actually cannot see, and that a hysterically paralyzed limb is in a different physiological condition from one that is not paralyzed but the physiological change is not the important factor in understanding the hysteria.

factors in the moment of stuttering[6] emphasizes the learned nature of the stuttering reaction and throws light on the question of why a stutterer stutters on certain words and phrases rather than others, but an understanding of the amount of stuttering in any larger behavior segment requires, as many other studies have shown, an understanding of the social situation as a whole and the emotional reactions of that particular subject to that situation.

A question almost sure to arise concerns children who begin to stutter from the beginning of speech or at early ages of two, three, or four years.

The work of Steer (7), Johnson (5), and Davis (3) shows that the speech of these so-called early stutterers, at time of first diagnosis of stuttering, is not significantly different from that of children of the same age who do not stutter. What is different, to a large degree, is the attitudes of parents toward these children. The easy bouncy repetitions of children are normal and are not similar to the phenomena we are treating here as stuttering. Further, it seems that many stutterers who state that they have stuttered since the beginning of speech or from a very early age, when questioned, report that they themselves have no memory of such stuttering but the parents looked back in retrospect and did remember that "Johnnie did seem to have trouble before." Any parent can look back at the speech of almost any child and come to the same conclusion.

The baffling question of why we have so many more male than female stutterers appears to have at least a theoretical solution along these lines. The earlier published article suggested that differences in training due to sex, differences which were minimized in the only child where the sex ratio was reduced, were an important factor in understanding the sex difference in frequency of stuttering. The goals that have to be given up in order to stutter may be more important to girls than to boys due to general cultural differences in our training of the sexes.

This discussion of various lines of evidence is not presented as proof of the theory, but more as a suggestion for further research. The specific needs or modes of availability listed are not intended to be all-inclusive nor is the factor of pampering believed to be operative in every case. Neglected, hated children, or children with organic defects may develop a strong need for a defense such as stuttering presents. Many questions remain to be answered. Exactly what are

---

[6] Many of the series of articles on the "Psychology of Stuttering," written or directed by Wendell Johnson, *J. Speech Disorders*, 1938, 1939, and 1940, are excellent examples of such studies.

the factors in training which produce these different systems of values between the sexes? How slight may the need be when the availability is very great? How weak may the availability be when the need is very great? The discussion may seem to slight the factors of availability but this is not the intention. In fact, the abundant evidence of how stuttering appears to run in families is taken here not as an indication of the inheritance of stuttering but as an indication of the importance of the psychological factor of availability.

There is nothing strikingly new about such a theory. Authors too numerous to mention have written about one or the other of these factors. If there is anything at all new about this theory it lies in its synthesis of two points of view and its systematization. It represents a framework not simply for stuttering but for all similar behavior disorders.

THERAPY

Once a person has stuttered the availability is always present. Any effective and lasting therapy, then, must concentrate on the need, although in some cases it may be necessary or at least a wise therapeutic measure to carry on some parallel work in the mechanics of speech.

If we accept the idea that the stutterer is using his stuttering as a defense of some kind and that he wishes, therefore, to protect the rationalization "that he can't help stuttering" (*i.e.*, by relating it to some physiological or hereditary cause) and will react emotionally to any theory that will "expose" this mechanism, we can develop more specific suggestions as to the procedure and nature of an efficient therapy. What will be described here is the actual procedure used on the first five cases described earlier.

The first step was the gathering of information. After several sessions of this the subject was forced without the therapist's doing anything but asking questions to reevaluate to some extent his own history and his rationalizations concerning stuttering. The first specific technique suggested was for the stutterer to do one hour's oral reading every day. After a few days he was told that the only purpose of this was to emphasize to him the fact that he did not have to stutter, and that if he was to understand his own stuttering he must look to psychological factors in terms of the situation that he is in. A second phase of the therapy was to go into the stutterers' own theories as to the nature of their stuttering or stuttering in general, discussing other therapies that they had been subject to, evaluating experimental evidence, and discussing cases. No effort was made at this stage to interpret their own history in full. The cases talked about were ones with elements common to their own history. Soon all these subjects were aware that perhaps a similar interpretation would apply to them. Cases were also examined who showed "personality disorders" other than stuttering. The general concepts of need, purpose, compensation, inferiority feeling, insecurity, etc., were analyzed. Reading assignments to literature in the field of personality theory and of stuttering were made and the material discussed.

The third phase of this therapy was that of interpretation. The subject's entire history and his day-to-day experiences were examined in terms of the theory already outlined.

At this time a group therapeutic situation was introduced. The five cases met once a week for two hours in addition to the three regular weekly individual interviews. Approximately the first half of that time was spent in a discussion of some abstract concept such as "style of life," "pampering," "preparation for a goal by building a defense in advance," "control through weakness," and others. The latter half of the session was taken over by one of the five, who discussed his own speech history in relation to the preceding discussion. This appeared to be a very valuable part of the therapy. It served to objectify the stuttering of the subject who was giving his own history and to strengthen the acceptance of the interpretation along similar lines by the others. They asked each other questions and tried to outdo each other in the extent to which they were able to probe beneath the surface for purposes and psychological motivations. The entire time spent with these cases was about three months, including the taking of histories which took up the first month.

In addition to the continuation of the interpretation phase and group sessions the last month was devoted mainly to building new, constructive attitudes. The old attitudes were described as a mistaken view by which the adults were meeting present-day situations with the same reactions they had had to childhood situations. They were encouraged in their ability to speak normally and to face life situations in the three fields of human endeavor—sexual and marriage, occupational, and social—without the need of the defense mechanism which they had used to avoid these situations. They were also directed to turn their attention away from themselves to the situation and ideas they wished to express. Specific "difficult" situations were examined objectively and the subjects were usually able to face these situations armed with a new attitude with little or no stuttering. Programs for dating, establishing friends, changing from an egocentric to an extrocentric social point of view, and planning for an occupational adjustment were instituted and carried out.

As the therapy progressed general factors of adjustment were stressed more and more and the emphasis changed from that of a stuttering therapy to a personality therapy wherein stuttering was used as an example of one of the individual's characteristic behavior reactions, a reaction which was related to and expressive of the personality as a whole.

In general, the results of this therapy give, at least, permissive evidence of the validity of the theory and therapy outlined here. At the conclusion of the study two of the cases (2, 3) did not stutter at all and were not stuttering after a period of one and a half years, when the last report on them was available. Both after the conclusion of the therapy and after a period of one and a half years, cases 1 and 5 are described by themselves and by the head clinician as no longer regarding themselves as stutterers nor feeling the need for any work on their speech, although they occasionally still have slight interruptions. The fifth case has improved his attitude towards his speech considerably, although the same improvement was not fully paralleled in his speech. However, in this case an additional three weeks would have been necessary to cut all intellectual and emotional ties to a shift-in-handedness therapy which he had completely accepted just prior to the beginning of this therapy. Unfortunately the extra time that was necessary in this case was not available.

SUMMARY

A working hypothesis for the understanding and treatment of stuttering has been presented in outline. The hypothesis is based on an intensive study of eight cases and an analysis of some of the experimental data in the field. The hypothesis arrived at is a general principle that holds for *all* stutterers rather than a statistical concept. The theory represents a systematic framework, in terms of availability and need, in which stuttering as well as many other behavior disorders may be viewed and which, rather than answering the experimental problems in the field, perhaps opens new ones. The theory presents a framework in which individual stutterers can be studied rather than one which attempts to give a single explanation for all stuttering. The therapy based on this psychological interpretation of stuttering is elastic and suited to the individual taken as a whole and not simply to the single symptom we call stuttering. It attempts, in most cases, to cure stuttering without relying on any techniques which are concerned purely with the mechanics of speech production.

REFERENCES

1. Adler, A. *Understanding human nature.* New York: Greenburg, 1927. Pp. 48–49.
2. Brown, F. W. Personality integration as the essential factor in the permanent cure of stuttering. *Ment. Hyg.,* 1933, **17**, 266–277.
3. Davis, D. M. The relation of repetitions in the speech of young children to certain measures of language, maturity and situational factors. *J. Speech Disorders,* 1939, **4**, 303–318.
4. Johnson, W. *Because I stutter.* New York: Appleton, 1930.
5. Johnson, W. The role of evaluation in stuttering behavior. *J. Speech Disorders,* 1938, **3**, 85–89.
6. Rotter, J. B. Studies in the psychology of stuttering: XI. Stuttering in relation to position in the family. *J. Speech Disorders,* 1938, **3**, 143–148.
7. Steer, M. D. Symptomatologies of young stutterers, *J. Speech Disorders,* 1937, **2**, 3–13.

Commentary to Chapter 3

The previous article reflects the influence of Alfred Adler in my thinking; the following one reflects the influence of Kurt Lewin, with whom I studied at the University of Iowa in 1937–1938. Although Lewinian psychology was attractive to me on several counts, it was the research on level of aspiration that excited me most, and in 1938 I began the work that ultimately became my dissertation. Lewin and his students were primarily interested in level of aspiration as a process variable; they were interested in the effects of success and failure on changes in the individual's goals and in the vectors that were involved in such changes. I was struck by the potential utility of this technique for studying an important aspect of individual differences in personality: the characteristic differences in the way in which individuals respond publicly to a self-evaluation problem following success and failure. Different responses seemed to reveal not only expectancies for future success and failure, but also characteristic defenses. From the beginning of my research in this area, I viewed expressed expectancies as different from implicit ones and became concerned with the methodology of measuring expectations as veridically as possible.

I quickly discovered that what was being called subjects' level of aspiration *seemed sometimes to reflect their hopes, sometimes their expectations, and sometimes defensive statements that might protect them from public failure. Often, responses could be interpreted as some combination of the three. It became clear that differences in instructions and testing situations could produce startlingly different results. As a result of these early studies on level of aspiration, I developed a strong interest in methodology. Personality constructs without clear and logical methods of measurement were either untestable or misleading. I also discovered in this work that expectancies could be reliably measured along a continuum.*

The following paper was the second of a series of four articles describing an attempt to develop a way of measuring expressed expectations and to determine the meanings, significance, and utility of such a measure.

3

Level of Aspiration as a Method of Studying Personality
Development and Evaluation of a Controlled Method

A recent trend in the testing of personality has been away from the inventories, towards more dynamic, behavioral methods. The level of aspiration technique has been one such approach that has aroused considerable interest.

Although differing among themselves, experiments concerned with level of aspiration have in common a specific, basic procedure. A subject is confronted with some task and either before or after practice he is asked to make a statement of how well he will do on the task. After failure or success in reaching this explicitly set goal he is asked to make another estimate. This may be repeated several times. Through this procedure it is possible to study, fairly objectively, the effect of success and failure on the explicitly set goals of an individual.

Unfortunately, a great deal of research, although showing the significance of certain social factors, has not yielded any definite results which would relate stable, specific personality variables to

Rotter, Julian B. Level of aspiration as a method of studying personality. II. Development and evaluation of a controlled method. *Journal of Experimental Psychology*, 1942, *31*, 410–422. Copyright 1942 by the American Psychological Association. Reprinted by permission of the publisher and author.

This article forms part of a dissertation submitted to the faculty of the Graduate School of Indiana University in partial fulfillment of the requirements for the degree, Doctor of Philosophy. I am indebted to Dr. C. M. Louttit, who directed the dissertation, and to Mr. David Shakow, Chief Psychologist at the Worcester State Hospital, who gave much aid and encouragement in the initial stages of this investigation.

Read in part before the American Psychological Association, September, 1940.

responses in this situation. The first article of this series (6), a critical review of the literature, points out several uncontrolled conditions in previous studies. This review (p. 472) concluded that:

> All in all, in every level of aspiration situation the nature of the situational factors and certain individual "personality" factors interact to determine the response. However, little or nothing is known about the stability or nature of these personality factors.
>
> In order to determine the nature of these personality variables it would be necessary to develop instructions that are not easily misinterpreted by the subject and in which previous experience with the task is controlled. It would also be necessary to examine all aspects of the individual's response, rather than limiting a description only to the difference between the expressed and achieved goals.

The purpose of the present study was to develop and evaluate an optimum method to discover those stable, individual personality factors, if any, which operate in the level of aspiration situation, following the suggestions for a controlled procedure given above. The instructions, task, and measures studied will be discussed separately.

I. METHOD

A. Selection of Instructions

In attempting to find satisfactory instructions, preliminary work was done with ten subjects using dart throwing as the task. Each subject made about ten trials with two sets of instructions and the results for the two different kinds of instructions were compared. The subjects were later interviewed to determine how they interpreted the instructions. In this way four different instructions were compared. These were (1) What do you *expect* to get next time? (2) What score will you *try* for next time? (3) What do you *think* you get next time? (4) The instructions of Hausmann (4). (These emphasize accuracy by penalizing for falling below one's estimate and giving no credit above the estimate.) It was found that subjects not only interpreted the above instructions differently but they also showed variations in the manner in which they interpreted the same instructions, with the exception of the instructions previously used by Hausmann.

The ideal set of instructions could not expect to eliminate the difference between explicit and implicit goals but simply to avoid misinterpretation on the part of the subject and to have all subjects approach the problem of estimate of future scores with a clear idea of what is expected of them. The subject need not follow the instructions but his deviation from them can only be significant if we are sure that he has understood them to mean what we assume they mean.

A slight modification of the instructions of Hausmann alone, of the four tried, seemed to fit this requirement. Gould (3), at the time that this preliminary work was completed, published a paper substantiating the criticism of the other instructions but rejecting Hausmann's instructions on three *a priori* grounds. (1) They may tend to reduce individual differences to a minimum. (2) The subject may only feel success when he makes his exact goal. Scoring over this can be considered as a failure. (3) Whatever individual differences do occur are rather an index of the subject's poor judgment than of basic personality trends. Preliminary work did not substantiate any of these criticisms. These instructions were used and methods for experimentally testing the validity of all three criticisms were included in the procedure.

The actual instructions used were:

This is a test of motor control. The idea is always to aim for the ten. Your score will depend on how close to the ten you come. You will be given a series of trials in which you should try to get as high a total score as possible. Before you start each trial, however, you will have to tell me the score you expect to get and you will not be credited with anything over that score. If your score is lower than your bid, then the score you will be credited with will be two points off your bid for every point you fall below in your actual score. For example, if you say you will score 15 and score 20, for the five trials, you will only get credit for 15; if you say 15 and score 10, then you will only get credit for 5. You can see that once your bid is made it is always to your advantage to score as high as possible.

B. Selection of the Task

If one is attempting to hold the situational factors as constant as possible, particularly attempting to hold the influence of the actual level of performance to a minimum, an analysis of the literature, consideration of all the purposes of the study, and preliminary work point to several criteria for the selection of the task. (1) The most important of these is that the task be novel so that the subject can have no idea of how other people score nor can he have built up previous attitudes towards his ability with the specific task. (2) The task should not be so easy or so difficult that any individual would feel himself at one or the other extreme of talent without having any immediate comparison with others. (3) Performance scores for all subjects should occupy a fairly narrow range just above the middle of the distribution of possible scores. (4) It would be necessary to find a task interesting enough to guarantee sustained and uniform attention so that it would be possible to have a sufficient number of trials for adequate quantitative results. (5) Performance scores should be variable enough so that the subject can only gauge his score approximately and is unable to avoid the conflict of whether to go up, down, or stay at the same level merely on the basis of a very stable score. (6) Similarly, the learning factor should be negligible so that the subject may not avoid the conflict simply by assuming a regularly increasing ability. (7) Finally, with a view toward use of this technique for general experimental and clinical purposes, general convenience, and adaptability to a wide range of age groups should be considered.

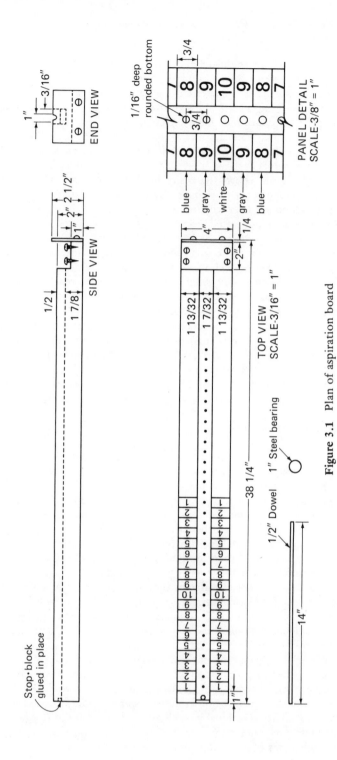

Figure 3.1 Plan of aspiration board

34

Dart throwing, although having a high interest value and other advantages, has the disadvantages of being familiar to some subjects and inconvenient for some clinical uses, particularly for use with psychotic patients. Another task, therefore, was devised which appeared to fit all the criteria. The apparatus for this task is shown in Figs. 3.1 and 3.2.

The board shown is of pine wood, 38 inches long with a square groove down the center. A steel ball is hit along the groove by a stick resembling a miniature billiard cue. Regularly spaced depressions preceding the numbered units and also one placed in the center of each numbered unit slow down the speed of the ball and provide a resting place for it when it comes to a stop. The score is dependent upon how closely to the central unit the ball comes to rest regardless of the direction. The central unit, painted in white with the black number ten on it, counts 10 points. The ones on either side count nine points and so on. The other units painted alternately blue and gray decrease to a value of 1 point.

Figure 3.2 View of the aspiration board with subject poised to roll the steel bearing.

In order to stabilize the scores somewhat, aspiration estimates were made for a group of five trials. The subject was given from fifteen to twenty-five practice trials, the number necessary for him to reach a somewhat flattened learning curve. Difficulty of the task could be controlled by adjusting the angle of the board in relation to the table it rested upon. Once set at the desired level the board was maintained at that level throughout the course of the entire study.

Although not of immediate interest to this study, the task also had the advantage of being readily adapted to control of success and failure by the experimenter. This adaptation has been reported in a paper by Rotter and Rodnick (5). In this apparatus the angle of the board was regulated by the use of a mechanical series of levers controlled by a foot pedal hidden under the rug. The movement of the board was not detected by the subjects as it was gradual and hidden by side supports. In this way it was possible to control the score within relatively narrow limits.

C. Test Measures

The work to date on level of aspiration has leaned very heavily on a single score, one that gives in one way or another some mathematical representation of the difference between the subject's estimates and his performances. However, there are many other ways of approaching the results and one of the purposes of this investigation is to evaluate the significance of some of these.

With the first group of fifty subjects 25 estimates were made by each subject. Later groups made 20 trials. With such a large number of trials, possibilities of numerical treatment of the results are unlimited. This study attempts to evaluate several measures indicating the relationship between estimates and performance, a measure of stability of estimates, scores indicating the nature of changes in estimates following success and failure, and, in a later article, one which takes into consideration the full pattern of the response.

D. General Procedure

The general procedure for all groups was as follows: (1) The subject was told simply to try to hit the ball so that it would stop at ten and to go ahead and practice for a while. (2) After 15 to 25 practice trials the subject was given the instructions to read. After the subject had read them, the experimenter went over the instructions verbally, giving as many examples of the scoring as was necessary to be sure the subject fully comprehended them. (3) If the subject inquired, he was told he could change his estimate as many times as he wished or could keep it the same all the time. (4) When the subject made his estimate, this was written down. The score for the five trials was written trial by trial, added, and the number of credits calculated. The credit score, not the actual performance score, was then written in large numerals where the subject could see it. (5) The instructions were not repeated after the first trial, the experimenter saying at the first regular trial, "You tell me each time what you are going to do." If the subject failed at any point to make an estimate before hitting the ball, he was stopped, reminded and the fact of his forgetting noted down. All spontaneous comments and exclamations were noted. (6) In Group I 25 trials of five hits apiece were given. In all the later groups 20 were given. In all cases a short rest was given when midway through the test. The usual time for the 20-trial test, including practice, was from 20 to 25 minutes. (7) All subjects were pledged not to discuss the test with anyone else.

Including all groups, 205 subjects were used in the study.

II. SUBJECTS AND SPECIAL PROCEDURES FOR THE DIFFERENT GROUPS

Group I

This group was used largely for exploratory purposes. The main intent was to determine whether or not the instructions and task fulfilled the criteria described earlier and avoided the *a priori* criticisms of Gould. A second function of this group was to test out the possible usefulness of certain measures and to determine their reliability. There were 22 male and 28 female subjects, all adults.

The men ranged in age from 21 to 56 with a mean age of 27.8. They were all hospital employees ranging in occupation from attendant to psychiatrist but the group was heavily laden with attendants. Of the 22 men 18 were attendants.

The women subjects ranged in age from 20 to 28. The mean age was 22.4. This group was heavily weighted with 16 nursing affiliates.

At the conclusion of the first test the entire 50 subjects were given, in addition to the regular aspiration procedure, three tests designed to determine their judgment. These were the Healy Picture Completion II, the Intermediate form of the Otis Self-Administering test of General Intelligence and two sections of the Alpha Common Sense Test.

At the end of one month all the subjects who were still available were retested. This included 32 of the original 50 cases. At the conclusion of the second test they were questioned about (1) the meaning of the instructions, (2) what they thought the test tested, (3) experiences of success and failure, (4) interest and involvement.

Group II

This, and the following groups were selected for special validity studies, which will be reported later, and were subject to additional procedures. Only a brief description of them is given here.

Group II consisted of 45 college students, 23 males and 22 females. The male subjects ranged in age from 18 to 30, with a mean age of 21.3. The female group ranged from 18 to 30 years with a mean age of 21.9. The subjects consisted of one whole class and parts of two other classes in clinical psychology.

Group III

Group III was made up of 21 crippled students attending college. These were selected from another experiment investigating college cripples as a group. Some were obviously deformed; in others the crippling was barely noticeable. There were 11 males and 10 females. The age range for males was 19 to 24, mean 21.2; for females it was 18 to 26, mean 21.1.

Group IV

Nine other subjects who are used in later validity studies were not included in any other group because of wide age differences, color differences, or ambiguity on the question of crippling.

Group V

Group V consisted of 80 male inmates of the Indiana State Penal Farm. These subjects all had short sentences, were white, from 16 to 35 years of age, and were all of average or better intelligence, as shown by the Henmon-Nelson Group Intelligence Test. Seventy-three of these were divided into three sub-groups upon the basis of personality characteristics. As these groups will be dealt with in some detail in a following article, reliability estimates will be reported for each sub-group.

VI. RESULTS

A. Evaluation of the Instructions

By correlating the scores of the three tests of judgment taken by Group I plus a composite score based on the subject's standing in all three tests with the two measures given below, it was possible to determine the validity of Gould's (3, p. 10) criticism of the instructions that "whatever individual differences do occur are rather an index of the subject's poor judgment than of basic personality trends."

The first measure gave the mean of the differences between the estimates and the preceding performance, *regardless of sign.* The second gave the difference between the mean aspiration and the mean achievement. None of the resulting eight coefficients showed any significant relation between the marked individual differences found and the measures of ability on judgment tests. The correlation coefficients ranged from .11 to −.25; the median coefficient was −.05. On all measures the spread of scores was as wide as that in data reported for previous studies and there was no evidence that individual differences were reduced in any way.

Thus far it appears that two of Gould's objections to these instructions are invalid. There remains to be considered the problem of scoring over one's bid. Interviews with the subjects of Group I at the end of the experiment indicate that when the subject scored over his bid he experienced a definite satisfaction in that he had made his contract, although if the actual performance was well over his bid the feeling of satisfaction was accompanied by some feeling of regret for not having bid higher. Success in daily life, however, is of the same nature, so that this technique may indicate how the individual reacts to the culturally defined successes and failures of daily life rather than some implicit "pure" feeling of success which may not exist at all.

B. Evaluation of the Task

These same interviews, as well as observation of verbal and non-verbal behavior in the situation showed that the task had high interest value for all subjects and, with very few exceptions, the ego involvement in the task was deep. The "aspiration board" is convenient for clinical use. It can be carried easily, set up anywhere, and is applicable to a wide age range.

In order to discover whether or not this was a novel task and whether the subject was bringing socially set standards into the test situation, it was necessary to determine whether or not the absolute level of performance was influencing the behavior in the situation. This was done by correlating the absolute level of performance with the mean of the differences between each estimate and the preceding performance (this, or a similar score, has been used as the chief measure in previous studies involving the level of aspiration technique), and also with the number of successes, for each subject. The latter score was used as it was reasoned that if subjects with higher performance do not actually succeed more often, there is little basis to believe that the absolute level of achievement is having any influence.

These correlations were determined for the 50 subjects of Gruop I and also for the 155 subjects of Groups II through V. The resulting four correlations, shown in Table 3.1, were all quite small. Only one (the largest coefficient shown in Table 3.1) was slightly greater than three times its probable error. There was no indication that the low *r*'s were due to a curvilinear relationship.

Table 3.1 Relation of Performance to the Difference Scores and the Number of Successes

	N	r between Performance and Difference Score	r between Performance and and Successes
Group I	50	−.21	.13
Group II–V	155	−.24	.15

Following the practice trials, learning was at a minimum. In Group I, where 25 trials were given, the average performance for the Group for the first ten trials was compared with the average for the last ten. This difference was only .66 of a point. The trial by trial learning was analyzed for the last 155 subjects, Groups II–V, who used the 20 trial test. Here the difference between the first ten and last ten trials for the whole group was only .84 of a point. The average score is given for each trial in Table 3.2. It will be noted that practically all of the little learning that took place occurred in the first four trials.

For the entire group of 205 cases the average performance was 28.05. The S.D. of the average preformances for all subjects was 3.63 and the range was 17 to 36. Eighty-five percent of the cases were included between the performance levels 23 and 32. It is evident that there was little difference in the height of performance level for the subjects of this investigation. Almost all performance scores were concentrated at a level slightly above the middle of the distribution of possible scores.

Table 3.2 Average Performance Scores for Groups II–V for Each Trial (155 Subjects)

Trial	Performance	Trial	Performance
1	25.1	11	28.0
2	26.8	12	28.9
3	27.8	13	28.7
4	27.2	14	28.3
5	28.0	15	29.3
6	28.0	16	28.1
7	28.3	17	28.1
8	28.7	18	28.3
9	28.1	19	27.5
10	28.0	20	29.2

Note: Average, first 10 trials = 27.60; average, second 10 trials = 28.44; average, all twenty trials = 28.07.

Although learning was at a minimum in the situation, there was for each individual subject considerable variability from trial to trial, so that the possibility of having to change his estimate always existed. The median S.D. of the individual S.D.'s for each of the 50 subjects in Group I was 6.25.

From these results it appears to be clear that this task fits to a very high degree the seven criteria outlined previously as necessary to provide optimum conditions to study the personality variables entering into the individual differences in level of aspiration situations.

C. Evaluation of Scores

Early studies have taken as their main measure the difference between the average aspiration and the median or average performance. It appears somewhat more meaningful psychologically, insofar as the object of study is the effect of success and failure on estimates of ability, to use a figure obtained by taking the *mean of the differences between each performance and the following estimate.* Test-retest reliability shows this latter measure to be slightly more reliable. This score will be referred to throughout the rest of this study as the *D-score.*

Clinical judgment indicated that the frequency of shifts or changes in the height of the estimate (similar to Frank's (2) measure of "rigidity") had a significant relationship to basic personality trends of the subjects. It was important, therefore, to determine whether or not this measure was being influenced by the variability of the performance. The frequency of such shifts was correlated with the S.D. of the performance for each of the 50 subjects in Group I. No relationship was found between these factors. The correlation obtained was less than twice its probable error.

Also shown to be of major importance is the nature of the changes following success and failure. This was recorded for all subjects. "Does the individual keep at the same level after success?," "Does he invariably go down after failure?" appear to be important questions.

The presence of unusual shifts, down after success and up after failure, appears to be of considerable clinical significance. These shifts cannot be treated in group statistical comparisons, however, because of their infrequent appearance. Less than half of the subjects showed any such shifts. When they were present at all, they had a significance that varied with the condition in which they arose.

A shift down after success had a different interpretation than a shift up after a failure. It also made a difference if it occurred in the beginning of the series of trials when the subject, in a sense, was still feeling his way, or in the latter half of the test. The same interpretation did not always apply if such shifts occurred when the subject's achievement was considerably different from his previous estimate or quite close to it.

The standard deviations of the aspiration estimates, the achievement scores, and the differences between performance and the following estimate were obtained for each subject in Group I, but not having any immediate applicability to the variables studied, they were not used further.

The frequency of successes (the number of times the subject reached or exceeded his estimate) gives roughly the same information as that given by the difference score and in later comparisons it almost invariably gave the same results as shown by using the D-score. Sometimes, however, differences were less marked. To avoid unnecessary repetition the figures giving the frequency of successes were dropped in later comparisons of groups. The correlation between the frequency of successes and the height of the D-score was .90 for the 50 cases in Group I, and .88 for the 155 cases in Groups II–V. A later article in this series will be devoted entirely to a consideration of the results in terms of whole patterns of response.

D. Reliability

It is extremely difficult to obtain a real measure of the reliability of the scores used. Test-retest reliabilities are particularly handicapped in that the first test introduces a standard for the second test and estimates in the second test are based on this standard. It would also be expected that if enough trials were given, eventually all subjects would make a greater and greater adjustment of their estimates to their performance but they would differ in the rate of this adjustment. This trend was clearly to be seen. The retest then cannot be considered a repetition of the first test but to a large extent a new situation. Odd-even or split-half techniques are not wholly applicable. These statistical methods were not designed for use with a task where the items are not discrete but each response depends upon the preceding one.

The major difficulty in applying such techniques with this task is that of patterning. One subject may fail, lower his estimate; succeed, raise his estimate; fail, lower his estimate, and so forth, for several trials. In such a case for all the odd trials the difference between performance and following estimate might be negative, for the even trials high and positive. Another subject might do the same thing but not shift his estimate until he had failed twice or succeeded twice. A split-half technique offers even greater difficulty due to differences in rate of adapting estimates to performance, as well as occasional complete changes during the course of the test of the pattern of behavior being exhibited. In spite of these difficulties the odd-even technique probably gives a better approximation of the reliability of measures than does the test-retest.

Nevertheless, it is interesting to see the relative consistency of different measures in a test-retest situation. These measures are based on the 32 subjects of Group I who were available for retest after a period of one month and are given in Table 3.3, along with the odd-even reliabilities.

In spite of the inadequacy of the test-retest measurement a certain amount of stability and consistency in the basic pattern of the response is shown by these coefficients. In order to determine the reliability of the changes up, down, or same, following success and failure, intra-class correlations (1) were obtained. These have the advantage of being readily changed to z scores, then averaged and changed back to a correlation. Six such correlations were obtained for the number of times the subject went up in his estimate, stayed the same, or went down after success and after failure. The coefficient .56 is obtained by changing the mean of the scores, for these six correlations, back to a correlation coefficient. The number of times the subject shifted his estimate was even more stable. Frequency of successes (number of times the subject reaches or passes his estimate) was more consistent in the test-retest figure than the D-score but less so in the odd-even coefficient where it was markedly affected by patterning in several cases where the subjects controlled their estimates in such a way that they managed to succeed every other trial.

Table 3.3 Reliability Measurements for Group I

Test-Retest (N = 32)	
Number of shifts	.70
Reactions following success and failure	.56[a]
Number of successes	.46
D-score	.32
Odd-Even (N = 50)[b]	
Number of shifts	.83
Number of successes	.63
D-score	.76

[a]Intra-Class correlation.
[b]Corrected by Spearman-Brown prophecy formula.

Table 3.4   Odd-Even Reliability Measurements for Groups II–V

Group	N	D-score	Shifts
II–V	155	.78	.80
II Men	23	.85	.70
II Women	22	.82	.75
III	21	.73	.72
V A	21	.82	.81
V B	21	.73	.84
V C	31	.75	.86

Note: Corrected by the Spearman-Brown prophecy formula.

Odd-even reliabilities for the frequency of shifts and for the D-score, the figures used mainly in the group comparisons to follow, are shown for the other groups in Table 3.4. These are based upon the shortened test of twenty trials.

These coefficients are not to be taken as true values of the reliability of measures. They are given only insofar as they may roughly suggest the true measures. The value and utility of these measures can only be determined by studies of the validity of the differences that appear in them.

VII. SUMMARY AND CONCLUSIONS

In an attempt to devise a level of aspiration technique which eliminated uncontrolled factors present in earlier studies, and which provided optimum conditions for the study of individual personality variables operating in the situation, a modified form of instructions originated by Hausmann and a simple but novel motor task were tested with 205 subjects.

These instructions were fairly successful in eliminating the possibility of misinterpretation upon the part of the subjects without involving judgment as a factor in the subject's reaction or reducing the extent of individual differences.

The task creates a great deal of interest, does not appear to be influenced by performance level, shows little learning after a short initial practice period, and appears to be free of attitudes and standards resulting from previous contact with this or a similar task. The task also allows for a large number of trials, providing adequate quantitative results, in a relatively short time. Several scores which attempt to represent the subject's full pattern of response appear to be reliably measurable.

Later studies in this series will describe attempts to determine the nature and stability of the personality traits which enter into the wide individual differences that appear in this level of aspiration situation.

REFERENCES

1. Fisher, R. A. *Statistical methods for research workers.* (6th ed.) Edinburgh: Oliver & Boyd, 1936.
2. Frank J. D. Individual differences in certain aspects of the level of aspiration. *Amer. J. Psychol.,* 1935, 47, 119–126.
3. Gould, R. An experimental analysis of "level of aspiration." *Genet. Psychol. Monogr.,* 1939, 21, 1–116.
4. Hausmann, M. F. A test to evaluate some personality traits. *J. Gen. Psychol.,* 1933, 9, 179–189.
5. Rotter, J. B., & Rodnick, E. H. A study of the reactions to experimentally induced frustration. (Abstract.) *Psychol. Bull.,* 1940, 37, 577.
6. Rotter, J. B. Level of aspiration as a method of studying personality. I. A critical review of methodology. *Psychol. Review,* 1942, 49, 463–474.

Commentary to Chapter 4

The following selection is taken from Social Learning and Clinical Psychology *(published in 1954). The two chapters present the basic working hypotheses of social learning theory, their rationale, and the early research testing their validity. The chapters speak for themselves. Earlier chapters in the book deal with the importance of theory in clinical psychology, major problems plaguing the field, criteria for a language of description, and general principles for a social learning approach to personality. Later chapters represent attempts to present an integrative approach to clinical psychology and include chapters on the relationship of this theory to other theoretical approaches, the clinical measurement of personality, psychological therapy, and the environmental treatment of children.*

The later chapters did not present some new omnibus measure of personality, a new descriptive psychopathology, or a new panacea for curing psychological ills. Rather, they tried to analyze, from a social learning point of view, what was being measured and what could be predicted from various approaches to personality measurement. Similarly, the characteristic practices of psychotherapy have been analyzed from a social learning viewpoint.

The basic concepts presented here have been refined, expanded, and added to, but they remain essentially the same. A 1955 Nebraska Symposium paper (Rotter, 1955) expanded on the difficult problem of defining and categorizing psychological situations. A current paper (Rotter, 1981) carries that quest further. The concepts of generalized expectancies for problem solving and the conception of simple cognitions as expectancies have been added and are described in later selections.

REFERENCES

Rotter, J. B. The role of the psychological situation in determining the direction of human behavior. In M. R. Jones (Ed.), *Nebraska Symposium on Motivation.* Lincoln: University of Nebraska Press, 1955. Pp. 245–269.

Rotter, J. B. The psychological situation in social learning theory. In D. Magnusson (Ed.), *The situation: An interactional perspective.* Hillsdale, N.J.: Lawrence Erlbaum Associates, 1981.

4

Social Learning
and Clinical Psychology
Basic Concepts

This social learning theory utilizes three basic constructs in the measurement and prediction of behavior. These are *behavior potential, expectancy,* and *reinforcement value.* In this chapter we shall describe a basic formula for behavior involving these three variables, additional constructs that are used in determination of these three variables, and more generalized formulas that are derived from the basic formula. The latter part of the chapter will deal with the actual measurement of the three variables and with experimental data now available regarding the conditions that affect or determine them.[1]

BEHAVIOR POTENTIAL

Behavior potential may be defined as the potentiality of any behavior's occurring in any given situation or situations as calculated in relation to any single reinforcement or set of reinforcements. The potentiality for the occurrence of any behavior may be ultimately determined from its actual occurrence in any situation where other alternatives are present. The measure obtained, then, would be rela-

Rotter, Julian B. Basic concepts. In J. B. Rotter, *Social learning and clinical psychology.* New York: Johnson Reprint Company, 1973, 1980. (Originally published, 1954) Broader conceptions. In Rotter, *Social learning and clinical psychology.* Reprinted by permission.

[1] The experimental data to be cited in detail will include only studies carried out to test these formulations. In a book like this that has the primary purpose of exposition it is not possible to describe all relevant research. The studies cited not only are most relevant but also serve the purpose of illustrating the concepts employed.

tive to other known alternatives. In any single situation the behavior potential may only be characterized as being stronger or weaker than some other behavior potentials. If the occurrence of any single behavior were to be calculated for a number of situations, the behavior potential might then be assigned a value at a number of possible points along a continuum. This value, however, would still represent a figure derived relative to other known alternatives.

The concept of behavior that we are utilizing is indeed a broad one. It includes any action of the organism that involves a response to a meaningful stimulus and that may be observed or measured directly or indirectly. Behavior that in other points of view may be referred to as emotional or implicit would be included in our definition, but we would not feel that it requires any special description or special laws to govern its occurrence. For example, we would include the behavior of looking around for cues in order to make a discrimination, clenching one's fist when frustrated, or making a verbal report or a verbal choice. We distinguish between a verbal statement and what the statement is supposed to represent. For example, if the subject is asked whether or not he is tense, we consider his verbal reply a predictable response in itself but not necessarily a description of his condition as it might be made by an objective observer. Similarly, if we ask a subject what he expects, his verbal report is a behavior that ultimately may be predicted, but it may *not* coincide with an observer's judgment based on the subject's subsequent behaviors.

Many of the psychoanalytic or Adlerian defense mechanisms are describable as behaviors; for example, avoiding particular stimuli, blaming others, and responding submissively to parents or strong figures. Operationally defined concepts such as repression, identification, and projection are all potentially describable as behaviors and predictable with the same set of constructs and laws as other behaviors. Some indirectly measurable behaviors have been described by Harlow (1949) as higher-level learning skills. Such behaviors as looking for alternatives, trying out a sequence of solutions, and withholding action until more cues are present may all be described as behaviors, even though they have to be measured indirectly by their consequent behaviors, which may be more readily observable.

EXPECTANCY

Expectancy may be defined as the probability held by the individual that a particular reinforcement will occur as a function of a specific behavior on his part in a specific situation or situations. Expectancy is independent of the value or importance of the reinforcement.

To understand fully this concept of expectancy, we should compare it with those of Lewin and Brunswik. Lewin (1951) has emphasized the subjective probability in the subject's estimate of the situation, and what is considered of psychological importance is the expectations of the subject rather than the actuarial or objective expectations that might be presumed to be present on the basis of past experience. Brunswik (1951), on the other hand, has emphasized objective probability: the subject's behavior is determined by a probability, i.e., a wager that he must make regarding outcomes; this probability is determined by the frequency of occurrence of objectively describable past events. The present point of view utilizes a principle of internal expectancy as its major intervening variable or construct. The term subjective, however, may perhaps be misleading and is avoided because of its connotations of introspection or inaccessibility to objective measurement. Objective probability, possibly as used by Brunswik, is *one* of several constructs used in the present formulation to calculate internal probability. Other constructs involving generalization, patterning, effects on expectancy as a function of number of past experiences, the unusualness of an occurrence, ambiguous cues, and so on, make up some of the variables that affect internal probability or expectancy. We are constantly concerned with obtaining objective measures of a variety of conditions in our continual efforts to improve the estimate of internal probability, which is not only one of the basic variables used to predict behavior but the variable most likely to change as a result of new experience.

REINFORCEMENT VALUE

The reinforcement value of any external reinforcement may be ideally defined as the degree of preference for any reinforcement to occur if the possibilities of their occurring were all equal. A simple example: a man might consistently choose to be paid ten dollars an hour for his work instead of one dollar an hour if it were only a matter of choice on his part, since the reinforcement value of ten dollars is consistently and significantly greater than that of one dollar in our culture. It can be readily demonstrated, for both individuals and cultures, that consistency or reliability exists in the degree to which any reinforcement is preferred by the individual or group. Such preferences can be demonstrated to exist independently of the expectancy of a forthcoming reinforcement. Like behavior potential, reinforcement value would have to be calculated in a choice situation and any obtained measure of reinforcement value would be relative only to other known alternative reinforcements. Since the act of choosing is itself a behavior, reinforcement value must be measured with expectancy held constant for the alternatives present.

BASIC FORMULAS

The statements above may be summed up in the following formula:

$$1.\ B.P._{x,\ s_1,\ R_a} = f(E_{x,\ R_a,\ s_1}\ \&\ R.V._a)$$

The formula may be read as follows: The potential for behavior x to occur in situation 1 in relation to reinforcement a is a function of the expectancy of the occurrence of reinforcement a following behavior x in situation 1 and the value of reinforcement a.

Note the sign & is used as the only indication of the nature of the mathematical relationship between expectancy and reinforcement value. The purpose of this is to avoid, for the time being, a more precise mathematical formulation because of an insufficient amount of experimental data. However, it seems fairly clear from data available that this relationship is a multiplicative one. Before a generalized mathematical formula may be evolved, it will be necessary to devise a technique for measuring all reinforcement values along the same scale, so that measurements made on a preference basis in one study or situation will be comparable with measurements made in other studies. For the most part, experimental investigations to date have attempted to hold one of the two constructs constant, thus avoiding the necessity for precise statement of the mathematical relationship between them. Current investigations are attempting to collect data that will permit a beginning formulation of a mathematical relationship. Studies now completed have been concerned with the development of adequate measures of expectancy and of reinforcement value, so that it is possible at this time to measure both variables in the same study for some kinds of experimental situations. The reader is cautioned, however, against presuming that the formula above and the ones to follow state some precise mathematical relationship. They are merely convenient forms of stating relationships between variables. Some mathematical prediction has been made in regard to the measurement of expectancy by Castaneda (1952); this will be described in a later section.

Prediction with such a formula does not lead to a statement of the potential occurrence of the behavior x in situation 1, since it considers only a single reinforcement a and not other possible consequences of behavior x. Should we be interested in calculating the potential of behavior x's occurring in situation 1 we would have to combine a set of such behavior potentials, each determined for a specific reinforcement. This behavior potential is expressed in the formula below:

$$2.\ B.P._{x, s_1, R_{(a-n)}} = f(E_{x, s_1, R_{(a-n)}} \,\&\, R.V._{(a-n)})$$

This may be read as follows: The potential of behavior x's occurring in situation 1 in regard to all potential reinforcements for which the individual has expectancies is a function of the expectancies of the occurrences of these reinforcements (a to n) in situation 1 and the values of these reinforcements.

Should we wish to broaden our prediction to include a variety or group of situations, the formula would then include additional situations. This may be expressed as in the formula below:

$$3.\ B.P._{x, s_{(1-n)}, R_{(a-n)}} = f(E_{x, s_{(1-n)}, R_{(a-n)}} \,\&\, R.V._{(a-n)})$$

This may be read as follows: The potentiality of behavior x's occurring in relationship to the reinforcements a to n in situations 1 to n is a function of the expectancies of these reinforcements' occurring in these situations and the values of these reinforcements.

We might wish now to broaden our prediction one more step and to include instead of a single behavior a group of functionally related behaviors (x-n) and not all their possible consequences but the degree to which these behaviors are used to obtain one of a set of functionally related reinforcements (a-n). This formula would be represented as follows:

$$4.\ B.P._{(x-n), s_{(1-n)}, R_{(a-n)}} = f(E_{(x-n), s_{(1-n)}, R_{(a-n)}} \,\&\, R.V._{(a-n)})$$

This may be read: The potentiality of the functionally related behaviors x to n to occur in the specified situations 1 to n in relation to potential reinforcements a to n is a function of the expectancies of these behaviors leading to these reinforcements in these situations and the values of these reinforcements.

These formulations are concerned with specific behavior-reinforcement sequences. From them we derive the broader constructs of *need potential, freedom of movement,* and *need value,* which are the important variables in what we refer to as psychological needs.

These concepts, introduced briefly here, will be described in much greater detail in Chapter VI [of *Social Learning and Clinical Psychology*, entitled "Broader Conceptions"].

The rather complicated formula (4) above may be reduced to a formula for more general prediction that may be expressed as follows: The potentiality of occurrence of a set of behaviors that lead to the satisfaction of some need (need potential) is a function of the expectancies that these behaviors will lead to these reinforcements (freedom of movement) and the strength or value of these reinforcements (need value). This may be given in the formula below:

$$5. \quad N.P. = f(F.M. \ \& \ N.V.)$$

Need potential is a function of freedom of movement and need value. In clinical work it is usually this formula in which we are essentially interested; that is, it is these constructs we are trying to measure in clinical predictions. The more specific formulas are used primarily in the experimental testing of hypotheses.

All the above formulas either state or imply that specific relationships among actual variables hold only for given specified situations. The situation itself is one of the variables in all of the formulas and requires definition. Perhaps one of the greatest weaknesses of current psychological theorizing and practice has been its failure to deal analytically with the situations or contexts in which humans behave. Although we are aware in animal studies that changing of lighting, texture of surface, and so on may result in considerably different behavior in trained animals, we have made little systematic progress in attempting to understand the behavior of humans as a function of the objectively describable situations in which they find themselves. Personality theory, on the contrary, has tended to try to predict behavior as a function of entirely internal characteristics—traits, types, drives, character fixations, and the like. Relatively little attention has been paid to the fact that there is probably more consistency or similarity in the behavior of twenty people sitting in a classroom than the behavior of the same people in twenty different situations including, say, a classroom, a party, a job interview, and a therapy session.

We mean by *s* a psychological situation or any part of it to which the individual is responding. Like Lewin (1951) and Kantor (1924), we define a situation as that which is experienced by the subject with the meanings that the subject gives it. The situation must also be describable in objective terms for scientific purposes. We do not let the matter rest with the statement that for each person the situation may have different meanings, since it is necessary to describe in some communicable way what it is that has different meanings for various persons.

Later in this chapter . . . we will describe in greater detail how the constructs defined thus far are measured; introduce secondary variables that may be utilized in analyzing how these basic constructs change, increase, decrease; and discuss some of the hypothetical relationships that govern these changes. Research testing and illustrating some of these hypotheses will be presented. Before going into the measurement of these constructs, it first seems necessary to discuss some of the primary principles of learning that we consider important in formulating hypotheses regarding the change in these variables. Such principles seem of prime importance in attempting to describe choice behavior of humans in complex social situations. These basic principles will be discussed under (1) the nature of reinforcement, (2) psychological directionality, and (3) the nature of functional relationships among behaviors.

The Nature of Reinforcement

[Earlier in *Social Learning and Clinical Psychology*] we discussed what was meant by reinforcement and adopted what might be called an empirical law of effect. That is, we can observe that the occurrence of some observable event changes the potentiality of occurrence of a behavior which has preceded that event; if this change in potential occurs with predictable regularity, we may say that the event or the occurrence of the event has changed in some way the behavior of the person under observation. Such an event is, by definition, a reinforcement. There is no problem of circularity here (i.e., a reinforcement is that which reinforces), since once we have made the observations, either in regard to a group or a culture or in regard to an individual, we may then make predictions about the effects of the same event when it occurs in the future. One thing that may be noted is that not only do we avoid in this way the theoretical difficulties of postulating physiological drives (which are difficult to measure in their strength, occurrence, and reduction) but we set up a concrete and measurable criterion for what a reinforcement is. A reinforcement is something that changes behavior in some observable way by either increasing or decreasing the potentiality of its occurrence. Should an event increase the potential for a response, it is by definition a positive reinforcement; should it decrease the potential, it is by definition a negative reinforcement.

We might distinguish at this time between reinforcement as it is experienced by the subject and reinforcement as it may be described by an experimenter or objective observer. The former we refer to as internal reinforcement; the latter, as external reinforcement.

Internal reinforcement may be ideally defined as a subject's experience (or perception) that an event has occurred which has some value for him. That is, an event has occurred that is pleasant or unpleasant or that the subject expects will lead to a pleasant or unpleasant future event. As we have indicated before, positive or negative value is determined by the resultant effects upon behavior.

External reinforcement is the occurrence of an event or act that is known to have predictable reinforcement value for the group or culture to which the subject belongs. Examples are: praising an adolescent for demonstrated skill in games, giving a child candy, giving affection to a group of children who are suffering from "love deprivation." The relationship between external and internal reinforcement is not assumed to be one-to-one for everybody; it varies with the subject and the conditions of reinforcement. When the study of the previous history of a person demonstrates that an act has previously resulted in internal reinforcement for that person, that act may be considered an external reinforcement for that person even though it has no known group or cultural value.

It does not seem necessary to illustrate experimentally the effect of a reinforcement upon behavior. Nevertheless a simple, brief illustration will indicate how the constructs described above are actually utilized in explaining a change in behavior. If a subject is asked to anticipate whether a red or a green light will be flashed on a board and is rewarded by being told he is correct if he alternates red and green, then the behavior of so alternating his responses will become more and more stable. This response will occur with regularity as long as it continues to be followed by an indication of its correctness. The verbal statement of correctness would be an external reinforcement, presumed in advance by the experimenter, to have a reinforcing value on the basis of previous experience with the cultural group to which this subject belongs. There might be an occasional subject who would not respond in this way; in order to obtain the desired response from such a subject a different reinforcement would be required. But for most members of the group to which he belongs, the verbal praise has a known effect of increasing the potentiality of occurrence of the responses preceding it. In this formulation it is hypothesized that each time a "correct" follows the behavior, the expectancy increases that the behavior will be followed by the reinforcement, "correct," in the future. As the expectancy increases, the behavior potential likewise increases, since it depends upon both expectancy and the value of the reinforcement. The occurrence of this behavior or the likelihood of its occurrence in this situation continually may increase till it approximates one or unity. This is a very simple situation; as complexities are added to the situation, other eventualities may occur. These will be described in greater detail later.

If two reinforcements of different value follow two different behaviors, it may be shown that the potentiality of the behavior that precedes the reinforcement of higher value will be increased to a greater extent than the potentiality of the behavior followed by the reinforcement of lesser value. Similarly, it may be shown that reinforcements of different value have effects on the same behavior proportionate to their value. In this way behavior potential may be increased or decreased by the occurrence of a reinforcement either as a function of increased expectancy or as a function of the difference between a present and previous reinforcement. Should a positive reinforcement not occur or should the event that follows the behavior be punishing to the subject, the potentiality of the behavior's occurring would decrease. Likewise, if the reinforcement were positive or rewarding but less so than previous reinforcements, it would result in a decrease in the potentiality of the behavior's occurring. Reinforcements function to change expectancies and, consequently, to change behavior potentials. They also affect behavior in that they have a value and a sign.

Psychological Directionality

[Earlier in *Social Learning and Clinical Psychology*] were presented a number of statements regarding the nature of needs. A restatement of some of them might serve as an introduction to a formulation of some working concepts of psychological needs.

1. The unit of study is the interaction of the individual with his meaningful environment.
2. The behavior of the organism has directionality.
3. When this directionality is looked upon from the point of view of the organism or individual, we speak of internal reinforcement or needs. When it is looked upon from the point of view of the objects or conditions of the environment, we speak of external reinforcements or goals.
4. Such descriptions of the behavior of organisms may be appropriately applied only at a particular stage of development. Relevant preceding or present conditions for some events that cannot be described from a psychological point of view may have to be made in other modes of description.
5. A person's behaviors may be functionally related in terms of the directionality of the behavior. That is, the functional relationships among a person's

various behaviors and goals may be described in terms of a need or the common directionality of responses.

6. More specifically, a need refers to the potentiality of occurrence of a group of functionally related behaviors in specified life situations directed toward a group of functionally related reinforcements. Its strength depends upon the variables of freedom of movement and need value.

THE ORIGINS OF PSYCHOLOGICAL NEEDS

In describing the first appearance of psychological needs, it is necessary to describe the antecedent conditions in physiological terms. That is, psychological needs appear to arise as learned in relation to the drives of the organism as described in physiological terms. This would include such drives as thirst, hunger, warmth, and pain avoidance. Originally the strength of such psychological needs (i.e., the potentiality of a person's making movements toward learned reinforcements or goals) may be a function of the strength of the drives, as physiologically described, with which they were associated, the frequency of such associations, and so forth. Once the learned needs are acquired, their strength can be increasingly better predicted from their relationship to other psychological goals rather than from their relationship to the primary drives. Following their first occurrence they differ from unlearned drives in that tendency toward movement or action is determined by the presence of the correct cues or stimuli rather than by some cyclical internal condition describable only at a physiological level.[2] That is, we may predict most efficiently at what time a dog will look for food in his dish by referring to some internal set of cues that are dependent upon some cyclical change in the organism. The behavior is consistent with the presumed internal cyclical changes. However, the dog seeks the *recognition* (psychological) of his master whenever his master is present unless there are competing needs that are stronger. The relevant condition for predicting behavior is something external to the organism. It is true, of course, that even the dog seeking food in his dish is responding to learned stimuli with learned behavior, and that such behavior as well as behavior directed toward avoiding negative reinforcement may be described entirely on the psychological level. The distinction to be made here is that psychological needs (i.e., directionality of response seen from a psychological mode of description) deal with the relationship of behavior to situations or cues or stimuli as a function of

---

[2] Dollard and Miller (1950, p. 88) have made a similar distinction between what they refer to as learned and unlearned drives.

experience. Explanation in terms of drive deals primarily with the relationship of behavior to the strength of cyclical internal changes in the organism, changes that are not dependent upon past learnings. In the case of the psychological need, what the subject has is not some impulse to action but rather a potentiality of response as a function of learned relationships.

This social learning approach rejects the theory that psychological goals must be explained in terms of their leading to the satisfaction or neutralization of a physiologically described drive and resulting in reduction of that drive. *We find it a sufficient basis for prediction to state that behavior directed toward the attainment of a learned goal or external reinforcement may be predicted through a knowledge of the situation the organism is in and from a knowledge of his past learning experiences.* It appears as if a theory that attempted to predict meaningful behavior through the description of the organism's physiological drive condition at a particular moment would hold not only no advantages but many disadvantages.

THE VALUE OF PSYCHOLOGICAL NEEDS

If a psychological need or acquired goal does not depend upon the reduction of a primary drive with which it was initially paired, what then does determine its strength, its value, its selective power, or its preference value for the subject? It is hypothesized that the value of any acquired reinforcement is a function of its relationship to other reinforcements. Each pairing of a reinforcement changes its value in the direction of the reinforcement with which it is paired. More specifically, the value of a reinforcement is determined by the value of subsequent reinforcements with which it has been associated and the expectancy or degree of relationship that has been developed between it and these subsequent reinforcements. That is, the value of a reinforcement or the strength of the psychological need, which is the internal referent for a reinforcement, is determined by the kinds of reinforcement it occurred in relation to, and is not *necessarily* lowered by the failure to continue to be associated with the original reinforcements.[3] It is true, however, that under certain conditions of

---

[3] In considering the change of any reinforcement value as the result of a failure to occur on the part of the original or any previous reinforcement to which it was attached, a variety of conditions are probably of significance. These would include previous pattern of associations (i.e., partial vs. 100 per cent reinforcement), the degree to which the original relationship was verbalized, and the degree to which the new failure of association is verbalized.

massing, the failure of a reinforcement to lead to another positive reinforcement with which it is currently associated will lead to diminution in behavior. It will be shown later that this may be explained as due to the reduction of expectancies that the original reinforcement will follow the present one. It is possible that any learned need or goal can have its value increased by new associations with the satisfaction of physiological drives or decreased by association with the frustration of these drives. Neither possibility, however, is necessary for the maintenance of the reinforcement, which may derive its value because of associations with other reinforcements of a *learned* nature—satisfaction coming not from the reduction of physiological drives but in perception of movement toward more generalized goals of security or psychological homeostasis. That is, the organism learns to move in the direction of specific environmental conditions and expects or obtains satisfaction by experiencing movement toward these goals. The organism is seeking a general state of continuous movement toward learned or acquired goals. It tends to prefer, therefore, the pathways or behaviors that lead more often to the reaching of the goal. This might be stated another way. The presence of a cue, stimulus, or situation that has previously been associated with satisfaction, negative or positive, is enough to enable us to predict the movement of the subject toward or away from that goal. However, it is not necessary that the state of the organism (described physiologically) at the time that the goal was originally learned be reproduced. Nor is it necessary in order for the goal to maintain itself that it lead to a reduction of the same drive or, for that matter, a different drive. Miles and Wickens (1953) have shown in a study with rats that the occurrence of secondary reinforcers had no demonstrable effect in reducing primary hunger drives.

This description of the way psychological goals acquire strength or value provides an explanation of some very interesting apparent paradoxes. For example, the paradox whereby originally the mother is associated with food; and, because of this association with food the mother's ideals take on a high positive value; finally, because of these ideals, a person will go without eating for long periods of time and will be ready, if the occasion demands, to starve. In the course of development these ideals have been tied so strongly to so many different satisfactions that they acquire a value or strength far in excess of any of the physiological drives to which they could be traced historically. Such a phenomenon of voluntary starvation may seem to be unusual or exceptional. It is possible, however, to find millions of men going into armies, experiencing extreme privation and continuous threats of death, primarily (as far as can be determined) because of such psychological motives as fear of public opinion, the need to demonstrate masculinity, and the need to maintain ideals.

If a learned reinforcement is attached positively to a physiological satisfaction and then subsequently becomes attached to other psychological satisfactions, it can become stronger than the original physiological drive to which it was related. If, on the other hand, a psychological need is associated with the satisfaction of a physiological drive and then becomes attached negatively or leads to the frustration of another psychological goal such as a learned need for affection or praise, it may become considerably weaker than the physiological drive to which it was originally related. If, once learned, a psychological need is no longer paired with any physiological satisfactions, it will maintain the same value that it had as a result of its original pairings providing it is not paired with any new reinforcements. If it continues to be paired positively, it may increase in value; if it becomes paired negatively, it will decrease in value. Generally speaking, *a goal or reinforcement that is learned or acquired and no longer paired with an original reinforcement will maintain its strength or value except as it changes on the basis of new pairings with other reinforcements physiologically described or psychologically described.* (An exception to this with which we are not concerned here is the change in Reinforcement Value that takes place as a result of the generalization of changes in values of functionally related reinforcements.) These learned and acquired goals, because they are so numerous, dominate more and more of a person's behavior as he develops and becomes aware of these relationships. In our culture, where there is rarely strong frustration of the hunger drive, it is not long in the development of the child before he becomes indifferent to the matter of who is now directly responsible for producing his food. More and more the importance of other people lies in their relationships in terms of such psychological goals as recognition, love, and dependence.

The Nature of Functional Relationships Among External Reinforcements

Up to this point, most of the discussion has centered around the value (or preference value) of a single reinforcement. Were prediction of behavior dependent on knowledge of the value of each potential reinforcement in the psychological environment, it would be extremely difficult to predict everyday behavior. It is hypothesized, however, that the value of various reinforcements may be predicted from the value of other reinforcements on the basis of functional relationships among them. These functional relationships are best described by means of various concepts of generalization.

In order to understand how functional relationships among a person's behaviors or goals occur, it is necessary to use three concepts of generalization as a hypothetical basis on which such functional relationships develop. These three concepts are: *primary stimulus generalization,* an extended version of *mediated stimulus generalization,* and a special case of the latter—*generalization of expectancy changes.*

On the basis of primary stimulus generalization we may speak of original functional similarity among external reinforcements or goals. To illustrate, by means of stimulus generalization a more or less uniform reaction may develop to the mother although she is seen in different dresses, and this reaction generalizes to some degree to all human beings.

The concept of mediated stimulus generalization accounts for the functional relationship among behaviors leading to the accomplishment of the same reinforcement. Emphasis at this point is upon mediation by means of the same reinforcement rather than by means of the same response; in practice this may not prove to be a significant difference. By leading to the same reinforcement, behaviors acquire a functional equivalence. For example, if screaming, kicking, and other similar behaviors all lead to expressions of annoyance on the part of a parent, some functional equivalence between these behaviors will arise. A strong reinforcement, positive or negative, of one of these behaviors will affect the potential of occurrence of any of the other functionally related behaviors to a greater degree than it will affect the potentials of behaviors not so functionally related. Both of the above concepts of generalization have been extensively described in psychological writings.

The third concept is somewhat novel, being distinctly related to an expectancy formulation of learning. This concept may be called generalization of expectancy changes and may be considered a special case of mediated stimulus generalization. It too depends upon mediation as a function of the similarity of reinforcements. Perhaps the best way to describe this kind of generalization is to pose an illustrative question. What happens to the child's expectancy of getting an ice cream cone after he has just been refused a candy bar? It can be demonstrated that the occurrence (or nonoccurrence) of a given reinforcement produces changes in expectancy for the occurrence of other reinforcements. It can also be demonstrated that changes in expectancy for other reinforcements follow a gradient, on which the child refused candy might have a lowered expectancy of getting ice cream while his expectancy of hurting his foot should he kick the door remains relatively unchanged. The nature of the generalization gradient of such expectancy changes would have to be determined empirically, although it may be hypothesized that the gradient would follow dimensions of similarity of reinforcement.

The generalization of expectancy along need-related lines has been tested and demonstrated by Crandall (1950), R. Jessor (1951), and Chance (1952). Crandall utilized three specific need areas of presumed functional relationship on the basis of cultural analysis. He selected (1) need for affection from opposite sex peers, (2) need for recognition through academic competence, and (3) need for recognition through physical coordination skills. The latter two were presumed to be more similar since they both could be included in a more encompassing need for recognition. The experimental variable was a frustrating situation introduced while the subject was attempting to gain recognition through physical skills. Pre- and post-measures of the expectancy for success or freedom of movement for these three needs were made; a balanced design with 18 specially constructed pictures was used, and the pictures were administered like the Thematic Apperception Test. Ratings of freedom of movement or expectancy for success in these three need areas were made by judges using the stories told by the subjects from these pictures. The judges were not told the subjects' names or whether the subjects were experimental or control. Control subjects went through the procedure of telling nine stories, resting for a while, and then telling nine more stories. Experimental subjects had nine stories; were placed in a situation in which they were required to do some very difficult tasks in motor coordination, after which they were shown fictitious printed norms to indicate that they had done poorly; and finally were presented nine more pictures. The reliability of the rating of the judges for the freedom of movement for the three needs resulted in an average correlation of .72. The actual results for the matched groups of control and experimental subjects are shown in Figure 4.1.

The difference between the experimental and control subjects for loss in freedom of movement for physical skills was significant at the .01 level; for academic skills it was significant at the .02 level; and for love and affection of opposite sex peers, significant only at the .20 level. The size of the decrements follows the predicted line of need-relatedness. However, the results of this study could be explained by other theoretical approaches or as a function of uncontrolled stimulus factors in the experimental design. The studies by Jessor and Chance, therefore, made further tests of this hypothesis.

Jessor utilized a more direct method of measuring expectancy, following the level-of-aspiration paradigm. He utilized four tasks:

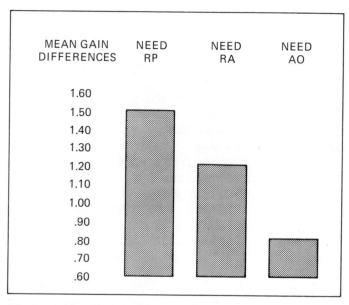

RP = Recognition Physical Skills
RA = Recognition Academic Skills
AO = Affection from Opposite Sex Peers

Figure 4.1 Differences of mean gains of experimental vs. control subjects from first to second thematic apperception testing in stories dealing with the three needs investigated (from Crandall)

task was the experimental task, the vocabulary task was an anagram test of increasing difficulty, the motor skill task utilized an epicyclic pursuit rotor, and the social skill task was described to the subject as a five-minute interview with one of the girls on the staff to determine general attractiveness to the opposite sex on the basis of a variety of personality characteristics. The subject was asked to estimate beforehand his expected scores on all four tasks on a 0-to-50 continuum and was told that an average score was 25. Jessor also asked the subjects to state a *minimal goal*. This was defined as the lowest score that they might receive and still feel satisfied with their performance. (A secondary interest in his study was to compare changes in expectancy scores with changes in minimal goal scores. These results will be dealt with elsewhere.) Following the initial statement of expectancy and minimal goal scores, the subject was given the arithmetic task; upon completion of this, he received a pre-arranged score that was either above or below his minimal goal score for the arithmetic task. In some cases this was more discrepant from the expectancy score than from the minimal goal score, and in some cases it was more discrepant from the minimal goal score than from the expectancy score. The subject was then asked to re-estimate his scores for another form of the same arithmetic task and, since he had not taken the other three tests yet, allowed to change his estimates on those if he wished. Since many of the subjects did not change scores, and since there was therefore a badly skewed distribution of changed scores, the results were analyzed in terms of the proportion of subjects who changed their expectancy scores on the four tasks. These results are given in Figure 4.2.

It may be noted that significant generalization effects took place which followed a gradient as predicted by the author in terms of the similarity of need or reinforcement based upon "common sense" or cultural knowledge. That is, the arithmetic and vocabulary tests were considered by the investigator to be closest together as two academic recognition tasks; the motor skill task next most similar, since it was a recognition task but of another area; and the social skill

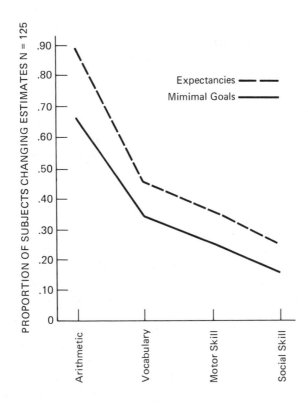

Figure 4.2 Gradients of generalization of expectancy changes for four tasks (from Jessor)

task most removed as a measure of recognition and also highly related to acceptance and love from opposite sex peers.

Chance (1952) recognized that the studies of Crandall and Jessor
were unable fully to control physical stimulus similarity as a basis for
prediction of generalization. She devised a third study, therefore, in
which the testing material was controlled for physical similarity.
Chance used two tests of an unstructured nature. One was a word
association test, the other an inkblot test, both described as measures
of personality. She employed four experimental conditions. In the
first condition the subjects were told that both tests measured
heterosexual adjustment. The second group was told that both tests
measured leadership potential. The third group was told that one
task measured leadership potential and the second one heterosexual
adjustment. In the fourth group the two tests were reversed—the subjects were told that the first test measured heterosexual adjustment
and the second test leadership potential. A procedure similar to
Jessor's was employed: the subjects stated expectancies for both
tasks, performed only one task (always the inkblot test), and then
were all given predetermined scores of either 7 or 14 points above
their estimate on the first task. Following this they were given their
second task and asked to restate their expectancies, which they were
given the opportunity to change if they wished. Chance's design was
balanced so that only the instructions regarding the nature of the
tasks differed for the different groups. She found that when the two
tasks were described as need-related, there was significantly greater
generalization than when they were described as measuring different
skills. She also found that the larger or 14-point increase resulted in
significantly greater generalization than the 7-point increase.

These three studies may be summed up as demonstrating the following: (1) generalization of expectancies takes place; (2) such generalization or the degree of generalization is a function of the amount
of change or increment in the original expectancy; (3) the generalizations follow a gradient; and (4) this gradient may be predicted from a
"common sense" or cultural knowledge of the degree of similarity
of the reinforcements or goals of the subjects. In all cases the gradient was determined or predicted before the study was made and veri-
fied without exception.

A recent study by Blumenkrantz (1953) has dealt with the problem of generalization of expectancy changes and at the same time
extended its implications to the area of recall after failure. His aim
was to investigate whether or not substitute successes after failure
have differential value in obviating the recall decrement and influ-

encing relearning on an originally failed task as a function of the degree of need-relatedness of the two tasks. He was able to show that there was a significant decrement in recall as a result of failure on the original task and that this recall decrement was obviated or diminished by an interpolated success experience. The interpolated success experience was a recognition test similar in need classification to the original failed task, and when this group with interpolated success was compared to a control group with no interpolated success but the same interpolated task, there was a strong tendency for the recall decrement to be diminished (for a two-tailed test $P = .10$ and $.08$). When the interpolated task was a social skills task, this success experience did not significantly reduce the recall decrement. The results of this study are more suggestive than conclusive. Theoretical analysis of the problem of memory and recall is being carried out by Jessor and others working with him. Such analysis, however, is now only in its initial stages.

These findings provide support for the idea that needs may be determined empirically rather than on an a priori, assumed, instinctual, or drive basis, and that such empirically derived needs may be quite useful in predicting how expectancies are generalized.

It seems logical that if such generalizations continue over a period of time so that expectancies for particular behavior-reinforcement sequences will have maximum generalization of one to the other, then these expectancies must also be correlated or be more similar to each other in level than to expectancies for a random selection of behavior-reinforcement sequences.

Assuming that the above formulations of the nature of generalization can be accepted, it could be predicted that the expectancy of a complex of behaviors leading to the same (or similar) reinforcements would tend to be similar for behaviors within the complex, since they are affected to a maximum degree by a generalization effect of one to the other. The expectancy of any one behavior's leading to positive reinforcement could then be estimated to some extent from the expectancy of any other behavior's leading to the same reinforcement. On this basis it would seem that the functional relationships among reinforcements and among behaviors may be approached profitably through concepts like psychological needs, which organize and classify behaviors and goals (external reinforcements) in terms of directionality (similarity of reinforcements). In this way an empirical and logical basis is provided for considering a person's behavior in terms of broader generalized categories (i.e., he is a highly dependent person) without necessitating a trait, faculty, typological, or instinctual approach to personality. Such descriptions, however, must be limited by some reference to the situations in which the behavior is presumed to occur.

Functional relationships like those proposed above must be determined empirically, and the classification or organization of reinforcements into psychological needs must be described as characteristic only of the particular culture in which the classification is made. Behaviors that bring love, approval, disapproval, praise, and so on in one culture will differ considerably from those that bring the same reinforcements in another culture.

Although it is true that a functional similarity will appear between behaviors or reinforcements, the amount of such similarity is determined by the degree to which these events have led to the same reinforcement, or to each other, in the experience of the particular subject. Consequently, one might expect that the more any classification scheme is broadened, the less functional similarity will exist between any two randomly selected behaviors or reinforcements included in that classification. Stated another way, intercorrelations of reinforcement values or of behavior potentials within any need will tend to be lower as the classification is more broadly conceived and made more inclusive. The more limited and specific the classification, the higher the functional similarity of any two randomly selected behaviors within the need, and the higher the predictability from one behavior potential or reinforcement value to another within the same classification. These inferences appear to be supported by Rockwell's (1950) study of the generality of needs.

THE CONCEPT OF HIERARCHY AND OF SYSTEMS OF NEEDS

Any behavior or any reinforcement may have a number of functional relationships. That is, any behavior may have a potential of leading to a specific reinforcement in one specific situation, and have another potential in relation to a different reinforcement in the same or a different situation. Abstractions regarding the potential of a set of behaviors all leading to the same kind of reinforcement (need potential) or abstractions of the similarity of a set of reinforcements in given situations are derived from specific behaviors and complex situations. Any single need abstraction is not the only representative of the values and relationships that could be derived from these behaviors or reinforcements. Any behavior may be a part of many systems of behaviors; any reinforcement may be a part of many systems of reinforcement. The psychologist treats those systems that are relevant to his particular purposes at any time.

From the previous paragraphs it may be seen that any group of reinforcements which may be considered similar may, in turn, be considered similar to a larger organization of reinforcements that is yet more inclusive. This process of broadening the classification of reinforcements may be continued until one arrives at a single over-all concept of directionality. Such a single organization may be referred to as *security* or *psychological homeostasis.* Within the framework of such an organization, all behaviors are to some degree functionally related to all other behaviors. However, the level of inclusiveness of generality in classifying behavior that one proposes to use in describing a person's needs will be determined by the breadth and/or exactitude required of one's prediction. The broader or the more inclusive the classification of the directionality of behavior (psychological needs), the greater the variety of behaviors about which predictions can be made, but the less accurate the predictions regarding any specific event. The more inclusive the category, the lower the correlation between any two randomly selected events included in the category.

Dean (1953) tested the hypotheses that the difference between a person's stated expectancies and his actual performance (what is usually referred to as a D-score in level-of-aspiration studies) could be predicted: (1) most accurately from previous experience or presumed expectancies in a situation similar to the one for which a prediction was to be made and involving almost the identical behavior-reinforcement sequences, (2) less accurately from a sampling of a variety of situations that involve the same skill but are abstracted from a more inclusive level of generality, and (3) least accurately from the subject's expectancy of success for behavior reinforcements in general from a sampling of almost any kind of situation excluding the specific category being predicted. More specifically, in a motor-skill level-of-aspiration task, Dean attempted to predict D-scores: (1) from previous performances in a similar task, (2) from expectancies for success determined through an interview for motor coordination tasks more generally, and (3) from an estimate of expectancy for success in general for all kinds of behaviors excluding motor coordination tasks. The interview for the two latter measures was made in a single setting but on different records so that the judges might evaluate them separately and without bias. Since the obtained correlation between these latter two measures (expectancy in motor coordination and expectancy in general) was not significantly greater than zero, the experimental procedure appeared to be successful in eliminating any bias between the two interview ratings.

It should be noted that Dean was attempting to measure not the stated expectancies but the expectancies resulting from generalization from functionally related experiences. He tried to predict behavior using three levels of abstraction, each one more inclusive than the preceding one. For each level of generality he selected one or more referents of behavior-expectancy-reinforcement sequences to predict the specific behavior in his experimental level-of-aspiration situation. The experimental task was the Level of Aspiration Board, which is shown in Figure 4.3.

His first category of a similar task was a modified level-of-aspiration board on which a plunger was substituted for the miniature pool cue used in the experimental task. Since the Level of Aspiration Board can be controlled within reasonably narrow limits, subjects were given a prearranged sequence of scores on a random basis to fit a normal distribution in the preliminary trial. In this way their uncontrolled performance in the experimental task would not

Figure 4.3   The level of aspiration board

be likely to be similar to that in the pre-task, but rather for the whole group it would have only a chance relationship.

Dean did find reasonably high prediction of the difference between a subject's performance and his stated expectancies from previous performance in the related task (Pearsonian r .70). In predicting from expectancy of success for motor coordination tasks in general, the difference between the performance and stated expectations could be predicted on the basis of an Eta (Eta .42).[4]

For Dean's measure of expectancy of success in general, with motor coordination tasks excluded, Eta dropped to .26. Apparently for the accuracy of the measuring instruments used, such a classification was too broad to allow for high prediction. In general his results strongly supported the hypothesis that the more inclusive or more general the category being utilized for predicting a specific behavior, the lower the prediction between any two or any set of independent referents within that category.

Since needs or directionality may be abstracted from different points of view and categorized at almost any level of inclusiveness or generality, we are faced in the problem of measurement and communication with an infinite variety of potential need names or categories. We must also be concerned with procedures for determining functional relationships of directionality. We must have terms that are not hit or miss, terms that will provide a language of description with good communicability or reliability and high functional utility or predictiveness. Where are we to find such terms?

Unfortunately, the point of view presented in this book is only a way of looking at the problem of personality and not a revelation from above in regard to the empirical facts of human nature. This point of view emphasizes the importance of testing empirically the functionality or utility of the concepts we use. It does not by mere theorizing provide the tremendous quantity of empirical findings necessary to a highly predictive, individual method of describing personality. We must, however, be able to state the procedures by which such a language would be developed and to make a start in its development. To begin the process of selecting concepts (abstractions regarding directionality) it is necessary to utilize the empirical in-

---

[4]The relationship between freedom of movement or expectancies for success in motor coordination tasks and stated expectancies is a curvilinear one, with some individuals with low freedom of movement underestimating and others overestimating in an unrealistic fashion—a finding consistent with previous research by Sears (1940, 1941) and Rotter (1943). Such "defensive behavior" might also be expected from this theoretical point of view, as we shall show in the discussion of low freedom of movement in the following chapter.

formation that is now available. Much of this is in the nature of the observations of clinicians and students of our culture. The concepts we may choose to work with originally should be those that seem most promising from the experience derived from the psychotherapeutic and general clinical experience of clinical psychologists. They should incorporate the experience of clinicians (whether Adlerian, psychoanalytic, Rankian, social learning, or whatever) and of sociologists such as Thomas who have been concerned with the problem for many years. The theory itself does not dictate in any way what these need category names should be. Concepts such as conformity, dependence, independence, status need, and need to dominate may all be highly useful; and all are subject to being broken down into lower levels of generality so that one may speak, for example, not merely of a need for dependence but of a need to depend upon parents, a need to depend upon peers, a need to depend upon the opposite sex, and so on. Eventually the reliability and the validity of many of these concepts will be tried out. Their utility for predicting specific behaviors will determine the preference accorded them. Attempts can then be made to develop high communicability regarding these terms and to develop instruments of known validity to apply in different situations for the purpose of measurement. However, the process itself of finding more refined or functionally useful abstractions of directionality and of developing new ones to deal with new problems as they arise is an endless one. Perhaps a merit of this point of view is that the psychologist will never work himself out of a job but will continually be faced with the problem of how to improve his language of description and his descriptive concepts. It is necessary to set up a language of description with communicability and functional utility. The realization that such description will always require improvement should help the clinician avoid wasting his efforts in defending any descriptive language as the "last word."

To begin this conceptual process some six need terms were developed in an attempt to define at a very broad level of generality most of the historically utilized concepts regarding drive, need, directionality of behavior, or motivational variables that have been useful to clinicians of many backgrounds. From these broad categories more specific terms or abstractions could be made, some of which could be almost entirely included in one of the broad categories, and some of which would be as obviously related to one broad category as to another. For example, for a category such as recognition, we could have a subcategory of academic recognition that might be almost entirely included in the broader classification. But a category such as the need to conform might be no more related to the need to be recognized than it is to the need to be accepted, approved, or loved. Six broad categories thought to be of relatively equal levels of inclusiveness were defined; the ideal definitions of these are given below:[5]

Recognition-Status: Need to be considered competent or good in a professional, social, occupational, or play activity. Need to gain social or vocational position—that is, to be more skilled or better than others.

Protection-Dependency: The need to have another person or group of people prevent frustration or punishment and to provide for the satisfaction of other needs.

Dominance: Need to direct or control the actions of other people, including members of family and friends. To have any action taken be that which he suggests.

Independence: Need to make own decisions, to rely on oneself, together with the need to develop skills for obtaining satisfactions directly without the mediation of other people.

Love and Affection: Need for acceptance and indication of liking by other individuals. In contrast to recognition-status, not concerned with social or professional position of friends, but seeks their warm regard.

Physical Comfort: Learned need for physical satisfaction that has become associated with the gaining of security.

Rockwell (1950) attempted to measure these six need constructs by utilizing a variety of measures in different situations and to determine the degree of predictability among the different measures. Correlations were obtained for the same concept measured in different situations and the intercorrelations or independence of these six concepts was determined. . . .

[Details of this study are deleted in order to conserve space.] Her results are of such complexity that they must be summarized (1950, p. 122):

Independence showed the greatest generality; Protection-Dependency and Dominance next; Love and Affection and Recognition-Status next; and

---

[5] Contrary to the way some would handle the concepts of dependence and independence, it will be noted that these two are considered not merely reciprocals of each other but independent ways of behaving that may not be highly correlated within the same person; since there are many other alternatives of action, it is possible for both to be relatively high or both to be relatively low. In addition to this, a person who shows a moderate amount of dependency behavior or dependency need potential and of independence need potential may still be characterized in one case as having a very high need value for independence but a low expectancy, but, on the other hand, as having a high expectancy for dependence but a low need value. That is, as measured within this system, two groups of behaviors are considered important enough to be measured separately; though they may frequently correlate negatively, such negative correlation is probably not any higher than the positive correlation between dependency and love and affection needs.

Physical Comfort practically none. A partial interpretation of the poor
Recognition-Status generality is that the homogeneous subject sample,
college students presumably high in Recognition-Status needs, prevented
much differentiation in respect to this concept. In the Incomplete Sentences Test and in the Interview few responses ratable as Physical Comfort
were elicited.   elicited.

The concepts were found to be interrelated in such a fashion as to
suggest two major clusters of needs with Protection-Dependency and Love
and Affection being one cluster and Independence and Dominance the
other cluster. Protection-Dependency and Love and Affection were frequently correlated positively; Independence and Dominance were frequently correlated positively and negatively related to the first two.
Recognition-Status tended to be related to the Independence and Dominance group but somewhat more equivocally. Physical Comfort seemingly
was of such unreliability as to show little relation with either group, but
was somewhat closer to Love and Affection and Protection-Dependency.

THE MEASUREMENT OF BEHAVIOR POTENTIAL

. . . The measurement of behavior potential can be direct or indirect.
Direct measurement would be accomplished by determining the
presence or absence or the frequency of actual occurrence of the
behavior. In any given situation it is presumed that the behavior that
occurs is the one with the highest potential. Behavior potential may
also be measured directly in terms of the frequency with which the
behavior occurs in a series of situations. In the first type of measurement, we are limited to an all-or-none representation. In the second
type of measurement, scores along a continuum may be calculated,
not only for the most frequently occurring behavior but also for
other behaviors.

What constitutes a behavior? We are concerned with psychological behavior or the changes that take place in a person or his relationship to the environment as a function of his response or reaction to
the acquired significance of his environment. We recognize, however,
the importance of implicit behavior, or behavior that is not readily
observed directly; such behaviors must frequently be determined by
the presence of other behaviors with which they are associated either
invariably or with high frequency. For example, in the study by
Schroder and Rotter (1952), a behavior of "looking for alternative
solutions" was presumed to be present and to be reinforced in some
experimental groups. The measures, however, for this behavior or the
test of its occurrence were measures of the time taken by the subjects for the solution of their problems.

The study by Schroder and Rotter will be presented below in

some detail as an illustration of how it is possible to measure indirectly an implicit behavior, in this case a behavior of *looking for alternatives*, which was presumed to be present with differing potential in four groups of subjects on the basis of initial training. The implicit behavior of looking for alternatives was considered to account for behavior that is frequently referred to as flexibility or the absence of "rigidity." This study will also have relevance for some of our later discussions in the chapter on psychotherapy. It is presented here in some detail, however, primarily to illustrate how the presence and strength of a behavior potential for an implicit behavior may be assumed from antecedent conditions and measured by subsequent observable behaviors.

The task consisted of grouping. On each trial the subject grouped six cards into three pairs on the basis of color, inside form, or outside form. The cards had different background colors (color) on which were large geometric figures (outside form), with smaller geometric figures inside the larger ones (inside form). Generally the cards were constructed so that grouping was possible on only one of the above bases. The experimental design is shown in Table 4.1. The table is read in terms of the following considerations: (a) Each letter (e.g., x_1) refers to a trial, i.e., when the subject is handed six cards to be grouped into three pairs on the basis of form or color. (b) x = grouping possible on outside form only; y = grouping possible on color only; z = grouping possible on inside form only; z' = grouping possible on inside and outside form. (c) No single grouping was difficult once the relevant principle was selected. (d) From x_1 to x_7 there was a progression from grouping on outside forms that are exactly alike to grouping on outside forms not so objectively similar. That is, the difficulty increased if difficulty is defined as greater objective dissimilarity of the forms to be grouped together. (e) x_5 was given last in each training sequence, so that comparisons between the groups were possible. (f) z_1, z_2, and z_3 contained inside form as the basis of grouping into pairs. (g) In z_4 the inside forms were the only basis for

Table 4.1 Experimental Design

Group	Training Trials 1 2 3 4 5 6 7	Experimental Trials 1 2 3 4 5 6 7 8 9
1	$x_1\,x_2\,x_3\,x_4\,x_6\,x_7\,x_5$	
2	$x_1\,x_2\,x_3\,x_4\,x_5$	$z_1\,z_2\,z_3\,z_4\,z'_5\,z'_6\,z'_7\,z'_8\,x_9$
3	$x_1\,y_1\,y_2\,x_2\,x_3\,x_4\,x_5$	
4	$x_1\,y_1\,x_2\,y_2\,x_3\,x_4\,x_5$	

Source: Schroder and Rotter, 1952.

grouping, but were less objectively similar than in z_1, z_2, and z_3. (h) From z'_5 to z'_8 there was a progression in that (1) inside figures as a basis for grouping became more dissimilar, and (2) outside figures as a basis for grouping became more similar.

For Groups I and II the training sequences consisted of training in grouping the cards on outside form for all trials. In Groups III and IV the training trials required grouping on outside form for some trials and color for others. The experimental sequence, which was constant for each group, demanded a new behavior or solution (inside form) on the first experimental trial. After four such trials the subject could change his basis of grouping back to outside form on any trial.

The four groups may be considered to make up a continuum in terms of the degree or amount of training they have in shifting to new solutions as opposed to solving each problem with the same solution. Group I was expected to be the most rigid since it had the most training in single solutions and no training in looking for alternatives. It had seven trials in which the correct solution was outside form. Group II is likewise a rigid group but one with not so much training and therefore not so high an expectancy for a solution for the same behavior. This group had five trials in which the correct solution was outside form. In Group III it was necessary for the subjects to shift to a color response for the second and third trials and then back to an outside form solution on the fourth trial, so they might be expected to have had reinforced at least twice the behavior of looking for alternative solutions. Group IV, which had the same number of color solutions as III but had them separated in such a manner as to require a Group IV subject to shift his solutions four times, would be the least rigid group.

It was thought possible to make four different tests of the hypothesis that the more training the group had in looking for alternatives the greater would be the potential of some behaviors occurring that would serve as an indirect measure of this implicit behavior. The first of these was that when the solution changed from outside form (x) to inside form (z) at the first experimental (z) trial, the time for solution would progressively decrease from Groups I to IV, since this would be the order in which the groups might be expected to give up trying to solve on the basis of outside form and would begin looking for new alternatives. The second hypothesis was that the groups trained to be more rigid would improve rapidly on the second trial since they would switch over to a new single solution but such improvement would progressively decline as the groups were trained to look for alternatives. The third hypothesis was that the more a group was trained to look for alternatives, even though they had less training on the outside form solution in the original training series, the quicker they would return to the original outside form solution, since they are looking for alternative ways of solving the problem. And the fourth hypothesis was that the more a group was trained to look for alternatives the more the subjects would fluctuate back and forth between x and z solutions during those trials where both are possible.

Results of this study relevant to these four hypotheses are given in Table 4.2 and Figures 4.4 and 4.5. All four hypotheses were supported at statistically significant levels.

It would be hard to account for these results on any basis other than that a behavior of looking for alternatives was differentially reinforced in the four groups, so that the behavior had differential expectancies of leading to reinforcement.

It is not necessary to set limits on the kinds of operations to be used in identifying behaviors. Although we are concerned with learned reactions to meaningful stimuli, the reactions themselves may be described by any kind of communicable language. Thus as an empirically determined operation, we would accept clenching of fists as an indication of aggressive behavior or flushing as an indication of a shame behavior if it could be demonstrated that the relationship between the behaviors is sufficiently high for one to indicate the

Table 4.2   Mean Time (Seconds) for Total Training Trials, x_5 and All Testing Trials

Trials	Group 1 Mean	SD	Group 2 Mean	SD	Group 3 Mean	SD	Group 4 Mean	SD
Training								
All	211.3	85.2	69.0	27.1	196.2	62.0	209.8	106.0
x_5	16.7	14.6	16.3	12.0	21.2	11.0	23.5	17.8
Testing								
z_1	24.00	11.80	19.77	10.42	15.42	8.77	11.59	4.42
z_2	12.19	6.50	12.50	4.11	13.19	6.12	14.88	7.74
z_3	12.80	8.08	13.80	9.14	13.54	8.60	16.14	6.72
z_4	17.80	14.00	14.15	4.14	26.53	23.60	20.73	15.76
z'_5	16.46	15.30	25.80	30.80	34.30	40.60	19.07	16.16
z'_6	14.04	8.40	13.96	7.21	15.50	6.80	14.19	7.30
z'_7	11.00	4.40	13.46	7.56	17.46	8.43	13.80	4.12
z'_8	12.85	7.80	15.46	10.04	17.69	10.70	16.53	9.24
x_9	13.81	6.10	18.34	14.50	14.76	7.18	16.34	10.40

Source: Schroder and Rotter, 1952.

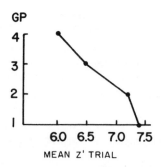

Figure 4.4 Mean trial at which each group changed back to grouping on *x* (outside form)

Source: Schroder and Rotter, 1952.

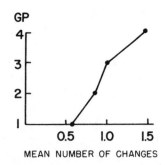

Figure 4.5 Mean number of alternations in solution for each group in testing series

Source: Schroder and Rotter, 1952.

presence of the other, or more accurately, for the readily observable behavior to indicate the presence of the presumed implicit behavior. In some cases we may be able to demonstrate how a specific behavior was acquired as a method of reaching a given goal. When our descriptive identification of a behavior, however, is by a physiological mode of description rather than a psychological, then this system would not be able logically to explain or describe the acquisition of the behavior. Consequently, we prefer to stay within the realm of psychological description where possible. However, it is entirely acceptable for practical purposes or for purposes of efficiency to define behaviors by any mode of description where we may obtain reliability and communicability and when our purpose is solely to account for or predict the acquired response of a person to his meaningful environment.

Another problem that arises concerns the determination of a unit of behavior. We may speak of the goal-directed behavior of a person—for example, going to a class. This may involve his finding his way through a crowded campus, stopping and talking to several people, finally entering a building, entering the correct classroom, sitting down, spreading out his books, and so on. At other times we may be concerned with whether the same person upon entering the class makes the choice of sitting down and opening a book to catch up on his reading assignment or whether he sits and talks to his neighbor instead. Obviously, we have no way of setting up an absolute criterion for determining units of behavior. Behaviors appear in sequences; the person who is at least awake is behaving continuously (from a psychological viewpoint), particularly when one includes implicit behavior. Behavior to be dealt with as a unit for purposes of either experimental or clinical prediction must of course be determined by the purposes of the investigator. Within this system we are concerned primarily with what may be called choice behavior, or the selecting of an alternative from a series of possible alternatives. When a sequence of acts requires only one such choice on the part of the subject, it seems logical to consider this as a single behavior unit even though the actions of the subject may be described as constituting a series of clearly differentiatable acts.

Tyler (1952), in a study of college students, has recently demonstrated that under certain conditions—particularly those when a first reinforcement is followed invariably by a second, and third, reinforcement—the behaviors leading to all of the reinforcements may be explained only in terms of a single unit or sequence, the reinforcement value for which is a total of the reinforcements which occur in that sequence. We usually choose as a unit of behavior an action that appears to be followed by some observable or measurable reinforcement, although this may constitute a long sequence of acts. Tyler's study, however, can also be analyzed to show that although we may sometimes consider sequences of acts followed by reinforcements as single units and treat them as such, it is possible even in such sequences to treat each reinforcement and each behavior separately to predict its occurrence (as long as we consider that the value of any reinforcement is determined by the other reinforcements that may be expected to follow from it either occasionally or invariably). For convenience, however, we may choose to treat a sequence of behaviors and reinforcements as a single unit, particularly when the sequence of events is of the invariable or 100 per cent kind.

THE INDIRECT MEASUREMENT OF
BEHAVIOR POTENTIAL

Direct measurement of behavior potential involves noting the occurrence of actual behavior in some specific situation. Behavior potentials may also be determined by the mathematical combination of expectancy and reinforcement value. Actually, all measurement from this point of view is measurement of behavior, whether we are attempting to measure expectancy, reinforcement value, behavior potential, or other variables. We are measuring something the subject says, does, or changes; something that constitutes part of his adjustment to the meaningful environment. Our measures of expectancy and reinforcement value are in reality measurements of behavior from which we may deduce expectancies and reinforcement values. They may never be measured directly but are only implied or determined from some observable act of the subject. Nevertheless, we may use these special behaviors, used to determine expectancies and reinforcement values, or special measurement situations to arrive at an estimate of the potentiality of some other behavior's occurring. For example, in the measurement of expectancy one typical technique is to provide choices in which the reinforcement value is constant. Similarly for the measurement of reinforcement value a common technique is to hold expectancy constant.

To the degree that we are able to control one of these two variables we may then assume that behavior potentials are directly proportionate to the magnitude of the variable that is allowed to vary. Thus, in a given situation, if the reinforcement value for six alternative behaviors is the same (this may be accomplished most easily by having the actual reinforcement the same for the six behaviors), it would be possible to measuure for these six behaviors the expectancy that the behaviors would lead to or be followed by the reinforcement. In this case we assume that the behavior potential for the six behaviors is directly proportionate to their expectancy values. Similarly for reinforcement value, if we hold expectancy constant for a variety of behaviors then we would presume that the behavior potentials would be proportionate to the reinforcement values, which might differ. Such techniques are satisfactory for prediction in carefully controlled experimental situations.

Obviously, before behavior potentials can be measured by combining expectancies and reinforcement values when neither variable is constant, we must begin to formulate precisely the nature of the mathematical relationship between these two variables. Although expectancy may be measured on an absolute scale, so that an expectancy of .60 will have comparable meaning for different subjects in different situations, we have as yet not devised a similar absolute way of measuring reinforcement values. The forced-choice and ranking techniques that have been used primarily to date do not provide measures that are comparable from subject to subject or from situation to situation when the actual reinforcements being measured are different. Methods of arriving at absolute measures, however, are not logically impossible; they are primarily laborious. At the present time experiments are being conducted to determine the feasibility of estimating such absolute measures at least on a preliminary basis. When it is possible to measure inforcement values so that they will be of comparable significance along some general continuum, comparable from situation to situation and from person to person, then it will be possible to develop a generalized formula in which expectancy and reinforcement value may be combined for the most efficient prediction of behavior potential.

Although a generalized formula for accurate prediction is not available at the present time, data now available indicate that within any single experimental situation with relative values for reinforcements and absolute values for expectancies some multiplicative mathematical relationship can be utilized to combine these two and make gross predictions of behavior potential. It could be readily demonstrated that when expectancy and reinforcement value are both high, behavior potential is greater than when they are both moderate or both low; that when expectancy is high and reinforcement value moderate, behavior potential is higher than when both are moderate; and so on. By using experimental conditions such as those described above or by holding either one of these two variables constant, it is possible to state and test hypotheses involving general principles of behavior. Such hypotheses would have to be stated in "more or less" terms for experimental groups undergoing different experimental conditions.

It should be clear that we still have far to go before accurate predictions of human behavior can be made. However, such a two-variable theory is an advance over a single-variable theory that attempts to predict behavior entirely on an expectancy principle or entirely on the basis of the strength of a drive or need.

The advantage of such a two-variable theory in understanding behavior can be illustrated by describing a common observation, apparently paradoxical, made by clinicians working in institutions for indigent or delinquent children. Often children sent to such institutions though differing considerably in their early environmental experiences, nevertheless have in common at the time of admission a history of aggressive or antisocial acts of some long standing. Some of these children, if they meet with an understanding and sympathetic professional worker, will continue to act aggressively and form no strong personal relationships to the worker. Other children, however, become quickly attached to this understanding adult and are anxious and willing to do everything possible to conform or to please the adult who gives them some direct understanding and affection. Most, if not all, of these cases have long histories of rejection, at least for some time before admission to the institution; it is difficult, therefore, if not impossible, to account for these differences entirely in terms of their expectancy or anticipation of affection from adults. In most of these cases it is rather obvious that such expectancies are close to the zero point. The differences are better accounted for in terms of the value or importance of the need for affection and the greater potentiality of some children to behave in a way that will result in such gratifications because of the high value for them of affection reinforcements.

On the other hand, if we were trying to explain behavior entirely on the basis of strength of need, we would be unable to explain the fact that both kinds of children (that is, those with high and low needs for affection) in a rejecting environment behaved in essentially the same way. Obviously to account for this we must consider that in their usual life situations, expectancies for the occurrence of such reinforcements were very low for both groups. If we are able to assess both of these measures, the expectancy for satisfaction and value of the satisfaction as well, then we might be able to predict that in a different situation, where it can be demonstrated that such reinforcements are available, these children would act in a differential manner. Their behavior would depend upon the value of these reinforcements (of adult affection) as compared with other needs such as, for example, status with a peer group.

Increments in Behavior Potential

Behavior potentials change. That is, increments of behavior potentials occur as a function of new experience. They change not only as a result of the occurrence of reinforcements following the behaviors but also as a result of generalization of changes in the behavior potentials of related behaviors. Such changes may take place either where the individual verbalizes the nature of the relationship between the behaviors, or where he does not. The mathematical expression of such increments resulting from changed expectancies or reinforcement values can be formulated only after a predictive mathematical relationship between the two variables is determined. Where it is possible to hold one variable constant, the measurable increments in either expectancy or reinforcement value would again be proportionate to any changes in behavior potential. It will be shown that it is possible, at least in some situations, to measure increments in expectancy with considerable accuracy. It should likewise be possible to determine increments in reinforcement value, at least in specific situations, with reasonable efficiency.

Of course, behavior potentials change as a result of pairing with new reinforcements. Whether on the basis of contiguity in time or space, or on the basis of verbal relationships, new reinforcements are continually being attached to behaviors. The calculation of any behavior potential, as has been stated earlier, must take into account all of the reinforcements that may occur in this situation for which the individual has an expectancy greater than zero. [A case history deleted here is similar to one presented in Chapter 2 of this book.]

THE MEASUREMENT OF
REINFORCEMENT VALUE

Reinforcements are identifiable events that have the effect of increasing or decreasing the potentiality of some behavior's occurring. It is assumed that when these events occur they have differential effects on the potentiality of the occurrence of behaviors that precede them or are related to them. A strong physical punishment has a greater effect in reducing the potentiality of the preceding behavior's recurring than does a mild criticism. The verbal statement of "that's nice" following a child's play behavior has considerably less effect on repetition of that or similar behavior than excited interest followed by discussion in which the description of the activity is repeated to others. The latter reinforcement may have so great an effect as to lead to the development of an occupational choice or of a prominent skill.

Since we often refer to reinforcement values, it is necessary to avoid the confusion of considering a reinforcement value and a reinforcement as synonymous. First, reinforcements may have the same value but still be quite different in nature and, second, for different persons the same reinforcements as objectively described may have considerably different values. When we discuss reinforcement value, we are referring to a mathematical statement of a preference on the part of the subject or subjects for this reinforcement or objectively describable event to take place.

It should be re-emphasized here that in any instance where we attempt to measure reinforcement value, we must make inferences from some behavior of the subject. If we do not control expectancy, our measure will be of the behavior potential of the response rather than of the reinforcement value with which we are concerned.

For example, if one should give a group of people whose financial need is great the choice of applying for a job that would pay one dollar an hour or applying for one that would pay ten dollars an hour, allowing them only a single choice with the potential of failure, it is quite conceivable that a large number would apply for the dollar-an-hour job. This could be predicted in a low-income group, where the expectancy of obtaining a position paying a dollar an hour would be much greater than the expectancy of obtaining a position paying ten dollars an hour. It could be demonstrated then that the behavior potential for the selection of the ten-dollar-an-hour alternative is different from the reinforcement value of the ten dollars. The value of reinforcements is a function of the value of reinforcements to which they have been paired in the past; the preference for ten dollars is due to the belief on the part of the subjects that in our culture more positive reinforcements of a variety of kinds can be obtained with ten dollars than with one dollar.

Frequently in experimental attempts to measure reinforcement value, the distinction has not been made between the verbal statement of preference and the value of the reinforcement as this variable is defined systematically. It is not infrequent that children (or adults, for that matter) will respond with a verbal response that they feel will lead to some other reinforcement. Thus, one might expect that the particular kinds of responses that will lead to approval from the experimenter may be made with greater frequency than should be anticipated on the basis of the "true values" of the things preferred.

This distinction is difficult to make clear. Suppose a child should be asked to vote in class whether he would prefer to practice fractions for another hour or to have a free play period. If he chooses fractions because he feels that in doing so he will ultimately learn the fractions and therefore get approval because of his skill, then his choice is based on the value of studying fractions for him. If, however, he has no anticipation that studying fractions *in itself* will lead to any further rewards but feels that *saying* that he wants to study fractions will lead to approval from the teacher, then the behavior of saying or selecting fractions is being followed by approval. That is, for this subject the voting may be a measure of the reinforcement value of teacher's approval rather than a measure of the value of being allowed to study fractions for an hour. In research attempting to measure reinforcement value, this distinction must be kept clearly in mind.

TECHNIQUES OF MEASUREMENT

A number of techniques have been used in the past to obtain a relative measure of goal-object preferences in a specific situation. Irwin and his students (Irwin, Armitt, and Simon, 1943; Irwin and Gebhard, 1946) as well as the Lewinian group have been active for some time in such measurements and in determining some of the conditions that make for object preference. Techniques may be so simple as to require only a statement of choice between two objects, i.e., "Which one do you want?" or "Which one would you prefer to have?" More elaborate techniques such as paired comparisons or forced choice probably give better results. Ranking procedures may provide sufficient discrimination, and recently methods have been described for converting ranks into continuum scores (Coombs, 1950; Guilford, 1936).

A study by E. Lotsof (1951) has contributed a somewhat indirect method of measuring differences in reinforcement values for pairs of reinforcements. Lotsof followed a design similar to Barker's (1946) but with some additional controls. He had subjects decide which of a pair of liquids they would prefer to drink in two kinds of situations—one where the choices were made on a hypothetical basis, and a "real" situation where they actually had to drink one cubic centimeter of the liquid of their choice. The results were quite clear-cut in demonstrating that (1) the greater the discrepancy in the reinforcement value of the two alternatives, the shorter the decision time, and (2) the more negative or unpleasant the choices, the longer the decision time. Matched pairs of reinforcements of a very close if not identical value required significantly longer decision times. Since Lotsof's choices were not extended far enough on the positive side, it can not be said definitively whether decision time gets shorter and shorter as the choices become more and more positive, or whether the relationship is a curvilinear one with the shortest decision time approximately at a mildly positive or neutral level.

Interestingly enough, Lotsof found the same principles to hold in the hypothetical or verbal choice situation as in the real situation. The negativeness, however, of the hypothetical alternatives tended to be decreased from the real situation. In other words decision time between strongly negative, hypothetical choices was quicker than for their "real" counterparts. Although these absolute differences occur, the results were encouraging for the use of the less cumbersome verbal choice technique for measurement of preference for reinforcements.

THE DETERMINANTS OF REINFORCEMENT VALUE

Although reinforcement values may be measured in preference situations, they may also be predicted from previous experience. It has been stated that the value of any reinforcement is a function of the reinforcements it has been paired with, or has led to, or is perceived as leading to, from previous experience. Such a formulation is consistent with almost any type of reinforcement theory. Secondary reinforcement as seen by the Hullian school similarly considers the determinants of a secondary reinforcement dependent upon its previous conditions of association with pre-existing reinforcements or reinforcers. Within this point of view this relationship itself may be stated in expectancy and reinforcement value terms. A generalized formula for this is given below:

$$6. \quad R.V._{a,s_1} = f(E_{R_a \to R_{(b-n)}, s_1} \ \& \ R.V._{(b-n), s_1})$$

This may be read: the value of reinforcement a in situation 1 is a function of the expectancies that this reinforcement will lead to the other reinforcements b to n in situation 1 and the values of these other reinforcements b to n in situation 1. It does not presume that these relationships may be easily or at all verbalized by the subject or that such expectancies correspond to an objective reality. Such expectancies may be built up entirely on the basis of past events, events that in some cases occurred many years previously and have no logical possibility of recurring. The conditions that make for the stability of reinforcement values, apparently independent of their continuing to lead to their original goals, have been a source of concern to psychologists for some time. Woodworth (1918), Allport (1937), and Murphy (1947) have all formulated theories that describe this partial or complete independence, but their theories do not adequately describe the conditions under which it takes place. Although we shall attempt here to hypothesize about the nature of some of the conditions that make for this apparent independence of reinforcement values, it is still an area of crucial interest and one requiring much ingenious research.

Formula 6 states that there are two major factors determining reinforcement value and that a change in either one will result in a change in reinforcement value. Expectancies for future reinforcements may change, the value of future reinforcements may change, or new and additional reinforcements may occur that will both affect the expectancy for that reinforcement to occur and introduce another value that will affect the value of reinforcement a. Complementary studies have been done by Hunt (1953) and Dunlap (1953), one varying the expectancy for reinforcements b to n to occur but holding the reinforcement value of the subsequent reinforcements constant, the other controlling the expectancy and varying the value of the subsequent reinforcements. . . . [A series of studies have been deleted here that describe research providing support for the general principles regarding determinants of reinforcement value. In addition to the Hunt and Dunlap studies, investigations by Schroder (1954), Austrin (1950), S. Jessor (1951), and Tyler (1952) were eliminated to conserve space.]

We might treat briefly here one other condition that appears to affect the value of reinforcements. This may be referred to as time delay. Various authors have characterized maladjusted, criminal, or neurotic persons by their inability to delay reinforcements or their tendency to seek immediate gratification. Perhaps the problem can be best stated by a simple example. If we were to offer a group of children a choice of penny candy today or a larger, five-cent candy of the same kind next week, at least some of the group will choose the immediate reward of apparently lesser value from an objective standpoint. This is a rather simple example, but a similar example could be constructed involving a clinical case and an apparent choice between an immediate gratification (which could be characterized as the avoidance of a punishment) and a possible later gratification of greater value should the patient give up some symptom or defense behavior.

It is doubtful that the apparent lower value of the reinforcement which may occur in the future is merely a function of time delay, or that the potential to maintain high values for reinforcements in spite of time delay is a variable which describes an important general personality characteristic as such. From this point of view it would seem logical that it is not the reinforcement itself which has a lower value in the present because it will not occur until some time in the future. Rather the behavioral choice made by the child or the adult for the present reinforcement is stronger because of a specific or generalized expectancy that future reinforcements that are promised are not likely to occur. Future reinforcements that are based not merely on someone else's keeping a promise but on some skill of the subject or on chance factors, may also be rejected because of lowered expectancy for their occurrence and not because of lowered reinforcement value as a function of time delay *per se.* There are, of course, specific reinforcements that may have more value in the current situation than in the future one simply because they would not be appropriate or lead to other possible satisfactions in the future situation. Similarly there are reinforcements which, occurring in the present situation, may have less value than in a future situation. If a man needs to pay his mortgage within 24 hours or lose his house, the sum of money involved has more value for him immediately than the same sum of money a week later.

What we are suggesting here is that the apparent lower value of reinforcements for some or all persons as a function of delay in time for their occurrence may be explained either (1) as a result of different situations in which they occur, or (2) as a result of a lower expectancy for the occurrence of the delayed reinforcement than for the occurrence of the immediate one.

THE INDEPENDENCE OF EXPECTANCY AND REINFORCEMENT VALUE

It has been stated earlier that expectancy and reinforcement value vary independently of each other. This statement seems to disturb some who feel, on the basis of clinical experience or limited experimental data, that these variables are, in fact, mutually influencing. We would maintain that there are specific conditions under which the size of an expectancy will affect the reinforcement value or the size of a reinforcement value will affect the expectancy. These are, however, specific conditions, and would be explained within social learning theory as a function of the given situation described. Stated otherwise, since both expectancy and the values of reinforcements are to some extent situationally determined, in specific situations the level of expectancy or the value of the reinforcement may in itself be a cue that determines the quantity of the other variable to some extent.

It is interesting to note that although many feel these variables are mutually dependent, hypotheses of the value of the relationship present include exact opposites. For example, some psychologists will point to the "fact" that things which are expected or occur frequently will lose their value; in other words, high expectancy tends to lower the reinforcement value. Others point to the "fact" that when the value is high, expectancy tends to be high as a function of "wishful thinking." In other words, one hypothesis is for a reciprocal relationship between the two, and the other is for a positively correlated relationship. It is true that specific kinds of reinforcements derive their value from their rarity, and that when they are demonstrated not to be rare they lose their recognition or status value. It is also true, as has been demonstrated in the level-of-aspiration research, that some people who have a relatively low expectancy for success tend to overestimate their performance considerably. This finding would imply at least that stated expectancies are subject to wishful thinking. Such findings, although undoubtedly true, are perhaps better dealt with in terms of a behavior of explicitly stating higher goals than as instances of actual effects of the reinforcements upon the "true" or internal expectancy.

A preliminary study by Rosenberg (1952), although not in itself definitive, has suggestive value for this problem. Rosenberg selected five penny candies that showed high reliability of ranking in pretesting over a two-week interval. She selected two of these candies and presented them in three sequences to three groups of approximately 20 children each. One group got Candy A half the time and Candy B the other half. A second group got Candy A 75 per cent of the time and Candy B 25 per cent of the time. A third group got Candy A 25 per cent of the time and Candy B 75 per cent of the time. A control group did not have any candy during this experimental period. The groups were taken from different schools to avoid complications resulting from communication among the groups. (The candies were merely passed out in school with the explanation that the experimenter was a representative of a candy company that was interested in "finding out what kinds of candy children liked best.") The children initially ranked the candies after eating them.

None of the experimental groups showed any increased or decreased preference for the experimental candies regardless of the frequency with which they obtained them. The control group showed a significant increase in preference for one candy. This increase reduced to the pretest level at a later retest. The basis for this increase in preference is unknown. Although in this initial study the actual occurrence of the reinforcement, which obviously changes expectancy for occurrence, did not apparently change its value, we must be quite guarded in assuming that independence of expectancy and reinforcement value exists because it has not been demonstrated. The dangers of attempting to prove a null hypothesis are obvious. Nevertheless, the results are suggestive and we may place some confidence in these findings since: (1) we know from the previously cited studies of Austrin, Hunt, and Dunlap that the occurrence of a reinforcement accompanied by additional reinforcements does affect re-rankings of preference, that is, we are able to demonstrate one condition that does affect reinforcement value; and (2) the rankings of candies were highly reliable, so that the failure to obtain results cannot be explained on the basis of the unreliability of the measure.

A number of studies such as those by Gebhard (1948) and Filer (1952) have shown or implied that the expectation for success in a task increases its attractiveness. These findings, of course, are not contrary to the notion of the independence of expectancy and reinforcement value expressed in our basic formula. As we would analyze such a situation, the choice value of the task itself as a reinforcement is increased as a result of the increased expectancy that play with a toy will lead to the occurrence of praise or some other reinforcement. In other words, we conceive of the toy itself as a reinforcement, the value of which will change as a function of other reinforcements that may occur as a result of playing with it or owning it.

Filer did find, however, that verbally induced expectancies in themselves did not significantly affect preferences for the goal-objects. A study by Marks (1951) indicated that stated expectancies of whether children would select a desirable or undesirable card from a pack showed a wishful effect or the tendency to increase the expectancy for the selection of the desirable outcome. However, since in this study the children were not in any way penalized for incorrect estimates, we would question whether what was being measured were the real expectancies or the behavior potential for *stating* that the outcome would be favorable. That is, in the study by Marks and perhaps some others like it, it may be asked whether the more valued reinforcements actually tend to increase the expectancy of their occurring or whether under certain conditions they may only increase the potential of the subject's stating that he thinks they will occur, partly because he has no need to differentiate his true expectancies from his wishes. It may also be true that in studies like that of Marks, where young children and relatively novel problems are used, the effect of generalized expectancies for successful outcomes (for prizes to occur, and so forth) may play a heavy role in the subjects' actual expectations as a function of their individual experience. This hypothesis might be tested by comparing a group of middle-class children with a group from a deprived socio-economic level, where generalized expectations for success, prizes, and gratifications might be considerably lower. However, the lower generalized expectancy for rewards in a deprived group may be compensated for by a higher tendency to give wishful or fantasy responses.

INCREMENTS IN REINFORCEMENT VALUE

The studies previously cited have demonstrated that increments in the value of a reinforcement (R_a) will follow as a function of the value of new reinforcements (R_{b-n}) that are related to them, and this appears to be true of either negative or positive subsequent reinforcements. Changes in the value of a reinforcement (R_a) also occur as a function of changes in the expectation for subsequent reinforcements (R_{b-n}) to occur.[6]

---

[6] It may be confusing that we have stated that expectancy and reinforcement value are not systematically related and then state that the value of a reinforcement is determined by the expectancy that it will lead to future reinforcements. The point here is that the relationship is between expectancy (E_2) and behavior potential in the case of the *B.P.* formula (Formula 1, p. 52) and with expectancy (E_2) and the prior reinforcement (R_a) in the *R.V.* formula (Formula 6, p. 52) but not between E_2 and $R_{(b-n)}$.

If the values of new reinforcements (R_{b-n}) are controlled, it would be presumed that increments of the original reinforcements (R_a) as a function of changes in expectancy would be proportional to the difference between the new or changed expectancy for the following reinforcement and the original expectancy. Similarly, if expectancy is controlled and the value of the new related reinforcement (R_b) is known as compared to the original reinforcement (R_a), then increments would be proportionate to the difference between the values of the original and the new reinforcement. If these factors are not controlled and we have to estimate the increment of value on the original reinforcement when both expectancies and the values of new reinforcements change, we are again faced with the problem of being able to combine these two variables mathematically. The problem is the same as that of measuring increments in behavior potential or changes in behavior potential, and at the present time we are faced with the same gross possibilities and limitations of estimation. Obviously, for accurate prediction in complex social situations, not only must we be able to state some mathematical relationship between expectancy and reinforcement value, but we must also be able to combine the expectancies and reinforcement values for the variety of possible reinforcements that may follow upon an original one. We must solve the same problem if we are to calculate a behavior potential in relationship to the variety of possible reinforcements that may occur. Nevertheless, the general principles for increasing or decreasing a reinforcement value are explicit, and preliminary tests of these principles or hypotheses seem quite favorable.

EXPECTANCY

Expectancy may be defined as a probability or contingency held by the subject that any specific reinforcement or group of reinforcements will occur in any given situation or situations. Expectancy is not a probability determined in actuarial terms but may be considered to be both (1) a function of probability, which can be calculated from past histories of reinforcements, necessitating the consideration of special problems such as patterning and reducing increments; and (2) a generalization of expectancies from other related behavior-reinforcement sequences. Such generalization effects may or may not be relevant to present conditions. That is, generalization-of-expectancy effects may represent the failure to make the differentiations that are necessary for adequate or efficient adjustment to any given situation. Such effects may be illustrated by the person who has been rebuffed or rejected by his parents and who therefore consistently expects rejection from other people even though such rejection is not likely to occur.

The formula for expectancy in a given situation then should be given as: expectancy (E_{s_1}) is a function of probability of occurrence as based on past experience in situations perceived as the same (E'_{s_1}) and the generalization of the expectancies for the same or similar reinforcements to occur in other situations for the same or functionally related behaviors (GE).

$$7. \ E_{s_1} = f(E'_{s_1} \ \& \ GE)$$

It would seem logical or in accord with common-sense observation that in a relatively novel situation a person's expectancies would be largely a function of such generalizations as we have described. Or, stated differently, that the GE effect will weigh more heavily in situations that might be described as novel than in those in which the subject has had a series of experiences. This point, perhaps, might be stated in differentiation terms: the more the subject tends to differentiate a specific situation from other situations as a result of more experience in that specific situation, the less significant the generalization effect from experience in other situations. If we represent frequency or number of trials or some mathematical function of number of trials by N, we can state this as a general formula as follows:

$$8. \ E_{s_1} = f\left(E'_{s_1} \ \& \ \frac{GE}{N_{s_1}}\right)$$

This may be read as follows: an expectancy (E_{s_1}) is a function of the expectancy for a given reinforcement to occur as a result of previous experience in the same situation (E'_{s_1}) and expectancies generalized from other situations (GE) divided by some function of the number of experiences in the specific situation (N_{s_1}).[7]

Such a formulation might be tested by comparing variability or

---

[7]This formula could be given in a more mathematically exact form as follows:

$$E = E' + \left(\frac{GE - E'}{N + 1}\right)$$

N in this formula would be some decelerating function of the number of trials. Stated in this form E is greater than E' when GE is greater than E', lower than E' when GE is lower, equal to E' when GE is equal to E', and equal to GE when there are zero trials in the situation or, in other words, when the situation is novel.

individual differences in expectancies for a group of subjects at the beginning of an experimental situation, in which N would be low, and at the end of the same situation, after many trials where all the subjects have gone through a similar pattern of reinforcements.

One experimental verification for the decreasing effect of generalized expectancy over a series of trials can be found in Dean's previously cited study of the effect of generalized expectancies on stated expectancies. It may be remembered that the correlation of the performance on the first task with the difference between the actual performance and the stated expectancies on the second task was .70 for the first trial. This correlation decreased regularly with increased trials until it dropped below the point of significance.

The importance of the generalization effect may be seen by referring to any experimental study of expectancy in human beings—for example, from the level-of-aspiration data, in which it can be demonstrated that marked and consistent individual differences occur following similar induced patterns of success and failure. Although it can be demonstrated that groups experiencing different patterns of success and failure will differ in their over-all means, some theoretical explanation is necessary to account for the marked differences between individuals in any group. In this formulation such initial and maintained individual differences should be predictable on a basis of generalization of expectancies from related behaviors directed toward the same or similar reinforcements in similar situations.

Generalization effects can be calculated by sampling expectancies for a group of behaviors that may be considered to be functionally related in that they lead to the same reinforcement or similar reinforcements. From such sampling an approximation of GE could then be calculated. Expectancies for such a group of functionally related behaviors have been described earlier as *freedom of movement.* That is, the freedom of movement for any need that is functionally related to the present behavior could serve as an estimate of the generalization effect. The more specific or circumscribed the need is conceived to be, the more accurate the calculations of the generalization-of-expectancy effect. For example, if we determine the generalization effect for the expectancy of success in a French course, it could be calculated from historically determined expectancies for other French courses, for other academic courses in general, or for recognition reinforcements in general. It would be hypothesized that the more limited need of obtaining recognition in other French courses would provide a more accurate basis for calculating the generalization effect than academic courses in general, or recognition in general. The calculation of freedom of movement for any need or need system will be described more fully in ["Broader Conceptions"]. The weighting of a generalization effect in terms of the novelty of situations and the identification of situations in terms of their novelty will have to be studied further, and more empirical data will have to be collected, before a more specific formulation may be made. Studies by Good (1952) and Castaneda (1952) have clearly indicated the importance of assessing the number of previous experiences in a situation for determining the effect of new experience.

It should be noted that behavior potential and reinforcement value are measured relative to other behavior potentials or reinforcement values of the subject. Expectancies, however, may be measured on an absolute scale and obtained figures are meaningful relative to other people. The sum total of reinforcement values or behavior potentials, measured in controlled choice situations, must always be the same for different subjects when preference methods are used to calculate them. However, subjects may differ widely: one may have low expectancies of success for all possible reinforcements; another may have high expectancies of obtaining the same positive reinforcements.

TECHNIQUES FOR MEASURING EXPECTANCY

One of the simplest techniques for measuring expectancy where only an approximate or crude measure is needed is that of simple choice behavior with reinforcement value controlled. As with reinforcement value, we may estimate expectancies from behavioral choices when the other variable is controlled. A good illustration of this technique is available in the study by Lasko (1952). Lasko used the Humphrey paradigm of having the subject state whether he expected a red or green light to go on in the next trial. In such a setting it is assumed that the subject, wishing to make the correct response, would have a reinforcement of equal value whether he was right with a green response or right with a red response. The determination, then, of whether he said "red" or "green" would be based upon whether his expectancy for red was greater than his expectancy for green or vice versa. For similar measurements, where verbal statements are undesirable for one reason or another, pressing of buttons or pulling of levers may be substituted for the verbal statement.

Attempts to arrive at finer measurement usually involve verbal techniques and are characterized by the types of experimental methodologies utilized in the studies frequently referred to as "level of aspiration" studies. The verbal techniques may be divided into several kinds. The first is one in which the subject states a probability on some scale of ten or one hundred for the occurrence of any specific score or reinforcement or event or for several different ones. For younger subjects, where there may be some doubt as to their understanding of the concept of probability, the ranking of which is most likely to occur, next most likely, and so on may be substituted. A more frequently used technique utilizes some task involving the possibility of a graded series of scores. The subject is asked to state what score he would expect to get. This technique was used in the previously quoted studies on the generalization of expectancies by Chance and R. Jessor. It is assumed that the reported score is the one of the highest expectancy, and usually assumed that the distribution of expectancies for scores on either side of the stated one fall away in a symmetrical gradient. So when a subject states an expectancy of 25 on one trial and of 27 on the next, it may be assumed that there was a lower expectancy for 27 on the first trial and that this expectancy had increased as the expectancy for 25 on the second trial had decreased.

It is possible (though it is rarely done) to combine the two methods mentioned above—that of stating probabilities for specific scores and that of stating the score most likely to occur. Subjects may be asked to state both (1) what score they expect to occur, and (2) their probability or confidence in their original bid.

These techniques have frequently led to justifiable criticism since, in social learning terms, the behavior of stating or indicating a goal in a social situation may be influenced by reinforcements other than the one of attempting to make the most correct estimate. Attempts to impress the examiner, to obtain satisfaction on a symbolic basis from the mere statement of high goals, or to save face by underestimating may all affect such bids. If it were possible to increase the reward value for accuracy of estimation or expectancy, the danger of these other reinforcements' affecting the stated expectancy would be lessened. With this in mind, Castaneda (1951, 1952), developed a betting technique where subjects were given objects of real value to bet on each trial. He used marbles with children and pennies with college students. The amount of the bet was presumed to be proportionate to their expectancy of success. Castaneda's studies will be described in greater detail in the section on increments in expectancy.

Since the measurement of expectancy plays such an important role in the testing of the theoretical constructions of this system, some of the studies representative of the approach to this problem in social learning theory will be presented in some detail. Preliminary attempts to assess and compare several operations for the measurement of expectancy with college student groups were made by Rotter, Fitzgerald and Joyce (1954).

In this investigation four groups of subjects were used, each group consisting of 30 undergraduate college students. Sex proportions were approximately equal in the four groups. The subjects were trained on a modified form of the Rotter-Jensen Group Level of Aspiration Test (Jensen and Rotter, 1947). This test consists of seven separate symbol substitution problems, each one quite complex and each one requiring a different key. Previous research with this test has indicated that scores on the seven tests remain approximately the same. It was possible to control the actual score obtained since the test is represented as a time test and it is possible to stop the subject when he has reached the number of substitutions set for that trial. All subjects obtained the same prearranged sequence of scores, which were, in order, 22, 29, 32, 27, 30, and 28. It may be noted that these scores give a mean of 28, and 28 appears once as a score at the end of the sequence. The work of Dean (1950) and Good (1952) has indicated that this would be experienced as a realistic score for most subjects. Following training, the four groups were provided with different instructions.

Group I were asked to indicate the score they expected to make on the next trial, with considerable emphasis being placed on accuracy and actual expectation. Instructions used were comparable to those of Festinger (1942). Following this, the subjects were asked to rate, on a ten-point scale, their probability of making that score.

Group II were asked to rate, on a ten-point scale, their *absolute* probability of making six different possible scores on the next trial. They were asked to rate their absolute probability of making the scores of 20, 25, 28, 30, 32, and 35.

Group III were asked to rate, on a ten-point scale, their probability of making *at least* 20 or more on the next trial and in the same manner for the remaining same scores.

Group IV, designated as the behavioral or betting technique group, were given 60 cents in six piles of 10 pennies each and were asked to bet up to 10 cents on making a score of *at least* 20 or more on the next trial and in the same manner for the remaining same scores.

The operational measurements of expectancy for Groups III and IV are identical, except that Group III stated a probability on a 10-point scale and Group IV bet up to 10 cents on each of the same six scores. The betting technique is essentially the same as that used by Castaneda.

Results are shown in Figure 4.6. Along the abscissa are the six possible scores on which the probability ratings were made. Along the ordinate is the rating scale of probability used. It can be seen that for Group I (large dot), which were asked to indicate the score they

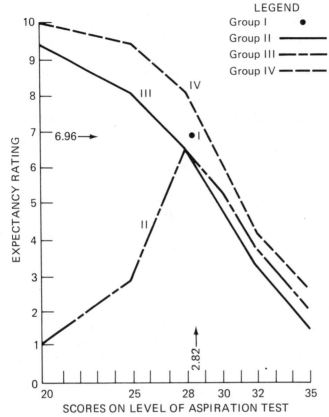

Figure 4.6 Mean expectancy scores for four groups with different instructions for reporting expectations (from Rotter, Fitzgerald, and Joyce).

expected to make on the next trial, there is a mean expectancy of 28.2—only slightly above the theoretical expectancy of 28. The probability they state that they will make this score is 6.96. It may be seen that this probability for the score of 28 intersects the curves for the remaining groups at somewhat comparable points.

Group II (broken line) were asked to rate their *absolute* probability of making each of six possible scores. These ratings result in a curve with the score having the greatest probability at the mean of the training trials and essentially the same as in Group I—that is, a score of 28. However, if we were to make a cumulative curve of probabilities at 28, the scores for this group would be well above the other groups at 28. Essentially, it appears the subjects were not able to respond to the instructions, since the sum of the cumulative probabilities would be well over 100 per cent. However, it is clear that the score given as expected in Group I is the score of the highest probability in Group II.

Group III (solid line) were asked to rate their probability of making *at least* the six same scores and Group IV (dashes) bet up to 10 cents on their chances of making *at least* the same scores. The curves for Groups III and IV were found to be significantly different at less than the 5 per cent level of confidence by an analysis of variance technique. The mean ratings at scores 20, 25, and 28 were found by test to be significantly different at less than the 1 per cent level of confidence.

It could be noted from the graph that in every instance the curve for the betting gave higher mean scores. Apparently, for this group of subjects and reinforcements of this value, the behavioral technique results in higher expectancy measures, the verbal technique being closer to the theoretical or actuarial expectancy. However, the curves for Groups III and IV correlated .99. This product moment correlation is based on the mean expectancy ratings for the two groups on each of the six possible scores.

Similarities of results in the four groups indicate that all four methods are tending to measure the same thing. The mean of statements of a single expected score coincides with the score given the highest probability of occurring on an absolute basis. However, students asked to estimate their scores on the basis of absolute probability apparently overestimated the probability for any specific score. When subjects were asked to state probabilities of obtaining at least a given score, the probabilities stated tended to be similar to those stated by subjects asked to give the most expected score.

MEASURING GENERALIZED EXPECTANCY

In level-of-aspiration studies one of the major scores dealt with, a score considered to have relevance for personality measurement—to represent, in other words, a generalized characteristic of the subject—is a difference score. This score may be calculated in several ways, but it represents primarily a discrepancy between the subject's actual performance and his stated expectations. The usual method for obtaining this difference score is to take the mean of the differences between each performance and the subsequent bid for the next trial. Such a technique, however, puts unrealistically high importance on the last trial, neglecting the effect of the earlier trials. Lezak (1950) has suggested a technique whereby the subject's mean performance up to a given trial is compared with his data on the subsequent trial. Such a technique, however, has an equal difficulty in that it counts early trials as important as later ones. An ideal, though laborious, method would base the performance estimate on all previous trials but would derive an empirical formula for weighting the significance of any trial so that proper weight could be placed on more recent experience. This point is particularly important in tasks in which practice effect is involved or in which the subject might assume that there is a practice effect likely to take place.

As we have discussed earlier, generalized expectancy may also be arrived at in a way similar to what we have termed freedom of movement or the mean of the expectancies for a group of related behavior-reinforcement sequences. A laborious method to calculate such expectancies is to produce them experimentally in a controlled situation. The more usual technique is to estimate them from interview material. Measurement of freedom of movement in this way will be discussed in greater detail [later in *Social Learning and Clinical Psychology*] .

INCREMENTS IN EXPECTANCY

The understanding and prediction of changes in expectancies is one of the more crucial aspects of this theoretical approach. Not only is it true from our formulations that behavior depends, in part at least, on expectations, but reinforcement values themselves depend upon expectations for subsequent reinforcements. Consequently understanding how expectations change becomes of crucial significance for any application of this theory to psychotherapy or any effecting of behavioral change. In addition we may consider the practical problems faced in effecting behavioral change—that it is frequently easier to change expectancies for immediate reinforcements than to change the value of reinforcements (or expectancies for reinforcements considerably removed in time). For example, it is easier to change a young woman's expectancy for her potential acceptability to the opposite sex than to change the value of this acceptability to her in a significant way. Although the changing of the reinforcement value may be accomplished by changing certain expectancies for subsequent reinforcements, these expectancies may be more difficult to change because of the continuous bombardment of cultural influences.

75204

It is hypothesized that there are two general variables that determine the size of changes in expectancy as a function of the occurrence of an external reinforcement. Analysis of the experimental writings in psychology reveals many studies supporting these two hypotheses. However, we shall present here in detail a few studies recently completed that were conducted as tests of the specific hypotheses given below.

Many people have noted that the surprise value of an occurrence determines to a large extent the degree of effect it may have in changing a person's usual behavior. Whether we are dealing with a positive reinforcing event or a negative one, this seems to hold true. A sheltered, overprotected child slapped in the face by a teacher may be traumatized into a considerable withdrawal in the school situation, a withdrawal that may be in marked contrast to his previous behavior. Or a neglected child characterized by bravado and "toughness" may break down and cry as the result of a show of affection on the part of some adult.

In the field of psychophysics it has been demonstrated numerous times that the discrimination of a change or a difference is a function of the strength of the original stimuli, or that the experience of difference is relative to the size or strength of the things being discriminated rather than a function of the absolute difference between the stimuli. These facts, which lead us to conclude that differences in a person's perception of situations are relative to his previous condition or previous experience, are formulated in expectancy terms as follows: The increment of expectancy following the occurrence of a reinforcement is a function of the formula $1 - E$ where 1 represents the actual occurrence (stated as an expectancy of 1.0) and E represents the previously held expectancy (stated as some decimal value). More generally, if we would want to apply this to more than one instance, we would say that the increment in expectancy is a function of the difference between the actual occurrence (stated as a decimal value) and the previously held expectancy. In the case of a decrement from a failure of a reinforcement to occur, zero would be substituted for 1 in the formula. Hull (1943) in dealing with a similar problem in relation to habit strength (sHr), has previously stated a similar principle.

Common sense also tells us that the effect of the occurrence of a reinforcement tends to decrease as a function of the number of previous experiences we have had in a given situation. Perhaps stated otherwise, the degree to which we base our expectancies on the most recent experience is a function of how much earlier experience we have had that is inconsistent with the recent one. As our experience becomes repetitive in a given situation, our expectancy becomes stabilized and a new occurrence has less effect in changing our behavior. For example, if we trade in a given grocery store over a long period of time and obtain good meat all of that time and then obtain poor meat on one day, we are not likely to change our place of buying meat. On the other hand, if we trade at a meat market only a couple of days and then obtain poor meat, this is likely to be enough to make us look around for an alternative place to obtain our food. If our expectations of intellectual adequacy are based on many high grades, the failure of that high grade to occur on one occasion will not have the same effect on establishing our future expectancies for grades as would the experience of a child in the first grade who is failed and made to repeat the class because of intellectual inadequacy.

This second principle may be formulated as follows: The increment of a specific expectancy (E') following the occurrence of any reinforcement diminishes as the subject has more experience in the specific situation. These two principles may be combined in the formula below for an increment of expectancy $(\Delta E')$ stated in general terms. In the formula, N represents some function of the frequency or number of previous experiences in a given situation; O, the occurrence of the reinforcement stated as a decimal (which in instances of a single reinforcement would be unity, or zero); and E, the expectancy for the occurrence of the reinforcement previously held by the subject.

$$9. \quad \Delta E' = f\left(\frac{O - E}{N}\right)$$

Good (1952) tested the effect of the number of previous experiences on changes in expectancy. Good had five groups of 25 male high-school students. The purpose of his design was to obtain groups of subjects all having the same expectancy for scores on a task and to have this expectancy based on different numbers of previous trials. On the basis of previous research and his own preliminary testing, it was predetermined that subjects who had no knowledge of a task but who were told that scores would range from 0 to 50 would have a mean expectancy or would state a mean expectancy of around 28. His first group, consequently, was merely asked to state an expectancy with no previous experience with the task at all. His second group was given a training trial and a reported score of 28. His third

group had five training trials all on one day and were given scores
of 25, 27, 29, 26, and 28. His fourth group had the same scores on
training trials as Group III except that trials were spaced one a day for
five days. His last group had fifteen trials spaced in three days and
all averaging a score of 28. Each group stated an expectancy at the
end of the training trials (or, in the case of the first group, immediately upon being presented with the task). They were all given one
more trial, in which a score was reported to them of ten points
higher than their last estimate regardless of their bid or expected
statement. Following this they were asked to make another statement of expectancy. Good's results showed that the number of trials
did not have apparent significance in determining the expectancy
statement at the end of the training period. However, it had considerable effect on the increment or raise in expectancy that followed the reinforcement of ten points higher than the expectancy
score. Groups I and II, the groups with no or only one trial previous
experience, raised their expectancies approximately the full ten
points as a result of the reinforcement. Groups III, IV, and V, however, all raised their scores roughly about five points. No significant
difference appeared between the five-trial groups and the group that
had five trials each for three successive days. It appears from Good's
data that, at least for this kind of score, the effect of the number of
previous experiences tended to diminish or approach zero after five
trials. Data collected from other sources would suggest that effects
may be measured after five trials.

    Two studies by Castaneda (1951, 1952) test the formula for in-
crements in expectancy, combining in a precise mathematical relationship the principles that expectancy changes are a function of
previous level and number of previous trials. It may be recalled that
Castaneda developed a betting technique for measuring expectancy.
In his first study with school children, the children were given eight
marbles on each trial and were permitted to wager eight or fewer
marbles on each trial's outcome. They received a prearranged sequence of successes and failure. Using other groups Castaneda demonstrated that accumulation effects or the effects of the number of
marbles accumulated before any wager did not significantly affect
the amount bet on any given trial for the conditions of his own experiment. He then was able to study the changes in expectancy of
groups who had different patterns of positive and negative reinforcements. Shown in Figure 4.7 are the amounts of marbles bet for two
sequences of reinforcements for two different groups, which differ
in the pattern or order of the reinforcements but contain the same
number of positive (+) and negative (−) reinforcements or successes

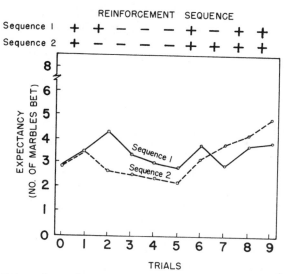

Figure 4.7 Comparison of expectancy curves for two groups with different reinforcement sequences but the same number of positive and negative reinforcements (from Castaneda).

Note: Read by finding the reinforcement (plus or minus) then read over to next column and down to find the level of expectancy after the occurrence of that reinforcement.

and failures (1951, p. 45). The fact that the number of marbles bet on the last trial of the two sequences was significantly different suggests that more than frequency must be considered in deriving an expectancy from previous experience.

In a later study Castaneda (1952), using as subjects college women attempting to do fine color matching from a distance of about seven feet, measured expectancies by the number of pennies (up to 10) they would bet on each trial. Again he found accumulation effects not to influence the betting on any given trial within the limits of the experiment. He tested the effect of frequency by repeating the same pattern of eight reinforcements and comparing the changes or increments of expectancy as a function of each new reinforcement for the first eight and for the second eight trials. Actual amounts bet are shown in Figure 4.8 (1952, p. 78). It can be seen that the curve for the second part is similar to but less accentuated than the curve for the first. The mean of the actual increments regardless of sign for the first eight trials, that is, the mean of the changes following each trial, was significantly greater than those for the repeated pattern of the second eight trials. From these and other groups, Castaneda de-

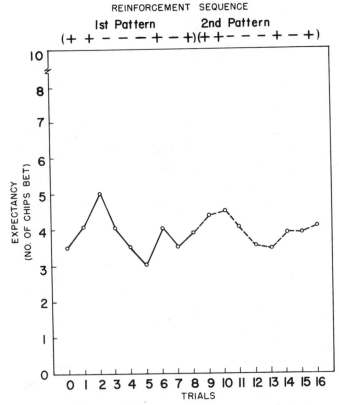

Figure 4.8 The effect of number of trials on increments of expectancy: Expectancy curve for Group IV (from Castaneda).

Note: Read by finding the reinforcement (plus or minus) then read adjacent column to find the level of expectancy after the occurrence of that reinforcement.

rived the following empirical equation (1952), p. 85):

$$10. \quad \Delta E' = \frac{1.0 - (E'_1)^2}{\sqrt{C^2 + N^2}}$$

It can be noted that a constant is included that represents an estimate of the previous experience of this group with the type of task in question. For different tasks this constant would be assumed to be different and would have to be derived empirically. In Castaneda's study this constant was 10. Subjects can rarely, if ever, be said to be dealing with an entirely novel situation or task; and in attempting to utilize the principle of frequency, it seems that a constant is necessary for different groups of subjects and for different kinds of experimental or life problems.

Castaneda cross-validated this equation by applying it to previous research and by testing it out on a new group. To do this, he began only with the first stated expectancy (the bet preceding the first trial) and using mean scores calculated a theoretical curve based on the sequence of positive and negative reinforcements, basing each calculation on the previous *theoretical* point rather than on an empirical point, so that any error in the curve would tend to be accumulative. A comparison of the obtained or empirical curve for a new group, who were given a long sequence of 23 trials in an attempt to carry their betting to extinction, with the actual mean scores obtained on the group is shown in Figure 4.9 (1952, p. 102). These two curves correlated .99 as determined from correlating the mean scores by Pearson Product correlation. This study provides strong support for both the frequency hypothesis and the 1 – E formula, indicating that the effect of both of these variables is to generate a negatively accelerated curve for successive expectancy increments of the same sign.

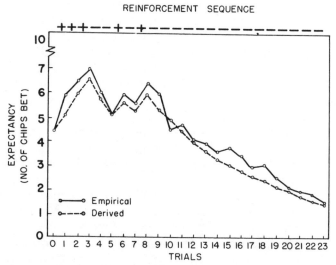

Figure 4.9 Application of a specific formula to expectancy increments: Empirical and derived expectancy curves for Group V (from Castaneda).

Note: Read by finding the reinforcement (plus or minus) then read adjacent column to find the level of expectancy after the occurrence of that reinforcement.

THE EFFECT OF PATTERNING OR SEQUENCE
ON EXPECTANCY

A study by Lasko (1952) approaches the problem of determining expectancies on the basis of patterning of previous reinforcements or experiences from a different point of view. Lasko hypothesized that a frequency or actuarial approach to expectancy neglected the tendency of a subject to project pattern or sequence into his experience even when the sequence itself was a random one. Essentially this introduces another variable, which may effect increments and decrements of expectancy in some instances.

Lasko used the Humphrey-type experimental situation; his subjects had to state whether they expected a red or a green light to go on. He characterizes the situation as one of intermittent reinforcement, where the same behavior is followed sometimes by a success and sometimes by a failure, differentiating it from the partial reinforcement situation, where behavior is sometimes followed by reinforcement and sometimes supposedly by non-reinforcement. Lasko also recognizes a distinction between learning in a situation where the effects following a behavior are a function of the behavior itself (for example, where a child's crying is reacted to by concern on the part of the parents) and learning in a situation where the subsequent effect or reinforcement is essentially controlled by someone else according to some prearranged sequence. In the latter case, the problem of the subject is to predict what someone else will do rather than to affect someone else's behavior by his own. Lasko argues, however, that in a life situation typically characterized by the subject's having some control over the effects of his own behavior, particularly with children, the reinforcements that occur are actually perceived as being controlled by others and not solely a resultant of their own behavior. That is, the subject is concerned with predicting the behavior of others as well as influencing or changing the behavior of others.

Lasko had three groups of subjects totaling 99 men and women students in elementary psychology courses. All three groups experienced the same percentage—25 per cent—of red and green lights during the 60 acquisition trials. The green lights occurred in what was apparently random sequence for all groups. The three groups differed in the maximum number of consecutive red lights that appeared in each sequence. For one group, the maximum number of red lights that occurred between green lights was four; in a second group, five; and for a third group, six. The acquisition trials were followed by 40 extinction trials.

Lasko found, as he had hypothesized, that during the extinction trials a maximum number of green responses would appear for the different groups on different trials. That is, the group that had sequences of no greater than four red lights between green lights would show their highest point of green light responses on the fifth trial; the group with five red lights as a maximum between greens would show it on the sixth; and the group with six red lights as a maximum number of consecutive trials would show it on the seventh. These hypotheses were supported by the data at a significant level of discrimination. Lasko also tested the results of Grant, Hake, and Hornseth (1951), which indicated that 25 per cent reinforcement in a Humphrey-type experimental situation could predict on an actuarial basis that subjects would continue to show or give 25 per cent responses of the same kind. Lasko felt that these results obtained only because the acquisition trials were not carried out in sufficient length, and tested an additional group with 120 acquisition trials. He demonstrated that when there is actually 25 per cent of a given response reinforced in a sequence, the frequency of that response will dip significantly below the 25 per cent level if the sequence is carried out for a sufficiently long number of trials.

In this chapter we have described hypotheses and research that may be thought of as of primary importance for establishing theoretical principles to predict or describe learned social behavior of human subjects. They tend to deal with specific behaviors or behavior sequences. ["Broader Conceptions"] will deal with constructs and hypotheses that are more readily applicable to clinical psychological problems.

BROADER CONCEPTIONS

The material discussed up to this point, although of considerable importance for the experimental testing of theoretical principles, is at a more specific level than the clinician is usually interested in. Although the concepts of behavior potential, expectancy, and reinforcement value may occasionally be applied to the understanding of a specific symptom, the clinician is usually interested in the broader or more general concepts of needs, the more broadly described stable behavior patterns, and the identification of the effects of life situations. In social learning theory these descriptive concepts are *need potential, freedom of movement, need value,* and the *psychological situation.* It is with these concepts that the clinician is usually concerned in his personality measurement or diagnosis and in his psychological treatment.

Since they are both of special importance in psychological treatment, we shall also discuss in this chapter the significance of language in learning and the development of minimal goal levels.

NEED POTENTIAL

The mean potentiality of a group of functionally related behaviors' occurring in any segment of the individual's lifetime is described by the concept of need potential. Such behaviors would be functionally related in that they lead to (or are directed toward) the accomplishment of the same (or similar) reinforcements. In other words, the functionality of the behaviors classified together in measuring need potential would be determined by the functional relatedness of the reinforcements for these behaviors. Behaviors that characteristically are directed toward the accomplishment of related goals or reinforcements are the behavioral referents for a need and are the behaviors we are concerned with in determining need potential.

Characteristics of behaviors that may be grouped together into need categories are the same as those we have discussed in regard to behavior potential. Implicit behaviors such as identification with authority figures might be grouped together into a need potential for identification with authority figures, or might be included in some other broader or more inclusive categories such as need potential for dependence or dominance. We have already discussed how behaviors may be classified into increasingly inclusive categories. The more inclusive the category, the less prediction may be expected from any randomly selected single referent to any other randomly selected single referent within the category. As long as we can specify direct or indirect objective referents for our behaviors, there are no restrictions on what kinds of need potential terms we can use other than their utility as determined by empirical tests.

As with freedom of movement and need value, for most purposes it would not be possible to make an exhaustive study of precisely when the subject utilizes behaviors leading to one reinforcement rather than another. To arrive at a practical estimate of need potential, some type of sampling procedure is necessary. For experimental purposes or in order to test general laws or principles, measurement is best accomplished by determining how the subject behaves in a select set of situations. Determination of which behaviors are directed toward the accomplishment of a particular need or goal is made initially on a cultural basis. This judgment may be made in a relatively free situation, as in the interpretation of projective material, or it may be made in a highly controlled situation. A controlled situation may be produced by having specific alternatives present in one or more situations, where each alternative has an established, culturally predetermined relationship to a given reinforcement or need. By *culturally predetermined* is meant that within a given group it is established that a particular behavior leads to (or is directed toward) the accomplishment of a particular goal or reinforcement for the majority of the people within the culture (or within any statistically agreed-upon proportion of that culture). So, for example, we might refer to grooming as culturally related to heterosexual acceptance, or to studying and doing homework as related to academic recognition. In a more controlled situation, if a subject were given a choice of getting a mild shock or being verbally insulted, these two behavioral choices might be considered culturally to be related to physical comfort and social recognition, respectively.

It should be emphasized at this point that such cultural definitions of the nature of external reinforcements do not take into account the individual deviations of the members of any culture. For purposes of measuring need potential, such deviations may be considered to be of two kinds:

(1) The reinforcements that make up a need are functionally related in a way which deviates from the culturally defined organization of reinforcements. Hence, the behaviors leading to these reinforcements would be likely to be different. For example, the behaviors of two people would be expected to vary if for one marriage is primarily a love and affection goal while for the other it is primarily a recognition goal.

(2) Behaviors that people use to reach the same reinforcements or needs vary with individual learning experiences. Thus, for example, a given adult might utilize skill in dancing as an important way to demonstrate independence from a parent who feels that dancing is wicked, rather than utilizing the more common pathway of establishing financial independence of the parent.

In order to make a measurement or an estimate of a person's need potential—particularly in a clinical situation—it would be necessary to have (a) a thorough knowledge of the subject's prior learning background, (b) the subject's own description of his needs and the significance of his behavior, and (c) a broad and general knowledge of all of the subject's behavior, and the cues and conditions to which he is responsive. Such elaborate measurement techniques are neither economical nor feasible for the study of groups or for the collection of group data in order to test theoretical hypotheses. For these latter purposes, the method described above using cultural referents would appear to be adequate.

TECHNIQUES OF MEASUREMENT
OF NEED POTENTIAL

In measuring need potential we are specifically interested in the frequency of the occurrence of *behaviors*. It is probably because of the confusion between behaviors and need values that much prediction in clinical psychology has failed. The clinician assessing need preferences from either his interviews or measuring instruments, frequently has presumed that behaviors which he associates with such need preferences will occur with high frequency in other situations. From a social learning point of view, this neglects entirely the concept of expectancy or freedom of movement. Although preferences may be high, behaviors may be relatively infrequent because of the subject's low expectancy that the behaviors will actually lead to the reinforcements. It is difficult for the clinician working in the laboratory or clinical situation to assess the frequency with which behaviors occur in the patient's life situations, since the patient's statements regarding his behavior are so frequently colored by his desires or by his expectancies.

Since the concepts of behavior and need preference have not been clearly separated by many, most clinical measuring instruments in general clinical practice obtain responses that are a mixture of both these variables. However, when the actions of the subject himself in the testing or clinical situation are analyzed as behavior, the clinician is better able to estimate need potential. The clinician frequently uses his opportunity for direct observation but rarely attempts to evaluate systematically. However, Cronbach (1948) and others have emphasized the importance in psychological testing of "process variables," that is, of attempting to assess what the patient actually does or how he reacts to the testing situation itself.

In addition to the direct observation of the subject over a period of time, the same techniques that are utilized in measuring behavior potential may be utilized in measuring need potential. Paper and pencil or verbal choice techniques, rankings, paired comparisons, forced choice, yes-no questionnaires, and so on are all ways of getting at how the subject actually behaves in some segment of his life. In measuring such potentials, the emphasis should always be on what the subject does or would do rather than on what he expects to happen or what he would like to happen.

More direct measures of observation, such as observational ratings of children in school or at home, the assessment of adults in problem situations as carried on by the O.S.S. during the war (O.S.S. Assessment Staff, 1948), and the Michigan assessment of clinical psychological trainees (Kelly and Fiske, 1951), have both advantages and disadvantages.

Projective tests have shown themselves historically to be poorly related to behavioral criteria, and many tests that impress the clinician with their validity fail to stand up under validation procedures involving independent behavioral criteria. Perhaps this failure occurs because such tests are not as well designed to measure behavior as to measure what we would characterize as freedom of movement and need value. Some of the more controlled instruments, such as the Incomplete Sentences Test, do provide some direct referents for need potential. . . .

Although one would not attempt to measure need potential for a highly specific single situation (one should rather measure behavior potential), higher predictability for need potentials and consequently greater utility would be obtained if some specification of the situation were made. More accurate prediction would result from the use of the concept of the need potential to demonstrate masculinity in same-sex situations than there would be for a more generalized concept of need potential to demonstrate masculinity in general. We are implying here not that the need potentials for masculinity in same-sex and opposite-sex situations would not be correlated in our society, but only that the behavior potentials for the specific behaviors classified or categorized together would be more like each other in the more restricted situationally bound categorizations than in the more general one.

Another approach to the measurement of need potential may be made by the use of sociometrics. A group of people who have opportunity to observe each other may be asked to make sociometric ratings that can be used as a measure of the degree to which the various persons use a particular kind of behavior in a given set of situations. Such a method has the advantage of permitting the behaviors to be assessed in a natural situation by people whose presence does not disturb or change the situation. When such sociometric ratings or nominations are used, it is particularly important that the behavior characteristics being rated be clearly defined with specific examples so that different raters and the experimenter have the same conception of what is being measured. Fitzgerald (1954) has employed a sociometric technique to measure dependence behavior or need potential in a college fraternity. He has been able to demonstrate high split-half reliability as well as significant correlation of his sociometric scores with projective test and interview ratings of dependence need potential.

NEED VALUE

Like need potential, need value is measured by determining the subject's preference for alternatives. Need potential is a matter of selecting one group of behaviors that lead to one of a given set of reinforcements over another group of behaviors leading to a different set of reinforcements. Need value involves the selection of one set of reinforcements over another set of reinforcements, when expectancy is held constant. *The mean preference value of a set of functionally related reinforcements is what is meant by need value.* It was described earlier how reinforcements become functionally related, primarily on the basis of two generalization principles: (1) through a similarity predictable by means of stimulus generalization principles (i.e., a slap on the wrist and a slap on the arm are two negative reinforcements that could become functionally related on the basis of stimulus generalization), and (2) through an extension of mediated stimulus generalization, in which a number of different reinforcements that tend to lead to the same reinforcement become related (i.e., a number of different responses of the mother, all of which lead to increasing the mother's attention, tend to develop some type of functional relationship).

Functionality of relationships can be demonstrated in two ways. One is readiness to accept substitutes (when one reinforcement is blocked, the subject tends to select another that he sees as similar and potentially possible in the same situation); the other, the generalization of expectancies among functionally related behaviors.

A study by A. Lotsof (1953) illustrates the use of substitution as a test of functional relationship. She worked with college women, presenting them with hypothetical situations in which, through no fault of their own, they were blocked in obtaining some satisfaction. She worked with the needs of academic recognition and acceptance from same-sex peers. Her typical blocking situations were ones where the library closed without notice or where a girl friend with whom the subject planned to spend an evening is unexpectedly called out of town to see her sick mother. After reading the hypothetical blocking situation, the subjects were asked to select from four alternatives what they thought they would do if this had happened to them. There were six such situations—three of them blocking academic recognition and three of them blocking acceptance from same sex peers. The four alternatives in each case included two academic and two social alternatives. All four alternatives were carefully matched in preference value, independently of the blocking situation, with a previous sample from the same population. Since this was a study of need value, in selecting the alternatives the subjects were instructed to make their choice as if each alternative were equally likely to take place. Given below is a sample of Lotsof's situations with the four alternatives (p. 114).

> You have made plans to take a short vacation with a girl friend over a week end. On Thursday your friend becomes seriously ill and cannot go. So instead:
>
> 1. You make up some work which you have missed to the satisfaction of the professor.
> 2. You do an extra good job on an assignment for which your professor compliments you.
> 3. You go to visit a girl friend in Cleveland.
> 4. You play tennis with a group of girls. (Assume you know how to play tennis.)

The same subjects were interviewed in an attempt to assess need value for the two needs being studied. The interviewer and other judges of the recorded interview had no knowledge of the choices made on the paper-and-pencil alternative test. Ratings on the two needs were made and the subjects were divided into two groups— those where, relative to the rest of that population, the academic was greater than the social need, and those where, relative to the rest of that population, the social was greater than the academic recognition need. Lotsof found that the group higher in academic recognition need had a significantly greater selection of academic recognition alternatives regardless of which need was being blocked, and that the social recognition group had a significantly greater selection of social recognition alternatives regardless of which need was being blocked. There was also a significant tendency present for the academic-recognition-blocking situations to result in more selection of academic recognition alternatives when both groups were combined than could be accounted for by chance. The same was not true, however, of the social-acceptance-blocking situations. This latter finding is interpreted as the influence of the experimental situation on the choices.

The fact that only the academic situation produced this effect seems to be explicable on the basis of the academic nature of the total cues in the situation—the experimenter was older and obviously associated with the University, the testing took place in an academic room in an academic building, and so on. It would seem that these influences provide cues that tend to increase the subjects' expectancy that behaviors leading to academic recognition have a greater likelihood for reinforcement in these situations.

It should be emphasized that Lotsof was careful to make the hypothetical blocking situations such that no blame or fault was implied for the subject. Blocking resulting from the subject's inadequacy might lead to considerably reduced expectancies of success in the area blocked and to defensive behaviors. In the latter case, a substitution criterion for functional relationship could be expected to break down in many cases.

Perhaps a more important demonstration of functional relationship is indicated in the concept of the generalization-of-expectancy changes, in which the occurrence of either positive or negative reinforcements has a generalization effect on the expectancy of reaching other reinforcements. When these reinforcements are functionally related, this effect is maximum; as the functional relationship is less, the effect is less. Functionality of relationship then could be measured by the amount of change in expectancy for any reinforcement to occur following the occurrence of a different reinforcement, as in the studies by Crandall, R. Jessor, and Chance.

Need value, then, is a preference value for a group of functionally related reinforcements, which may be measured by a sampling method. For group and experimental purposes, one could again determine culturally the nature of these functionally related reinforcements and then determine their preference value in one or more choice situations where expectancy is controlled (or is known and can be accounted for). In this way we may offer a subject a series of alternatives either verbally or nonverbally, and on the basis of his choices determine a relative need value. For example, culturally we may define the acquisition of marbles for a sixth-grade child as a peer recognition reinforcement; we may define the goal of an ice cream cone as a physical comfort reinforcement. We may define a desire to be a boss or to give orders as a domination goal, a desire to avoid help or direction from adults as an independence goal, and so on. The nature of these goals is determined by analysis of the culture to which the subjects belong. If the subjects whom we measure are drawn from the same culture, we are able to arrive at adequate referents for needs for predictive or experimental testing purposes.

As in the case of need potential, of course, individuals may differ from the group norms or modal tendencies, and specific reinforcements may belong to organizations of reinforcements that are different from those to which they usually belong in the given culture. For individual prediction an exhaustive study of the subject—his learning background, his behavior in known situations, his verbal productions, and so forth—is necessary in order to reach an accurate estimate of need value. To determine the meaning or relationships of a given reinforcement, it is desirable to know: (1) when it became a reinforcement for the subject; (2) what pre-existing reinforcement did it lead to, and under what circumstances; and (3) what the subject sees as substitutes (or as related reinforcements).

TECHNIQUES OF MEASURING NEED VALUE

Like need potential, need value may be measured with interview, objective, and projective tests. Direct observation of behavior can be used when it is possible to set up a series of situations where expectancy or freedom of movement is controlled. Such control is not likely to be possible in life situations, but it may be set up in behavioral test situations.

Although it has usually been difficult to assess actual behavior from projective tests, it is quite likely that they may provide a good opportunity for the measurement of need value. Clinicians who have utilized instruments such as the TAT with adolescents are familiar with the fact that extremely aggressive, hostile stories may appear with considerable frequency in the well behaved, "normal" boys or girls who are selected as part of a control or normal population to compare with disturbed children. Sheer counting of the number of aggressive themes, for example, has frequently failed to differentiate between a child who seems unaggressive and a delinquent whose main symptom is one of hostile and aggressive behavior. One can resolve this problem only by discriminating between the potentiality of occurrence of a particular kind of behavior and the value or the preference the subject might have for reinforcements that he anticipates will follow. It is quite possible that the so-called normal child will have the same need value for hostile and aggressive behavior as the delinquent but a much lower need potential. This may occur because the expectancy of satisfaction from hostile behavior tends to be much lower; it is just as likely to occur because the expectancy of satisfaction for other behaviors tends to be much higher. Clearly the latter reason frequently carries no weight with the rejected and neglected delinquent child.

Rafferty (1952) has devised a manual for scoring an interview and two projective tests for measurement of need value in three need areas. Her study will be described more fully in the next section on freedom of movement, since it encompasses measurement of both of these variables.

In the measurement of need value by paper and pencil, forced choice, paired comparisons, or ranking methods, it is necessary to attempt to hold expectancy constant by means of verbal instructions. These instructions characteristically state, "If you could have any one," "If the chances of getting them are all equal," and so on. The only way of testing the effectiveness of such instructions would be to compare such verbal choice situations with ones where the subject could actually make choices and obtain the reinforcement often enough to be convinced that the expectancy of obtaining any one of his choices was 100 per cent. The previously cited study by E. Lotsof did indicate that verbal instructions may be expected to produce the same results as the real choices in the framework of the experimental design and subjects that he used.

FREEDOM OF MOVEMENT

The measurement of freedom of movement is of particular interest to the clinical psychologist, since the concept of freedom of movement in relation to a specific need (or, in more general terms, covering all needs) is probably most closely related to variables that in other points of view deal with the adjustment-maladjustment continuum.

An ideal definition of freedom of movement can be stated as: *The mean expectancy of obtaining positive satisfactions as a result of a set of related behaviors directed toward the accomplishment of a group of functionally related reinforcements.* A person's freedom of movement is low if he has a high expectancy of failure or punishment as a result of the behaviors with which he tries to obtain the reinforcements that constitute a particular need.

It will be asked why the term *Freedom of movement* is used instead of *mean expectancy,* which is probably more descriptive although perhaps more prosaic. We have selected the term *freedom of movement* in order to convey the relationship of this concept to some of the frequently used concepts of maladjustment, since freedom of movement deals with expectancy for a variety of behaviors for positive satisfaction. High freedom of movement implies an expectancy of success for many different behaviors in different situations; low freedom of movement implies the opposite.[8] *Freedom of*

---

[8]Although there is a relationship between the number of pathways or behaviors leading to satisfaction and freedom of movement as we have defined it, the use of the term itself does not indicate the number of such pathways available to the subject. Rather freedom of movement refers to the expectancy for gratification of the behaviors actually used by the subject whether they be many or few in number.

movement seems to be more similar in its connotations to concepts in other points of view which are used to imply important aspects of adjustment, concepts such as *anxiety* and *inadequacy feelings.*

Whereas need potential and need value must always be measured relative to other needs, freedom of movement may be measured on absolute or relative scales by using either indirect or direct methods of measurement. If it were possible to control (or equalize) reinforcement values in two or more different need areas, we could measure freedom of movement on a relative basis by assuming that a subject will direct his behavior toward the accomplishment of the reinforcement for which he has the greatest expectancy.

Other direct approaches to freedom of movement, yielding an absolute rather than a relative measure, would be by the use of verbal statements of expectancy (such as those used in level-of-aspiration studies), through behavioral indications of expectancy (such as the number of marbles bet in Castaneda's study), and through decision time, if it proves to be a useful measure of expectancy. These measures do not require comparison with the subject's other needs, but allow direct comparison of the subject with other persons within the same culture. By comparing a particular subject's responses with those of other persons, we may say (for example) that he has low freedom of movement not only for some specific need but in all needs, if we have measured all needs. In this sense, then, it is possible to obtain an absolute measure of freedom of movement as contrasted with the relative measures of need value or need potential. Both of the latter are always relative to the subject's other need potentials and need values and must summate to unity. Freedom of movement as defined above can be low for one person for all needs and high for another person for all needs.

Dean, in the study previously described, used a single measure for freedom of movement derived from the level-of-aspiration paradigm. If we accept the formula for expectancy, the degree of underestimation or overestimation in a relatively novel situation should be a function of the over-all level of expectancy for related problems or tasks (generalized expectancy).[9] The difference then between performance and stated expectancies might well be a short-cut measure of freedom of movement for that need area. A difficulty of this method as demonstrated by several studies is the tendency for people

---

[9] For any given need *GE* or generalized expectancy would be the basis for calculating freedom of movement, except that freedom of movement depends upon expectancy for positive satisfaction and requires also knowing the subject's minimal goal level. Generalized expectancy for *satisfaction* or *success* is equivalent to freedom of movement.

with low freedom of movement to behave defensively and to make use of the stated expectancy itself as a source of satisfaction. Subjects characterized as maladjusted, inadequate, or having low expectancies for success are frequently characterized by having either very low or very high difference scores. Although such types of defensive behaviors limit the use of this type of measure as a simple and direct measure of freedom of movement, it may still be quite useful for some purposes, particularly if combined with other measures of freedom of movement.

One method of measuring freedom of movement has already been extensively relied on in other personality theories and may be considered to be an indirect method of measuring freedom of movement in this system. Such a method depends upon identifying the frequency with which the subject, when seeking a potential goal, resorts to avoidance behavior or to irreal methods of satisfying or reaching the goal. Characteristically such avoidant and irreal behaviors have been referred to as "defense mechanisms." They are exemplified by *rationalization, projection,* development of symptoms for the purpose of avoiding crucial test situations as described by Adler's concept of *distance,* and so on. To understand how frequency of such behavior may be used as a measure of freedom of movement, it is necessary to accept some preliminary assumptions and to clarify the definition of avoidant and irreal or symbolic behaviors.

Although all goal-directed behavior may be considered to lead toward psychological homeostasis, satisfaction, or security, one can speak of avoidant behavior in contrast with positive or constructive behavior that is directed toward the accomplishment of some positive satisfaction. The child who avoids another aggressive child or a dog he fears will bite him, the college student who avoids taking examinations he expects to fail, the adult who avoids heterosexual situations because he expects rejection from the opposite sex—all are engaging in avoidant behavior. Although it is possible to determine for each individual whether a given behavior is avoidant or positive, avoidant behavior may also be defined culturally.

Similarly, where some behaviors are often oriented toward positive satisfaction but are considered by others actually not to achieve such satisfactions, these behaviors may be called irreal. Some examples are the avoidance of blame through projection, the accomplishment of goals through rationalization or daydreaming, and the achievement of superiority through identification. Again, the determination of whether a particular behavior may be thought of as an irreal method or a real and constructive one for reaching satisfaction must be determined by the culture in which a subject lives. Praying and knocking on wood are symbolic methods only if they are symbolic in the culture to which the subject belongs.

Having defined avoidant behavior and symbolic behavior in cultural terms, we may go on to one of the basic assumptions in utilizing such behavior as the basis of a method of measurement. This assumption may be stated as follows: These behaviors, defined culturally as avoidant or symbolic and therefore not constructive, do not lead to direct positive satisfactions from other members of the culture and almost invariably lead ultimately to negative reinforcement. Behaviors that serve to avoid potential failures in job-getting, in making a marital adjustment, in making a social adjustment, and so on ultimately lead to relatively strong negative reinforcements from other members of the culture. Irreal behaviors, although they may not immediately lead to negative reinforcement, are characterized by the absence of behavior that is satisfying on the part of other people in the environment. When irreal behaviors become excessive, so that they interfere with or take the place of constructive behaviors, they lead to strong negative reinforcement on the part of other people in the society.

Our second assumption is that people who use such behaviors experience or become aware of this negative reinforcement. If this assumption is true, any person who uses behaviors that he knows will result in negative reinforcement or that have become associated with negative reinforcement must do so because the strength of that particular negative reinforcement or the expectancy for it is less than the expectancy for negative reinforcement that might follow positive and realistic methods of reaching these goals. That is, if a person's avoidant and irreal behaviors are frequently followed by negative reinforcement, he will use them only if his expectancy for *failure* or *punishment* for positive behavior directed toward a given set of goals is higher than his expectancy for failure or punishment for the avoidant or irreal behavior.

To return to our original definition of freedom of movement, we may say that the extent to which avoidant or irreal behaviors are used provides an indirect measure of freedom of movement since it indicates the degree to which a person has an expectancy of obtaining positive satisfactions in some need area. It may be concluded that people who, in the face of potential reinforcements of love and affection, seek to avoid situations with members of the opposite sex or who set up barriers and methods of rejecting the opposite sex, do so because through their earlier experience they have developed strong expectancies for punishment or failure in such situations.

TECHNIQUES OF MEASURING FREEDOM
OF MOVEMENT

Measurements of freedom of movement by assessing defense behavior may be made in controlled situations. For example, in the
level-of-aspiration technique it is possible to identify certain patterns
of behavior as characteristic of avoidance of failure or of symbolic
methods of achieving success. Freedom of movement can be measured by unstructured methods such as projective techniques and
interviews. Crandall (1950) successfully used TAT stories from specially constructed pictures for the measurement of freedom of
movement and was able to predict a gradient of generalization-of-
expectancy changes. Similarly, it is possible to use either a controlled
or free interview to obtain a sample of behaviors from which the
amount of dependence upon avoidant or irreal behaviors in relation
to different needs could be estimated, as has been done by Rockwell
(1950) and Rafferty (1952).

Rafferty, using the need areas of love and affection from opposite sex peers and academic recognition, obtained measures of freedom of movement and need value from an interview, a modified
TAT, and the Incomplete Sentences Blank. Preliminary group
manuals were constructed for the measurement of these two variables for each of the three kinds of testing situations. Ratings were
made by Rafferty and by two other judges. She found, as did Rockwell and A. Lotsof, that reliabilities for judgments on these variables
are relatively high for the interview and for the Incomplete Sentences
method. In Rafferty's study, reliability of ratings for freedom of
movement derived from the modified TAT was somewhat lower
than that found by Crandall. Some estimate of the utility of these
measures could be obtained from the intercorrelation, if any, between the same measures derived from three different kinds of
material—interview, Incomplete Sentences, and modified TAT. Her
correlations are shown in Table 4.3. In general these measures show
significant intercorrelations in the three different types of testing situations where the specific material obtained has little or no overlap.

It may be asked why so many of these studies deal with the need
for academic recognition and acceptance from the opposite sex,
needs that may have little significance in the general population.
That is, one may question the generality of the findings from such
studies to other needs—ones that' are frequently considered less
socially acceptable, such as for sexual gratification, or for dominance
through hostile or aggressive behavior. Generality of these findings
cannot be assumed. The reason for their choice is that for the college

Table 4.3 Correlation Coefficients (Pearson *r*) between Each Measure

	AR-NV	AR-FM	LA-NV	LA-FM
Interview & TAT	.46‡	.36§	.44‡	.36§
Interview & ISB	.66*	.38§	.36	.25
TAT & ISB	.36	.19	.41§	.04
Combined TAT-ISB				
& Interview	.64*	.48†	.46+	.42§

Source: Rafferty, 1952.
* .001 level of confidence
† .01 level of confidence
‡ .02 level of confidence
§ .05 level of confidence

AR—academic recognition
LA—love and affection
NV—need value
FM—freedom of movement

student population, the population most readily available for testing, they represent real and important goals. Furthermore, it has been possible to devise instruments for the measurements of such goals that can be utilized by subsequent investigators. Essentially we are testing theoretical principles, and there seems to be no logical reason why the principles that obtain for one set of goal-directed behaviors should not be predictive of another set of goal-directed behaviors.

The reader who has used the concept of need in other contexts may be confused as to what a need *really* is from this systematic viewpoint. It should be repeated here, therefore, that the term *need* is used synonymously with need potential. The concept is a behavioral one; it describes a person's tendency to behave in a given fashion. It depends upon the value of the reinforcements toward which the functionally related behaviors are directed and the expectancies that these behaviors will lead to the reinforcements.

THE PSYCHOLOGICAL SITUATION

If this social learning theory is to utilize the principle stated in the first postulate that its basic datum is the interaction of the individual and his meaningful environment, we have yet to consider in detail the specific ways we distinguish or describe differences in the meaningful environment or psychological situation. We need to develop a method of describing the situation, *s* in our basic formula (p. 52) in order to determine the degree of similarity in any two objectively described situations and to use the categorization of situations in prediction and control.[10]

---

[10] The determination of the principles describing the nature of the simple act of discriminating characteristics of a stimulus situation along physical dimensions such as color, size, and form is a more molecular problem than the ones we are interested in at this time.

It is presumed that the manner in which a person perceives a given situation will determine for him which behaviors are likely to have reasonable probability or the highest probabilities of leading to some satisfaction. Thus a person reacting to another person whom he classifies as an enemy is more likely to utilize behaviors aimed at harm avoidance than behaviors directed toward love and affection. Should his perception of the situation change, the expectancy that given behaviors will lead to satisfaction will change markedly. In some instances the value of a given reinforcement will change if the situation is recategorized. This occurs when the value of the first reinforcement is dependent upon some immediately following reinforcement that is more or less likely to occur in one situation than in another.

Specific cues that have acquired meanings and that will determine expectancies may be aspects of objects or they may be verbal in nature. The facial expression of a stranger and the expensiveness of office furniture are examples of object cues determining expectancies. Instructions in an experimental situation (as in the study of Tyler) are an example of a verbal cue leading to categorization. What we refer to here as a cue might be referred to as an external reinforcement in another context. In any situation there will be present a large variety of cues and possibilities for many different expectations for behavior-reinforcement sequences.[11]

CATEGORIZING THE PSYCHOLOGICAL SITUATION

Psychologists have for a long time been interested in categorizing the behavioral or internal state of their human subjects. Although they have at the same time recognized that behavior of the human subjects changes in different situations or, as a matter of fact, is even characteristically different in different situations, they have almost universally neglected to set up descriptive categories for describing

---

[11] The distinction between a cue and reinforcement would not be of any great importance were it not for the fact that many aspects of situations (tables, chairs, eyeglasses, high foreheads) affect expectancies but their occurrence does not appear to lead to changes in behavior potential carried over into other situations. *Although almost all reinforcements are also cues for new reinforcements, not all cues are reinforcements.* It seems at this time that a distinction can be made on a common-sense basis. A cue that is not a reinforcement is an aspect of the situation, the occurrence of which a person does not relate to his own behavior—that is, the person does not feel that it occurs as a result of his own behavior. A cue is merely present; a reinforcement happens to someone.

different kinds of situations. It surely has long been recognized that the average or normal man's behavior is to a large extent determined by the situation he is in, or that when he fails to "adjust" and react differentially in different situations, he is called abnormal. It seems apparent that there is a greater similarity of behavior among a group of people watching a baseball game than among the behaviors of the same people in widely different situations. One learns over the course of time that the behavior that brings reward in one situation may bring punishment in another, and he learns to classify situations accordingly.

Fuller (1950) is cognizant of the importance of the situation for prediction in his work with subhuman species. Prediction of the behavior of individual animals in a variety of situations requires categorization of the situation by the experimenter. He proposes a classification based on two variables, incentive value and complexity.

One major problem facing the psychologist is the development of terms to describe situations, terms that are communicable, that (like our other descriptive constructs) may be reliably and objectively measured, and that have utility. To say that a man will act aggressively in a threatening situation is better than to say that he is an aggressive man, but it is only better if the words, *in a threatening situation,* convey and communicate meaning so that a group of observers would all be able to predict when he would act hostilely and when he would not.

We would propose that we describe situations by their cultural meanings in terms of the characteristic reinforcements that are likely to occur in those situations, that is, that we characterize situations parallel to the way we characterize psychological needs. The concepts that are useful in a given culture for characterizing functionally related reinforcements would probably be most useful in describing situations. Of course, it is clear that no situation always brings one kind of reinforcement. Situations can be characterized as mixed or can be described in terms of the dominant, usual, or most frequent reinforcements likely to occur in a given culture. Situations may also be characterized as unstructured or unfamiliar in cases where the expectancies for any particular kind of reinforcement tend to be low.

As in the case of needs, we have no *a priori* list of terms based on instinct or armchair theorizing; the problem is an empirical one. For the time being, therefore, we will have to characterize situations in the same terms in which we try to characterize behavior: academic recognition situations, love and affection situations, conformity situations, dominance situations, and so on. In this sense people, too, may be thought of as situations; it makes good sense to speak of authority figure situations, heterosexual situations, and so forth when these terms imply that a particular kind of reinforcement is likely to occur.

In describing the situation itself or the cues in the situation merely for purposes of identification, we are faced with the same problem as we are faced with in describing behavior. This in itself requires no systematic treatment but only the use of objective communicative language for the purpose of identifying what it is we may be talking about. The constructs we use may be from any mode of description as long as they serve the purpose of reliable communication.

Obviously the meaning of the situation, the cue, or the stimulus for the subject may vary sharply from that of its cultural value or meaning either for very specific situations or for very large groups of them. The subject may make finer discriminations than the average person in the culture, or he may not have learned to make discriminations where others make them. A person's experience with a given situation may show such variations because of differences in his parents, because of his previous sub-culture, or as a result of his own special characteristics. *The clinician does not assume that the individual classifies situations in the same way as the majority of the culture or that the situations the individual is likely to see as similar are the same ones likely to be seen as similar by the culture.* Rather, the clinician's problem is to find out what this specific situation means to the individual and what situations he is likely to see as similar. This end is accomplished by observation of the patient's behavior, through interviews dealing with past experiences and present attitudes, and from other information the clinician obtains about the subject.

We have discussed the psychological situation and sometimes substituted *cue* or *stimulus.* We would hold, with Lewin and the Gestalt psychologists, that a person reacts to the totality of his psychological environment. However, he also reacts to specific aspects of it, and within a given situation the presence of different cues may set up conflicts or expectancies for quite different outcomes for the same behavior. As psychologists, we may be interested in his reaction to the situation as a whole, and we may also be interested in analyzing this down to its specific cues. How we describe a specific situation must be determined by our immediate purpose and the degree of predictive efficiency we are willing to sacrifice for reasons of economy of time. If for a given purpose it is sufficient to fasten upon some specific cue or stimulus object to make the necessary predictions, other aspects of the situation may well be neglected. If it is found empirically that other aspects of the situation when considered result in significantly higher prediction, then description of the psychological situation must be extended to include these cues as well.

THE RELATIONSHIP OF BEHAVIOR
TO THE SITUATION

How does the situation specifically enter into our basic formula for behavior? *The individual's expectancy that a given behavior will be followed by a given reinforcement is dependent upon how he characterizes the situation.* That is, we might say that we may determine a subject's expectancy accurately only after we know how he characterizes his psychological situation. Since his expectancy is determined by the variables E', GE, and N, in order to calculate E' we must know what previous situations he sees as being similar to or the same as the present one. His generalized expectancy for particular reinforcements to occur is also to some extent situationally bound, and we must know whether he classifies the present situation as one where reinforcements of a given category are likely to occur. We must also know how many times previously he has been in a situation that he would characterize as the same or similar.

There can be little doubt that a person expects different outcomes for the same behavior in different situations. The rabid and aggressive partisanship of the football spectator, highly acceptable and positively reinforced in the stadium, might be strongly negatively reinforced in the social bridge game. Dependent, help-seeking behavior may be strongly reinforced for a man when alone with a wife or girl friend but rejected with peers of the same sex. A male in our society would usually accept a compliment regarding his aesthetic appeal with pleasure when alone with a woman but he is likely to be embarrassed by it when there are other males present.

In other words, it appears not only that the situation determines what reinforcements are most likely to occur in a given situation for a given behavior but also that the value of the reinforcements themselves are frequently different in different situations as they may be expected to lead to different further reinforcements. In our example of a man who finds a compliment rewarding in one situation but not in another, the reinforcement has changed value because he has learned to expect that when other men are present this reinforce-

ment may well be followed by kidding, rejection, or doubts regarding
his masculinity. We may refer to the expectancy for the reinforcement to occur as E_1 and the expectancy that a given reinforcement
will be followed by subsequent reinforcements as E_2. The study by
Schroder and Rotter previously cited (p. 136) illustrates how the
situation affects E_1 and, consequently, choice behavior. The experimental design of this study was such as to demonstrate that differential training led to predictable differences in expectations with
several groups of subjects, although the objectively described situation or stimuli were the same. Of course, this has been demonstrated
in a great number of previous learning studies. It would also be possible to cite many studies where the same subjects were involved in
different situations. However, the principle is the same, that previous
experience in any situation determines the expectations for future
behavior-reinforcement sequences.

Expectancies set up by cues in the situation are not always simple expectancies for some one thing to occur; they frequently may
be for the occurrence of a sequence of events. For example, some
cues on a task may lead to an expectation that "I will get better with
practice," or "I will get worse because of fatigue," or "There is a
trick to this thing; when I learn it I will be able to solve the problem." These may be thought of as expectations that particular kinds
of behavior such as persistence, being on one's guard, or avoiding the
obvious will lead either to some specific known reward or to satisfaction in a more general sense. It is in part because human subjects
are so capable of utilizing the cues in the situation in just this complex fashion that many psychologists prefer to work with naive subhuman species.

In general the values of reinforcements are not as greatly affected
by situational changes as are the expectancies that specific behaviors
will lead to specific reinforcements. This difference is due in part to
the fact that the value of most reinforcements as related to future
reinforcements is itself not readily changed, since the future reinforcements are frequently quite delayed and therefore not part of
the specific situation itself. However, many reinforcements change
in their value in a specific situation, particularly when the relationship to reinforcements expected to follow the original is likely to
have been verbalized by the subject and when the subsequent reinforcement is likely to occur relatively soon. The study by Phares
(1953) illustrated differences in the preference for reinforcements
in different situations (or how the situation affects E_2). It should
be noted, however, that although Phares found significant differences, a remarkable consistency from situation to situation was also
apparent.

Phares standardized a list of reinforcements (getting the best grades in class, making the football team, being able to fix my father's car, and so on) on a group of 99 seventh- and eighth-grade school children. On the basis of judges' agreement on the nature of the reinforcements, he selected 18 of them and made up three matched groups of six each, each group having the same mean preference value in his standardizing group. The three categories were comprised of recognition reinforcements in the athletic skills area, recognition reinforcements in the academic skills area, and recognition reinforcements in the manual skills area. He then obtained rankings for these 18 reinforcements in three different school situations involving random selections of other seventh- and eighth-graders since they were all required course situations. The ranking instrument was administered by the English teachers in English classes, by the gym teachers in gym classes, and by the manual training teachers in the manual training classes. Since in each of the three situations a different 50 boys ranked the full list, Phares had a total of 150 subjects in the experimental phase of his study. He studied the reliability of his instrument by using a split half technique on the academic items in the academic situation, the athletic items in the athletic situation, and the manual skill items in the manual training situation. His reliabilities were .91, .79, and .83, respectively.

Since his differences were slight, he used difference scores and found that the difference between mean ranks of the academic and athletic reinforcements in the academic situation as compared with that difference in the athletic situation was highly significant. A similar result was found for differences between the athletic and the manual reinforcements in those two situations. No significant difference, however, was obtained between the rankings of the reinforcements in the academic and manual situations. Some of the failure to show a difference between the latter two situations may be explained by the fact that these two situations were more similar to each other than either one of them was to the gym situation, where the students and teacher were all in gym clothes and the rankings were done on the gym floor. Also Phares' analysis of the actual manual items showed that many of them had little in common with the activities of the manual training classroom, as many of his items had to do with mechanical skills or skills involving knowledge of motors and electrical devices. These values actually received little reinforcement in the manual training classroom. However, the study sufficed to show that a very simple paper-and-pencil test, when administered in different physical conditions with different administrators, can produce significantly different results. Such a finding, though perhaps expected, is of considerable significance for both clinical and experimental psychology in that the physical setting of the test or experiment and the cue values of the clinician or the experimenter are frequently neglected, both in research designs and in clinical practice, in attempting to analyze the significance of the subject's responses. At the present time there is accumulating in the field of projective testing considerable evidence regarding the importance in test results of such variables as the sex and manner of the examiner as well as the physical situation in which projective tests are given. These studies may be interpreted essentially in a fashion similar to that of Phares.

THE PSYCHOLOGICAL SITUATION AND SOCIAL ROLES

Sociologists have long recognized that a subject's behavior in certain social situations is determined by the expectancies that others have regarding his behavior. They have referred to a person's social role as that person's assumption of one or more of a limited series of behaviors that he believes to be appropriate to the expectations of others. We might say that the subject learns on the basis of objective cues that particular kinds of behavior are more likely to be reinforced in one situation than another. Where social situations are relatively clearly identified in a similar manner by members of the same culture, uniformity of categorization and behavior increases. Analysis of sociological treatises on role behavior may provide important leads in determining what behaviors are likely to be associated with particular ways of identifying situations.

AMBIGUOUS AND UNSTRUCTURED SITUATIONS

It seems important to differentiate between ambiguous and unstructured situations. We refer to ambiguous situations as ones in which the important cue or cues are not readily identified or recognized by the subject. Some of the experiments on perception and need using tachistoscopic presentation might fit this description, or a TAT picture in which it is difficult to make out the sex or the facial expression of a character. It would seem that in such situations there would be a tendency to identify the stimulus or cue as one leading to a need of greater value to the subject, whether this is negative or positive. Stated otherwise, the identification of the stimulus follows the principle of generalization, and the subject who has already identified many more cues as potentially leading to a given satisfaction or, in our terms, the subject with the strongest need potential in a given area, would be more likely to see this stimulus as he has seen other stimuli.

An unstructured stimulus situation might be identified as one in which the expectations that particular behaviors will lead to particular reinforcements whether negative or positive are all low, or, stated in common-sense terms, the situation is a new one. Again we may expect that the selection of behaviors in such a situation will be a function of generalization. We might be more interested in expectancy in this instance and anticipate that behavior would follow the normal lines of the greatest generalized expectation for reinforcement. If the subject had a high expectancy for failure in many situations, his behavior in the novel situation would tend to be irreal or avoidant. If he had a high general expectation for recognition gratifications, his behavior would be one leading to recognition reinforcements. Such unstructured situations would also be characterized by the ease of change in behavior as a function of experience.[12] That is, going back to our formula for expectancy increments, changes in expectancy as a result of a single new experience are maximal when the number of previous trials in a situation approaches zero.

CHANGES IN THE CATEGORIZATION OF SITUATIONS

Although the situation as objectively described may remain relatively the same, it may, in the course of an experiment or a segment of time, change considerably in its meaning to the subject. These changes result in behavioral changes that cannot be accounted for by the use of the regular formula for increments in expectancy or reinforcement value. For example, if we measured the expectancy for success of a college student on a mechanical puzzle that he had failed at six times and then mastered on the seventh trial, he would probably express an expectancy of 100 per cent on the eighth trial, an expectancy that could hardly be predicted on an incremental basis. But he has previously learned that when such a task is solved once, it may be solved any number of times after that. He would now place the task in a category different from the category he had placed it in when it was not solved.

Another example would be that of a person who at social gather-

---

[12] Expectancy for a particular reinforcement to lead to a particular reinforcement may be relatively high after one or two trials in a new situation. Although expectancies in such *relatively* novel situations would change readily, the situations would not be considered unstructured.

ings usually behaves with excessive politeness. In a novel situation he begins to behave politely, but after observing the host for a short time he changes over to practical joking. What happens in these situations is that the occurrence of the reinforcement not only has an incremental function on expectancy for some behavior-reinforcement sequences but also serves as a cue or a stimulus for expectations for future reinforcements. When this happens in an experiment, the experimenter must, as the subject already has, recategorize the situation and calculate his expectancies in terms of a new and different situation. We are saying simply that reinforcements when they occur, not only serve an incremental function on expectancy but also are in themselves cues that may lead to the recategorization of the situation. Frequently psychologists find that this takes place both in the laboratory and in life only after it has occurred and find it extremely difficult to predict. However, the problem is no different from the problem of predicting from the situation originally. Cues have cultural meanings that we may use to set up preliminary predictions; we may then correct these meanings from empirical evidence as we study groups in more controlled conditions. For a given subject we may learn the meaning of specific cues through our clinical procedures. In any case, the implications are obvious that a thorough knowledge of the culture is necessary to predict behavior of human beings as it relates either directly or indirectly to other humans.

Some of the findings of the partial versus 100 per cent reinforcement studies that are difficult to explain on other bases may be explained on just such a shift in categorization of the situation as a function of the occurrence of the new reinforcement. Viewed in this way the new reinforcement is the first extinction trial in the case of a 100 per cent reinforced group, a trial that results in a marked and sometimes total drop in expectancy. This drop does not seem to be accountable for on a simple decremental basis, whereas for the partial reinforcement group the extinction seems more nearly to fit a simple decremental function as has already been demonstrated in Castaneda's data. The study by Lasko (1950) with children illustrates this sharply. . . . [Details of this study were deleted to conserve space.]

SOCIAL ATTITUDES AND THE
PSYCHOLOGICAL SITUATION

Categorizations regarding a group of people or events of social significance have been referred to in psychological writings as an attitude or *social attitude*. From a social learning point of view, in considering social attitudes, instead of placing the emphasis on grouping situations functionally on the basis of similarity of reinforcements, the emphasis is on some common objective characteristic of the stimulus or situation. In this instance the stable behavior-expectancy-reinforcement sequences of concern are determined by the subject's reactions to such stimuli as Negroes, religious beliefs, and political beliefs. There are certain practical reasons why, for the purposes of the social psychologist, such an approach may have maximum utility. However, the social psychologist must empirically demonstrate that the basis for placing a group of behavior-reinforcement sequences in the same category is useful for prediction. For example, the concept of an attitude toward war must allow prediction of behavior from referent to referent for a subject or from one sample to another. *Like the concept of need in the field of personality study, the failure to separate the concept of behavior from those of expectancy and reinforcement value limits the utility of the construct of social attitudes.* Sometimes the failure to discriminate between test response behavior (involving the examiner as a social stimulus who has his own value to the subject) and the subject's internal or private beliefs leads to discouraging results.

It seems that to speak of social attitudes as a way of *behaving* toward a group or class of external events or cues with empirically demonstrated functional meaning would be of considerable value in this field.[13] In terms of our behavior potential formula, the stimulus, whether it is a Negro or a religious idea, is a cue that determines for the subject the expectancy or expectancies that specific behavior will lead to specific outcomes. When there is empirical evidence that the expectancies for behavior-reinforcement sequences aroused by the stimuli identifying the object of the attitude are functionally related, then utility for that concept of a social attitude would be demonstrated.

A further comment in regard to social attitudes should be made. A person's behavior in relationship to some stimulus, from the social learning point of view, is determined not merely by his expectations regarding the nature of the stimulus but by his expectations of what behavior toward this stimulus will be rewarded and the value of these rewards. The subject is concerned not merely with predicting some event accurately but with behaving in such a way as to provide himself with maximum satisfaction. If only the former characteristic of making accurate predictions were involved, it would be hard to

---

[13] Hovland, Janis, and Kelley (1953) have recently described one general approach of this kind.

understand why some southerners fail to make certain kinds of distinctions among Negroes and to see some of them as social equals. Their failure to do so, which cannot be accounted for by their inability to "recognize facts," can be readily understood in terms of the negative reinforcement that would follow from other whites for a change of behavior either in expressed verbal attitudes or in direct relationships. If this analysis is valid, emphasis on changing the reinforcements resulting from the behaviors involved might be more effective in changing social attitudes than the emphasis sometimes placed on merely providing more or more accurate information. Information is only likely to influence when the status of the information giver is unusually high, or, as rarely may be the case, where the need for intellectual consistency is unusually strong.

MINIMAL GOAL LEVELS

If one were to consider the potential outcomes for a series of alternative behaviors in a specific situation or for some sequence of life situations, it would be possible to place the outcomes or external reinforcements on a continuum in terms of preference. Some of these outcomes will be experienced as satisfactions, some as failures or punishments. *The minimal goal level is defined as the lowest goal in a continuum of potential reinforcements for some life situation or situations which will be perceived as a satisfaction.* Operationally, it would be the lowest goal in a continuum of possible reinforcements that would strengthen or increase the behavior potential of the response leading to it, following its occurrence. Common-sense experience indicates that this point may vary widely for different persons. Brief attention may be rewarding to one child and frustrating to another; similarly, the effect of a minimum passing grade, a casual compliment, or a small raise in salary will differ among adults. If by maladjustment we mean a state of dissatisfaction or the absence of positive reinforcements, it can be seen that a person whose minimal goal levels are consistently above the reinforcements that follow his behavior will regularly fail to achieve satisfaction. Therapy is frequently concerned with finding new ways of reaching pre-existing goals, but perhaps more often it is concerned with changing goal values or need values, particularly minimal goal levels. That is, an attempt may be made to increase the value of reinforcement acts below the minimal goal level.

Minimal goals, like other goals, change. A reinforcement act that is associated primarily with other negative reinforcement acts takes on a negative value. Those associated with other positive acts take on a positive value. If a parent rewards a child with praise only when he is better than everyone else in some competition and criticizes any other performance, then the child may achieve satisfaction only in being first. Any other outcome of competition is a failure, to be avoided at all cost. Similarly, if a child has learned that his wants may be fulfilled by maintaining the constant attention of adults, then any less attention is a threatening situation. It is the pre-existing goals or the reinforcements which are perceived to follow any newly acquired reinforcement that determine whether it is positive or negative, strong or weak.

Frequently minimal goals fluctuate with experience. Such a fluctuation occurs as a result of the changing standards of *others*, actual or anticipated, rather than as a direct and automatic effect of success or failure on the minimal goal. That is, other people modify their behavior toward a person as they learn to know what behavior is typical of him. The mother who wanted her child to have all A's but whose child gets mostly C's changes her standards, perceives a B as progress and rewards it appropriately. The wife who wanted to be rich but finds herself struggling in a lower-income group sees a small raise as a step up and praises her husband correspondingly. This behavior is typical of a culture where there are constant efforts at improvement, self-betterment, and so forth, so that progress at almost any level has become in itself something to be rewarded.

The opposite is frequently, but perhaps not as consistently, as true. Minimal goals have a tendency to shift up following repeated success, since the failure to improve can be negatively reinforcing and a goal, once positive, gradually takes on a negative value. The studies by Dean (1951) and R. Jessor (1951) tend to indicate that minimal goals are to some degree free of expectancy but do fluctuate with success and failure in a controlled situation.

Dean (1951), in a study using the Level of Aspiration Board, gave subjects a continuous series of failure experiences, controlling their performance so that it reduced gradually over a series of trials. He asked for estimates of expectancy before each trial and also "for the lowest score they would accept and still feel satisfied." He found that expectancy scores dropped significantly more than minimal goal scores, indicating some independence of these two measures and a greater resistance to changing the minimal goals.

R. Jessor (1951) also requested minimal goal statements as well as expectancy statements in his investigation of the generalization-of-expectancy changes. Like Dean he found that minimal goals dropped significantly less on negative reinforcement than did expectancy scores, although the minimal goals did show a significant drop. Minimal goals also followed the same gradient of generalization as did expectancy scores. In an earlier study, Preston and Bayton (1941) asked for a somewhat similar score in a level-of-aspiration situation. They asked for three statements of aspiration—wished-for scores, expectancy, and the score that represented the lowest score they expected to achieve. Although the latter is not the same as the minimal goal score in Dean's and Jessor's studies, it is comparable. Preston and Bayton found that the "least" score did not fluctuate with the other two and that the other two scores showed significant correlation.

Although some minimal goals fluctuate with experience, most cultures provide relatively inflexible standards for some situations; failure to meet these standards usually results in some subsequent negative reinforcement. One must obtain at least passing grades, have a minimum aesthetic appeal, and so on in order to avoid rather strong punishments. Each larger culture and each subculture has many such absolute standards. Many parents, too, are rigid or inflexible in one or more areas and withhold satisfaction regardless of the child's persistent failure to meet their standards.

When the parents, in terms of their own standards or as representatives of the culture, set too high standards or demands (including the moral standards and goals that are stressed by the psychoanalysts), or teach a child by example or didactically that satisfaction lies only in goals that are out of his reach, the child is being prepared for a life of dissatisfaction. Similarly, when a parent is overdemonstrative, overprotective, or overindulgent, the child learns to find security or satisfaction in a relationship that no one else can duplicate. The characteristic behavior of others then is equated to the parent's behavior when the child's needs were about to be frustrated rather than met.

We have stressed how minimal goals are established historically on the basis of the reinforcements by others. This does not mean that a person does not experience "self standards" or that he does not set for himself standards which if not met lead to an experience of failure. It would not be denied that such self standards exist as they are perceived by the individual; they are, however, a result of his experience with others. Sometimes a person finds himself in a social situation where no other people are present who have the reinforcement value for him that former associations did. The minimum goals of a dead mother or the standards she may have set may persist over a long period of time in spite of the difference between these standards and those of immediate associates. As in the case of changing the values of other reinforcements, it is frequently true that when the subject cannot establish relationships with others as important to him as his earlier ties, a change in his minimal goals or moral standards may come about only through setting up a strong relationship with a psychotherapist. To say that a person's standards are self standards is only to say that he can no longer verbalize how these standards came to be, and that he differentiates them from the standards of others who are perhaps now in face-to-face association with him.

CHANGING MINIMAL GOALS

A minimal goal refers to some external reinforcement. Its value is positive but approaching zero or negative value. To make an external reinforcement that is perceived as a failure or below the minimal goal no longer a negative reinforcement becomes a problem essentially of changing the reinforcement values for a group of related reinforcements. At the theoretical level, this has been discussed under changing reinforcement values. Much of the problem of therapy obviously is concerned with this issue. Johnson (1946) has stressed the importance of high goals in leading to frustration and demoralization in his "IFD" pattern. Adler (1924) has made the same point in his emphasis on fictional goals of superiority, and the Freudian psychoanalytic school has emphasized the high moral standards or "strong superego" characteristic of many neurotic people. Changing minimal goals or reinforcement values will be discussed on a more practical basis in Chapter IX [of *Social Learning and Clinical Psychology*] in the discussion of psychotherapeutic techniques.

THE SIGNIFICANCE OF LANGUAGE
IN SOCIAL LEARNING

In the previous discussions we have mentioned from time to time the importance of language in the learning process. Nonverbalized relationships seem to be resistant to extinction. Language may either provide cues that will determine behavior or provide a rein-forcement. Language functions to direct attention to specific cues. Although it is a difficult problem to define implicit language opera-tionally, it seems apparent from numerous learning studies of human beings that implicit language in problem solving is characterized by the use of symbols or abstractions. There is evidence from several studies that the use of language will enhance or speed up learning, even in conditioning experiments that are thought of as involving a nonverbal or automatic learning. Apparently verbalizing what is hap-pening will speed up both acquisition and extinction of a conditioned response (Hilgard, Campbell, and Sears, 1938; Razran, 1949; Leeper, 1951).

Language as a stimulus may be readily defined operationally. It is like any other stimulus except that it may represent not only pres-ent objects but events of both past and future. We are referring to the use of language here as a process of symbolizing or abstracting from the environment to represent objects and events not physically present and to characterize the relationships between objects and events not physically present. We are not able to present a compre-hensive theory of language and its development at this time; we can merely accept the manipulation of symbols or abstractions as an im-portant variable that relates to behavior.

Referents for language as a cue or stimulus are relatively easily specified. Implicit language presents greater difficulties. The ability of the subject to verbalize events or relationships communicably after they have occurred would be one important referent for im-plicit language. It is doubtful that this abstracting or symbolizing process can be represented as an all-or-none affair. The amount of implicit symbolizing a person performs in one situation may be measured by the degree to which he carries over or can apply experi-ence in one situation to experience in a new or different situation. When we are considering whether or not the subject uses symbols to represent his experience, that is, the degree to which he categorizes, classifies, or abstracts his experience, it seems likely that we shall end up with a continuum. We may also distinguish levels of abstraction in terms of the number and broadness of the classifications used. These are problems which, in themselves, will require the development of an extensive theoretical system to provide the necessary framework for fully understanding language behavior. We may discuss, however, at a more empirical level the effect of language on the variables we have already constructed, when it is empirically possible to demon-strate that explicit or implicit language is present.

LANGUAGE AS A CUE OR REINFORCEMENT

A person learns to associate words, ideas, and statements, like any other stimuli, with future events. Words spoken, written, or conveyed through gesture are signals for future occurrences. Not only may they serve as a major cue but they may direct attention to specific cues in a complex situation. Through the use of instructions, a problem that might be a trial-and-error problem running to hundreds of trials can be changed to a one-, two-, or three-trial learning problem. One of the major functions of language in a social situation is to direct a person's attention to the relevant cues and consequently to avoid the irrelevant cues. A person may then apply previous experience to a current situation by dealing with a few cues rather than having to treat each situation as a Gestalt, new and different from anything that has ever preceded it. Sometimes the effect of language is misleading, since it may direct one's attention to too few cues. Nevertheless it is a technique by which a person may react quickly to a situation without having to understand it on the basis of extended trial-and-error behavior.

In the research cited, we have referred to praise as a reinforcement. Praise obviously is primarily a verbal event. Like any other reinforcement that has acquired its value, language too acquires values—frequently values far stronger than the original nonverbal stimuli that serve as satisfiers. Statements of recognition, love, rejection, shame, can be much more profound in their effect on the mature human in our culture than food deprivation and the absence of irritation on the skin.

THE ROLE OF IMPLICIT LANGUAGE
IN CHANGING EXPECTANCIES
AND REINFORCEMENT VALUES

Since the potentiality of any behavior's occurring is a function of the expectancy that it will lead to some reinforcement and the value of that reinforcement, and since the value of the reinforcement is a function of what other reinforcements it has been associated with in the past, this relationship between events and their consequences is a determiner of behavior. It would follow from the previous discussion that the verbalization of these relationships or the degree to which a person symbolized them would be an important determiner of their susceptibility to change. Normally a person's behavior is

based upon many previous experiences, which follow a partial reinforcement paradigm.[14] The behavior of crying to get help, for example, may be reinforced in the average child in the first couple of
years of life hundreds of times, but not every time.

However, language serves to bring to bear previous experience
that in itself may represent many, many trials, or to allow for recategorization of the situation so that it is seen as more similar to some
new group of experiences. By verbalization, then, one can quickly
bring about major changes in expectancies. One can build up a person's expectancies for new or different reinforcements by directing
his attention to new and previously neglected consequences of behavior. Or one can change a person's expectancies by analyzing his
previous experiences to show that he has fastened in a sense on the
wrong cues, and that his present situation is more similar to something else in his experience than to the past events to which he has
related it. Such a conception, of course, justifies the importance of
insight in learning or in therapy. However, it does not make it a *sine
qua non* for change, or learning. Language may serve to create new
expectancies (and thus effect considerable changes in behavior) without analysis of how old ones were mistakenly built up. We shall
discuss these problems more thoroughly in Chapter IX [of *Social
Learning and Clinical Psychology*]. It is important at this point only
to indicate that the verbalization of relationships *may* increase the
speed with which expectancies for reinforcements may be changed,
and consequently help change the behaviors affected by those
expectancies.

Research on set, learning attitude, or higher-level learning skills
such as that by Harlow and others (Harlow, 1949; Siipola, 1941;
Rees and Israel, 1935) may be thought of in these terms as the effect
of language in reducing irrelevant cues or acting as a selecting device
for relevant cues. It can be shown in many complex problem-solving
tasks, such as the Luchins' (1942) studies on water jar problems, that
a subject can solve apparently insolvable problems very quickly when
his attention is directed to the proper cues in the situation.

Since the effect of language is to classify, to categorize, or to

---

[14] The importance of the reinforcements' being partial rather than 100 per cent was implied in the section on the importance of the stimulus or the psychological situation. In a
partial reinforcement series, non-reinforcement itself develops or has an expectancy and the
non-occurrence of the reinforcement does not change the categorization of the situation. In
this kind of learning, future behavior is dependent only upon increments of expectancy,
increments that tend to become relatively small as the number of trials on which the expectancy is based becomes greater. Consequently, a behavior that is learned over a great
many trials by a partial reinforcement sequence may change very slowly merely as a result
of non-reinforcement.

abstract similarity in events, it serves, therefore, to determine and enhance the nature of generalization. If an event is symbolized, it will increase generalization to other events that are similarly abstracted. Not only does language determine generalization or mediate generalization on the basis of the subject's implicit categorizing, as Razran (1949) has shown, but the language of others may be used by the observer as a stimulus to determine, control, or enhance generalization. It allows the teacher or therapist to generalize in terms of principles or to affect many behaviors rather than a single one in a single situation. Language also allows one to deal with behavior in terms of generalities or groups or classes without specifying single or separate referents, although an important question is involved in the degree to which specific referents are communicated.

It presents the interesting experimental problem of how generalization will take place more effectively: as a result of a direct reinforcement of a behavior of the subject and his own implicit abstracting and generalizing, or as a result of dealing verbally in terms of generalities or classes. This is a problem that obviously has important implications for psychotherapeutic practice.

Since language may function to deal with non-present objects and events, it allows for the building up of expectancies for subsequent reinforcements that may be delayed considerably in time. The student in graduate school works assiduously at a task that would lose its reinforcement value for him if he did not anticipate that it might be related four years hence to a Ph.D. degree, an event that for him has never occurred but which he is able to anticipate through the use of language. Language may be utilized by the observer, therapist, or parent to create or change reinforcement values by communicating relationships between present events and potential future events. With language, we can negate or neutralize, perhaps to a large extent, the effect of delayed reinforcement on learning. Where in nonverbal learning the delay of reinforcement is highly correlated with the efficiency of acquisition and performance, language may be used to reduce this relationship considerably. . . . [A section on "complexity-simplicity" was deleted as the material is covered in other chapters of this book.]

REFERENCES

Adler, A., 1924. *The practice and theory of individual psychology.* New York: Harcourt, Brace & Co., Inc.

Allport, G. W., 1937. *Personality; a psychological interpretation.* New York: Henry Holt & Co., Inc.

Austrin, H. R., 1950. "The attractiveness of activities as determined by different patterns of negative and positive reinforcement," Unpublished doctor's dissertation, The Ohio State University.

Barker, R. G., 1946. "An experimental study of the relationship between certainty of choice and relative valence of the alternatives," *J. Pers., 15,* 41–52.

Blumenkrantz, J., 1953. "Post failure recall as a function of successes in degree of need relatedness to the failed task," Unpublished doctor's dissertation, University of Colorado.

Brunswik, E., 1951. "The probability point of view," in M. H. Marx (ed.), *Psychological theory.* New York: The Macmillan Company.

Castaneda, A., 1951. "A method for measuring expectancy as conceived within Rotter's Social Learning Theory of Personality," Unpublished master's thesis, The Ohio State University.

——, 1952. "A systematic investigation of the concept expectancy as conceived within Rotter's Social Learning Theory of Personality," Unpublished doctor's dissertation, The Ohio State University.

Chance, June E., 1952. "Generalization of expectancies as a function of need relatedness," Unpublished doctor's dissertation, The Ohio State University.

Coombs, C. H., 1950. "Psychological scaling without a unit of measurement," *Psychol. Rev., 57,* 145–158.

Crandall, V. J., 1950. "A preliminary investigation of the generalization of experimentally induced frustration in fantasy production," Unpublished doctor's dissertation, The Ohio State University.

Cronbach, L. J., 1948. "A validation design for qualitative studies of personality," *J. Consult. Psychol., 12,* 365–374.

Dean, S. J., 1950. "The effects of a cultural standard on minimal goal level and level of expectancy," Unpublished master's thesis, The Ohio State University.

——, 1953. "Sources of variance in individual statements of expectancy," Unpublished doctor's dissertation, The Ohio State University.

Dollard, J., and N. E. Miller, 1950. *Personality and psychotherapy; an analysis in terms of learning, thinking, and culture.* New York: McGraw-Hill Book Co., Inc.

Dunlap, R. L., 1953. "Changes in children's preferences for goal objects as a function of differences in expected social reinforcement," Unpublished doctor's dissertation, The Ohio State University.

Festinger, L., 1942. "Wish expectation and group standards as factors influencing level of aspiration," *J. Abnorm. Soc. Psychol., 37,* 184–200.

Filer, R. J., 1952. "Frustration, satisfaction, and other factors affecting the attractiveness of goal objects," *J. Abnorm. Soc. Psychol., 47,* 203–212.

Fitzgerald, B. J., 1954. "The relationships of two projective measures to a sociometric measure of dependent behavior," Unpublished doctor's dissertation, The Ohio State University.

Fuller, J. L., 1950. "Statistical analysis; a classification of organism-field interaction," *Psychol. Rev., 57,* 3–18.

Gebhard, Mildred E., 1948. "The effect of success and failure upon the attractiveness of activities as a function of experience, expectation, and need," *J. Exp. Psychol., 38,* 371–388.

Social Learning and Clinical Psychology

Good, R. A., 1952. "The potentiality for changes of an expectancy as a function of the amount of experience," Unpublished doctor's dissertation, The Ohio State University.

Grant, D. A., H. W. Hake, and J. P. Hornseth, 1951. "Acquisition and extinction of a verbal conditioned response with differing percentages of reinforcement," *J. Exp. Psychol., 42,* 1–5.

Guilford, J. P., 1936. *Psychometric methods.* New York, London: McGraw-Hill Book Co., Inc.

Harlow, H. F., 1949. "The formation of learning sets," *Psychol. Rev., 56,* 51–56.

Hilgard, E. R., R. K. Campbell, and W. N. Sears, 1938. "Conditioned discrimination; the effect of knowledge of stimulus-relationships," *Amer. J. Psychol., 51,* 498–506.

Hovland, C. I., I. L. Janis, and H. H. Kelley, 1953. *Communication and persuasion; psychological studies of opinion change.* New Haven, Conn.: University Press.

Hull, C. L., 1943. *Principles of behavior: an introduction to behavior theory.* New York: Appleton-Century-Crofts, Inc.

Hunt, D. E., 1953. "Reinforcement value as a function of expectancy for subsequent social reinforcement," Unpublished doctor's dissertation, The Ohio State University.

Irwin, F. W., F. M. Armitt, and C. W. Simon, 1943. "Studies in object-preferences. I. The effect of temporal proximity," *J. Exp. Psychol., 33,* 64–72.

Irwin, F. W., and Mildred E. Gebhard, 1946. "Studies in object-preferences; the effect of ownership and other social influences," *Amer. J. Psychol., 59,* 633–651.

Jensen, M. B., and J. B. Rotter, 1947. "The value of thirteen psychological tests in officer candidate screening," *J. Appl. Psychol., 31,* 312–322.

Jessor, R., 1951. "A methodological investigation of the strength and generalization of verbal reinforcement," Unpublished doctor's dissertation, The Ohio State University.

Jessor, Shirley G., 1951. "The effects of reinforcement and of distribution of practice on psychological satiation," Unpublished doctor's dissertation, The Ohio State University.

Johnson, W., 1946. *People in quandaries.* New York and London: Harper and Brothers.

Kantor, J. R., 1924. *Principles of psychology,* vols. i, ii. New York: Alfred A. Knopf, Inc.

Kelly, E. L., and D. W. Fiske, 1951. *The prediction of performance in clinical psychology.* Ann Arbor, Mich.: University of Michigan Press.

Lasko, A. A., 1950. "A theoretical study of partial reinforcement within the framework of Rotter's Social Learning Theory of Personality," Unpublished master's thesis, The Ohio State University.

——, 1952. "The development of expectancies under conditions of patterning and differential reinforcement," Unpublished doctor's dissertation, The Ohio State University.

Leeper, R. W., 1951. "Cognitive processes," in S. S. Stevens (ed.), *Handbook of experimental psychology,* pp. 730–757. New York: John Wiley & Sons, Inc. London: Chapman and Hall.

Lewin, K., 1951. "The nature of field theory," in M. H. Marx (ed.), *Psychological theory*, pp. 299–315. New York: The Macmillan Company.

Lezak, M. D., 1950. "A new method of analyzing data in an experiment on level of aspiration," *Amer. J. Psychol., 63*, 617–618.

Lotsof, Antoinette B., 1953. "A study of the effect of need value on substitution," Unpublished doctor's dissertation, The Ohio State University.

Lotsof, E. J., 1951. "A methodological study of reinforcement value as related to decision time," Unpublished doctor's dissertation, The Ohio State University.

Luchins, A. S., 1942. "Mechanization in problem solving—the effect of einstellung," *Psychol. Monogr., 54*, 1–95.

Marks, Rose W., 1951. "The effect of probability, desirability, and 'privilege' on the stated expectations of children, *J. Pers., 19*, 332–351.

Miles, R. C., and D. D. Wickens, 1953. "Effect of a secondary reinforcer on the primary hunger drive," *J. Comp. Physiol., 46*, 77–79.

Murphy, G., 1947. *Personality: A biosocial approach to origins and structure.* New York, London: Harper and Brothers.

O.S.S. Assessment Staff, 1948. *Assessment of men.* New York: Rinehart & Company, Inc.

Phares, E. J., 1953. "Situational factors in the determination of reinforcement values," Unpublished master's thesis, The Ohio State University.

Preston, M. G., and J. A. Bayton, 1941. "Differential effect of a social variable upon three levels of aspiration," *J. Exp. Psychol., 28*, 351–369.

Rafferty, Janet E., 1952. "Use of two interpretive projective techniques for prediction within Social Learning Theory of Personality," Unpublished doctor's dissertation, The Ohio State University.

Razran, G., 1949. "Attitudinal determinants of conditioning and of generalization of conditioning," *J. Exp. Psychol., 39*, 820–829.

Rees, H. J., and H. E. Israel, 1935. "An investigation of the establishment and operation of mental sets," *Psychol. Monogr., 46*, (210), 1–26.

Rockwell, Anne F., 1950. "The evaluation of six social learning need constructs," Unpublished doctor's dissertation, The Ohio State University.

Rosenberg, Margery R., 1952. "The effect on the value of a reinforcement as a function of occurrence," Unpublished master's thesis, The Ohio State University.

Rotter, J. B., 1943. "Level of aspiration as a method of studying personality. III. Group validity studies," *Charact. and Pers., 11*, 254–274.

——, 1944. "The nature and treatment of stuttering; a clinical approach," *J. Abnorm. Soc. Psychol., 39*, 150–173.

——, B. J. Fitzgerald, and J. Joyce, 1954. "A comparison of some objective measures of expectancy," *J. Abnorm. Soc. Psychol., 49*, 111–114.

Schroder, H. M., 1954. "The development and maintenance of the value of a reinforcement," Unpublished doctor's dissertation, The Ohio State University.

——, and J. B. Rotter, 1952. "Rigidity as learned behavior," *J. Exp. Psychol., 44*, 141–150.

Sears, Pauline S., 1940. "Levels of aspiration in academically successful and unsuccessful children," *J. Abnorm. Soc. Psychol., 35*, 498–536.

——, 1941. "Level of aspiration in relation to some variables of personality; clinical studies," *J. Soc. Psychol., 14,* 311–336.

Siipola, E. M., 1941. "The relation of transfer to similarity in habitstructure," *J. Exp. Psychol., 28,* 233–261.

Tyler, F., 1952. "A methodological investigation within the framework of Rotter's Social Learning Theory of the validity and utility of conceptualizing behaviors sequentially," Unpublished doctor's dissertation, The Ohio State University.

Woodworth, R. S., 1918. *Dynamic psychology.* New York: Columbia University Press.

Commentary to Chapter 5

Like many of the selections presented in this book, the following paper is a theoretical analysis of some broad problem or problems. I have chosen the theoretical papers as more important because articles describing single experimental studies often raise more questions than they answer. It is only in trying to make sense out of a large number of studies, all with their individual flaws, that new insights occur and progress is made in the field.

This paper deals with the use of tests for predictive purposes. Of course, in interpreting prediction broadly to include postdiction, there could be no other reason to give tests. At the time this paper was written, diagnostic testing took up most of the time of practicing clinical psychologists. Yet when controlled studies were done, much of the evidence to support the utility of such testing was severely disappointing. This paper represents an attempt to analyze the reasons for the failure. It does not provide a simple solution. It does point to careful construction and interpretation of test results consistent with a useful theory of personality that can be applied to test-taking behavior as well as to the specific variable being measured and the behavior to be predicted.

Devising useful measures takes time as well as an adequate theory of personality. For the most part, in the past two decades clinical psychology has tended to play down the importance of testing rather than to develop better measures. Although clinical psychology has thrived nevertheless, I am of the opinion that there will be a day of reckoning. The inefficiency of applying therapeutic methods to individuals without a careful, thorough understanding of individual differences before deciding on the method and the therapist will catch up with clinical psychology eventually. In the future, better methods of measurement will have to be devised, rather than "new" therapeutic panaceas.

5

Some Implications of a Social Learning Theory for the Prediction of Goal Directed Behavior from Testing Procedures

Many sophisticated observers are aware that a wide gap exists between personality theory and the techniques or procedures used to measure personality variables. The low level of prediction of such testing procedures may well be a function of the failure to apply the theories themselves to the methods of measurement. Particularly, it is a failure to apply an analysis of the determinants of behavior in general to the specific test taking behavior of the subjects (Ss).

The gap itself may be described as having three aspects. The first of these relates to the question of the constructs used in the theory and the constructs which the tests were developed to measure. In many instances rather than devising tests which measure specific theoretical constructs which are carefully defined and for which the test behavior can be understood as a logical referent, the descriptive constructs used to classify test response do not logically relate to the new theoretical constructs but are bent or twisted to measure the new variables. That is, test constructs which were used to classify test responses developed earlier are "translated" to be measures of the new variables. Examples of this are use of Rorschach variables such as color, movement, and shading which arose from imagery-

Rotter, Julian B. Some implications of a social learning theory for the prediction of goal directed behavior from testing procedures. *Psychological Review*, 1960, *67*, 301–306. Copyright 1960 by the American Psychological Association. Reprinted by permission of the publisher and author. I am indebted to Shephard Liverant for his helpful comments and suggestions about this paper.

type theory, to measure such constructs as "ego strength," "rigidity," and "tolerance for ambiguity." The Rorschach was not developed to assess such variables and in translating or twisting older methods of Rorschach scoring to measure these variables it is quite likely that a loss of prediction results.

A second aspect of this gap between personality theory and methods of measurement of personality lies in the testing procedure itself. For example, where the theory may emphasize the significance of differences in behavior in the presence of authority figures vs. peers or males vs. females, the formal test procedure assumes no such variables are important. That is, no difference in interpretation of test results follows from the fact that the examiner may have a different social stimulus value in one case than in another or under one set of conditions rather than another. In such an instance although the theory itself recognizes (and experimental data such as Gibby, Miller, & Walker, 1953, and Lord, 1950, support) the importance of the effect on behavior of the nature of the social stimulus, the test procedure itself does not take it into account. An example would be in the application of Murray's theory (1952) which sees behavior as a function of internal *needs* and environmental *presses*. Tests have been developed using this theory (Thematic Apperception Test, as clinically used; Edwards Personal Preference Schedule) which presume to measure the strength of various needs but fail to account for the test behavior as a function of the testing situation itself (an environmental press) as one of the variables determining the test behavior. Other characteristics of this discrepancy between theory and test taking procedure will be discussed more fully later.

A third aspect of the gap lies in the area of inference from test behavior. The issue here is that there is an absence of logic or contradiction in the assumed relationship between what the S does, or test behavior, and what is inferred from such behavior. Peak (1953) and Butler (1954) among others have discussed this problem earlier. Jessor and Hammond (1957) have noted such a gap in the inferences made from the Taylor Anxiety Scale. Another example could be drawn from the Edwards Personal Preference Schedule (Edwards, 1953) in which Ss are asked to state their preferences for different kinds of goals but there is no theoretical basis provided to allow one to make predictions about *nontest behavior* from such preferences. Of course, it can be assumed that the preferences have some one-to-one relationship with some criterion behavior, but is unlikely that even the test authors would make such a theoretical commitment. In other words, it is not clear exactly what can be predicted or should be predicted from the test responses. Individuals using such tests, however, can defend themselves by stating that prediction is after all an empirical matter and one has to find out what can or should be predicted. It is likely, however, that the construction of tests which are systematically or theoretically pure, in that they are devised to measure specific variables or to make specific predictions, with the method of measurement and inference consistent with the theory will ultimately provide much better predictions of behavior as well as a test of the utility of the theory itself.

The purpose of this paper is to explicate some of the implications of a social learning theory of personality for the measurement of personality variables. The particular point of emphasis is the measurement of goal directed behavior conceptualized in social learning terms as *need potential.* Secondarily, the paper aims at illustrating the nature of the relationship between testing procedures and inference about behavior more generally.

In social learning theory (Rotter, 1954) the basic formula for the prediction of goal directed behavior is as given below:

$$BP_{x,s_1,R_a} = f(E_{x,R_a,s_1} \ \& \ RV_{a,s_1}) \quad [1]$$

The formula may be read as follows: The potential for behavior x to occur in Situation 1 in relation to Reinforcement a is a function of the expectancy of the occurrence of Reinforcement a following Behavior x in Situation 1 and the value of Reinforcement a, in Situation 1. Such a formula, however, is extremely limited in application for it deals only with the potential for a given behavior to occur in relationship to a single specific reinforcement. The prediction of responses from personality tests requires a more generalized concept of behavior and the formula for these broader concepts is given below:

$$BP_{(x-n),s_{(1-n)},R_{(a-n)}} = f(E_{(x-n),s_{(1-n)},R_{(a-n)}} \ \& \ RV_{(a-n),s_{(1-n)}}) \quad [2]$$

This may be read: The potentiality of the functionally related Behaviors x to n to occur in the specified Situations 1 to n in relation to potential Reinforcements a to n is a function of the expectancies of these behaviors leading to these reinforcements in these situations and the values of these reinforcements in these situations. For purposes of simplicity of communication, the three basic terms in this formula have been typically referred to as need potential, freedom of movement, and need value as in the third formula below:

$$NP = f(FM \ \& \ NV) \qquad\qquad [3]$$

In this formula the fourth concept, that of the psychological situation, is implicit. The variables referred to above and operations for measurement have been defined and further explicated in a previous publication (Rotter, 1954).

In order to illustrate the social learning theory implications for measurement of personality and for the measurement of goal directed behavior, it seems expedient to consider three basic approaches to this problem based on the number of determinants used theoretically to predict such goal directed behavior and the problems, limitations, and advantages of each approach.

STRENGTH OF NEED AS A BASIS FOR PREDICTING BEHAVIOR

Although many esoteric systems of prediction utilize essentially the strength of need, drive, or instinct approach, this method can be described as the simplest or least complicated approach. Basically a series of constructs are formulated more often on an a priori basis than empirically, or at least on a presumed clinical rather than experimental basis. These descriptive terms may refer to instincts, drives, needs, factors, entities, or vectors of the mind (i.e., the Minnesota Multiphasic Personality Inventory, Edwards Personal Preference Schedule, Rorschach, Humm-Wadsworth, etc.). They all have in common that there is more than one basic characteristic, that these two or more characteristics are in some way measurable along a continuum and presumably the individual's behavior can be predicted from the characteristics which are "stronger" and the characteristics which are "weaker."

Sometimes the personality disposition can be predicted from the strength of other constructs according to either simple or complex statements of relationship formally postulated, hypothesized, or informally asserted. These relationships can become quite complex as in psychoanalysis or quite esoteric as in Szondi's explanation that motivated behavior is a result of the interaction of dominant and recessive genes. Because the methods of measurement in some instances cannot be direct, as in the assessment of unconscious drives in psychoanalysis, an impression of great complexity is given but regarded entirely from the point of view of the prediction of behavior, the system may still have a simple character. The potential for a given kind of behavior is still directly predictable from the strength of the drive, instincts, needs, or energies postulated.

There is another form of this model in which the various drives, dispositions, or needs are considered to interact. For example, the individual may be conceived of as being controlled by his intellect and his emotions, but his behavior must be understood in light of the interactions of these two forces with a third variable, the will as in the Rorschach Test (1942). Again, this makes complex the calculation of strength or weakness but does not change the overall method of making predictions. Whether dealing with will, intellect and emotions or ego, superego and id, the effect of interaction is only to increase or decrease the tendency of one of the needs to function or to strengthen or weaken one of them or perhaps to produce a fourth or fifth additional need. The basic method of prediction stays the same although the calculation of strength or weakness in such a model becomes more difficult.

The obvious problem, of course, for such rudimentary method of prediction is how to predict anything at all. If a system included five instincts or needs and these are ordered on some metric system from high to low, does one assume that the person will always act in the fashion to be predicted from his strongest or highest need? If an S is more oral than anal, does he always act in an oral fashion? Actually the most logical assumption in regard to any specific instance is that he will always act the same way. One might presume on a statistical basis, as it is sometimes done, if the individual is at the 70th percentile on Need A and at the 30th percentile on Need B, 70% of the time he would act in one fashion and 30% of the time in the other over some undefined period of time. However, the only sensible statistical or logical prediction in any specific instance, if no other variables are concerned, is that he would act in accordance with the higher need. This might still give fairly good prediction if only 2 variables are involved, but if 20 variables are involved and many of them are very close in value or "strength," then the amount of error begins to increase. In fact, it becomes a problem to predict even slightly above chance and, indeed, except for some limited and highly controlled experimental situations, this is the problem in psychology now. A recent illustration of this failure is reported in a carefully controlled study by Little and Shneidman (1959) who failed to find much relationship between interpretations of psychological tests (Rorschach, MAPS, TAT, and MMPI) and anamnestic data. Loevinger (1959) summarizing the predictiveness of individual tests in the recent *Annual Review of Psychology* states, "To date the only tests which

meet standards for individual prediction are those of general ability"
(p. 305). Previous reviewers have made similar statements.

Another problem which arises in the prediction of behavior with
this simple model is that it soon becomes apparent that the strength
of a wish, need, or drive to achieve some goal such as being taken
care of, obtaining love, or injuring someone is not a good predictor
of the occurrence of behavior directed towards the achieving of that
goal. To some extent this problem can be dealt with by the notion
of interaction of needs, but usually in order to account for the discrepancy between need or wish and behavior, constructs of the same
order do not provide sufficient explanatory basis. It is actually necessary to postulate some other kinds of internal constructs to account
for the discrepancy between what might be called wish, desire, need,
or instinct and observable behavior.

In the measurement of these need strengths all varieties of tests
and devices have been used. To some extent, the personality questionnaire is utilized a little more by people adopting such a predictive
scheme as that described above, but also projective tests, observation,
interviewing, and many other techniques of personality measurement
have been used in this fashion. Test construction methodologies may
currently be more sophisticated in that they control for social desirability of items, motivation, faking, lying, and inability to understand directions. Recent tests may also rely on purification of
factors, cross-validation, or item analysis. However, with all these
"modern improvements" in test design one is still left with a series
of figures which are of doubtful utility for the actual prediction of
behavior at a level satisfactory for either practical application or for
the clarification of theoretical issues.

THE ADDITION OF AN EXPECTANCY
CONSTRUCT IN THE PREDICTION OF
GOAL DIRECTED BEHAVIOR

The absence of additional variables explicitly defining the relationship of need and behavior appears to be not so much a matter of
simple theoretical structure as it is merely the absence of any real
explicit theory about human behavior. The development of a predictive model which recognizes the discrepancy between need and behavior and tries to systematically take it into account represents a
second level of sophistication.

At an earlier date perhaps psychoanalysis dealt with this problem
most effectively in introducing concepts such as repression, sublima-

tion, suppression, defense, reaction formation, etc., to account for the discrepancy between observed behavior and the presumed internal drive, need, or instinctual urge.

At this level of theorizing some systematic variable is added to the internal motivational state in order to predict behavior. Perhaps another way of saying this is that in addition to some measure of preference or value of a specific goal another systematic concept must be introduced, not only in a hit-or-miss fashion but perhaps directly into our assessment procedure. The psychoanalytic solution has been criticized because many specific concepts are introduced to account for a discrepancy between drives, urges, or needs and observable behavior, but these concepts are not readily measurable. In addition, one does not know when one explanation, i.e., reaction formation, is the explanatory concept or another such as sublimation or simple repression.

In social learning theory (Rotter, 1954) it is presumed that the relationship between goal preference (reinforcement value) and behavior can be determined only by introducing the concept of the individual's expectancy, on the basis of past history, that the given behavior will actually lead to a satisfying outcome rather than to punishment, failure, or, more generally, to negative reinforcement. Since the early formulations of Tolman (1932), expectancy theories have become more and more widely relied upon both in human learning and personality theories. It is possible to conceptualize more specific constructs such as repression and reaction formation as only special cases of an expectancy for severe punishment and that a more general relationship holds which includes perhaps all of these and also expectancies for punishment or failure of which the individual is quite aware. For example, an individual may wish very much to be a good dancer and to dance with members of the opposite sex. He makes no attempts, however, to dance at a party or a dance because he can tell you "but I look like a fool when I go out on the dance floor." We need, in other words, to introduce no specific construct involving the "unconscious" to explain the discrepancy between his wish and his behavior. The S may or may not be aware of expectancies which influence his behavior. Whether or not he is aware of them may affect the degree to which these expectancies change with new experience as well as other variables. The degree of awareness may be an important additional variable; however, the level of expectancy itself is the broader variable which bears a direct relationship to the potential occurrence of a specified behavior.

The question arises, then, of how one takes into account such factors in an actual testing situation. It could be said that no one is really so naive as to believe that the strength of an internal motivational condition or need is a direct predictor of behavior. Somehow or other, whether or not the individual had learned a given behavior or expected it to work is also an important aspect of prediction. However, more often than not this aspect of prediction has been treated as a source of error, something to be eliminated if possible, both in testing or in the validation of a test instrument. As a matter of fact, many currently used instruments attempting to assess the strength of motives, drives, or needs are usually confounded. Although they may be quite sophisticated in methodology, the test items or the test variables usually refer in part to what the individual did, i.e., overt behavior ("I frequently lose my temper"), in part to what he wished ("I would like to have more friends"), and in part to what he expected to be the outcome of his own behavior ("I feel that other people do not appreciate my good intentions"). To some extent these impure items probably add to prediction by providing more than one kind of referent for behavior, but the nonsystematic way in which they are used also limits prediction.

In trying to predict goal directed behavior from tests, two possibilities are open. One of these is to attempt to predict behavior from other behavior which presumably is functionally or predictively related to the test behavior. What this involves is analyzing test situations as behavioral samples under a given set of test conditions. For example, to assess dependent behavior one could use direct observation techniques, perhaps in problem solving situations, in which the S is scored for help-seeking behavior (cf. Naylor, 1955). In questionnaires the items should refer to what the S does, not to what he expects, wishes, or feels. The use of behavior samples for predictions or the regarding of all kinds of tests including projective tests essentially as samples of behavior to be analyzed in terms of what the S does under these conditions has been described elsewhere (Rotter, 1954). Like the work sample test in industry it undoubtedly provides the best prediction to a limited specific behavioral criterion since it requires the fewest intermediate constructs and the fewest assumptions regarding the action of other variables.

However, there are many problems, both theoretical and clinical, when it is important to break down this behavioral measure into its major determinants of reinforcement value and expectancy for the occurrence of the reinforcement. For example, in psychotherapy an understanding of how some behavior or group of behaviors may be most readily changed requires analysis into at least these two components. Even when strictly concerned with predictions of behavior in a broad band of life situations, rather than change, analysis into separate determinants may provide greater prediction than a work sample or behavioral technique. In this second alternative it is important either to control or systematically vary the other variable or measure both. For example, Liverant (1958) has measured some needs by presenting pairs of items involving goal preference matched for social desirability, and Jessor and Mandell (Mandell, 1959) are developing a similar test to measure expectancy for success in satisfying the same needs.

In using projective material such as the TAT, Crandall (1951) has demonstrated that expectancy for need satisfaction, for which the term freedom of movement is used in social learning theory, can be reliably measured by selecting particular kinds of referents. The work of Mussen and Naylor (1954), Kagan (1956), and Lesser (1957) gives strong evidence that the relationship between theme counts of aggression on the TAT and overt aggressive behavior depends to a large extent on whether or not that overt behavior is socially acceptable in the *S*s' own homes or social climates. The relationship between theme count and overt aggressive behavior appears to hold only when the *S*s do not have a high expectancy that aggressive behavior will be punished. Atkinson and Reitman (1956) report that in a number of studies of need achievement, it has become clear that prediction of behavior is enhanced if, in addition to taking a measure of need achievement based upon achievement theme counts in TAT-like material, an additional measure of expectancy for success is also taken into account.

In dealing with this type of testing material the recently published study of Fitzgerald (1958) provides a more systematic analysis. Using a highly reliable sociometric technique of nomination of fraternity brothers as his behavioral criteria and dealing with the need dependency, Fitzgerald found no relationship between theme counts and overt behavior. Presumably, dependent behavior is not socially acceptable among male college students. He had, however, independent interview ratings of need value, that is preference or desire for dependency satisfactions and of freedom of movement, or expectancy that behavior directed toward achieving dependency would be satisfied.

He found that by using these measures he did obtain a significant correlation between theme counts and the *discrepancy* between need value and freedom of movement. More specifically, what he called a conflict score or score indicating the degree to which the individual preferred dependency or desired dependency satisfactions but expected that he could not achieve them correlated with theme counts for dependency.[1] On the other hand, an Incomplete Sentences Blank measure of dependency which utilized behavioral referents as well as reinforcement value and expectancy referents did show a low but significant relationship of the number of completions dealing with dependency with both the sociometric and interview measures of need potential or actual dependent behavior. Although an actual analysis was not made, it seems very likely that the reason for the correlation in the case of the ISB and not the TAT is that at least some of the ISB completions were descriptions of actual behavior. Possibly a purer measure of behavior would have shown a greater relationship to the sociometric and interview rating assessment of actual dependent behavior in life situations.

Should we build two instruments or at least two sets of testing operations to separately assess need value and freedom of movement, or should we attempt to use behavioral measures in order to make our predictions about behavior, we would still be faced with the problem of predicting in a specific situation. Given measures of six behavior potentials, however arrived at, the problem remains that of knowing which of these is likely to be the behavior preferred in some specific situation. One is again forced to predict that the behavior with the highest potential always occurs and one is limited again in prediction to a very low level of accuracy. In the laboratory situation where we can reduce the possible alternatives to two, significant, although not predictive results, are possible. In the life situation where the alternatives are very frequently of a large order, the question arises of whether or not any useful prediction is possible. This leads us to a third level of sophistication, one in which the psychological situation is one of the variables on which prediction is based.

THE PSYCHOLOGICAL SITUATION
AS A THIRD DETERMINANT
OF GOAL DIRECTED BEHAVIOR

Few would deny that the psychological situation will affect the potential of occurrence of any behavior or class of behaviors. However, the fact that behavior will vary from situation to situation is most often treated as a source of error, something to be avoided. If possi-

---

[1] Whether or not the relationship between theme count and high reinforcement value and low expectancy is general is not yet known. It appears at this time to possibly depend on whether or not the test material and testing situation is conducive to the free expression of fantasy.

ble, one should construct tests or find personality variables which rise somehow above the situation. It is probably no exaggeration to say that thousands of hours of wasted work have been done by psychologists in the vain goal of finding either tests or variables which would, somehow or other, predict regardless of the situation in which the test is given or regardless of the situation in which the predicted behavior is expected to occur.

There are three separate problems here which will be discussed as one basic problem. The first problem is to understand the effect of the testing situation on test results. For example, Sarason (1950) has provided an excellent discussion of some of the influential situational variables in intelligence testing. The second problem is to understand the nature of the criterion situation which affects the criterion measures. The third and ultimately most important problem is to devise our tests with full consideration of the nature of the test situation in order to predict behavior in other situations for which the test was constructed. In other words, we need to devise tests not to predict personality or needs or behavior in the abstract but in specified situations or classes of situations if we want high prediction. *We need to know and take into account the dimensions of situation similarity in devising test procedures.*

Cronbach (1956) has criticized the failure to regard differentially the criterion situations in which tests are applied. In regard to the test situation we have only attempted to standardize the test procedure but usually have ignored the importance of the social context in which the test is given. Perhaps the most important thesis of this paper is that the psychological situation needs to be understood and systematically considered in our predictive formula, not treated as a source of error or something that can be ignored because part of the total situation is standardized.

Recently there have been a number of studies which demonstrate that almost all tests are subject to faking, to instructional variation, to examiner influences, to testing conditions, etc., regardless of the type of test (Borislow, 1958; Green, 1951; Gross, 1959; Mussen & Scodel, 1955; Rotter, 1955). The general inference drawn from these studies is that the tests are poor. Actually the implication of such findings is that we are making inefficient use of our tests. If the test situation for many personality tests is one in which social conformity or acceptability is easily achieved and no other satisfactions are given up in achieving acceptability, then for some purposes this motive should be controlled. However, the test situation can also be utilized to measure the importance of social conformity for the individual. *What we call faking is only our recognition of the fact that the S is taking the test with a different purpose or goal than the one the ex-*

aminer wants him to have. For some purposes it might be important to understand what kind of goals he exhibits in this kind of situation. More often than not we simply try to control what we should be studying. For example, in giving intelligence tests it might be better to study systematically the effect on performance of encouragement and discouragement rather than to attempt some mythical neutral attitude which is presumably the same for every examiner. Knowledge of the effects of situational variations would be of particular value in understanding the frequently diverse and contradictory results of apparently similar research investigations. For example, Henry and Rotter (1956) found that large, predicted differences were obtained between two comparable groups on the Rorschach test if one group was reminded before the regular instructions that the test had been used frequently to study psychopathology. An obvious implication of this study is that investigators using this same test in the college laboratory and in the clinical setting may well produce diverse results.

Another example of how the situation can be used in testing is provided by the patient who is being assessed for possible benefit from psychotherapy. If the clinic or hospital can provide both male and female therapists and also therapists who rely on support and direction as well as therapists who remain distant and passive, then the testing procedures can be varied so that those situational influences are present. The testing could provide information to indicate what kind of therapy and what kind of therapist is likely to provide *this* patient with the most efficient conditions for relearning. For more conventional purposes of clinical testing, it is still more important to know under what conditions the patient behaves in a paranoid fashion and under what conditions he does not, than it is to know how many percentiles of paranoia he has.

Not only can the test situation itself be analyzed as a behavioral sample but situational referents can be incorporated into the content of items by systematic sampling. For example, questionnaire items can deal with the *conditions* under which the S feels tense, nervous, happy, has headaches, etc. as Mandler and Sarason (1952) have done for some intellectual test taking situations. Similarly, projective methods, particularly TAT-type tests, can systematically vary the situation through the selection of test stimuli as has been done by Crandall (1951) and McClelland, Atkinson, Clark, and Lowell (1953). More recently Murstein (1959) has suggested a conceptual model for stimulus variation with thematic techniques.

The many studies indicating marked effects of testing conditions suggest that it is of great importance in the publication of any test that descriptions of the differences in test results that are likely to be associated with different kinds of testing situations be provided. No test can be adequately understood unless the data regarding its standardization or use includes systematic descriptions of the differences in test results which are a function of different kinds of testing conditions and different kinds of purposes in taking the test for similar samples of *S*s. Only when we know whether an *S* is likely to produce different test results when he is taking the test to demonstrate how imaginative he is as compared to taking it to prove that he needs help will we be adequately able to understand the meaning of test results and to predict future behavior from them.

There have been personality theorists who have made much of the importance of the individual's life space. Kantor (1924) was one of the first to emphasize that the basic datum of psychology is the interaction of an individual and his meaningful environment. For Kantor, people do not have internal characteristics in the same sense as for other theorists; rather they have a reactional biography of interactions with the environment. Lewin (1951) has also emphasized the importance of the life space or psychological situation in the determination of human behavior. Brunswik (1947) has repeatedly called for analyses of and sampling of psychological situations for predictive purposes. Helson (1948) has applied his theory of Adaptation Level to social psychology stating that the effect of the total field can be quantified by careful ordering of the field of exposed stimuli. Recent concern with the importance and need for systematic study of situation variation has been expressed by Allport (1958) and Cronbach (1957).

In a more limited and less systematic way, psychoanalysis has suggested, in a few areas, that certain kinds of goal directed behavior depended upon the psychological situation. This is done in making distinctions between the individual's potential response to authority figures vs. nonauthority figures and males vs. females. Beyond this, little systematic analysis of differences in life situations has been made by the traditional analyst. Murray's (1952) formulation of the nature of personality stresses that behavior is a function of the interaction of an individual with a psychological situation which he felt could be categorized as "press." At a more specific level Atkinson and Raphelson (1956) have shown the value of including situational variables in studying achievement behavior. This general point of view has also been represented in sociology by Thomas (1951) and Coutu (1949).

In social learning theory, it has been hypothesized that the situation operates primarily by providing cues for the *S* which are related to the magnitude of his expectancies for reinforcement for different behaviors. The effect on the value of the reinforcement itself operates through expectancies for associated or subsequent reinforcements which may differ from situation to situation. It has also been hypothesized that situations may be usefully categorized in terms of the predominant reinforcements as culturally determined for any large or small culture group. There are many other possible ways of categorizing situations depending upon the predictive purposes involved.[2] Methods of determining generality or determining the dimensions of similarity among situations have been described in an earlier paper (Rotter, 1955).

Two illustrative studies of an increasing number of experimental analyses of behavior which vary both internal characteristics and the psychological situation systematically in the same study are described below. These studies follow the basic paradigm that the presumed relevant individual (personality) and situational (experimental manipulations) variables can be observed simultaneously and their interaction studied.

ILLUSTRATIVE STUDIES VARYING
BOTH THE SITUATION AND
INTERNAL CHARACTERISTICS

A recent doctoral dissertation by James (1957) illuminates very clearly the potential of greater prediction when both the situation and the internal characteristic are varied in the same study. The behavior being studied by James involved a variety of learning variables, including acquisition, changes or shifts, extinction, generalization, and recovery of verbalized expectancies for gratification. Two general hypotheses were involved in this study growing out of previous

---

[2] Several writers have pointed out the difficulty of identifying situations independently of behavior. That is, how can one describe a situation as one would a physical stimulus independently of the S's response? The problem is not different from that of describing stimuli along dimensions of color although perhaps vastly complicated in social or other complex situations. In the case of color stimuli ultimately the criterion is a response of the scientist or observer, sometimes a response to an intermediate instrument, and one that is at the level of sensory discrimination and so leads to high observer agreement. In the case of the social situation, the level of discrimination is common sense based on an understanding of the culture rather than the reading of an instrument. As such, reliability may be limited but still be sufficiently high to considerably increase prediction. In this way specific situations could be identified as school situations, employment situations, girl friend situations, etc. For the purpose of generality various kinds of psychological constructs could be devised to arrive at classes of situations which have similar meaning to the S. The utility of such classes would have to be empirically determined depending on the S's response. The objective referents for these situations, which provide the basis for prediction, however, can be independent of the specific S. That is, they can be reliably identified by cultural, common sense terms.

work by Lasko (1952), Phares (1957), Neff (1956), and James and Rotter (1958). Hunt and Schroder (1958) have also dealt with what appears to be a related variable. The first of these hypotheses might be stated as a situational one. That is, that the nature of a learning process differs depending upon whether or not the situation is one in which the reinforcements that occur are a direct outcome of some internal characteristic of the individual such as skill, a physical characteristic, or whatever, versus a situation where the reinforcements are essentially controlled by someone else or by chance or by conditions or powers beyond the *S*'s control. Perhaps a good example of the latter would be a dice game or the winning of a door prize or having soup spilled on one because a waiter tripped, etc. James utilized line and angle matching tasks reinforcing each *S* positively on his guesses in six of the eight training trials. He specifically hypothesized when the situation is structured in such a way that the *S* expects the occurrence of reinforcements to be beyond his control or partly beyond his control, increments and decrements in expectancy for gratification as a result of experience are smaller, the number of unusual shifts, that is, shifts up after failure or down after success, are greater, extinction is faster, and there is less generalization from one task to another and greater recovery following extinction.

The measurement of individual differences in this study followed from the previous work of Phares which suggested that individuals can be differentiated in the degree to which they see the world and the things that happen to them as controlled by others or as determined by chance or unpredictable forces. The second hypothesis, then, was that all the differences which would occur as a result of the situational conditions would also be true of individuals within all groups as a function of their general attitude towards "control of reinforcement."

In order to predict the individual differences in attitude, James enlarged and revised the questionnaire first devised by Phares. This was given to all *S*s at the end of each experiment. The results are most striking. All of the predicted outcomes hypothesized above resulting from the differences in instructions or situations were obtained and all were statistically significant with the exception of recovery following extinction, which showed a strong trend in the predicted direction. Similarly, within each group the individuals high as compared to low on the questionnaire differed significantly in exactly the same way as did the groups themselves as a result of the different instructions or situations presented. Although individual prediction was not the concern of this investigation, it is quite clear that a simple formula could be devised which could predict all of the learning variables involved in this study with a fair degree of accuracy. Certainly it is clear that a greater degree of accuracy is possible when both the situational and individual variables are taken into account. Perhaps far more important, this study indicates that various experimental paradigms in studying human learning are likely to produce different kinds of results. Whether or not a given learning task is one in which the S feels that success is dependent upon the experimenter's manipulation (for example, when he is expecting to predict a random sequence of red or green lights) or is the result of his own skill provides a crucial difference in the nature of the learning process itself.

The study of James, however, does not provide a satisfied feeling that it illustrates all of the problems of prediction involving both the individual's characteristics and the situation from which the prediction is made. It gives an almost too simple picture of the interaction of these two variables. Another recent dissertation by Moss (1958) suggests that this relationship can be more complex, and illustrates more clearly the effect of the testing situation on more commonly used types of assessment procedures.

Moss studied a general behavioral characteristic which he called cautiousness. Essentially this was defined as the avoidance of risk, the selection of the safest alternative in a situation where failure or negative reinforcement was possible. He varied the situation by reacting differently to three groups following the administration of a questionnaire which he described as a measure of social acceptability. One group was shown false norms at the conclusion of the questionnaire that indicated that they were in the ninetieth percentile of social acceptability for a college group. Another group of Ss was shown that they were at the tenth percentile, and a third group was given no information about the results of this supposed test of social acceptability. He hypothesized that cautious behavior would increase with negative reinforcement. Immediately following this procedure, the Ss were given two projective type tests and behavior on these tests was analyzed as to degree of cautiousness.

Prior to the giving of the "social acceptability" questionnaire the Ss had been tested on the level of aspiration board. Behavior on the level of aspiration board (Rotter, 1942) was categorized into cautious or noncautious patterns.[3] The general tendency to seek safe alternatives in the obtaining of satisfactions then was measured in a

---

[3] Cautious and noncautious behavior was characterized according to the patterns described by Rotter (1954, pp. 318–324). Patterns 1 and 3 were considered as noncautious and 2, 4, 7, and 8 as cautious patterns. The latter group are characterized by a variety of techniques presumably aimed at avoiding failure to reach explicit goals. Patterns 1 and 3 are characterized by higher expectancies than performance but within "normal" bounds and consequently a higher number of failures to reach one's estimates.

situation in which the *S* himself has some control over failure or success.

One kind of behavior studied was that of sorting figures taken from the MAPS test. The *S* was presented the figures and asked to sort them into two piles any way he wished. The procedure was repeated a second time asking for a different kind of sort, and a third time. The sorts themselves were characterized as being safe or cautious in that they dealt with highly objective characteristics of these figures, or less safe in that they dealt with characteristics which were more abstract or had to be read into many of the figures. For example, sorts based on personality characteristics were considered as noncautious as opposed to safer or more cautious sorts such as those into groups of men and women, children and adults, Negroes and whites, etc.

A second kind of behavior studied was the *S*'s response to a series of four TAT pictures. In this case the *S*'s stories were treated as Weisskopf (1950) has treated them with her measure of transcendence. A cautious or safe interpretation was one sticking close to the characteristics of the picture and one in which the theme itself was a common one.

Moss found some differences among his groups in the direction he had hypothesized, that is, that the threatened group, the group that was told that it was at the tenth percentile, showed greater cautiousness than the other two groups. The differences between groups, however, although consistently in the direction he predicted, only approached significance and were not large. However, when Moss divided his *S*s within groups into cautious and noncautious on the basis of their level of aspiration patterns, he found some highly significant differences. The cautious *S*s showed no significant differences among the three conditions. However, the noncautious *S*s showed significant differences between conditions. That is, noncautious *S*s in one condition responded differentially from noncautious *S*s in another condition. These differences were primarily due to greater noncautious behavior in the no-information group. Differences in test behavior between cautious and noncautious *S*s were also highly significant on both tests within the no-information group but not in the other groups.

In spite of the complexity of this study, a few findings seem relatively clear from an analysis of group means as well as significance of differences. *S*s who were cautious on the level of aspiration test, which is a somewhat free situation, were also cautious in the other test conditions. Of course, this does not mean that they were cautious in situations which were not perceived by them as evaluation situations. On the other hand, *S*s who were noncautious on the level of aspiration test appeared to maintain this greater risk taking behavior under test situations where no information about results was given. However, when they were negatively reinforced, they became more cautious and they also did not appear to be different from cautious Ss under conditions where they were quite successful. Perhaps this is related to the presumed conservatism which follows from success. There was no consistent prediction from the level of aspiration situation to the two "projective tests" which could be made without considering the situation. In at least two of the situations the cautious Ss were not significantly different from the noncautious Ss. On the other hand, the psychological situation or the three different situations seemed to have no effect on the cautious Ss. Only in the interaction of the noncautious Ss with the situational variables was prediction possible from the level of aspiration test.

A similar type of result to that of Moss was recently reported by Lesser (1959). Lesser found that intercorrelations among various measures of aggression were significantly higher under experimental conditions of low anxiety than under conditions of high anxiety about aggression.

James's results suggest a rather simple relationship between dispositional and situational variables, but it is clear from the study of Moss and other studies that a simple additive or multiplicative relationship will not always describe the nature of the interaction. An important implication of this principle is that there is a general lack of efficiency in research studies in which only one set of variables, that is only dispositional or situational, are systematically varied, since the conclusions of the two sets of studies cannot be put together in a simple fashion. Unless both kinds of variables are systematically varied *within the same investigation,* both an understanding of the determinants of behavior and the prediction of it may suffer.

A striking example of the importance of studying the effects of dispositional and situational influences simultaneously is provided by Helson, Blake, Mouton, and Olmstead (1956). In applying Adaptation Level theory to a study of attitude change they found important interactional effects when situations were varied in external influence pressure and individuals were distributed on a measure of ascendancy–submissiveness.

It is true that many of the above propositions are obvious. Most psychologists recognize that there is a difference between overt behavior directed toward certain goals and the desires that individuals have to obtain these goals. Similarly, most psychologists know that the psychological situation is a determinant of the occurrence of a given behavior. The thesis here, however, is not merely that this is the case but that all of these variables must be ordered and studied systematically, in order to make predictions.

SUMMARY

The major contention of this paper has been that the prediction of goal directed behavior of human subjects from test procedures has been and will continue to be at an extremely low hit-or-miss level because of inadequate conceptualization of the problem. Findings are frequently not replicatable because of the failure to systematically differentiate behavior, reinforcement value, and expectancy as internal variables and to recognize that these variables are affected by the psychological situation.

The psychological situation of the patient in the clinic is so different from that of the elementary psychology student taking a test as part of an experiment that it is possible that the kinds of predictions which can be made in one situation would hardly hold in the other. The evidence that faking is possible and that different norms obtain when subjects are job applicants, employees, or volunteers does not necessarily mean that a test is no good. Nor is prediction essentially hopeless because it can be demonstrated that two experimenters, whether the same sex or opposite, or slight changes in the wording of instructions, will differentially affect test or experimental results. All of these things indicate only that the psychological situation, perhaps acting primarily through the expectancies they arouse by the cues present, considerably affect behavior. It is necessary that we do not consider such influence as error to be ignored, as difficulty to be avoided or as the problem of some other profession to investigate. Rather it is necessary to study these influences and consider them regularly and systematically in a predictive schema. That is, for some purposes, factors such as social desirability of items, examiner's behavior, and the subject's goals in the test situation should be controlled, and in other cases they should be allowed to vary. In all cases, however, they must be systematically considered.

Implicit in this entire paper is the belief that a satisfactory theory of goal directed behavior is a primary prerequisite for developing adequate tests. Knowledge of statistics and test construction procedures can be valuable but they cannot supplant an adequate theory of behavior which is applied to the test taking behavior itself.

To arrive at a fully systematic model for relating these general or high order constructs and to coordinate them in turn to lower level sets of content variables, devised for different purposes, will be a long and arduous but rewarding task.

REFERENCES

Allport, G. W. What units shall we employ? In G. Lindzey (Ed.), *The assessment of human motives.* New York: Rinehart, 1958.

Atkinson, J. W., & Raphelson, A. C. Individual differences in motivation and behavior in particular situation. *J. Pers.,* 1956, **24**, 349–363.

Atkinson, J. W., & Reitman, W. R. Performance as a function of motive strength and expectancy of goal attainment. *J. abnorm. soc. Psychol.,* 1956, **53**, 361–366.

Borislow, B. The Edwards Personal Preference Schedule and fakability. *J. appl. Psychol.,* 1958, **42**, 22–27.

Brunswik, E. *Systematic and representative design of psychological experiments.* Berkeley: Univer. California Press, 1947.

Butler, J. M. The use of a psychological model in personality testing. *Educ. psychol. Measmt.,* 1954, **14**, 77–89.

Coutu, W. *Emergent human nature.* New York: Knopf, 1949.

Crandall, V. J. Induced frustration and punishment-reward expectancy in thematic apperception stories. *J. consult. Psychol.,* 1951, **15**, 400–404.

Cronbach, L. J. Assessment of individual differences. In P. R. Farnsworth and Q. McNemar (Eds.), *Annu. Rev. Psychol.,* 1956. Stanford, Calif.: Annual Reviews, 1956. Pp. 173–196.

Cronbach, L. J. The two disciplines of scientific psychology. *Amer. Psychologist,* 1957, **12**, 671–684.

Edwards, A. L. *Manual of the Edwards Personal Preference Schedule.* New York: Psychological Corp., 1953.

Fitgerald, B. J. Some relationships among projective test, interview and sociometric measures of dependent behavior. *J. abnorm. soc. Psychol.,* 1958, **56**, 199–204.

Gibby, R. G., Miller, N. R., & Walker, E. L. The examiner's influence on the Rorschach protocol. *J. consult. Psychol.,* 1953, **17**, 425–428.

Green, R. F. Does a selection situation induce testees to bias their answers on interest and temperament tests? *Educ. psychol. Measmt.,* 1951, **11**, 503–515.

Gross, L. R. Effects of verbal and nonverbal reinforcement in the Rorschach. *J. consult. Psychol.,* 1959, **23**, 66–68.

Helson, H. Adaptation level as a basis for quantitative theory of frames of reference. *Psychol. Rev.,* 1948, **55**, 297–313.

Helson, H., Blake, R. R., Mouton, Jane S., & Olmstead, J. A. Attitudes as adjustments to stimulus, background, and residual factors. *J. abnorm. soc. Psychol.,* 1956, **52**, 314–322.

Henry, Edith M., & Rotter, J. B. Situational influences on Rorschach responses. *J. consult. Psychol.,* 1956, **20**, 457–462.

Hunt, D. E., & Schroder, H. M. Assimilation, failure-avoidance, and anxiety. *J. consult. Psychol.,* 1958, **22**, 39–44.

James, W. H. Internal versus external control of reinforcement as a basic variable in learning theory. Unpublished doctoral dissertation, Ohio State Univer., 1957.

James, W. H., & Rotter, J. B. Partial and one hundred percent reinforcement under chance and skill conditions. *J. exp. Psychol.,* 1958, **55**, 397–403.

Jessor, R., & Hammond, K. R. Construct validity and the Taylor anxiety scale. *Psychol. Bull.,* 1957, **54**, 161–170.

Kagan, J. The measurement of over aggression from fantasy. *J. abnorm. soc. Psychol.,* 1956, **52**, 390–393.

Kantor, J. R. *Principles of psychology.* Vols. 1, 2. New York: Knopf, 1924.

Lasko, A. A. The development of expectancies under conditions of patterning and differential reinforcement. Unpublished doctoral dissertation, Ohio State Univer., 1952.

Lesser, G. S. The relationship between overt and fantasy aggression as a function of maternal response to aggression. *J. abnorm. soc. Psychol.,* 1957, **55**, 218–222.

Lesser, G. S. Population differences in construct validity. *J. consult. Psychol.,* 1959, **23**, 60–65.

Lewin, K. The nature of field theory. In M. H. Marx (Ed.), *Psychological theory.* New York: Macmillan, 1951.

Little, K. B., & Shneidman, E. S. Congruencies among interpretations of psychological test and anamnestic data. *Psychol. Monogr.,* 1959, **73**(6, Whole No. 476).

Liverant, S. The use of Rotter's social learning theory in developing a personality inventory. *Psychol. Monogr.,* 1958 **72**(2, Whole No. 455).

Loevinger, Jane. Theory and techniques of assessment. In P. R. Farnsworth (Ed.), *Annu. Rev. Psychol.,* 1959. Palo Alto, Calif.: Annual Reviews, 1959. Pp. 287–316.

Lord, E. E. Experimentally induced variations in Rorschach performance. *Psychol. Monogr.,* 1950, **64**(10, Whole No. 316).

McClelland, D. C., Atkinson, J. W., Clark, R. A., & Lowell, E. L. *The achievement motive.* New York: Appleton-Century-Crofts, 1953.

Mandell, Elizabeth E. Construct validation of a psychometric measure of expectancy. Unpublished master's thesis, Univer. Colorado, 1959.

Mandler, G., & Sarason, S. B. A study of anxiety and learning. *J. abnorm. soc. Psychol.,* 1952, **47**, 166–173.

Moss, H. The generality of cautiousness as a defense behavior. Unpublished doctoral dissertation, Ohio State Univer., 1958.

Murray, H. A. Toward a classification of interaction. In T. Parsons & E. A. Shils (Eds.), *Toward a general theory of action.* Cambridge: Harvard Univer. Press, 1952.

Murstein, B. L. A conceptual model of projective techniques applied to stimulus variations with thematic techniques. *J. consult. Psychol.,* 1959, **23**, 3–14.

Mussen, P. H., & Naylor, H. K. Relationship between overt and fantasy aggression. *J. abnorm. soc. Psychol.,* 1954, **49**, 235–239.

Mussen, P. H., & Scodel, A. The effect of sexual stimulation under varying conditions on TAT sexual responsiveness. *J. consult. Psychol.,* 1955, **19,** 90.

Naylor, H. K. The relationship of dependency behavior to intellectual problem solving. Unpublished doctoral dissertation, Ohio State Univer., 1955.

Neff, J. Individual differences in resistance to extinction as a function of generalized expectancy. Unpublished doctoral dissertation, Ohio State Univer., 1956.

Peak, Helen. Problems of objective observation. In L. Festinger & D. Katz (Eds.), *Research methods in the behavioral sciences.* New York: Dryden, 1953.

Phares, E. J. Expectancy changes in skill and chance situations. *J. abnorm. soc. Psychol.,* 1957, **54,** 339–342.

Rorschach, H. *Psychodiagnostics.* New York: Grune & Stratton, 1942.

Rotter, J. B. Level of aspiration as a method of studying personality: II. Development and evaluation of a controlled method. *J. exp. Psychol.,* 1942, **31,** 410–422.

Rotter, J. B. *Social learning and clinical psychology.* New York: Prentice Hall, 1954.

Rotter, J. B. The role of the psychological situation in determining the direction of human behavior. In M. R. Jones (Ed.), *Nebraska symposium on motivation,* 1955. Lincoln: Univer. Nebraska Press.

Sarason, S. The test situation and the problem of prediction. *J. clin. Psychol.,* 1950, **6,** 387–392.

Thomas, W. I. (Collected writings) In E. H. Volkart (Ed.), *Social behavior and personality: Contributions of W. I. Thomas to theory and social research.* New York: Social Science Research Council, 1951.

Tolman, E. C. *Purposive behavior in animals and men.* New York: Appleton-Century, 1932.

Weisskopf, E. A. A transcendence index as a proposed measure of projection in the Thematic Apperception Test. *J. Psychol.,* 1950, **29,** 379–390.

Commentary to Chapter 6

The monograph presented next is interesting both in terms of its content and the impact it has had on the social sciences. According to Citation Classics (Garfield, 1978), during the years 1969–1977 it was referred to in the published social science literature some 1,345 times. Not only was it the most cited article of the period, but it was cited more than twice as often as any other. At this writing the popularity of this concept appears to continue unabated. One can only guess at the reasons for this popularity, but some speculations may be instructive.

The monograph itself, published in 1966, was an analysis of work begun many years earlier, first as part of graduate student research and then as a four-year project supported by the Air Force Office of Scientific Research. The dissertations of E. Jerry Phares and William James were important starts in test construction and initial data gathering; and two colleagues and coinvestigators of the research grant, Melvin Seeman and Shepherd Liverant, made important conceptual as well as empirical contributions. The work and ideas of many others went into the formulations and conclusions of the monograph, but special acknowledgment should be made to Douglas Crowne, Virginia and Vaughn Crandall, Pearl Mayo Gore, and Bonnie Strickland. The forced choice personality test (I-E Scale) presented in the monograph was the fifth revision of a test that first appeared in Phares's dessertation and was revised in that of James. Subsequently it was revised three more times on the basis of accumulated empirical data. The late Shepherd Liverant was particularly involved in the last three revisions. Although the final product of this test-development research had its own appeal, it seems to me that there were additional reasons for the interest in this monograph, some of which might be of concern to anyone interested in the sociology of knowledge.

By my own estimate the most important reason for the interest in internal versus external control of reinforcement was the "real world" sociopolitical concerns of psychologists and other social scientists of the times. My own original interest was theoretical— that is, a discovery that changes in expectancies were systematically predictable from whether or not the person perceived his or her own actions as the cause of rewards or saw rewards as not contingent on his or her own behavior. By the time this work was published, how-

ever, the country was feeling the impact of the Vietnam War, the student revolution, the urban riots, and the assassinations. Interest in social action ran high, and a great deal of disillusionment accompanied people's awareness of their inability to control events important to their lives. The interests of social scientists often reflect their sociopolitical concerns.

Many graduate students and colleagues at Ohio State University were intrigued by the I-E construct. The result of this interest was a rapid accumulation of data, which quickly expanded the range of empirical problems that might be viewed as related to individual differences in internal versus external control. Many of these problems— such as social-action-taking behavior in blacks, response to political appeals, efficiency in the practice of psychotherapy, and the effectiveness of self-treatment regimes in medical rehabilitation—had potentially important applications, this gave them a special appeal.

Finally, a word should be said about the form of publication. Some of the research reported in the monograph was previously published, some in press or being prepared for publication, and some available only in the form of unpublished theses and dissertations. Some data were presented only in the monograph. Thus the whole represented more than the sum of the parts. Without the monograph most readers would have seen only a small part of the data; they might have been interested but probably not overly impressed. Programmatic research suffers when it is published only piecemeal so that the reader does not get in one place and at one time the overview of history, theory, empirical data, and potential applications.

If this analysis is true, it follows that less publication of individual, isolated nontheoretical articles and more frequent publication of programmatic empirical-theoretical articles and monographs might increase the rate of which stable, major increments in knowledge occur in psychology.

REFERENCE

Garfield, E. The one hundred articles most cited by social scientists, 1969–1977. *Current Contents*, 1978, 32, 5–14.

6

Generalized Expectancies for Internal Versus External Control of Reinforcement

The role of reinforcement, reward, or gratification is universally recognized by students of human nature as a crucial one in the acquisition and performance of skills and knowledge. However, an event regarded by some persons as a reward or reinforcement may be differently perceived and reacted to by others. One of the determinants of this reaction is the degree to which the individual perceives that the reward follows from, or is contingent upon, his own behavior or attributes versus the degree to which he feels the reward is controlled by forces outside of himself and may occur independently of his own actions. The effect of a reinforcement following some behavior on the part of a human subject, in other words, is not a simple stamping-in process but depends upon whether or not the person perceives a causal relationship between his own behavior and the reward. A perception of causal relationship need not be all or none but can vary in degree. When a reinforcement is perceived by the subject as following some action of his own but not being entirely contingent upon his action, then, in our culture, it is typically perceived as the result of luck, chance, fate, as under the control of powerful others, or as unpredictable because of the great complexity of the forces surrounding him. When the event is interpreted in this way by an individual, we have labeled this a belief in *external control*. If the person perceives that the event is contingent upon his

Rotter, Julian B. Generalized expectancies for internal versus external control of reinforcement. *Psychological Monographs*, 1966, *80*, 1–28. Copyright 1966 by the American Psychological Association. Reprinted by permission of the publisher and author.

own behavior or his own relatively permanent characteristics, we have termed this a belief in *internal control*.

It is hypothesized that this variable is of major significance in understanding the nature of learning processes in different kinds of learning situations and also that consistent individual differences exist among individuals in the degree to which they are likely to attribute personal control to reward in the same situation. This report is concerned with reviewing a number of studies which have been made to test both hypotheses; to present some heretofore unpublished experimental results; and to present in detail new data regarding the development, reliability, and validity of one measure of individual differences in a generalized belief for internal versus external control of reinforcement.

THEORETICAL BACKGROUND

Social learning theory (Rotter; 1954, 1955, 1960) provides the general theoretical background for this conception of the nature and effects of reinforcement. In social learning theory, a reinforcement acts to strengthen an *expectancy* that a particular behavior or event will be followed by that reinforcement in the future. Once an expectancy for such a behavior-reinforcement sequence is built up the failure of the reinforcement to occur will reduce or extinguish the expectancy. As an infant develops and acquires more experience he differentiates events which are causally related to preceding events and those which are not. It follows as a general hypothesis that when the reinforcement is seen as not contingent upon the subject's own behavior that its occurrence will not increase an expectancy as much as when it is seen as contingent. Conversely, its nonoccurrence will not reduce an expectancy so much as when it is seen as contingent. It seems likely that, depending upon the individual's history of reinforcement, individuals would differ in the degree to which they attributed reinforcements to their own actions.

Expectancies generalize from a specific situation to a series of situations which are perceived as related or similar. Consequently, a generalized expectancy for a class of related events has functional properties and makes up one of the important classes of variables in personality description. Harlow's (1949) concept of high-level learned generalized expectancies involving relationships between a learned generalized expectancies involving relaionships between a wide variety of behaviors and their possible outcomes. A generalized attitude, belief, or expectancy regarding the nature of the causal relationship between one's own behavior and its consequences might affect a variety of behavioral choices in a broad band of life situations. Such generalized expectancies in combination with specific expectancies act to determine choice behavior along with the value of potential reinforcements. These generalized expectancies will result in characteristic differences in behavior in a situation culturally categorized as chance determined versus skill determined, and they may act to produce individual differences within a specific condition.

Specific expectancies regarding the causal nature of behavior-outcome sequences in different situations would also affect behavior choice. From social learning theory one would anticipate that the more clearly and uniformly a situation is labeled as skill or luck determined, in a given culture, the lesser the role such a generalized expectancy would play in determining individual differences in behavior.

RELATED CONCEPTIONS

In learning theory it has been recognized that differences in subject behavior are related to task differences along a dimension of skill and chance. Goodnow and Postman (1955) and Goodnow and Pettigrew (1955), for example, present data to show that probabilistic learning theory is not applicable where the subject feels that the occurrence of the reinforcement is lawful. Wyckoff and Sidowsky (1955) similarly felt that their subjects' behavior changed when they no longer felt that the task was a "guessing" problem. Cohen (1960) has extensively studied differences in subjects' behavior or strategy in choice and skill games noting the tendency for the "gambler's fallacy" to appear in chance games . . . an effect opposite to the usual effect of reinforcement. A somewhat different approach to chance and skill task differences is assumed by Feather (1959) who felt that motivation was lessened in chance tasks as compared to skill tasks. In general, however, a *theoretically based, systematic study* of chance and skill differences in acquisition and performance has not been made prior to the series of studies to be reported here.

The literature of personality theory does contain discussions of a number of variables which may have some relationship to the one of major concern in this paper. The significance of the belief in fate, chance, or luck has been discussed by various social scientists over a long period of time. Most of their concern, however, has been with differences among groups or societies rather than individuals. Typical of an early discussion of this kind is that of Veblen (1899), who felt that a belief in luck or chance represented a barbarian approach to life and was generally characteristic of an inefficient society. Although Veblen was not concerned with individual differences, his discussion implied that a belief in chance or luck as a solution to one's problems was characterized by less productivity and, consequently, bears some parallel to the hypothesis that a belief in external control of reinforcements is related to a general passivity. Veblen also stated, "In its simple form the belief in luck is this instinctive sense of an unscrutable, teleological propensity in objects or situations." In other words, Veblen states that the belief in luck is related to or similar to a general belief in fate.

More recently, Merton (1946) has discussed the belief in luck more or less as a defense behavior, as an attempt "to serve the psychological function of enabling people to preserve their self esteem in the face of failure." He states it "may also in some individuals act to curtail sustained endeavor," or, in other words, he too suggests a relationship between passivity and the belief in chance or luck.

The concept of alienation which has played an important role in sociological theory for many years does seem related at a group level to the variable in internal-external control. The alienated individual feels unable to control his own destiny. He is a small cog in a big machine and at the mercy of forces too strong or too vague to control. Marx, Weber, and Durkheim place great importance on this concept, and more recently Merton (1949) has stressed it importance in the study of asocial behavior. Seeman (1959) has linked the concept of alienation as it refers to *powerlessness*, to internal-external control as a psychological variable. Some sociologists (Nettler, 1957; Srole, 1956) have developed a crude individual measure of alienation.

In psychology, White (1959) in discussing an alternative to drive reduction has noted how the work of many authors has converged on a belief that it is characteristic of all species to explore and to attempt to master the environment. He has labeled this concept *competence*. While White was not specifically interested in individual differences he has noted that such a motive or drive is not explained by primary drive and although perhaps not as strong as some primary drives it is moderate in strength and persistence. Angyal (1941) has also noted the significance of the organism's motivation towards *autonomy*, or the active mastery of the environment.

There are a number of other psychological variables which appear to bear some relationship to the concept under investigation.

Some of these are undoubtedly related, but, for others, it is possible that the relationship is more apparent than real.

Perhaps one of the major conceptions which bears some relationship to the belief in internal versus external control of reinforcements is that of need for achievement. The work of McClelland, Atkinson, Clark, and Lowell (1953) and of Atkinson (1958) and their colleagues working primarily with adults, and Crandall (1963) with children, suggests that people who are high on the need for achievement, in all probability, have some belief in their own ability or skill to determine the outcome of their efforts. The relationship is probably not linear, however, since a person high on motivation for achievement might not be equally high on a belief in internal control of reinforcement, and there may be many with a low need for achievement who still believe that their own behavior determines the kinds of reinforcements they obtain.

Another variable which may bear some genuine relationship to the variable of internal versus external control of reinforcement is the concept of "field determined" versus "body oriented." The work of Witkin, Lewis, Hertzman, Machover, Meissner, and Wapner (1954) suggests that people can be ordered on a continuum, in some perception experiments, describing whether they derive most of their cues from the field or from internal sources. A study by Linton (1955) suggests that people who are "field oriented" or "field dependent" tend to be more conforming. However, unpublished data of the author indicate no relationship between an individual measure of internal-external control and the Gottschalk Figures Test, a measure frequently used as an operation for "field determined."

Perhaps less clear is the relationship of internal versus external control of reinforcement to the notion of "ego control." Although the concept of ego control is not always defined similarly, it seems to contain the ideas of confidence and ability to deal with reality. While it seems likely that the individuals at both extremes of the internal versus external control of reinforcement dimension are essentially unrealistic, it is not as likely that the people toward the middle of the distribution are less confident. We do have indications, however, that the people at either extreme of the reinforcement dimension are likely to be maladjusted by most definitions, and, to the extent that ego control is another type of definition of maladjustment, it would bear some curvilinear relationship to the variable we are concerned with here.

Similar to the conception of Witkin et al. is that of Riesman (1954), who has attempted to describe an apparently comparable distinction. Riesman's conception is based on the degree to which people are controlled by internal goals, desires, etc. versus the degree to which they are controlled by external forces, in particular social forces or conformity forces. Although this variable may bear some relationship to the one under investigation, it should be made clear that the apparent relationship is not as logical as it appears. Riesman has been concerned with whether the individual is controlled from within or from without. We are concerned, however, not with this variable at all but only with the question of whether or not an individual believes that his own behavior, skills, or internal dispositions determine what reinforcements he receives. While the conformist (the opportunist, in particular) who is actively trying to learn and adjust to the rules of the society he lives in is at one end of Riesman's continuum, he is likely to be in the middle of the continuum with which we are concerned.

Finally, a word should be said about the general concept of causality. This psychological dimension is one which has been neglected for some time, although it is one of the strong interests of Piaget (1930), who studied how the notion of causality developed in children. Pepitone (1958) has recently discussed several aspects of the attribution of causality in social interactions. However, individual differences in how causality is assumed to relate events has not been a subject of investigation. It would seem that some relationship would exist between how the individual views the world from the point of view of internal versus external control of reinforcement and his other modes of perception of causal relationships.

STUDIES OF COMPLEX LEARNING

The notion that individuals build up generalized expectancies for internal-external control appears to have clear implications for problems of acquisition and performance. If a human can deal with future events with the use of verbal symbols and can perceive an event as following a preceding behavior of his own, then the strength of that connection will depend at least in part on whether or not he feels there is a causal or invariable relationship between his behavior and the event. Once a person has established a concept of randomness or chance the effects of reinforcement will vary depending upon what relationship he assigns to the behavior-reinforcement sequence.

A person who is looking for an unusual brand of tobacco and is finally able to find it will return to the same place where he was reinforced before when he needs tobacco again. However, an individual who needs money and finds a five dollar bill in the street is not likely to return to that spot to look for a five dollar bill when he needs money. A behavior of looking on the ground may be strengthened to some degree in the latter case. However, the individual is selective in what aspects of his behavior are repeated or strengthened and what aspects are not, depending upon his own perception of the nature of the function as the result of a series of trials. It is evident and the preceding behavior.

In its simplest form, our basic hypothesis is that if a person perceives a reinforcement as contingent upon his own behavior, then the occurrence of either a positive or negative reinforcement will strengthen or weaken potential for that behavior to recur in the same or similar situation. If he sees the reinforcement as being outside his own control or not contingent, that is depending upon chance, fate, powerful others, or unpredictable, then the preceding behavior is less likely to be strengthened or weakened. Not only will there be a difference of degree but also a difference, in some instances, in the nature of the fuctions as the result of a series of trials. It is evident that if this analysis is correct then different kinds of learning paradigms or situations are going to produce different kinds of learning functions. A learning situation such as that in which the experimenter arbitrarily determines the right response for whether or not food is given, regardless of the behavior of the subject, will produce a different kind of learning than one where the subject believes his behavior determines whether or not the reinforcement will occur. In other words, learning under *skill* conditions is different from learning under *chance* conditions.

To test this hypothesis a series of studies was undertaken comparing verbal expectancies for future reinforcement under conditions of chance and skill learning. In this group of studies it has been necessary in order to compare skill and chance learning tasks directly to provide a similar sequence of reinforcement in both cases which was controlled by the experimenter without the subject's knowledge of such control. Two strategies are used. The first is to provide a relatively ambiguous task under two conditions, one in which the subject is *instructed* that it is skill determined. Obviously in these studies we are dealing with a continuum in which in one situation the task is likely to be perceived as relatively more skill determined. The second strategy is to present different tasks which are also surreptitiously controlled by the experimenter and which are defined as skill and chance essentially through previous cultural experience. For example, although they have certain problems of comparability, dice throwing is generally recognized as a chance task, while solving arithmetic problems and throwing darts are generally recognized as skill tasks.

The first of these studies was undertaken by Phares (1957).

Phares used color matching as an ambiguous task and instructed half of the subjects that the task was so difficult as to be a matter of luck and the other half of his subjects that success was a matter of skill and that previous research had shown that some people were very good at the task. The subjects matched samples to finely graded standards. He used a second task of matching lines of slightly varying lengths to standards placed on cards at different angles. For both tasks a fixed order of partial reinforcement (right or wrong) was used and the measure of expectancy was the number of chips a subject would bet on his probability of being correct on the succeeding trial.

Phares found, as hypothesized, that the increments and decrements following success and failure, respectively, were significantly greater under skill instructions than under chance instructions. Reinforcements under skill conditions had a greater effect on raising or lowering expectancies for future reinforcements. He also found that subjects shifted or changed their expectancies more often under skill conditions. (Another measure of the same data described above.) Finally he showed a strong trend toward unusual shifts in expectancies, that is, up after failure or down after success (the gambler's fallacy) under chance conditions. The significance of this last finding was marginal ($p = .07$, two-tailed test).

This study was followed by one by James and Rotter (1958). In this study the emphasis was on the extinction of verbal expectancies. Under conditions of partial and 100% reinforcement an extrasensory perception (ESP) type of task was used with experimenter control, and the exact same sequence of 50% partial reinforcement was given to two groups of subjects (two other groups had 100% reinforcement) for 10 training trials. Two groups were told that guessing in the task had been shown by scientists to be entirely a matter of luck, and two groups were told that there was evidence that some people are considerably skilled at the task. While the groups did not differ significantly at the end of the training trials, the chance and skill groups did differ significantly in the number of trials to extinction. Extinction was defined as stating an expectancy of 1 or 0 on a scale of 10 for three consecutive trials.

The interesting thing about the results of this investigation was that the usual findings of superiority of partial over 100% reinforcement in trials to extinction was true only of the group with chance instructions, but under skill conditions the mean number of trials to extinction for 100% reinforcement was longer (22.9) than under 50% reinforcement (19.8). Trials to extinction under partial reinforcement were significantly longer for chance than for skill instructions, and trials to extinction for 100% reinforcement were significantly longer for skill than for chance instructions. The findings were interpreted to indicate that under chance conditions the extinction series was interpreted as a change in the situation, a disappearance of previous lucky hits in the 100% reinforcement condition but not in the 50% reinforcement conditions. For the subjects with skill instructions, the greater the previous reinforcement the longer it took the subject to accept the fact that he was not able to do the task successfully.

A further check on these studies was made by Rotter, Liverant, and Crowne (1961), who studied the growth and extinction of expectancies in chance-controlled and skilled tasks. This study involved using two tasks, one the ESP task referred to above and, the second, a motor task presumably involving steadiness which would typically be perceived as a skill task. Again in both tasks similar sequences of reinforcement were used. In this case instructions were identical, the difference in the cultural perception of the tasks being the experimental variable. This study utilized eight groups, four chance and four skill with 25%, 50%, 75%, and 100% reinforcement over eight training trials followed by an extinction series. This study confirmed the previous findings of both Phares and James and Rotter. During the training trials, subjects (except the 100% reinforcement groups) showed greater increments or decrements following success and failure respectively under skill conditions than under chance conditions. Major differences in extinction were obtained independently of the expectancy levels at the end of the training trial. In this study, extinction curves for the two groups crossed over completely, so that all of the findings of the James and Rotter studies were replicated, but, in addition, 100% reinforcement took significantly longer to extinguish than 50% reinforcement in the skill task. Differences between the groups were smaller at the 25% and 75% reinforcement schedules than at 50% or 100%. The latter findings were interpreted as suggesting that at the 25% and the 75% levels the chance task was being rewarded or reinforced more often or less than could be accounted for by chance alone. The frequency of reinforcement itself may tend to make the task appear more like a skill task. In the case of 100% chance reinforcement, however, the abrupt change from continuous positive reinforcement to continuous negative reinforcement suggests a change in the nature of the situation.

The question could arise as to whether or not differences in extinction patterns would be the same with a behavioral criterion other than verbalized expectancies. To test this, Holden and Rotter (1962) again used the ESP task instructing one group of subjects that it was a skill task and the other group that it was determined entirely by luck. Subjects were given two dollars in nickels and told they could bet a nickel on each trial on whether or not they would succeed until they wished to discontinue and keep the remaining money or until they ran out of nickels. Three groups all given 50% partial reinforcement were used, one with skill instructions, one with chance instructions, and one with ambiguous instructions. Results showed a clear difference, with the subjects given chance instructions and those who were not told it was either a chance or a skill task having significantly more trials to extinction (almost twice as many) than the skill group. Extinction was defined as voluntarily quitting the experiment.

An unpublished dissertation by Bennion (1961) using the same tasks as in the Rotter, Liverant, and Crowne study, rather than instructions to produce the skill and chance difference, examined a partial reinforcement sequence that was predominantly positive but in which reported scores differed in variability to two groups. Overall mean score and frequency of success and failure as defined by the experimenter were controlled. Bennion hypothesized that greater variability of scores either under chance or skill conditions would produce results similar to that of the difference between the chance and skill conditions. There would be greater responsiveness in changes in expectancy to success and failure under the less variable conditions. He found support for this hypothesis as well as replicating the difference in responsiveness under chance and skill conditions obtained by Phares and by Rotter, Liverant, and Crowne in previous studies.

In another unpublished dissertation, James (1957) studied some of the same variables and in addition the generalization of expectancies and the "spontaneous recovery" of expectancies. He used both a line-matching and an angle-matching task. Two groups, one with chance and one with skill instructions, were given 75% reinforcement for a sequence of eight trials and then were tested for generalizations of expectancies by having one trial on the new second task. Two other groups were given the same 75% reinforced eight training trials followed by a series of extinction trials, then given a 5-minute rest and given two additional trials on the same task. These latter groups were examined for "spontaneous recovery." James' findings again replicated the differences between chance and skill groups in the growth of acquisition of expectancies. He found, as hypothesized, significantly greater generalization of expectancies from one task to another under skill instructions than under chance instructions. He also found more "spontaneous recovery" under skill instructions, but the difference in this case only approached significance.

Bennion's study of the effect of variability in scores on a task can be interpreted as defining one of the conditions which make for the perception that the task is in fact skill or chance determined. Other conditions affecting such a perception were studied by Blackman (1962). Blackman used the well-replicated finding that under chance conditions extinction in a 50% reinforcement sequence is likely to be considerably longer than under skill conditions. In a counterbalanced design he used numerous sequences of presumably random appearing lights, controlling for the percentage of reinforcement. The task was one of attempting to predict whether a red or a green light would appear on the following trial. He varied the length of sequences in which the same light would appear consecutively, and he varied the degree of patterning from presumably purely random through an easy pattern to a complicated pattern. Extinction began when the red light ceased to go on, and the measure of extinction was based upon the elimination of subject predictions of red responses. He found, as he hypothesized, that the length of sequences significantly affected the number of red responses in extinction and the expectancies associated with them. The longest sequences extinguished more quickly. Similarly, the easy but not the complicated pattern, which was apparently not perceived, also resulted in quicker extinction. These results are interpreted to indicate that longer sequences and recognizable patterns suggest to the subject that there is not a random pattern but an experimenter-controlled one. Consequently, when extinction begins and the red light no longer appears the subject interprets the situation as one in which the experimenter has changed the sequence of lights. If, however, the subject interprets the original sequence as random, he will persist much longer before extinguishing on anticipation that the red light will appear again.

Implications from the studies of Rotter, Liverant, and Crowne (1961), Bennion (1961), and Blackman (1962) can be summarized. Subjects are more likely to see a sequence of reinforcement as *not* being chance controlled when the percentage of reinforcement significantly deviates from a 50-50 percentage in a right-wrong situation, when the sequence of reinforcements appears to have a pattern, when unusually long sequences of one of two alternative events occur, and when variability of performance is minimal in a task allowing for scoring along a continuum.

A somewhat different variable was investigated by Phares (1962), who studied perceptual thresholds for shock-associated stimuli in chance-controlled versus skill situations. Phares used a tachistoscopic exposure of nonsense syllables, some of the stimuli being accompanied by shock. The skill group was told that the shock could be escaped by pressing the correct button which could be learned. The chance group was instructed that they could press any of the sequence of buttons and this may or may not avoid the shock depending upon chance. The skill group was run first and then the chance groups. In this way the experimenter could control the number of shocks, so that he was able to match the chance group with the skill group in the total number of shocks obtained during the 10 training trials. Recognition thresholds for the syllables were taken before and after the training. He found, as hypothesized, that the recognition thresholds dropped significantly more in the skill-instructed than in the chance-instructed groups although they had had the same number of shocks on the same trials and for the same nonsense syllables. Phares concluded that subjects who feel they have control of the situation are likely to exhibit perceptual behavior that will better enable them to cope with potentially threatening situations than subjects who feel chance or other noncontrollable forces determine whether or not their behavior will be successful.

Investigations of differences in behavior in skill and chance situations provide relatively clear-cut findings. When a subject perceives the task as controlled by the experimenter, chance, or random conditions, past experience is relied upon less. Consequently, it may be said that he learns less, and under such conditions, he may indeed learn the wrong things and develop a pattern of behavior which Skinner has referred to as "superstitious." These studies strongly imply that the interpretation of investigations of acquisition and performance must be made in light of the position on the continuum of complete chance control to complete skill control at which the particular task falls. Differences in learning are not merely a matter of degree but also of nature or kind as indicated by the dramatic reversal of extinction curves as demonstrated by Rotter, Liverant, and Crowne (1961). Perhaps more important are the implications for the learning theory favored by psychologists in general. Such theory is often based upon experimental paradigms which involve experimenter control. That is, they use tasks where the experimenter decides in a more or less arbitrary fashion when he will reinforce or where he will reinforce but not ones where the subject feels that his own performance determines primarily whether or not he will be successful at the task. However, many, if not the majority of learning situations of humans in everyday life situations, are in fact perceived as skill controlled. The direct application of theories of learning based upon experimenter controlled tasks to such learning is in grave doubt.

Although there is no direct proof that "experimenter control" is equivalent to "chance control," it would seem logical that the subject perceiving no regularity or predictability to the reinforcement would regard it similarly. This conclusion is supported by the earlier mentioned Blackman (1962) experiment . . . a typical "experimenter control" paradigm . . . where he obtained longer extinction times when the training sequence of partially reinforced red and green lights lacked discernible patterns. It is also supported by the fact that tasks with chance instructions produce the same kind of differences between 100% and 50% partial reinforcement in extinction rates as do the typical experimenter control experiments.

INTERNAL VERSUS EXTERNAL CONTROL
AS A PERSONALITY VARIABLE

Development of Measures of
Internal-External Control

The first attempt to measure individual differences in a generalized expectancy or belief in external control as a psychological variable was begun by Phares (1957) in his study of chance and skill effects on expectancies for reinforcement. Phares developed a Likert-type scale with 13 items stated as external attitudes and 13 as internal attitudes. The scale was developed on a priori grounds, and he found some suggestive evidence with his first crude attempt at measuring individual differences that prediction of behavior within a task situation was possible. In particular, he found that the items stated in an external direction gave low predictions, approaching statistical significance, that individuals with external attitudes would behave in a similar fashion as did all subjects when placed in a chance situation versus a skill situation. That is, they tended to show more unusual shifts, smaller magnitude of increments and decrements, and a lower frequency of shifts of expectancy in any case than did subjects who scored low on these 13 items.

Phares' work was followed by James' (1957) dissertation, previously referred to. James revised Phares' test still using a Likert format and wrote 26 items plus filler items based on the items which appeared to be most successful in the Phares study. He similarly hypothesized that within each of his groups, regardless of chance or skill instructions, those individuals who scored toward the external end of the continuum would behave in each group in the same way as the difference between the chance group and the skill group for all subjects. James was able to find low but significant correlations between his test and behavior in the task situation. External subjects had smaller increments and decrements following success and failure, generalized less from one task to another, and recovered less following the period of extinction. They also tended to produce more unusual shifts (up after failure and down after success) in expectancy.

The James-Phares scale has been used in some research involving correlates of individual differences in a generalized expectancy for internal-external control. However, the late Shephard Liverant in association with J. B. Rotter and M. Seeman undertook to broaden the test; develop subscales for different areas such as achievement, affection, and general social and political attitudes; and control for social desirability by the construction of a new forced-choice questionnaire. The earliest version of this scale included a hundred forced-choice items, each one comparing an external belief with an internal belief. The scale was item analyzed and factor analyzed and reduced to a 60-item scale by Liverant on the basis of internal consistency criteria.

Item analysis of the 60-item scale indicated that the subscales were not generating separate predictions. Achievement items tended to correlate highly with social desirability, and some subscales correlated with other scales at approximately the same level as their internal consistency. On this basis, items to measure more specific subareas of internal-external control were abandoned.

Data were collected for a large group of subjects to provide item correlations with the Marlowe-Crowne Social Desirability Scale (Crowne & Marlowe, 1964). The overall correlation of the scale with the Social Desirability scale for different samples ranged from .35 to .40 which was deemed to be too high. Reduction and purification of the 60-item scale was undertaken by S. Liverant, J. B. Rotter, and D. Crowne. Validity data from two studies were used along with internal consistency data. Item validity for most of the items was available from a study of Seeman and Evans on tuberculosis patients who had evidenced greater self-effort towards recovery versus those who were more passive. Item validity for the prediction of individual differences in trials to extinction in the previously cited study of Rotter, Liverant, and Crowne (1961) was also available. In this final revision, wording of some items was changed to make the items appropriate for noncollege adults and upper level high school students.

By eliminating those items which either had a high correlation with the Marlowe-Crowne Social Desirability Scale, a proportional split so that one of the two alternatives was endorsed more than 85% of the time, nonsignificant relationship with other items, or a correlation approaching zero with both validation criteria, the scale was reduced to 23 items. The final version of the scale, the one on which most of the subsequent data to be reported are based, is a 29-item, forced-choice test including 6 filler items intended to make somewhat more ambiguous the purpose of the test. This measure will be referred to in the remainder of this article as the I-E scale.

The I-E scale is presented in Table 6.1. Instructions for administration are presented in Appendix A. Biserial item correlations with total score *with that item removed* are given for 200 males, 200 females, and the combined group. It can be seen that these are moderate but consistent. The letter preceding the external choice in every item is italicized. The score is the total number of *external* choices.

Table 6.1   The I-E Scale with Correlations of Each Item with Total Score, Excluding That Item

	Biserial Item Correlations		
Item	*200 M*	*200 F*	*400 M + F*
1.a. Children get into trouble because their parents punish them too much.		(Filler)	
b. The trouble with most children nowadays is that their parents are too easy with them.			
2.a. Many of the unhappy things in people's lives are partly due to bad luck.	.265	.250	.260
b. People's misfortunes result from the mistakes they make.			
3.a. One of the major reasons why we have wars is because people don't take enough interest in politics.			
b. There will always be wars, no matter how hard people try to prevent them.	.214	.147	.182
4.a. In the long run people get the respect they deserve in this world.			
b. Unfortunately, an individual's worth often passes unrecognized no matter how hard he tries.	.238	.344	.289
5.a. The idea that teachers are unfair to students is nonsense.			
b. Most students don't realize the extent to which their grades are influenced by accidental happenings.	.230	.131	.179

Table 6.1 (continued)

Item	Biserial Item Correlations		
	200 M	200 F	400 M + F
6.a. Without the right breaks one cannot be an effective leader.	.345	.299	.319
b. Capable people who fail to become leaders have not taken advantage of their opportunities.			
7.a. No matter how hard you try some people just don't like you.	.200	.262	.229
b. People who can't get others to like them don't understand how to get along with others.			
8.a. Heredity plays the major role in determining one's personality.		(Filler)	
b. It is one's experiences in life which determine what they're like.			
9.a. I have often found that what is going to happen will happen.	.152	.172	.164
b. Trusting to fate has never turned out as well for me as making a decision to take a definite course of action.			
10.a. In the case of the well prepared student there is rarely if ever such a thing as an unfair test.			
b. Many times exam questions tend to be so unrelated to course work that studying is really useless.	.227	.252	.238
11.a. Becoming a success is a matter of hard work, luck has little or nothing to do with it.			
b. Getting a good job depends mainly on being in the right place at the right time.	.391	.215	.301
12.a. The average citizen can have an influence in government decisions.			
b. This world is run by the few people in power, and there is not much the little guy can do about it.	.313	.222	.265
13.a. When I make plans, I am almost certain that I can make them work.			
b. It is not always wise to plan too far ahead because many things turn out to be a matter of good or bad fortune anyhow.	.252	.285	.271
14.a. There are certain people who are just no good.		(Filler)	
b. There is some good in everybody.			
15.a. In my case getting what I want has little or nothing to do with luck.			
b. Many times we might just as well decide what to do by flipping a coin.	.369	.209	.288

Table 6.1   (continued)

Item	Biserial Item Correlations		
	200 M	*200 F*	*400 M + F*
16.a. Who gets to be the boss often depends on who was lucky enough to be in the right place first.	.295	.318	.307
b. Getting people to do the right thing depends upon ability, luck has little or nothing to do with it.			
17.a. As far as world affairs are concerned, most of us are the victims of forces we can neither understand, nor control.	.313	.407	.357
b. By taking an active part in political and social affairs the people can control world events.			
18.a. Most people don't realize the extent to which their lives are controlled by accidental happenings.	.258	.362	.310
b. There really is no such thing as "luck."			
19.a. One should always be willing to admit mistakes.		(Filler)	
b. It is usually best to cover up one's mistakes.			
20.a. It is hard to know whether or not a person really likes you.	.255	.307	.271
b. How many friends you have depends upon how nice a person you are.			
21.a. In the long run the bad things that happen to us are balanced by the good ones.	.108	.197	.152
b. Most misfortunes are the result of lack of ability, ignorance, laziness, or all three.			
22.a. With enough effort we can wipe out political corruption.			
b. It is difficult for people to have much control over the things politicians do in office.	.226	.224	.227
23.a. Sometimes I can't understand how teachers arrive at the grades they give.	.275	.248	.255
b. There is a direct connection between how I study and the grades I get.			
24.a. A good leader expects people to decide for themselves what they should do.		(Filler)	
b. A good leader makes it clear to everybody what their jobs are.			
25.a. Many times I feel that I have little influence over the things that happen to me.	.521	.440	.480
b. It is impossible for me to believe that chance or luck plays an important role in my life.			

Table 6.1 (continued)

| | Biserial Item Correlations | | |
Item	200 M	200 F	400 M + F
26.a. People are lonely because they don't try to be friendly.			
b. There's not much use in trying too hard to please people, if they like you, they like you.	.179	.227	.195
27.a. There is too much emphasis on athletics in high school.		(Filler)	
b. Team sports are an excellent way to build character.			
28.a. What happens to me is my own doing.			
b. Sometimes I feel that I don't have enough control over the direction my life is taking.	.331	.149	.238
29.a. Most of the time I can't understand why politicians behave the way they do.	.004	.211	.109
b. In the long run the people are responsible for bad government on a national as well as on a local level.			

Note: Score is number of underlined items.

A careful reading of the items will make it clear that the items deal exclusively with the subjects' *belief* about the nature of the world. That is, they are concerned with the subjects' expectations about how reinforcement is controlled. Consequently, the test is considered to be a measure of a generalized expectancy. Such a generalized expectancy may correlate with the value the subject places on internal control but none of the items is directly addressed to the *preference* for internal or external control.

Test data on the I-E scale have been obtained in a series of samples. Results are summarized in Table 6.2. Where no source is given, the data have been collected by the author and are being reported here for the first time.

Internal consistency estimates are relatively stable as shown in Table 6.2. While these estimates are only moderately high for a scale of this length, it should be remembered that the items are not arranged in a difficulty hierarchy, but rather are samples of attitudes in a wide variety of different situations. The test is an additive one and items are not comparable. Consequently, split-half or matched-half reliability tends to underestimate the internal consistency. Kuder-Richardson reliabilities are also somewhat limited since this is a forced-choice scale in which an attempt is made to balarce alternatives so that probabilities of endorsement of either alternative do not include the more extreme splits.

Table 6.2   Internal-External Control Test Data: Reliability and Discriminant Validity

Sample	Type	N	Sex	r	Source
		Internal Consistency			
Ohio State University	Split half	50	M	.65	
Elementary	Spearman-	50	F	.79	
psychology	Brown				
students					
Sample 1		100	Combined	.73	
	Kuder-	50	M	.70	
	Richardson	50	F	.76	
		100	Combined	.73	
Ohio State University	Kuder-	200	M	.70	
Elementary	Richardson	200	F	.70	
psychology					
students					
		400	Combined	.70	
National stratified	Kuder-	1000	Combined	.69	Franklin (1963)
sample	Richardson				
Purdue opinion			M & F ap-		
poll			proximately		
10th, 11th, and			Equal *N*s		
12th grades					
		Test-Retest Reliability			
Ohio State Universtiy	1 month	30	M	.60	
Elementary	Group	30	F	.83	
psychology	administra-				
students	tion				
		60	Combined	.72	
Prisoners	1 month	28	M	.78	Jessor (1964)[a]
Colorado					
Reformatory					
Ohio State University	2 months	63	M	.49	
Elementary	1st group				
psychology	administra-				
students	tion	54	F	.61	
	2nd individual				
	administra-				
	tion	117	Combined	.55	
		Correlation with Marlowe-Crowne Social Desirability Scale			
Ohio State University		166	M	−.16	
Elementary		140	F	−.32	
psychology					
students					
		306	Combined	−.21	

Table 6.2   (continued)

Sample	Type	N	Sex	r	Source
Ohio State University Elementary psychology students		136	M	−.22	Schwarz (1963)
Ohio State University Elementary psychology students		180	F	−.12	Strickland (1962)
Ohio State University Elementary psychology students		103	M	−.17	Watt (1962)
		77	F	−.35	
		180	Combined	−.29	
Kansas State University Elementary psychology students		113	45M, 68F Combined	−.28	Ware (1964)[a]
Ohio Federal prisoners Ages 18–26, 8th grade plus reading		80	M	−.41	Ladwig (1963)

Correlation with Intellectual Measures					
Ohio State University Elementary psychology students	Ohio State Psychological exam.	107	F	−.09	Strickland (1962)
Ohio State University Elementary psychology students	Ohio State Psychological exam.	26	M	.03	Cardi (1962)
		46	F	−.22	
		72	Combined	−.11	
Ohio Federal prisoners Ages 18–26, 8th grade plus reading	Revised beta IQ	80	M	.01	Ladwig (1963)

[a]Personal communication.

Test-retest reliability for a 1-month period seems quite consistent in two quite different samples. The somewhat lower reliabilities for a 2-month period may be partly a function of the fact that the first test was given under group conditions and the second test was individually administered. In the studies of test-retest reliability, means for the second administration typically dropped about 1 point in the direction of less externality.

Correlations of the 60-item I-E scale with the Marlowe-Crowne Social Desirability Scale were obtained in a number of college student samples and typically ranged between -.35 and -.40. The attempt to reduce this correlation in the new scale was moderately successful. The correlations for the new scale range from -.07 to -.35. The greater range may reflect differences in testing conditions. A correlation of -.22 represents the median for the different samples of college students where males and females are combined.

The unusually high correlation between the Marlowe-Crowne Social Desirability Scale and the I-E scores for the prisoner population is probably best understood in terms of the testing conditions. These prisoners were tested shortly after entering the reformatory in the admission building during the same period of time when they were receiving other classification tests. They were told that the test was not being given for administrative but experimental purposes and that the test scores would not become part of their permanent records. It is doubtful, however, that many of them believed these instructions. This interpretation tends to be supported (see Table 6.3) by the fact that the mean score for these prisoners was significantly lower than for college students although one might naturally expect them to be more external than the college student population.

Both the Strickland (1962) sample and Ladwig's (1963) sample of male prisoners show negligible correlations with intelligence. Cardi's (1962) sample, however, suggests a somewhat different relationship for male and female and is consistent with earlier studies of the 60-item scale and the James-Phares scale. In any case, the correlations with intelligence are low.

Means and standard deviations of the I-E scores for a variety of populations are given in Table 6.3. As in Table 6.2, if no other source is given the data have been obtained by the author. Appendix 6.B provides cumulative frequencies for 575 males and 605 females of the Ohio State sample. This sample reported in Table 6.3 and in the appendix includes tests obtained at different times of the year over a 2-year period in a variety of experiments. In all cases, however, the test was given in group administration in psychology classes and does not overlap other samples reported in Table 6.3.

Table 6.3   Means and Standard Deviations of I-E Scores for Samples of Several
Populations

Sample	Testing Conditions	N	Sex	Mean	SD	Source
Ohio State University	Group	575	M	8.15	3.88	
Elementary psychology students (combined samples)	Experimental	605	F	8.42	4.06	
		1180	Combined	8.29	3.97	
Kansas State University	Group	45	M	7.71	3.84	Ware (1964)[a]
Elementary psychology students	Experimental	68	F	7.75	3.79	
		113	Combined	7.73	3.82	
University of Connecticut	Group	134	M	8.72	3.59	
Elementary psychology students	Experimental	169	F	9.62	4.07	
		303	Combined	9.22	3.88	
Florida State University	Group	116	Combined	9.05	3.66	Gore and
Negro students, psychology classes	Experimental		62M, 54F			Rotter (1963)
Peace Corps trainees (three programs combined)	Group	122	M	6.06	3.51	
	Assessment	33	F	5.48	2.78	
		155	Combined	5.94	3.36	
Prisoners, age 18–26	Individual					
8th grade plus reading	Experiment (?)	80	M	7.72	3.65	Ladwig (1963)
Columbus, Ohio 12th grade, college	Small groups (3–12)	41	M	8.46	3.89	Stack (1963)
applicants	Experimental	32	F	7.31	3.64	
		73	Combined	7.96	3.80	

Table 6.3 (continued)

Sample	Testing Conditions	N	Sex	Mean	SD	Source
National stratified sample, Purdue opinion poll 10th, 11th, and 12th grades	Various	1000	Combined M & F Approximately equal Ns	8.50	3.74	Franklin (1963)
18-year-old subjects from Boston area	Individual	32 25 57	M F Combined	10.00 9.00 9.56	4.20 3.90 4.10	Crowne and Conn (1965)[a]

[a]Personal communication.

Sex differences appear to be minimal except in the case of the University of Connecticut sample. In this sample the means tend to be somewhat higher generally than in Midwestern samples, but it is not clear whether this is in fact a sectional difference or results from other factors of selection or testing. One important difference between the University of Connecticut sample and the others was the large size of the University of Connecticut classes, with 303 subjects comprising a single class. The difference between male and female means for this sample was significant.

Although the college Negro population was obtained from psychology classes in an equivalent fashion to the other college samples, it does appear to be slightly more external than the Mid-western college sample but not more external than the University of Connecticut sample. However, significant differences between Negroes and whites in mean I-E scores were obtained by Lefcourt and Ladwig (1965) with comparable samples. They used 60 white and 60 Negro inmates from two correctional institutions who were not significantly different in social class, age, intelligence, or reason for incarceration. Negroes were significantly more external (Means, 8.97) than white offenders (Means, 7.87).

The very low scores for Peace Corps volunteers can be accounted for in two possible ways. The data do not allow determination for which variable was playing the greater role. As a select group we would expect from a validity point of view that a group of Peace Corps volunteers would be highly internal overall, and, in fact, they were. However, the test was given in three different training groups as part of an assessment battery, and the subjects knew that scores on this as well as other tests would determine in part whether or not they would be judged to be acceptable for appointment as Peace Corps volunteers and sent overseas on assignment. It seems natural that they would interpret the internal response as more desirable under these circumstances. Whether in fact Peace Corps volunteers are more internal than unselected college students will have to be determined under comparable testing conditions.

While we would expect Peace Corps trainees to be more internal than unselected college students, we would also expect that young male prisoners, most of whom were incarcerated for car stealing, would be more external. This is clearly not the case. However, more internal mean scores can be accounted for on the basis of the high correlation with social desirability under the particular testing conditions (see previous discussion). There seems to be little doubt that scores on this test, as on all personality measures, can be significantly affected by the testing conditions.

The Franklin sample of high school students taken from the Purdue Opinion Poll differs on two important grounds from the samples of Crowne and Conn[1] and Stack (1963). One difference lies in the fact that the administration procedures are essentially unknown and vary from school to school for the Purdue Opinion Poll sample, but probably include many instances where the tests were administered by the pupils' own teachers or principals. Secondly, and more important, is the fact that the Purdue Opinion Poll is an anonymous poll in contrast to all our other samples in which the subject's name is recorded.

While the Stack sample appears to agree with the anonymous Franklin sample, they are not actually comparable. The Stack study was concerned with reactions to acceptance and rejection for college admission, and his sample was drawn from a group of subjects all of whom were applying for college. The Crowne and Conn sample was drawn from a follow-up of the subjects studied by Sears, Maccoby, and Levin (1957). They were all about 18 years of age, a few were freshmen in college, a few had dropped out of school, but most were seniors in high school.

In summary, it seems most logical that the somewhat higher

---

[1] Personal communication, 1965.

external scores obtained by Crowne and Conn would be more characteristic of unselected high school students who are given a test under experimental conditions by an examiner who does not have other authority relationships to them. The difference between the Stack sample and the Crowne and Conn sample suggests that students in high school seeking to go to college are more internal than is an unselected high school population.

This interpretation is supported in fact by one of Franklin's (1963) findings that among his subjects those students who intended to go on to college were significantly more internal than those who did not so intend.

Additional Test Characteristics

Two factor analyses have been completed. The first, based on the same 400 cases for which the item correlations are given in Table 6.1, indicated that much of the variance was included in a general factor. Several additional factors involved only a few items, and only a small degree of variance for each factor could be isolated. These additional factors, however, were not sufficiently reliable to suggest any clear-cut subscales within the test. Franklin (1963) also factor analyzed his 1,000 cases of high school students and obtained essentially similar results. All of the items loaded significantly on the general factor which accounted for 53% of the total scale variance.

In considering discriminant validity, the question of the relationship of the scale to adjustment comes up. Theoretically, one would expect some relationship between internality and good adjustment in our culture but such a relationship might not hold for extreme internal scores. However, there is clearly an interaction between internality and experience of success. The internal subject with a history of failure must blame himself. In regard to the other end of the distribution, externality may act as an adequate defense against failure, but very high scores toward the external end may suggest, at least in our culture, a defensiveness related to significant maladjustment. Extreme scores which were also true scores would suggest a passivity in the face of environmental difficulties, which, at least for many subjects, would result in maladjustment in our society.

In substance, the relationship between I-E scores and adjustment would not be a linear or a clear one from a theoretical point of view. We might expect seriously maladjusted groups to have more variability on I-E scores and probably more frequently to have high scores in the direction of externality. Within a relatively homogeneous (normal) group such as unselected college students or high school students theoretical expectation would be for a low linear correlation.

Several samples of Ohio State elementary psychology students have been examined for the relationship between the I-E scale and the Rotter Incomplete Sentences Blank (Rotter & Rafferty, 1950). In general, linear correlations have not been significant, and, while some curvilinear correlations have been significant, they are not U-shaped distributions and cannot be explained simply. Ware (1964)[2] found a correlation of .24 between the I-E scale and the Taylor Manifest Anxiety scale for his 111 subjects (significant at the 5% level). Efran (1963) used a shortened form of the Taylor Manifest Anxiety scale and of the I-E scale and examined the relationship for 114 combined male and female tenth-, eleventh-, and twelfth-grade high school students. His obtained correlation was .00.

In summary, the test shows reasonable homogeneity or internal consistency, particularly when one takes into account that many of the items are sampling a broadly generalized characteristic over a number of specific or different situations. However, at least with the relatively homogeneous sample studied the test is limited in ability to discriminate individuals. Other populations may provide a greater spread of scores but for college students in the middle 50% of the distribution the test is more suitable for investigations of group differences than for individual prediction. Whether or not a more refined measure of such a broad characteristic can be developed is an open question. Relationships with such test variables as adjustment, social desirability or need for approval, and intelligence are low for the samples studied and indicate good discriminant validity.

Multimethod Measurement

Campbell and Fiske (1959) have indicated the importance of multimethod measurement in the determination of construct validity of personality tests. Earlier studies with the 60-item scale of the forced-choice I-E test typically produced correlations between .55 and .60 with the earlier James-Phares Likert-type scale. The largest sample studied was that of Blackman (1962), who obtained a correlation of .56 for his 151 elementary psychology student subjects. Florence Johnson (1961) obtained a correlation of .58 for 120 subjects.

Two studies of nonquestionnaire approaches to the measurement of internal-external control have been made with the 23-item

---

[2] Personal communication, 1964.

scale. Adams-Webber (1963) compared the forced-choice I-E scores with scores from a story-completion test. The story beginnings involved a central character who initiates an "immoral" course of action. Scoring was based upon whether the consequences of this act in the story completions appeared to follow from the individual's behavior or were caused by it or were more a function of external conditions or agents. Judges rated story endings from a crude manual. Adams-Webber analyzed his data by dividing his 103 subjects into groups based on the number of external endings for his three story completions. Analysis of variance indicated a highly significant difference among the groups ($p = <.001$). The "projective" test of tendency to see punishment for moral transgression as being externally imposed or as being the result of the immoral behavior was significantly related to I-E scale scores.

In a study of academic failure, Cardi (1962) developed a measure of internal-external control from a semistructured interview which ranged from 35 minutes to an hour. Judges' ratings following a manual were correlated with I-E scale scores obtained at an earlier time and independently of the interview. As in the Adams-Webber study the judges' ratings were satisfactorily reliable. She obtained a biserial correlation of .61 ($p = <.002$) for her 25 subjects between subjects rated high or low from the interview data and I-E scale scores. The variable being studied here is capable of reliable measurement by a variety of test methods.

Social Class Differences in Internal-External Control

When the Warner scale based on father's occupation was used, studies of the Ohio State samples of elementary psychology students did not show significant social-class differences. However, the college student population utilized was highly homogeneous. Similarly, Gore and Rotter (1963) failed to find significant social-class differences in a somewhat lower social class but similarly homogeneous grouping at a southern Negro college. Studies with younger or noncollege age samples, however, have shown differentiation. Franklin (1963) recorded a significant relationship between higher socioeconomic class and internality based on his national stratified sample of 1,000 cases. Battle and Rotter (1963), using Negro and white sixth- and eighth-grade children and a projective type test, did find a significant social-class effect with race and intellectual level controlled. There was also a significant effect for race, but most of the variance was accounted for by an interaction in which the lower-class Negroes were considerably more external than the groups of middle-class Negroes or upper- or lower-class whites. This finding is similar to the Lefcourt and Ladwig (1965) study of Negro and white prisoners, most of whom were lower socioeconomic class.

Political Affiliation

One analysis of the relationship of the test to political identification has been made. This study included 114 Ohio State elementary psychology college students. No significant differences were found in the mean scores of 49 students who identified themselves as Republican, 20 who identified themselves as Democrats, and 45 who said they were independent or not identified with either major party. With the earlier 60-item scale Johnson (1961) found no significant differences in I-E scale scores between 73 college student supporters of Nixon and 47 supporters of Kennedy. However, such results may not be typical of another geographical area where there are sharper differences in political liberalness between the two major parties.

Children's Tests of
Internal-External Control

Three measures of internal-external control for children have been devised. The first of these by Bialer (1961) was modified from the James-Phares scale. It is a 23-item questionnaire with yes-no responses. With younger children the items are read, and the child answers yes or no. A typical item is, "Do you really believe a kid can be whatever he wants to be?"

Crandall, Katkovsky, and Preston (1962) developed a scale (Intellectual Achievement Responsibility—IAR) for "self-responsibility" in achievement situations. The items dealt with whether or not the child felt that he, rather than other persons, usually caused the successes and failures he experienced in intellectual achievement situations. The child chose between alternatives as in the following example: "Suppose you did better than usual in a subject at school. Would it probably happen (a) because you tried harder, or (b) because someone helped you?"

A third test for children, more projective in nature, was developed by Battle and Rotter (1963). This test presented the subject with six situations modeled on the Rosenzweig picture frustration approach. The child was told how he would fill in the balloon, as in comic strips, for an outline drawing: for example, where one child is saying, "How come you didn't get what you wanted for Christmas?"

A reliable scoring manual for this test was developed. This projective measure correlated significantly (.42) with the Bialer questionnaire in a group of 40 white and Negro children. Data obtained from all three of these tests will be referred to in the following section.

PERSONAL CORRELATES OF A GENERALIZED EXPECTANCY FOR INTERNAL-EXTERNAL CONTROL: CONSTRUCT VALIDITY OF THE I-E MEASURES

Performance in Controlled Laboratory Tasks

The first investigations of individual differences in the I-E variable were made in connection with learning or performance tasks in which skill and chance instructions were given. Phares (1957) obtained prediction bordering on significance for 13 chance-oriented items for individual differences in the size of the increments or decrements following success and failure and in the frequency of unusual shifts within conditions: that is, those shifts in expectancy where the subject raises his expectancy after a failure or lowers it after a success.

James (1957), in the previously cited experiment, found low but significant prediction with revised scale and individual differences *within* each condition. In each case the behavior of externals differed from that of internals in the same way that the overall population differed under chance instructions as compared with skill instructions. James found that the size of increments and decrements in expectancies following reinforcement, the frequency of unusual shifts, the tendency to generalize from one task to another, and the number of trials to extinction were significantly related to his questionnaire of internal-external control.

Later studies using task differences rather than instructions and in some cases other types of tasks have not been as successful as James in predicting individual differences within conditions using either the James-Phares scale or the more recent I-E scale. More consistent prediction has been made of the frequency of unusual shifts during a controlled reinforcement sequence. Several investigations have found this difference to be significant or near significant and the trend is always in the same direction, namely, that externals tend to produce more unusual (or gambler's fallacy) shifts. Battle and Rotter (1963) also found that the Bialer scale significantly predicted the number of unusual shifts for sixth- and eighth-grade Negro and white children.

Liverant and Scodel (1960) examined the preferences for bets in a dice-throwing situation using the earlier 60-item version of the I-E scale. They found that subjects scoring toward the internal end of the scale tended to prefer intermediate probability bets or extremely safe bets over the long shots and that they tended to wager more money on safe as against risky bets when compared to those subjects scoring at the external end of the continuum.

In general, individual prediction in competitive laboratory situations for college students has been only partially successful. Apparently, the rather narrow range of internal-external control attitudes in college students and the strong situational determination of the competitive laboratory tasks limits prediction. The behavior most susceptible to individual prediction is that which deals most directly with risk taking and expectancies of the real influence of luck as demonstrated by belief in the gambler's fallacy.

Attempts to Control the Environment

In the following sections for the sake of brevity subjects in the upper half of the distribution of scores on the I-E scale or other measures will be referred to as externals and those in the lower half as internals. It should be made clear that we are dealing here with only one variable affecting behavior and that we are *not* implying a typology of any kind. In fact, in some of the studies involving college populations those subjects being characterized as relatively more external may in fact be more internal on the average than the mean of the population at large.

Perhaps the most important kind of data to assess the construct validity of the internal-external control dimension involves the attempts of people to better their life conditions, that is, to control their environment in important life situations. It is in this sense that the I-E scale appears to measure a psychological equivalent of the sociological concept of alienation, in the sense of powerlessness. The first study of this type was undertaken by Seeman and Evans (1962), who employed a revision of the 60-item I-E scale not too different from the later-developed 23-item scale. They investigated the behavior of patients in a tuberculosis hospital, measuring how much they knew about their own condition, how much they questioned doctors and nurses about their own condition, and how satisfied they were with the amount of feedback they were getting about their medical status. They used 43 matched pairs of white male patients, each pair being matched for occupational status, education, and ward placement.

As hypothesized, they found that the internals knew more about their own condition, questioned the doctors and nurses more (according to doctors' and nurses' independent ratings), and expressed less satisfaction at the amount of feedback or the information they were getting about their condition from the hospital personnel.

Seeman (1963) followed this study with one of reformatory inmates, investigating memory for various kinds of information which they were exposed to in incidental fashion. He found a significant correlation, independent of intelligence, between internality-externality and the amount of information remembered about how the reformatory was run, parole, and long-range economic facts which might affect the persons after they left the reformatory.

Gore and Rotter (1963) obtained signed commitments from students at a southern Negro college regarding activities to be undertaken during vacation in behalf of the civil rights movement. Students who were willing to take part in a march on the state capitol or to join a freedom riders' group were clearly and significantly more internal than those who were only willing to attend a rally, were not interested in participating at all, or avoided even filling out the requested form. Since these were all-Negro students who must have had high involvement in the integration issue, the willingness of some to take part in active attempts to change, and others not to must have been related to their own generalized expectancy that their behavior could, in fact, effect a change in the prejudice which surrounded them as well as other variables. While this study had strong face validity, in that the students who signed up for these activities expected to take part in them, no follow-ups were made as to whether or not they actually did take part. A study by Strickland (1965) investigated activists in a Negro civil rights movement in a different state in comparison to Negroes matched for education and socioeconomic status who did not take part in such issues. She again found a significant difference with the activists more internal on the I-E scale.

Phares (1965) in a more stringent test of a generality of internal-external control attitudes selected two samples, one internal and one external, on the I-E scale but matched for the attitudes towards maintaining fraternities and sororities on campus. He instructed both groups to act as experimenters to change the attitudes of other students. He found, as hypothesized, that his internal subject-experimenters were significantly more successful in changing attitudes of others than the external subject-experimenters, who did not differ significantly in the amount of change achieved from a control group who were not subject to any influence condition.

In two separate studies the author has investigated the relationship between petition signing and internal-external control. In both instances, subjects were given the opportunity to sign petitions pro or con some issue such as Red China's being admitted to the United Nations or pro or con postseason football games, on the pretext that only by providing both alternatives could the petitions be passed out in classes. It was hypothesized that internality on the test would relate to signing the petitions in either direction versus non-signing. In both cases, the I-E scale failed to predict who would be signers and who would not. Whether or not the signing of a petition under classroom conditions involves other variables which were not taken into account and masked any internal-external control variance was not clear. In any case, the test failed to predict petition signing under these conditions.

A recent investigation in this area involves a different cultural population. Seeman (1964)[3] studied workers in Sweden with a translated version of the I-E scale. Seeman's results seem to point clearly to the fact that membership in unions versus nonmembership, activity within the union, and general knowledge of political affairs were all significantly related to internality. Correlations were low but significant and held up when controlled for variables such as education, age, and income.

Perhaps related to this feeling that one can control the environment is also a feeling that one can control himself. Some studies of the relationship of internal-external control to smoking perhaps are relevant. Straits and Sechrest (1963) found that non-smokers were significantly more internal than smokers, and James, Woodruff, and Werner (1965) replicated that finding and in addition reported that following the Surgeon General's report, among male smokers, those who quit and did not return to smoking in a specified period of time were more internal than those who believed the report but did not quit smoking. The difference was not significant for females who apparently were motivated by other variables including, for example, the tendency to gain weight when not smoking.

This group of studies lends strong and relatively consistent support to the hypothesis that a generalized expectancy—that one can affect the environment through one's own behavior—is present in at least two different cultures, can be reliably measured, and is predictive of logical behavioral construct referents.

While significant correlations have been referred to throughout this section, it should be made clear that for the most part they are low and leave room for much in the way of specific attitudes in the·

---

[3] Unpublished manuscript.

particular areas of behavior that were investigated. Perhaps some explanation may be called for here for the fact that variance due to the specific situation was not accounted for by the two factor analyses of the test. In the factor analyses done by the author, several factors involving small but significant variance were isolated, each involving only two or three items with significant loadings. These factors, however, were highly specific and did not constitute broad enough *subareas* to appear useful to the author. It must also be remembered that most items involving achievement had to be dropped from the scale because of their apparently great susceptibility to social desirability influence.

Internal-External Control and Achievement Motivation

It would seem a logical extension of the notion of internal-external control that those at the internal end of the scale would show more overt striving for achievement than those who felt they had little control over their environment. However, there are two limitations on the potential strength of this relationship, particularly as it applies to college students or adults. One of these is that among college students and adults, particularly with males, there are more defensive externals or people who have arrived at an external view as a defense against failure but who were originally highly competitive. Many such people still maintain striving behavior in clearly structured competitive situations but defensively account for failures by expressed external attitudes. The other limitation is one of specificity in that internal-external control attitudes are obviously not generalized across the board, and in the highly structured academic achievement situation there is probably more specificity determining response than in other kinds of situations. With children who have less experience in the competitive academic situation, a higher relationship could be anticipated than with a select population of college students.

The Crandall et al. (1962) scale (IAR) developed for use with children is specific to the achievement area and Crandall et al. did find free play achievement behavior and achievement test scores in boys but not in girls related to test scores. Neither the Children's Manifest Anxiety scale nor the Thematic Apperception Test (TAT) achievement measure predicted either boys' or girls' achievement behavior.

Cellura[4] found a direct relationship between the SRA academic

---

[4] Unpublished manuscript, "Internality as a determinant of academic achievement in low SES adolescents," Syracuse University, 1963.

achievement test, with IQ partialled out, of lower socioeconomic status boys and the IAR scale. Crandall's subjects were predominantly middle class, and Cellura's were all in Hollingheads' fourth and fifth categories.

In Franklin's (1963) study of high school students involving the national stratified sample of 1,000, he hypothesized 17 relationships of the I-E scale to *reported* evidences of achievement motivation. These included such things as early attempts to investigate colleges, intention to go to college, amount of time spent doing homework, parents' interest in homework, etc. He found a significant relationship in the predicted direction in 15 of his 17 relationships.

A study by Efran (1963) produced an indirect but extremely interesting indication of the relationship between striving for achievement and internal-external control. Using a balanced-order controlled procedure he studied high school students' tendency to forget (repress) failures versus successes and found that the tendency to forget failures was significantly related to scores towards the internal end of the dimension. It is possible that the functional value of a defensive tendency towards externality is indicated by these findings. The results suggest that the external has less need to "repress" his failures since he has already accepted external factors as determining his success and failure to a greater extent than those subjects scoring as more internal on the I-E control scale.

A study by Rotter and Mulry (1965) also supports the stronger motivation of internals in achievement situations. In this study, 120 male and female unselected subjects were placed in an angle-matching situation of extreme difficulty. Half of the subjects were instructed that the task was so difficult as to be chance determined and half that it was difficult but that previous data had shown that some people were very good at it. All subjects were then given eight trials of which 75% were positively reinforced, followed by an extinction series of no correct answers until their verbalized expectancies reached 1 or 0 for two consecutive trials. Within the skill and chance groups, subjects were divided into internals and externals at the median. Decision time was measured for all subjects from the time they were given the sample for judging until they selected a standard. The subject was unaware that he was being timed. Analysis of variance produced a significant interaction. Internals took longer to decide on a matching standard under skill conditions than did externals but took a shorter time under chance conditions than did externals. Most of the difference was attributed to the internals who have very long decision times under skill conditions and very short times under chance conditions, these being significantly different. The externals took longer under chance conditions than under skill conditions but the difference was not significant. The result not only shows the greater involvement of internals under skill conditions but in general suggests that internals tend to value reinforcements for skill much more than chance, and if the opposite cannot be said for the more external subjects of this study, it is at least clear that there is no significant differentiation for them.

In summary, the expected relationship between the tendency to perceive what happens to a person as dependent upon his own actions and greater motivation in achievement is generally supported although prediction was not consistent for boys and girls using the Crandall et al. scale with children.

Internal-External Control and Resistance to Subtle Suggestion

One other area of construct validity has been investigated in some depth. This involves the variables of independence, suggestibility, and conformity as related to internal-external control. It seems that internals would be more resistive to manipulation from the outside if, in fact, they are aware of such manipulation. If they were aware, they would feel deprived of some of their control of the environment. Externals expecting control from the outside would be less resistive. One special consideration here, however, is in the area of conformity. If the internally oriented person perceives that it is to his advantage to conform he may do so consciously and willingly without yielding any of his control. It is only where it might be clearly to his disadvantage that he would resist conformity pressures.

An investigation of the latter hypothesis was carried out by Crowne and Liverant (1963). They studied unselected college students, dividing them at the median into internals and externals and observing them in an Asch conformity situation. Under one set of conditions the usual Asch instructions were used. In the second set of conditions, subjects were given a certain amount of money and allowed to bet on each of their judgments. Subjects could choose to bet or not to bet and could determine the amount they were willing to bet on each judgment. In the normal Asch situation, there were no differences between internals and externals in the amount of yielding. However, under betting conditions the internals yielded significantly less than the externals. They also bet more on themselves when going against the majority than did externals on their independent trials. The internals had no significant differences between their bets on conforming and independent trials, but the externals bet significantly less on independent trials than they did on trials on which they yielded.

Other tests of the tendency to yield to external influence were obtained from studies of Strickland (1962) and Getter (1962) relating scores on the I-E scale to verbal conditioning. On the basis of a thorough postexperimental interview, Strickland divided her subjects into those who were aware of the reinforcement contingency and those who were not. In addition, of those who were aware she divided those who conditioned from those who did not. While she found no overall relationship between conditionability and I-E scale scores, she did find large and significant differences between those subjects who were aware and did not condition and those subjects who were aware and did condition. As expected, the subjects who were aware and did not condition were considerably more internal than those who were aware and did condition.

The study by Getter involving a somewhat different technique produced a fairly large number of latent conditioners. That is, subjects who showed no significant evidence of conditioning during the training trials, but during extinction when no reinforcement was given, showed a significant rise in the reinforced response. Again, these subjects were significantly more internal than either subjects who did not show such latent conditioning among non-conditioners or who conditioned during the training trials.

Both of these studies suggest a kind of negativism to external manipulation on the part of internals. However, a study by Gore (1962) helps to clarify this issue. Gore used an experimenter influence paradigm in which she presented TAT cards to three groups of subjects, ostensibly to determine which cards produced longer stories. One condition involved overt influence in which she specified which card she thought was the best. The second condition involved subtle influence in which she presented the same card, saying to the subjects and smiling, "Now let's see what you do with *this* one." The third condition was a control condition of no influence. She also used unselected subjects dividing them at the median into internals and externals. Her results showed no significant differences between internals and externals under the overt suggestion condition and control condition, but under the subtle suggestion condition the internals produced significantly shorter stories than did externals and significantly shorter stories than did control subjects in the no suggestion condition. It is under the subtle suggestion conditions they reacted by telling shorter stories or were, in fact, negativistic. However, in the overt condition, there were no traces of this negativism. Apparently, when given the conscious choice the internal is not resistive. However, when he is aware that an attempt is being made to subtly manipulate him he does become resistive.

The four studies taken as a whole support one another. The individual who percieves that he does have control over what happens to him may conform or may go along with suggestions when he chooses to and when he is given a conscious alternative. However, if such suggestion or attempts at manipulation are not to his benefit or if he perceives them as subtle attempts to influence him without his awareness, he reacts resistively. The findings have considerable significance for the general area of persuasion and propaganda.

Antecedents of Internal-External Attitudes

Relatively little work has been done on antecedents for developing attitudes of internal versus external control. The consistent indication that lower socioeconomic level groups are more external allows for a number of alternative explanations. Graves (1961) predicted and found differences among Ute Indians, children of Spanish-American heritage, and whites in an isolated triethnic community. As he expected the Indians are most external, the Spanish-Americans in the middle, and the whites more internal. The implication is for direct cultural teaching of internal-external attitudes since, in fact, the Spanish-Americans were financially more deprived than the Indians although it is true that the Indians who were partially supported by the government had fewer occupational outlets. In support of this interpretation of the influence of direct teaching, Shirley Jessor (1964)[5] found a correlation of .38 between mothers' coded answers to interview questions of internal-external attitudes and responses of their high school children to a 23-item questionnaire similar to the 23-item scale described here. Her sample included 81 pairs drawn from the same cross-cultural sample.

In the previously cited study by Battle and Rotter (1963), the highly external group was the low-socioeconomic-level Negro group in contrast to Middle-class Negroes or whites of either lower- or middle-class identification. Interestingly enough, within this group there was a significant relationship between intelligence and externality. This relationship was counter to the socioeconomic level findings. It was the more intelligent Negro children in the lower socioeconomic level who were the most external. The findings are based on a small N and may be regarded as only suggestive. However,

---

[5] Personal communication, 1964.

what they imply is that the perception of limited material opportunities and of powerful external forces is one variable making for an external attitude. Similarly, Cellura (See Footnote 4) found that with both the Bialer scale and the Crandall et al. IAR scale the parents of the more external children had significantly lower education levels.

One investigation with college student subjects attempted to relate orthodoxy of religious beliefs to internal-external control (Rotter, Simmons, & Holden, 1961[6]) using the McLean scale which measures belief in the literalness of the Bible. No relationship was found. With other college student groups there were no significant differences between individuals of one religious faith versus another. Interviews with individual subjects in a college population at least suggest that religion may well have a role in the development of internal or external attitudes. However, it is the specific emphasis that is placed upon the role of external fatalistic determination by parents which is more likely to determine the attitude than the abstract doctrines of the sect. These studies bearing on the problem of antecedents of internal-external beliefs are indirect, and work needs to be done in this area of investigation. One obvious antecedent worthy of study would be the consistency of discipline and treatment by parents. Clearly it would be expected that unpredictable parents would encourage the development of attitudes of external control.

SUMMARY

The studies reported here represent an unusually consistent set of findings. For most findings there are replications sometimes in other laboratories, sometimes with other kinds of populations, and sometimes with different methods of measurement and techniques of producing condition or situational effects. The broad findings are summarized below.

1. People in American culture have developed generalized expectancies in learning situations in regard to whether or not reinforcement, reward, or success in these situations is dependent upon their own behavior or is controlled by external forces, particularly luck, chance, or experimenter control, which are fairly consistent from individual to individual. If subjects perceive a situation as one in which luck or chance or experimenter control determines the rein-

---

[6] Unpublished manuscript, 1961.

forcements, then they are less likely to raise expectancies for future reinforcement as high following success, as if they perceived the reinforcement to be dependent upon skill or their own efforts. Similarly, they are less likely to lower expectancies as much after failure. They are less likely to generalize experiences of success and failure or expectancies of future reinforcement as much from one task to another similar task. The pattern of extinction is markedly different involving a reversal of the typical 100% versus 50% partial reinforcement findings. When perceived as skill determined, 100% reinforcement takes longer to extinguish than does 50% reinforcement. Finally, under conditions where they perceive the task as luck, chance, or experimenter controlled they are more likely to raise expectancies after a failure or to lower them after a success. In general, under skill conditions behavior of a subject follows what might be considered a more logical or commonsense model. It is particularly important that many of the learning paradigms utilized by psychologists are of the type where reward is experimenter controlled. These results suggest that generalizing "laws of learning" from such studies is a dangerous procedure. In substance, one main interpretation of these studies is that research in human learning should be understood or interpreted in light of the position on a continuum of internal to external control that the task and procedure will be perceived by the subjects.

2. Not only do subjects in general differentiate learning situations as internally or externally determined but individuals differ in a generalized expectancy in how they regard the same situation. Such generalized expectancies can be measured and are predictive of behavior in a variety of circumstances. These characteristic differences in viewing behavior-reinforcement contingencies can be measured in children and adults by different methods with reasonably high intercorrelations between different methods of measurement.

3. Data are presented on one scale for measuring individual differences in generalized expectancy for internal-external control which has been used in the largest number of studies of this variable. This is a forced-choice 29-item scale including 6 filler items. Item analysis and factor analysis show reasonably high internal consistency for an additive scale. Test-retest reliability is satisfactory, and the scale correlates satisfactorily with other methods of assessing the same variable such as questionnaire, Likert scale, interview assessments, and ratings from a story-completion technique. Discriminant validity is indicated by the low relationships with such variables as intelligence, social desirability, and political liberalness. Differences

in means of selected populations is generally a weak criterion of validity. Nevertheless, differences obtained for different types of populations are generally consistent with expectancies.

4. Most significant evidence of the construct validity of the I-E scale comes from predicted differences in behavior for individuals above and below the median of the scale or from correlations with behavioral criteria. A series of studies provides strong support for the hypotheses that the individual who has a strong belief that he can control his own destiny is likely to (a) be more alert to those aspects of the environment which provide useful information for his future behavior; (b) take steps to improve his environmental condition; (c) place greater value on skill or achievement reinforcements and be generally more concerned with his ability, particularly his failures; and (d) be resistive to subtle attempts to influence him.

APPENDIX 6A
INSTRUCTIONS FOR THE I-E SCALE

This is a questionnaire to find out the way in which certain important events in our society affect different people. Each item consists of a pair of alternatives lettered a or b. Please select the one statement of each pair (and only one) which you more strongly believe to be the case as far as you're concerned. Be sure to select the one you actually believe to be more true rather than the one you think you should choose or the one you would like to be true. This is a measure of personal belief: obviously there are no right or wrong answers.

Your answers to the items on this inventory are to be recorded on a separate answer sheet which is loosely inserted in the booklet. REMOVE THIS ANSWER SHEET NOW. Print your name and any other information requested by the examiner on the answer sheet, then finish reading these directions. Do not open the booklet until you are told to do so.

Please answer these items carefully but do not spend too much time on any one item. Be sure to find an answer for every choice. Find the number of the item on the answer sheet and black-in the space under the number 1 or 2 which you choose as the statement more true.

In some instances you may discover that you believe both statements or neither one. In such cases, be sure to select the one you more strongly believe to be the case as far as you're concerned. Also try to respond to each item independently when making your choice; do not be influenced by your previous choices.

APPENDIX 6B

Table 6B.1 Distribution of I-E Scale Scores for 575 Males and 605 Female Ohio State Elementary Psychology Students

	Males[a]			Females[b]	
I-E score	f	Cum. %	I-E score	f	Cum. %
			21	1	100.00
20	1	100.00	20	1	99.83
19	1	99.83	19	3	99.67
18	4	99.65	18	7	99.17
17	10	98.96	17	10	98.02
16	10	97.22	16	8	96.36
15	10	95.48	15	17	95.04
14	15	93.74	14	23	92.23
13	31	91.13	13	37	88.43
12	32	85.74	12	31	82.31
11	32	80.17	11	42	77.19
10	49	74.61	10	42	70.25
9	53	66.09	9	64	63.31
8	73	56.87	8	53	52.73
7	52	44.17	7	50	43.97
6	52	35.13	6	66	35.70
5	41	26.09	5	37	24.79
4	43	18.96	4	42	18.68
3	29	11.48	3	37	11.74
2	22	6.43	2	22	5.62
1	10	2.61	1	8	1.98
0	5	0.87	0	4	0.66

[a]$N = 575$; Mean $= 8.15$; $SD = 3.88$.
[b]$N = 605$; Mean $= 8.42$; $SD = 4.06$.

REFERENCES

Adams-Webber, J. Perceived locus of control of moral sanctions. Unpublished master's thesis, Ohio State University, 1963.

Angyal, A. *Foundations for a science of personality.* New York: Commonwealth Fund, 1941.

Atkinson, J. W. (Ed.) *Motives in fantasy action and society.* Princeton: D. Van Nostrand, 1958.

Battle, Esther S., & Rotter, J. B. Children's feelings of personal control as related to social class and ethnic group. *Journal of Personality,* 1963, **31**, 482–490.

Bennion, R. C. Task, trial by trial score variability of internal versus external control of reinforcement. Unpublished doctoral dissertation, Ohio State University, 1961.

Bialer, I. Conceptualization of success and failure in mentally retarded and normal children. *Journal of Personality*, 1961, **29**, 303-320.

Blackman, S. Some factors affecting the perception of events as chance determined. *Journal of Psychology*, 1962, **54**, 197-202.

Campbell, D. T., & Fiske, D. W. Convergent and discriminant validation by multitrait-multimethod matrix. *Psychological Bulletin*, 1959, **56**, 81-105.

Cardi, Miriam. An examination of internal versus external control in relation to academic failures. Unpublished master's thesis, Ohio State University, 1962.

Cohen, J. *Chance, skill and luck*. Baltimore: Penguin Books, 1960.

Crandall, V. J. Achievement. In Harold W. Stevenson et al. (Eds.), *National Society for the Study of Education Yearbook: Part I. Child psychology*. Chicago: Univer. Chicago Press, 1963.

Crandall, V. J., Katkovsky, W., & Preston, Anne. Motivational and ability determinants of young children's intellectual achievement behaviors. *Child Development*, 1962, **33**, 643-661.

Crowne, D. P., & Liverant, S. Conformity under varying conditions of personal commitment. *Journal of Abnormal and Social Psychology*, 1963, **66**, 547-555.

Crowne, D. P., & Marlowe, D. *The approval motive*. New York: Wiley, 1964.

Efran, J. S. Some personality determinants of memory for success and failure. Unpublished doctoral dissertation, Ohio State University, 1963.

Frather, N. T. Subjective probability and decision under uncertainty. *Psychological Review*, 1959, **66**, 150-164.

Franklin, R. D. Youth's expectancies about internal versus external control of reinforcement related to *N* variables. Unpublished doctoral dissertation, Purdue University, 1963.

Getter, H. Variables affecting the value of the reinforcement in verbal conditioning. Unpublished doctoral dissertation, Ohio State University, 1962.

Goodnow, Jacqueline J., & Pettigrew, T. F. Effects of prior patterns of experience upon strategies and learning sets. *Journal of Experimental Psychology*, 1955, **49**, 381-389.

Goodnow, Jacqueline J., & Postman, L. Probability learning in a problem-solving situation. *Journal of Experimental Psychology*, 1955, **49**, 16-22.

Gore, Pearl Mayo. Individual differences in the prediction of subject compliance to experimenter bias. Unpublished doctoral dissertation, Ohio State University, 1962.

Gore, Pearl Mayo, & Rotter, J. B. A personality correlate of social action. *Journal of Personality*, 1963, **31**, 58-64.

Graves, T. D. Time perspective and the deferred gratification pattern in a tri-ethnic community. Unpublished doctoral dissertation, University of Pennsylvania, 1961.

Harlow, H. F. The formation of learning sets. *Psychological Review*, 1949, **56**, 51-65.

Holden, K. B., & Rotter, J. B. A nonverbal measure of extinction in skill and chance situations. *Journal of Experimental Psychology*, 1962, **63**, 519-520.

James, W. H. Internal versus external control of reinforcement as a basic variable in learning theory. Unpublished doctoral dissertation, Ohio State University, 1957.

James, W. H., & Rotter, J. B. Partial and 100% reinforcement under chance and skill conditions. *Journal of Experimental Psychology,* 1958, **55**, 397–403.

James, W. H., Woodruff, A. B., & Werner, W. Effect of internal and external control upon changes in smoking behavior. *Journal of Consulting Psychology,* 1965, **29**, 184–186.

Johnson, Florence Y. Political attitudes as related to internal and external control. Unpublished master's thesis, Ohio State University, 1961.

Ladwig, G. W. Personal, situational and social determinants of preference for delayed reinforcement. Unpublished doctoral dissertation, Ohio State University, 1963.

Lefcourt, H. M., & Ladwig, G. W. The American Negro: A problem in expectancies. *Journal of Personality and Social Psychology,* 1965, **1**, 377–380.

Linton, Harriet R. Dependence on external influence: Correlations in perceptions, attitudes and judgment. *Journal of Abnormal and Social Psychology,* 1955, **51**, 502–507.

Liverant, S., & Scodel, A. Internal and external control as determinants of decision making under conditions of risk. *Psychological Reports,* 1960, **7**, 59–67.

McClelland, D., Atkinson, J. W., Clark, R. A., & Lowell, E. L. *The achievement motive.* New York: Appleton-Century-Crofts, 1953.

Merton, R. *Mass persuasion.* New York: Harpers, 1946.

Merton, R. Social structure and anomie. In *Social theory and social structure.* Glencoe, Ill.: Free Press, 1949, 125–149.

Nettler, G. A measure of alienation. *American Sociological Review,* 1957, **22**, 670–677.

Pepitone, A. Attributions of causality, social attitudes and cognitive matching processes. In R. Taguiri & L. Petrillo (Eds.), *Person perception and interpersonal behavior.* Stanford, Calif.: Stanford University Press, 1958. Pp. 258–276.

Phares, E. J. Expectancy changes in skill and chance situations. *Journal of Abnormal and Social Psychology,* 1957, **54**, 339–342.

Phares, E. J. Perceptual threshold decrements as a function of skill and chance expectancies. *Journal of Psychology,* 1962, **53**, 399–407.

Phares, E. J. Internal-external control as a determinant of amount of social influence exerted. *Journal of Personality and Social Psychology,* 1965, **2**, 642–647.

Piaget, J. *The child's conception of physical causality.* New York: Harcourt, Brace, 1930.

Riesman, D. *Individualism reconsidered.* Glencoe, Ill.: Free Press, 1954.

Rotter, J. B. *Social learning and clinical psychology.* Englewood Cliffs: Prentice-Hall, 1954.

Rotter, J. B. The role of the psychological situation in determining the direction of human behavior. In M. R. Jones (Ed.), *Nebraska symposium on motivation.* Lincoln: Univer. Nebraska Press, 1955. Pp. 245–269.

Rotter, J. B. Some implications of a social learning theory for the prediction of goal directed behavior from testing procedures. *Psychological Review,* 1960, **67**, 301–316.

Rotter, J. B., Liverant, S., & Crowne, D. P. The growth and extinction of expectancies in chance controlled and skilled tests. *Journal of Psychology,* 1961, **52**, 161–177.

Rotter, J. B., & Mulry, R. C. Internal versus external control of reinforcement and decision time. *Journal of Personality and Social Psychology,* 1965, **2**, 598–604.

Rotter, J. B., & Rafferty, Janet E. *The Rotter Incomplete Sentences Blank manual: College form.* New York: Psychological Corporation, 1950.

Schwarz, J. C. Factors influencing expectancy change during delay in a series of trials on a controlled skill task. Unpublished doctoral dissertation, Ohio State University, 1963.

Sears, R. R., Maccoby, Eleanor, & Levin, H. *Patterns of childrearing.* Evanston: Rowe Peterson, 1957.

Seeman, M. On the meaning of alienation. *American Sociological Review,* 1959, **24**, 782–791.

Seeman, M. Alienation and social learning in a reformatory. *American Journal of Sociology,* 1963, **69**, 270–284.

Seeman, M. Social learning theory and the theory of mass society. Paper read at the annual meeting of the American Sociological Society. Los Angeles, 1963.

Seeman, M., & Evans, J. W. Alienation and learning in a hospital setting. *American Sociological Review,* 1962, **27**, 772–783.

Srole, L. Social integration and certain corollaries: an exploratory study. *American Sociological Review,* 1956, **21**, 709–716.

Stack, J. J. Individual differences in the reduction of cognitive dissonance: an exploratory study. Unpublished doctoral dissertation, Ohio State University, 1963.

Straits, B. C., & Sechrest, L. Further support of some findings about characteristics of smokers and non-smokers. *Journal of Consulting Psychology,* 1963, **27**, 282.

Strickland, Bonnie R. The relationships of awareness to verbal conditioning and extinction. Unpublished doctoral dissertation, Ohio State University, 1962.

Strickland, Bonnie R. The prediction of social action from a dimension of internal-external control. *Journal of Social Psychology,* 1965, **66**, 353–358.

Veblen, T. *The theory of the leisure class.* New York: Macmillan, 1899 (Modern Library edition, 1934).

Watt, N. F. The relation of public commitment, delay after commitment, and some individual differences to changes in verbalized expectancies. Unpublished doctoral dissertation, Ohio State University, 1962.

White, R. W. Motivation reconsidered: The concept of competence. *Psychological Review,* 1959, **66**, 297–333.

Witkin, H. A., Lewis, Helen B., Hertzman, M., Machover, Karen, Meissner, Pearl B., & Wapner, S. *Personality through perception.* New York: Harper, 1954.

Wyckoff, L. B., & Sidowski, J. G. Probability discrimination in a motor task. *Journal of Experimental Psychology,* 1955, **50**, 225–231.

Commentary to Chapter 7

The concept of internal versus external control of reinforcement (or locus of control) *was from the first a potentially important idea for both learning theory and the fields of personality and psychopathology. Thus, though not surprising, it was somewhat disappointing that the excitement this concept created in the fields of personality, psychopathology, psychotherapy, and medical rehabilitation was not mirrored in traditional learning theory.*

It seemed to me that these studies provided clear-cut evidence that the principles of acquisition, performance, and extinction differed markedly in contingent and noncontingent learning situations—that is, where outcome was contingent on the subject's behavior or independent of it. Whereas the former kind of learning seemed more important for humans, it was the latter kind, using animal subjects, that characterized the majority of studies on which learning theories were based. Perhaps it was at this time that learning psychologists began to recognize the limitations of the conditioning paradigm and animal studies and turned instead to studies of verbal learning, memory, and information processing. Consequently, they were less interested in revising their old theories than in producing new ones in their current areas of interest. In any case, the interest in internal versus external control of reinforcement as a major variable in learning theory never came close to the experimentation it stimulated in personality theory and clinical psychology.

The paper presented here—done with two colleagues, Shepherd Liverant and Douglas P. Crowne—was one of a large number of studies (including masters theses, dissertations, and independent studies) performed by me, my colleagues, and graduate students. These studies make up a solid and well-replicated set of experiments that, taken together, clearly show that learning under noncontingent reinforcement conditions differs from contingent or skill learning not only in degree but also in the laws governing such learning. This study was itself a replication of two previous investigations (James & Rotter, 1958; Holden & Rotter, 1962). It introduced additional schedules of reinforcement and used different tasks rather than different instructions for the same task.

REFERENCES

Holden, K. B., & Rotter, J. B. A nonverbal measure of extinction in skill and chance situations. *Journal of Experimental Psychology*, 1962, *63*, 519–520.

James, W., & Rotter, J. B. Partial and one hundred percent reinforcement under chance and skill conditions. *Journal of Experimental Psychology*, 1958, *55*, 397–403.

7

The Growth and Extinction of Expectancies in Chance Controlled and Skilled Tasks

A series of previous studies (Phares, 1957, James & Rotter, 1958, James, 1957) have shown that the growth and extinction of verbalized expectancies for reinforcement are affected by the nature of the task. More specifically, whether or not human Ss see success in a task as being determined or controlled by chance, random or other factors beyond their control, or see the reinforcement in the situation as an outcome of their own characteristics or skills, appears to have systematic effects on changes in their expectations for future reinforcements. The distinction may be an extremely significant one for learning theory, since it appears that many of the paradigms (such as conditioning, verbal conditioning and probability learning) that are applied to human learning are based partially or entirely on the chance, luck or experimenter controlled situation. However, the behavioral situations to which these models may be applied typically involve mature humans performing in skill tasks.

Differences in learning in two kinds of situations are not solely a

Rotter, Julian B., Liverant, S. & Crowne, D. P. The growth and extinction of expectancies in chance controlled and skilled tasks. *Journal of Psychology*, 1961, 52, 161–177. Reprinted by permission.

Received in the Editorial Office on April 5, 1961, and published immediately at Provincetown, Massachusetts. Copyright by The Journal Press.

This research was supported in whole by the United States Air Force under Contract No. AF 49 (638)-741 monitored by the Air Force Office of Scientific Research of the Air Research and Development Command.

We should like to gratefully acknowledge the assistance of Miss Alice Gordon, Miss Bonnie Strickland and Miss Yvonne Johnson in testing subjects and collating data for this investigation.

matter of degree. The James and Rotter (1958) study indicated a reversal in the rate of extinction of verbalized expectancies under conditions of 50 per cent and 100 per cent reinforcement when the same task was described to the subjects as a skill task, or as a luck task.

Two questions have been raised about these results. One question concerns whether or not the findings are limited to verbalized expectancies and the other deals with the problem of whether or not the findings are in effect the result of the instructions and could not be systematically duplicated by studying the nature of individual tasks. Holden (1960) has recently completed a study using betting behavior rather than verbalized expectancies. Extinction was considered to have occurred when S was no longer willing to bet on his success. His results replicated the study of James and Rotter in regard to 50 per cent reinforcement and demonstrated that the differences between skill and chance are not limited to measures of verbalized expectancies.

The present study is concerned with a more thorough investigation of the skill-chance dimension as regards both the growth and extinction of expectancies under four different reinforcement schedules. In this study the differences hypothesized in the growth and reduction of verbalized expectancies are based on the nature of the task itself rather than instructions or statements by the experimenter regarding the task.

The studies referred to earlier have taken their point of departure from social learning theory (Rotter, 1954). In this theory, it is assumed that the situation produces or is composed of cues to which the subject has attached expectancies on the basis of previous experience. These are expectancies that specific behaviors will lead to specific consequences or reinforcements. The expectancies themselves are determined by the past history of reinforcement with those same cues, and generalized expectancies which may relate either to the nature of the behaviors involved, the reinforcements, the nature of the cues, or all three. Generalized expectancies for specific kinds of behaviors leading to similar reinforcements are described by the concept of freedom of movement. Some generalized expectancies, however, cut across specific kinds of reinforcements and have to deal with what might broadly be called problem solving skills or perhaps what Harlow (1949) has referred to as higher level learning skills. Such generalized expectancies might include, for example expectancies related to concepts of causality, delay of gratification, the consequences of trial and error behavior, looking for alternatives, etc. There is some evidence to support the notion (Rotter, Seeman & Liverant, 1961) that such a generalized expectancy is present in adult subjects in regard to the implications for the future occurrence of reinforcements which appear to result as a function of their own stable characteristics versus chance.

It should follow from the above assumptions that in a given task if S regards the task as being more controlled by luck or chance he is likely to "learn" less about future behavior-reinforcement sequences from the occurrence of the reinforcement following the behavior. In other words, his expectancies for future reinforcement are likely to change less when he regards the occurrence of the reinforcement to be beyond his control. It was hypothesized, then, that if a subject regards success in a particular task as determined by luck, chance or external control his expectancies for future positive reinforcement would, (1) rise less after positive reinforcement, (2) fall less after negative reinforcement, (3) be more subject to the gambler's fallacy (the occurrence of a negative reinforcement increases the probability of a subsequent positive reinforcement or vice versa) and (4) in an extinction series (continuous negative reinforcement) would be slower to extinguish as a consequence of (2) and (3). In the case of 100 per cent or near 100 per cent reinforcement the individual who regards the reinforcement as dependent upon some kind of external control would assume early in the extinction trials either that luck had turned against him or that the experimenter was no longer rewarding the same behavior.

On the other hand, a subject who regarded reinforcement as a function of his own skill would extinguish more slowly under 100 per cent reinforcement than under partial reinforcement because it would take him longer to accept the fact that his presumably stable skills had diminished. He is not anticipating external changes in the situation which will account for failure. The present study is designed to provide one or more tests of all these hypotheses.

A. SELECTION OF TASKS

In order to test these hypotheses, we needed to find one task that Ss in a given culture would regard as being primarily luck or chance determined, and one in which the subject would feel that his performance was primarily a matter of skill. The two tasks at least had to be discriminable on a continuum of skill versus chance control. The design produced some difficult requirements. In order to make the two tasks comparable the same series of reinforcements during an acquisition or growth of expectancy phase would have to be presented. Consequently, both tasks must be controlled by E, but in one case S should believe that performance is a matter of his own skill and in the other that it is a matter of luck. In the extinction phase it would be necessary for S, under one condition, to change from 100 per cent success trials to no success without being suspicious that E was, in fact, controlling the task.

A number of tasks were tried out in an attempt to meet these conditions and finally tasks were found for female Ss which appeared to work with a minimum of suspicion of experimenter control.

The task selected as a skill controlled or internally controlled task was adapted from Cromwell's (1959) modification of Sky's (1950) apparatus. We will refer to it here as the Vertical Aspiration Board. The apparatus is shown in Figure 7.1. In this task the subject is asked to pull on a string connected with a platform on which a steel-bearing ½" in diameter is placed. The subject is required to lift the platform smoothly to a specified height before the ball rolls off. The ball itself is held on the platform by an electromagnet which can be switched on and off by a silent knee switch underneath the table. Since the platform itself slopes forward, the ball falls off instantaneously after the current is cut off by the knee switch. Complete control of scores is thus obtainable. The apparatus is constructed so that there are no wires in evidence, the current being supplied to the moving platform via contact with a strip of copper not visible to the subject. The current is supplied by a dry cell hidden in a false bottom on the table. A detailed description of the apparatus may be obtained from the authors.

The chance or luck task is similar to the one used by James & Rotter (1958) in their previous report. The subject is shown a number of stacks of five cards with X's and O's on them. His problem is to guess each card in a group and to obtain a better than chance (four or five) number of correct guesses in order to succeed. The cards are placed in a simple tachistoscope and immediately following each guess a window raises and the subject can see whether he is correct or not. However, none of the actual stacks of cards are used by the experimenter hidden behind the tachistoscope. Instead, a single card with an X and an O on it is moved back and forth silently before the window rises and immediately after the subject has stated his guess. With a little practice our experimenters carried this off so well that in our large group of subjects not a single one verbalized any suspicion that the experimenter was controlling his success in guessing. While it is true in this task that some subjects in some degree may have felt that a true ESP skill might be involved, our over-all assumption was that such a task for the group as a whole would be considered to be much more determined by chance, luck, or random factors than the task utilized as a skill task.

Figure 7.1 The vertical aspiration board

B. SUBJECTS

In pre-testing the skill tasks a number of the men expressed some suspiciousness, primarily in the 100 per cent reinforcement group. Consequently, it was decided to run this experiment entirely with female
Ss. The men who did express suspiciousness did not know what was
happening but felt that in some way the experimenter was controlling the outcome. The design called for eight groups or conditions
of twenty Ss each. All Ss were from the elementary psychology
courses at The Ohio State University where Ss are required to serve
in one or more experiments although they have a choice of the type
of the experiment in which they wish to participate.

C. DESIGN AND PROCEDURE

The 160 Ss were randomly assigned to eight groups. For each task
there was a 100 per cent, 75 per cent, 50 per cent, and 25 per cent
positively reinforced group. Positive reinforcement and failure are
defined herein as reaching or not reaching a criterion score. Each
group was given eight training trials and in each group the first and
last trial was positively reinforced. Following the training trials, extinction trials were instituted in which S continuously failed to
achieve the necessary standard on every trial. In summary the experimental design, shown in Table 7.1, was a two by four factorial for
which analysis of variance was employed to assess the dependent
variables.

If the S did not extinguish earlier the experiment was terminated
on the 50th extinction trial. In every case, after being shown the
task and explained what was required, each S stated on a scale of 0
through 10 his expectation of succeeding on the following trials.

Table 7.1 Experimental Design

Group		N	1	2	3	4	5	6	7	8	
						Training Trials					
25%	Chance	20	+	−	−	−	−	−	−	+	Extinction
25%	Skill	20	+	−	−	−	−	−	−	+	Extinction
50%	Chance	20	+	−	−	+	+	−	−	+	Extinction
50%	Skill	20	+	−	−	+	+	−	−	+	Extinction
75%	Chance	20	+	+	−	+	+	+	−	+	Extinction
75%	Skill	20	+	+	−	+	+	+	−	+	Extinction
100%	Chance	20	+	+	+	+	+	+	+	+	Extinction
100%	Skill	20	+	+	+	+	+	+	+	+	Extinction

These verbalized expectancies for success provide the data for this study. The criterion for extinction was two consecutive trials with a verbalized expectancy for success of 0 or 1. Instructions and the detailed procedure are given below.

1. Vertical Aspiration Board Instructions

This experiment is to see how well you can succeed in raising this ball without its falling off (demonstrate) and also to see how accurate you are in estimating your success.

The object of this task is for you to try by pulling this string to raise the ball on the platform as high as possible before the ball drops off. You will be given a number of trials. The apparatus is built with a very slight tilt forward so that the ball is more likely to fall off the platform the higher it is raised. Of course if you raise the platform very quickly the ball can't drop off because of the momentum, therefore the platform must be raised slowly. Now, in order to be clearly successful you must score 80 or better on a given trial.

Before each trial I would also like you to estimate how certain you are that you can succeed, i.e., get 80 or better. You are to estimate your degree of certainty of success on a scale going from 0 to 10. For example, if you feel fairly sure that you will succeed, that is, that you will get 80 or higher, you may rate yourself with a nine or ten. If you feel moderately sure that you will succeed you may rate yourself with a 4, 5, or 6. If you feel pretty sure you will *not* be successful, i.e., not get 80, you may rate yourself with a 0 or 1. Use any numbers on the scale (0, 1, 2, 3, 4, 5, 6, 7, 8, 9, 10) to indicate how successful or unsuccessful you think you will be. It is important that you select your estimates carefully on the 0 to 10 scale and that they correspond closely with how certain you *really* are. They should be an accurate description of the degree to which you really feel that you will or will not succeed.

Do you have any questions so far? All right——, do as well as you can. Now, before we begin, make an estimate on the scale from 0 to 10 as to what you think the likelihood is of your getting 80 or better on the first trial.

2. T Scope Instructions

This experiment is to see how well you can do at telling me beforehand which of two kinds of cards will be exposed in this opening (pointing) and also to see how accurate you are in estimating your success.

In this box (show box) we have a large number of cards marked with either an X or an O (show one of each). These cards are divided into sets of five. Each set has been *shuffled* and there are not necessarily the same number of X's and O's in each set. Each time I will select *at random* one of these sets of five cards and place it behind this closed shutter (point). (Remove box.) You are to tell me whether the top card is an X or an O. After you tell me, this shutter will open and you will know whether you were right or wrong. I will remove that card and the next card in the set will be in front of the closed shutter and again you will tell me whether it is an X or an O. In this way we will go through a number of these sets of 5 cards. I will also be keeping score and will let you know how well you did at the end of each trial, that is, at the end of a set of five cards.

Now in order to be successful on a trial you must get at least four or more cards right out of five. Four or five cards correct will mean that you have succeeded. Any number of cards correct below four will mean that you have *not* succeeded.

The remainder of the instructions are identical with those of the Vertical Aspiration Board.

D. RESULTS

1. Training

Our over-all hypothesis specified that when S perceives a task to be controlled by external forces he "learns" less from the occurrence of a reinforcement than if he perceives the reinforcement in a situation to be exclusively, or to a greater degree, a function of his own behavior and efforts. Four tests of this hypothesis were made on the training trial data.

The first test applied was the change in verbalized expectancies from the first to the second trial. All eight groups were positively reinforced on the first trial. At the beginning of the second trial, then, all the subjects were comparable in percentage of reinforcement and it was possible to compare the four skill task groups with the four task groups in the degree to which a positive reinforcement resulted in a rise in expectancy for the subsequent trial.

A second test of our over-all hypothesis was made by comparing the expectancies at the end of the training sequence. In this case, four separate comparisons were made between the 25 per cent, 50 per cent, 75 per cent, and 100 per cent skill and chance groups. If changes in expectancies were differential for the two tasks, cumulative effects of the eight training trials could best be shown at the beginning of the 9th trial.

The third test of differences in approach to learning in the two kinds of situations was a measure of unusual shifts, that is, shifts up after failure or down after success in the verbalized expectancy for future success. It was hypothesized that such shifts would be greater in a situation perceived as being controlled by external factors or chance.

A fourth test involved a more complicated measure. In this case we were interested in the extent to which the individual varied his expectancies as a function of his new experience in a manner consistent with the previous reinforcement. The measure which we will refer to as Total Amount of Change was then taken simply to include all of the appropriate shifts in expectancy which followed from the previous reinforcement. That is, the total amount or sum of relevant shifts or changes up after success and down after failure in verbalized expectancies was computed for each subject. In this measure, unusual shifts (see above) were excluded. These four tests of differences between skill and chance groups are obviously not independent.

The means and standard deviations for expectancy statements during the training trials are given in Table 7.2. In order to make

Table 7.2 Means and Standard Deviations of Expectancy Statements During the Training Trials

Group			1	2	3	4	5	6	7	8	9
			\multicolumn{9}{c}{*Training Trials*}								
25%	Chance	M	4.0	5.4	4.5	3.3	3.3	3.1	4.0	2.9	4.5
		SD	2.0	2.1	2.0	1.6	1.5	1.8	1.7	2.1	2.0
25%	Skill	M	4.0	7.8	7.2	6.0	4.6	4.3	4.4	3.5	5.8
		SD	2.1	1.7	1.6	1.9	2.4	2.6	2.2	2.1	2.0
50%	Chance	M	3.9	5.1	4.5	4.6	5.6	6.2	5.9	5.1	6.0
		SD	1.2	1.6	1.2	1.3	1.7	1.6	1.7	1.6	1.9
50%	Skill	M	3.5	7.3	6.7	5.3	7.6	7.5	7.1	6.3	7.4
		SD	1.6	1.6	1.4	1.7	1.3	1.6	1.4	1.5	1.2
75%	Chance	M	3.9	5.6	7.0	5.8	7.6	8.1	8.8	6.7	7.0
		SD	2.0	1.3	1.2	1.5	1.0	1.2	.9	1.4	1.5
75%	Skill	M	3.2	7.4	7.9	7.0	8.2	8.3	8.4	7.6	8.2
		SD	1.8	1.9	1.6	2.0	1.7	1.5	1.5	2.1	1.7
100%	Chance	M	3.8	5.6	6.7	7.5	8.4	8.7	8.8	9.0	9.0
		SD	2.0	1.8	1.8	2.0	1.6	1.7	1.5	1.4	1.5
100%	Skill	M	3.8	7.8	8.4	8.4	9.3	9.3	9.1	9.2	9.4
		SD	1.7	1.1	.9	1.0	.7	.7	.9	.8	.8

comparisons between groups for subsequent trials it is first necessary to demonstrate that there are no significant differences in initial means which might account for later differences. Consequently, an analysis of variance was made for the initial statements of expectancy for the eight groups. The over-all F was not significant for initial expectancies. As can be very clearly seen from Table 7.2, the amount of rise for Ss in the skill tasks for all four groups was considerably greater following the first positive reinforcement than for any of the chance groups. Here the analysis of variance was highly significant ($F = 69.91$; df = 1 & 152; $p = <.001$). The consistency of the differences between comparable groups is striking. It is clear that when faced with the tasks which most of them regarded as one involving skill to begin with, the first reinforcement led to a much sharper rise in expectancy for future success.

The analysis of variance for expectancies at the end of the training trials yielded a significant F for the difference between skill and chance groups and for reinforcement schedules. (Skill-Chance, $F = 17.11$; df 1 & 152; $p = <.001$) Reinforcement schedules, F $= 42.96$; df = 3 & 152; $p = < .001$.) In every case, higher expectancies were stated at the end of the training sequence for the skill groups than for the chance groups. These differences are significant for the 25 per cent ($p = < .05$), 50 per cent ($p = < .01$), and 75 per cent ($p = < .05$) reinforcement schedules but not for the 100 per cent groups where both groups were beginning to asymptote at the upper limit of the expectancy scales.

The number of unusual shifts in the eight groups were not subjected to analysis of variance and the hypothesis of difference was rejected on inspection. There were a total of 47 unusual shifts in the four skill groups and 46 in the four chance groups. Only 42 per cent of the subjects had one or more unusual shifts.

An analysis of variance was computed on the total amount of

Table 7.3 Analysis of Variance of Total Change in the Direction of Previous Reinforcement

Source	df	MS	F
Skill vs. Chance	1	117.30	6.69*
Reinforcement Schedules	3	114.62	6.54**
Skill vs. Chance ×			
Reinforcement Schedules	3	78.36	4.47**
Within (error)	152	17.53	
Total	159		

   * p < .02
   ** p < .01

change in the direction of the previous reinforcement which yielded, as shown in Table 7.3, a significant interaction.

Table 7.4 presents the means and standard deviations for the eight groups and the significance of the difference for the skill versus chance paradigms. Again it can be seen that there was more relevant changing of expectancies in all four skill groups than in the comparable chance-task groups. These differences are significant for the 25 per cent and 50 per cent groups, but not for the 75 per cent and 100 per cent groups where there was, in general, less shifting since more subjects reached an asymptote for their verbalized expectancies before the end of the training series.

2. Extinction

The major measure of the differences in learning in the two kinds of situations was the number of trials to extinction under continuous failure to achieve the specified level of performance. Figure 7.2

Table 7.4 Means, Standard Deviations, and Differences Between and Within Skill and Chance for the Amount of Change in the Direction of Previous Reinforcement

Group	N	Mean	SD	Difference	t
Between Skill and Chance					
25% Skill	20	11.95	4.55	4.55	3.44***
25% Chance	20	7.40	4.11		
50% Skill	20	11.10	4.37	3.35	2.53**
50% Chance	20	7.75	4.78		
75% Skill	20	9.10	5.44	1.70	1.28
75% Chance	20	10.80	4.41		
100% Skill	20	6.65	2.49	0.65	0.49
100% Chance	20	6.00	2.37		
Within Skill and Chance					
25%– 75% Skill				2.85	2.15**
50%– 75% Skill				2.00	1.51
50%–100% Skill				4.45	3.36***
75%–100% Skill				2.45	1.85*
75%– 25% Chance				3.40	2.57**
75%– 50% Chance				3.05	2.30**
75%–100% Chance				4.80	3.63***
50%–100% Chance				1.75	1.32

* p < .10
** p < .05
*** p < .01

shows the mean number of trials to the extinction criterion of 0 or
1 expectancy for two continuous trials for the four skill and four
chance groups. From Figure 7.2 and the analysis of variance given in
Table 7.5 it can be seen that a complete reversal takes place in trials
to extinction for skill versus chance groups. Neither the skill-chance
dimension itself or the reinforcement schedule is significant alone,
but the interaction between reinforcement schedule and the skill
chance variable is highly significant. Homogeneity of variance was
established by the F Max test (Walker & Lev, 1953).

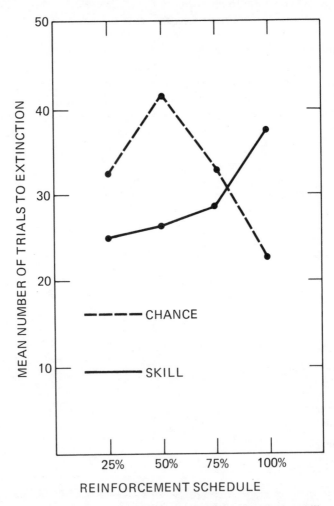

Figure 7.2 Mean number of trials to extinction for skill
and chance groups under the four reinforcement schedules

Table 7.5 Analysis of Variance of Trials to Extinction

Source	df	MS	F
Skill vs. Chance	1	409.60	1.41
Reinforcement Schedules	3	214.30	0.74
Skill vs. Chance X Reinforcement Schedules	3	1835.03	6.30*
Within (error)	152	291.06	
Total	159		

* p < .001

Table 7.6 presents the significance of the differences of the means of standard deviations and significance of the differences between comparable groups for the eight conditions. It can be seen from Table 7.6 that not only does the reversal between 50 per cent and 100 per cent or partial and continuous reinforcement take place but the differences between comparable chance and skill groups are significant at both the 50 per cent and 100 per cent levels. Under skill conditions the number of trials to extinction rises with increased

Table 7.6 Means, Standard Deviations, and Differences Between and Within Skill and Chance for the Number of Trials to Extinction

Group	N	Mean Trials	SD	Difference	t
Between Skill and Chance					
25% Skill	20	24.60	19.64		
25% Chance	20	32.60	19.12	8.00	1.48
50% Skill	20	26.30	13.65		
50% Chance	20	42.05	16.97	15.75	2.92***
75% Skill	20	28.10	17.06		
75% Chance	20	33.10	17.71	5.00	0.93
100% Skill	20	38.70	16.00		
100% Chance	20	22.75	15.56	15.95	2.95***
Within Skill and Chance					
100%– 75% Skill				10.60	1.96*
100%– 50% Skill				12.40	2.30**
100%– 25% Skill				14.10	2.61**
50%– 25% Chance				9.45	1.75*
50%– 75% Chance				8.95	1.66
50%–100% Chance				19.30	3.58***
75%–100% Chance				10.35	1.92*

* p < .10
** p < .05
*** p < .01

reinforcement in the training sequence. Under chance conditions, extinction is protracted at the 50 per cent level and, relative to all other groups, quite short at the 100 per cent level.

E. DISCUSSION

Although the number of training trials was relatively short, major differences appeared between the groups tested on the skill apparatus and on the chance apparatus. These differences must be attributed to the ways the groups perceived the two tasks as a function of common cultural experience. The considerably greater rise for the four skill groups following the first positive reinforcement makes sense in line with our original hypothesis that the subject will change his expectancies for future reinforcement to a larger extent if he attributes the occurrence of this reinforcement to some permanent characteristic of himself, such as a skill.

The second test involving expectancies at the end of the training sequence likewise showed differences in the same direction between all of the comparable reinforcement schedule groups. It is clear enough why this should be true of the 75 per cent and 100 per cent groups, but not equally clear of why it would be true of the 25 per cent and 50 per cent groups. The 25 per cent group in particular, under skill conditions, should not have been expected to rise to an expectancy level so much higher than the actual frequency of previous reinforcement. It seems likely that the best explanation for this rise is that in all the skill groups with the exception of the 100 per cent group (in which some people typically asymptote at an expectancy level of nine presumably not being willing to state the highest possible expectancy), that an overestimation took place as a result of previous experience with skill tasks. A level of aspiration study by Sutcliffe (1956) in which he compares skill and guessing random events gives strong support to this interpretation. In other words, if the subject perceived the task as one of skill, he habitually expected to do better as a function of practice on subsequent trials. Having succeeded once he anticipates he can do it again because he possesses the necessary skill. Although there may be other explanations for these findings, this appears to be the most logical alternative.

The failure to find differences in unusual shifts in the chance versus the skill groups cannot readily be explained. Phares (1957), using 13 trials and a single task, in which instructions differentiated his chance from his skill groups, was able to find a difference approaching significance ($p = .07$). It appears that for the tendency to commit the gambler's fallacy, at least in regards to this measure of unusual shifts, verbally designating a task as being controlled by skill or by luck appears to be a more effective method of producing differences than taking two tasks differentiated on the basis of presumed common cultural experiences.

The fourth test of total changes in verbalized expectancies in the two comparable groups yielded results as predicted. What this difference between skill and chance groups indicates is that under skill conditions subjects lower their expectancies more after failure and raise them more after success over all the eight trials. In other words, past reinforcement is a clearer cue to future reinforcement when the subject believes that his own skill determines outcome.

One of the more interesting aspects of the extinction data is that differences between chance and skill groups is much smaller at 25 per cent and 75 per cent reinforcement schedules than at 50 per cent and 100 per cent. One hypothesis to account for this finding is that the 25 per cent and 75 per cent group in the chance task were being rewarded or reinforced less or more often than could be accounted for by chance alone. The frequency of reinforcement itself may tend to make the task appear more like a skill task. In a recent dissertation, Blackman (1960) was able to demonstrate that non-obvious patterning of reinforcements apparently affected the perception of a task as skill or chance controlled. The greatest difference among the partially reinforced groups is at the 50 per cent level where an even distribution of successes and failures in the chance task might enhance the notion that the task is in fact being controlled by luck. This does not account, of course, for the fact that the 100 per cent chance group would not also see the task as skill controlled because of the high frequency of reinforcement. Our hypothesis here is that the nature of the task is such that although the subjects may tend to eventually regard the task as skill determined during the training trials, the non-occurrence of the reinforcement in the first few trials of extinction quickly strengthens the original notion that it is a luck task or one subject to external control. That is, they quickly hypothesize that the experimenter has, in fact, changed something about the task or that the early successes were in fact a matter of luck which has run out. Such an explanation invokes two different principles to account for the differences between chance and skill groups. Although this explanation is not parsimonious it has at least the virtue of fitting the data.

F. SUMMARY AND CONCLUSIONS

Previous studies by Phares (1957), James and Rotter (1958), and James (1957), have demonstrated that major differences in the growth and extinction of verbal expectancies take place when a task is perceived as one being controlled by chance or luck versus being controlled by skill or internal factors. That is, these differences obtain when S anticipates that reinforcement occurs as a function of something external to himself in contrast to his belief that reinforcement is a function of his own behavior. Obviously, tasks could differ along this dimension in degree as well as kind. These previous studies suggest that the differences in behavior in the two kinds of tasks are not merely a matter of degree but, in fact, different principles of learning apply. This is shown particularly in the reversal of partial versus 100 per cent reinforcement conditions in the chance versus skill groups, with the typical finding (Lewis, 1960) of superiority of resistance to extinction in the partially reinforced condition found only in the externally controlled or chance task. Such findings are of considerable importance both in learning theory and in the application of learning principles to a complex life situation.

However, the findings described above were all based on the use of a single task or tasks in which the difference between chance control and internal control was established by differential instructions. In the present study an attempt was made to study the differences in the growth and extinction of expectancies using two different tasks which we hypothesized would be regarded as skill and chance controlled tasks on the basis of the previous cultural experience of the subjects, rather than by instructions. Eight groups of subjects were studied with an apparatus involving a motor skill of steadiness and one of guessing cards. For each task a group of 20 subjects were given 25 per cent positive reinforcement, 50 per cent positive reinforcement, 75 per cent positive reinforcement, and 100 per cent positive reinforcement, for eight training trials. On nonreinforced trials the subject failed to achieve a criterion score. Following this all groups were given continuous failure until they extinguished by stating expectancies for future success of 1 or 0 for two consecutive trials.

The general hypothesis tested was that under chance conditions the occurrence of reinforcement leads to less learning in that previous experience is a less stable predicter of the future occurrence of the event. In general, the results strongly supported the two hypotheses. First, that under skill conditions positive and negative reinforcement leads to greater increments and decrements in verbalized expectancies. Second, that the extinction of expectancies under continuous negative reinforcement will reverse under chance and skill conditions so that 50 per cent is more resistant to extinction than 100 per cent reinforcement under chance conditions, and 100 per cent reinforcement is more resistant to extinction than 50 per cent reinforcement under skill conditions.

REFERENCES

Blackman, S. Some factors affecting perception of events as chance determined. Unpublished doctoral dissertation. The Ohio State University, 1960.

Cromwell, R. A methodological approach to personality research in mental retardation. *Amer. J. Ment. Defic.*, 1959, **64**, 333–340.

Harlow, H. F. The formation of learning sets. *Psychol. Rev.*, 1949, **56**, 51–65.

Holden, K. B. A non-verbal measure of differences in extinction in skill and chance interactions. Unpublished doctoral dissertation, The Ohio State University, 1960.

James, W. H. Internal versus external control of reinforcement as a basic variable in learning theory. Unpublished doctoral dissertation. The Ohio State University, 1957.

James, W. H., & Rotter, J. B. Partial and one hundred per cent reinforcement under chance and skill conditions. *J. Exp. Psychol.*, 1958, **55**, 397–403.

Lewis, D. J. Partial Reinforcement: A selective review of the literature since 1950. *Psychol. Bull.*, 1960, **57**, 1–28.

Phares, E. J. Expectancy changes in skill and chance situations. *J. Abnorm. Soc. Psychol.*, 1957, **54**, 339–342.

Rotter, J. B. Social Learning and Clinical Psychology, New York: Prentice-Hall, 1954.

Rotter, J. B., Seeman, Mr. R., & Liverant, S. Internal versus external control of reinforcement: A major variable in behavior theory. In (N. F. Washburne, Ed.) Decisions, Values and Groups, Vol. 2., London: Pergamon Press, 1961.

Sky, A. W. An apparatus for a frustration task. *Australian J. Psychol.*, 1950, **2**, 116–120.

Sutcliffe, J. P. Random events as a function of belief in control. *Australian J. Psychol.*, 1956, **8**, 128–139.

Walker, H. M., & Lev, J. Statistical Inference. New York: Henry Holt, 1953.

Commentary to Chapter 8

The 1954 book (Social Learning and Clinical Psychology) included two chapters on psychotherapy. They were organized around a SLT analysis of current practices in psychotherapy, such as making interpretations, offering assurances, showing acceptance, suggesting alternative behaviors, and so forth. These chapters also included some recommendations for efficient practice of psychotherapy and comments on what seemed to be inefficient practices from an SLT point of view.

 Changes in behavior or ideation can occur in many different ways; a simple, cookbook approach to psychotherapy is actually antagonistic to this theory, which stresses that, even when one is dealing with patients showing similar symptom patterns, individual differences need to be considered in order to work out effective treatment plans. Nevertheless, there has been a constant pressure to provide more structure for people who wanted to apply SLT to the problems of psychotherapy. The following paper was written with that purpose in mind, although it still does not come close to providing any simplified approach to psychotherapy.

 A word should be said about the detailed inclusion of my own ethical values as applied to the psychotherapy interaction. Many promoters of specific therapeutic approaches leave such value statements implicit; others present their own values disguised as "facts" of human nature. SLT is a theory about learned behavior—not good behavior or bad behavior or adjusted or maladjusted behavior. To apply such a theory to psychotherapeutic practice, one must make an explicit statement of one's values. Therapists with different values would go about applying this or any other theory in different ways.

 This paper was originally published in 1970. Since then, two brief papers have been published on psychotherapy practice. One is a series of brief comments in a comparative study done by Marvin Goldfried (Rotter, 1980). The other provides a more detailed approach to teaching problem solving skills in psychotherapy (Rotter, 1978).

REFERENCES

Rotter, J. B. Generalized expectancies for problem solving and psychotherapy. *Cognitive Therapy and Research,* 1978, *2,* 1–10.

Rotter, J. B. Some views on effective principles of psychotherapy. In M. R. Goldfried (Ed.), Special issue: Psychotherapy process. *Cognitive Therapy and Research,* 1980, *4,* 271–306.

8

Some Implications of a Social Learning Theory for the Practice of Psychotherapy

The problems of psychotherapy may be viewed as problems in how to effect changes in behavior through the interaction of one person with another. That is, they are problems in human learning in a social situation or context. In spite of this, there has been until recently relatively little application of formal learning theory and of laboratory research on human learning to the techniques of psychotherapy. Where learning theory has been used at all, it frequently has been applied in one of two ways. The first of these is as a justification for therapeutic procedures developed from other theoretical approaches rather than as a basis for deriving new methods and techniques. This approach frequently fails to make use of the implications of a considerable body of knowledge regarding human learning but rather selects particular principles to justify favorite therapeutic procedures. The second approach follows a restricted conditioning model that is limited in the kinds of problems to which it can be applied and which frequently fails to take into account much of what the individual has already learned when he comes to therapy. It fails to recognize that the complex attitudes, goals, skills and behaviors of the individual significantly affect what he will learn and under what conditions he will learn most efficiently. In such an approach the ab-

Rotter, Julian B. Some implications of a social learning theory for the practice of psychotherapy. In D. Levis (Ed.), *Learning approaches to therapeutic behavior change*. Chicago: Aldine, 1970. Reprinted by permission.

I am grateful to Miss Dorothy Hochreich for her helpful suggestions in the preparation of this manuscript.

sence of functional content variables for stable human behavior, that is a personality theory, often reduces the efficiency of therapy because of failure to understand the gradients of generalization of behavior changes and to understand the nature of "hidden" reinforcements which strengthen an apparent maladaptive response.

This failure to fully apply learning theory can be explained in part because many individuals involved in studying complex *human* learning as a general area of investigation are not concerned with the application of their findings to psychotherapeutic practice. A more serious barrier to application, however, is that there is too great a disparity between the kind of laboratory situations in which human learning is typically studied and the complex social interactions which characterize psychotherapy.

The gap between theory and laboratory research, and the prediction of behavior in complex social interactions is a great one and cannot be closed by a single leap. The purpose of this paper, however, is to lessen that hiatus somewhat by illustrating some implications of one social learning theory for the practice of psychotherapy, as specifically as the present state of the theory and research allows. Since no special laws are assumed that are peculiar to psychotherapeutic interactions many of the hypotheses generated here regarding psychotherapeutic change would apply equally to effecting social change.

In order to derive either implications or predictions from a behavior theory to the problem of psychotherapy, one must have available a theory suitable to the complex phenomena concerned and sufficiently developed that at least all of the major variables and their relationships are known and measurable, so that prediction can be made or control exercised. Second, one must know the dimensions along which behaviors may be categorized, generalizations predicted, etc. In other words, one must have integrated with such a learning theory, a content theory (sometimes called a personality theory) which presumes to have abstracted from such social interactions the relevant aspects of behavior into functional categories (i.e., needs, traits, habit families, etc.). There must be a useful descriptive terminology to characterize the generalized aspects of behavior as well as a theory which describes the process of change.

Behavior theories vary in the degree to which they fit this ideal. The degree to which they deviate may account for the apparent minimum connection between the theories of personality and/or learning and the psychotherapeutic methods which presumably derive from them. For example, both Kelly (1955) and Rogers (1951) have in common a phenomenological theory with many points of similarity. Yet the implications each sees from theory to psychotherapeutic practice are so different that in many instances they would have to be placed at opposite ends of a set of continua used to describe therapeutic techniques. A bewildering variety of practices have been advocated by therapists who justify them as stemming from something they all refer to as "psychoanalytic theory" (Rotter, 1960). Similarly, Wolpe, among learning theorists, (1958) describes a learning and neurophysiological theory of behavior of Hullian origin and goes on to advocate therapeutic practices which have only a loose connection with his theory and appear opposed in many major ways to Dollard and Miller's (1950) application of presumably the same theory. Although awareness of this problem has led to an attempt to exercise caution in drawing implications from theory to practice in this paper, it should be stated at the outset that these implications are also loose and although they seem logical to the author, they may well not be so perceived by others.

There is a second difficulty in the drawing of specific implications from a personality theory for the problem of psychotherapeutic practice or of social change. An adequate theory of behavior may explain how changes take place or how to achieve the control of some behaviors, but a scientific theory does not specify what kinds of changes are good or bad from the point of view of social or ethical values. What constitute adequate goals for psychotherapy or social change and what constitute ethical means of achieving these goals is not a part of a scientific theory but of a value system. (That is, a set of judgments dealing with what is good and what is bad.) Different value systems utilizing the same theory might well lead to very different methods of practice. When one advocates a specific method of psychotherapy, one has explicitly or implicitly made a commitment to a specifiable set of values. For example, such a commitment might take the form that the therapist is ethically justified in helping the patient arrive at a better understanding of himself but should assiduously avoid affecting in any other way the kinds of changes that may take place in the patient's goals or behavior. Whether or not this is possible is a matter of controversy. However, it is clear that the methods that such a therapist would use would be quite different than those of another therapist, operating with the same theory, who explicitly states that the goal of psychotherapy is to increase the patient's capacity to love others. It is because of this latter point that it seems necessary to emphasize that the applications of social learning theory to follow have to be regarded as only one set of possible techniques.

Since social learning theory has not reached the stage where it is possible to make completely unambiguous deductions to specific complex social phenomena, it is not always possible to talk about implications at a highly specific level. The purpose of this paper is to illustrate at some middle level of generality one possible application of social learning theory to psychotherapy for a particular set of values. The intention is to apply a complex learning theory of personality as directly as possible to the problems of psychotherapy, rather than to use learning principles as post-hoc explanations of techniques derived from other points of view. The goal is to not only apply the abstract processes of learning to psychotherapy but also to take into account what the individual has already learned in order to determine what kinds of change will be most beneficial to him and under what circumstances he can learn most effectively. Before proceeding, it is necessary to indicate what value commitments are involved in the illustrative application that follows.

SOCIAL VALUES IN PSYCHOTHERAPY

Briefly stated, there are three implicit or explicit general positions that psychotherapists take in regard to the goals of treatment. Particular therapists may combine these goals in a variety of ways.

The first of these goals is one of conformity or normalcy as the ideal outcome of treatment. From this point of view the object of treatment is to help the person change so that he is more like other people, particularly in regard to any characteristics which are considered to be detrimental to himself or others. A special case of this orientation is the disease approach which considers that the patient's difficulty is characterized by certain symptoms. The descriptions of these illnesses are to be found in textbooks. As in medicine, the purpose of treatment is to eliminate the illness as evidenced by the reduction of symptoms.

The second general goal might be called one of subjective happiness. The purpose of treatment is to help the patient reach a state of greater happiness or comfort or pleasure. The emphasis is on internal feelings, resolution of internal conflict, acceptance of self, etc.

The third value orientation in psychotherapy might be called the socially constructive one. Here the goals of psychotherapy are seen as helping the patient to lead a more constructive life, to contribute to society, to maximize his potential for achievement, to maximize his feeling of affection or contribution to others.

It is a combination of the last two which forms the ethical or

value background for the general suggestions regarding psychotherapy which follow. Briefly and more specifically, the following
value commitments are made:

1. The therapist understands that his behavior has a definite effect
on the patient, not only in regard to the patient's self-understanding,
but also his behaviors, his specific goals, and his ethical judgments.
The therapist is willing to accept *some* of the responsibility for these
changes and to attempt to direct or control them.

2. The therapist seeks to provide the patient with a greater potential for satisfaction. That is, the therapist seeks to direct the
patient's behavior to goals which the patient values or which provide
him with satisfaction within the limitations expressed below.

3. The therapist seeks to eliminate, or to keep the patient from
acquiring behaviors or goals which he feels are *clearly* detrimental to
others in society.

4. The therapist believes that the patient should "carry his own
weight" in society, at least to the extent that he makes some contribution to the welfare of others in return for the satisfactions he receives from others.

Applying such values to the particular patient is obviously not a
cut and dried affair but will depend on the judgment of the therapist.
It should be emphasized again that these are only the values of one
person. They do not follow from social learning theory nor are they
part of it, but it is necessary to have some explicit set of values before application of any theory to the practice of psychotherapy can
be logically considered.

BASIC TERMS IN SOCIAL LEARNING THEORY

It is not possible to present all of the theoretical concepts relevant
to the problem of psychotherapy. In one way social learning theory
is a far more complex personality theory than most and requires the
analysis of four variables in order to make a prediction, where many
theories require only one or two. In some theories explanation and
prediction is based on identifying a strongest trait or internal characteristic of the individual or the conflict between two traits. It is possible in a brief paper such as this to give only a rather disjointed
account, hoping that this will provide at least the flavor of a more
systematic and comprehensive exposition.

Social learning theory may be briefly characterized as an expectancy learning theory which utilizes an empirical law of effect. In

this theory (Rotter, 1954) the basic formula for the prediction of goal directed behavior is as follows:

$$1.\ \text{B.P.}_{x,s_1 R_a} = f(E_{x,R_9 s_1} \ \& \ RV_{a,s_1}).$$

The formula may be read: The potential for behavior x to occur in situation 1 in relation to reinforcement a is a function of the expectancy of the occurrence of reinforcement a following behavior x in situation 1, and the value of reinforcement a in situation 1. It is assumed that expectancies can be measured along a continuum. Such a formula, however, is extremely limited in application for it deals only with the potential for a given behavior to occur in relationship to a single specific reinforcement. Practical clinical application requires a more generalized concept of behavior and the formula for these broader concepts is given below:

$$2.\ \text{B.P.}_{(x-n),s(1-n),R(a-n)} = f(E_{(x-n),s(1-n),R(a-n)}$$
$$\& \ R.V._{(a-n),s(1-n)}).$$

This may be read: The potentiality of the functionally related behaviors x to n to occur in the specified situations 1 to n in relation to potential reinforcements a to n is a function of the expectancies of these behaviors leading to these reinforcements in these situations and the values of these reinforcements in these situations. For purposes of simplicity of communication, the three basic terms in this formula have been typically referred to as need potential, freedom of movement and need value as in the third formula below:

$$3.\ \text{N.P.} = f(\text{F.M.} \ \& \ \text{N.V.})$$

In this formula the fourth concept, that of the psychological situation, is implicit. Some of the content variables of this theory are empirically determined needs, arrived at by grouping behaviors which have some functional relationship on the basis of their leading to the same or similar reinforcements. The generality or breadth of such concepts depend on one's purpose. For example, at a very general level we may use terms such as need for recognition and status, need for love and affection, need for dependence, need for independence, need for dominance and need for physical comfort. At a more specific level typical concepts might be need for academic recognition, need for aggression towards authority figures, need for love and affection from the same sex peers, etc. The basis for such groupings derives not from presumed instincts or drives but is empirically deter-mined and follows from the learning experience of the individuals of a given culture.

The variables referred to above and operations for measurement have been defined and further explicated in previous publications (Rotter, 1954, 1955, 1967a, 1967b).

SOME MAJOR HYPOTHESES AND
THEIR IMPLICATIONS

In psychotherapy we are usually concerned with classes of behaviors or more general characteristics. Consequently, this paper will deal primarily with the formula that *need potential* is a function of *freedom of movement* and *need value* for a particular class of situations. A crucial part of this theory for the problem of psychotherapy is that there are specific hypotheses regarding the behavior of an indi-vidual with low freedom of movement and high need value for a particular class of satisfactions. When such an individual has low freedom of movement and places high value on some class of rein-forcements, he is likely to learn behaviors to avoid the failure or punishments that he anticipates in this area and may make attempts to achieve these goals on an irreal level. The person anticipating punishment or failure may avoid situations physically or by repres-sion or may attempt to reach the goals through rationalization, fantasy or symbolic means. Most of the great variety of behaviors commonly regarded as defenses or psychopathological symptoms are here referred to as avoidance or irreal behaviors. Such avoidance and irreal behaviors themselves may frequently start a vicious cycle and lead to both immediate and delayed additional negative reinforce-ments. Expectancies for punishment may give rise to a number of implicit behaviors, thoughts or cognitions, that can be observed only indirectly. Such implicit behaviors might include awareness of dis-turbed body states, fixation on the punishment, narrowing the field of attention, rehearsal of obsessive thoughts, etc., which can seri-ously interfere with constructive behavior or problem solution. In other words, frequently at the bottom of a problem involving either lack of feeling of satisfaction, conflict, anticipation of punishment, irreal behavior, or lack of constructive activity, is a condition of low freedom of movement and high need value.

Low freedom of movement may result from the patient's lack of knowledge or ability to acquire adequate behaviors to reach his goals or may be a consequence of the nature of the goal itself (such as the desire to have others take all responsibility for one's actions) which frequently results in strong punishments in a specific society. Low freedom of movement may also result from "mistaken" evaluations of the present as a consequence of early experience. For a given person sometimes the behaviors, sometimes "erroneous" expectations, and sometimes the nature of the person's goals may be considered to be the primary source of difficulty.

An important aspect of the problem of low freedom of movement concerns the concept of minimal goal level in social learning theory. In any given situation the possible outcomes of behavior can be ordered from a very high positive reinforcement or goal to a very high negative reinforcement or goal. The theoretical point at which, in this ordering, the outcome changes from one which is positive or reinforcing to negative or punishing is called the minimal goal level. Such a concept can be applied either to a series of goals that are functionally related, e.g., all achievement goals, or to any combination of outcomes possible in a given situation or set of situations. An individual may have low freedom of movement although from the viewpoint of others he appears to succeed often because his reinforcements usually are below his own minimal goal level. Such internalized high minimal goals are frequently involved in problems of low freedom of movement. It should be stressed at this point that the goals referred to can be of any kind: moral, ethical, achievement, sexual, affectional, dominating, dependent, etc. In social learning theory any functionally related set of reinforcements toward which the individual moves is considered the basis for assuming a need and for which a need potential, freedom of movement, and need value can be determined.

In order to increase the patient's freedom of movement for goals he values highly, one possible approach is to change the values of the goals themselves. This might be necessary under conditions in which the person has two or more goals of high value but of such nature that the satisfaction of one involves the frustration of the other, as in the case of individuals with strong desires for masculinity and dependency satisfactions in the same situations. Another instance would be one in which the goals of the patient, such as the desire to control and dominate others, lead to conflict with others' needs and eventuates in both immediate and delayed punishment. A third instance of changing the value of goals would involve the lowering of minimal goals when they are unrealistically high, such as in the case of an individual who regards any indication of fear in himself as proof that he is not sufficiently masculine.

To understand how minimal goal levels can be changed, one has to consider how reinforcement values, or the values attached to reinforcement, are acquired, maintained, or changed. In social learning theory, the value of reinforcement in a given situation is hypothesized to be a function of the expectancy that the reinforcement will lead to subsequent reinforcements, and the value of those subsequent reinforcements as in the formula below:

$$4. \ R.V._{a,s_1} = f(E_{R_a} \rightarrow R_{(b-n),s_1} \ \& \ R.V._{(b-n),s_1})$$

If a child believes that when he gets an "A" in school it will lead to affection, then the value of the "A" is dependent upon the value of the affection and the expectancy that the affection will be forthcoming. If he feels that a "B" will lead to rejection, a similar analysis holds. For most goals each reinforcement is related to several consequent reinforcements rather than one.

The problem in changing minimal goals, then, or in changing the value of any goal or set of goals, is frequently one of changing expectancies for subsequent reinforcement. Adler (1939) has long emphasized the importance of discussing life goals with the patient in order to change immediate goals and behaviors. Many times the values of goals are maintained over a long period of time with the expectancy for subsequent reward relatively stable because the relationships have not been verbalized and the subject is not aware of them. In many instances delayed negative reinforcement follows from achieving an earlier reward but the subject fails to relate these to the prior goal. For example, a woman seeking to control her husband fails to recognize that the consequences of her behavior and her successful attempts at control, although bringing immediate gratification, also lead to subsequent negative reinforcements because of the hostility or rejection on the part of the husband. In other words, the value of goals can be changed sometimes by examining the early rewards with which they were associated but which may no longer be operating, and also by analysis of present and future consequences which the person has never associated directly with the goal.

One implication of such an analysis is that insight into the acquisition of particular goals may be helpful in changing their values if the subject sees that expectancies for subsequent reinforcements have changed since the time of acquisition or were mistaken in the first place. Such a conception is not different from any other insight type of therapy. However, a further implication is that it may be of equal importance to analyze also the consequences of present behaviors and goals which are frequently delayed but nevertheless result from the behaviors the individual uses or reinforcements which he seeks. It is frequently important not only to discover why it is, for example, that one seeks to demonstrate superiority over members of the opposite sex in terms of early experience but also important to discover what are the present and long term consequences of such goals and of the behaviors used to achieve them.

These comments deal with one method of changing freedom of movement or increasing freedom of movement by lowering minimal goals, or having the individual place greater value on alternative goals. There are other ways in which freedom of movement can be increased and presumably as a result both personal feelings of satisfaction as well as more constructive behavior will be increased. As Mowrer (1948) has pointed out in his discussion of the neurotic paradox, sometimes expectancy of punishment remains high because the individual fails to learn that what he fears is no longer realistic since he avoids the situation in which he can learn anything to the contrary. If his experience with competitive scholastic activity is such that it was negatively reinforcing as a child, he may never learn that he is capable of reaching satisfying goals in this area because he avoids involvement or competitive striving in situations involving academic or scholastic achievement. In this instance freedom of movement may be increased, sometimes by the therapist's own direct reinforcements, and by interpretation of how such an attitude came about and why it is no longer appropriate to present life situations. The emphasis here is on changing the expectancies directly and it may be possible not only to do this by the therapist's behavior and by interpretation but also by control, manipulation or use of other environmental influences. The studies on verbal conditioning (Krasner, 1958) suggest how important the role of the therapist may be as a direct reinforcer of behavior. Changes in the attitudes and behaviors of teachers, parents, spouses, supervisors, etc. may achieve the same effect as face to face therapy and in fact do so more effectively because they are not part of the temporary and artificial situation of the therapy room.

In some instances, although the patient's goals are realistic enough and appropriate enough for his social group and his expectancies are based accurately on present situations, the problem is one of having learned inadequate pathways to achieve these goals or perhaps of not having learned more effective methods of reaching his goals. Here the problem can be regarded as more pedagogical. The search for alternative ways of reaching goals must frequently be taught to the patient as a general technique of dealing with his problems and as a method of finding specific ways of achieving more satisfaction in current life situations.[1] The assumption that once the patient is free from some kind of internal disorganization, conflict, repression, etc. he will automatically be able to find adequate ways to reach his goals, does not appear useful to this writer. It is often precisely because the patient does not have alternate pathways that he frequently holds on to his less effective behavior in spite of insight into his situation. Frequently, the therapist then labels his failure to progress as due to "intellectual" but not "emotional" insight. Rather, the patient needs to know what the alternate pathways are and needs to have the experience of trying them out and finding them successful before he is willing to give up ineffective behaviors.

Although the warmth, understanding, interest and acceptance of the therapist are important in order to have the patient verbalize his problems and express himself freely, they also result in his becoming an important source of reinforcement for the patient in his present life circumstances. It should be noted that if the therapist is a powerful reinforcer for the patient, whether he is aware of it or not, then he should know a great deal about the life circumstances and the cultural milieu in which the patient lives. Only with such knowledge can he use his position as a reinforcer efficiently. To obtain this knowledge he must spend much time discussing these life situations. His independent knowledge of subcultures is an important aspect of his skill as a therapist.

Another pedagogical problem is frequently one of helping patients differentiate the nature of varied social situations. Low freedom of movement may not result so much from the use of·ineffective behaviors in general as from the use of behaviors inappropriate for a given situation. The kind of behavior which may be admired and respected and reinforced in a situation calling for efficiency and the solution of a specific task (for example, a combat team or a committee seeking to make some change in the community) may lead to rejection at a party or in a bedroom. Sometimes because of the distortions of parents or the limited or protective environment of childhood, a particular person fails to learn or to make these discriminations among social situations which are necessary for obtaining satisfactions. When placed in these circumstances in later life he falls back on the techniques he has learned in other situations which may in fact be quite inappropriate. Analysis of what actually transpires in social situations, how other people feel and think, what are the purposes for which particular interactions take place in a

---

[1] It can be seen here as in other discussions of implications that the value commitments described earlier are an implicit filter between theory and practice.

variety of present day life situations, may help the patient make these discriminations which he has failed to make in the past. The low freedom of movement one may have in regard to a particular need, such as the desire to have others take care of one, may be a result of attempts to satisfy such needs at inappropriate times. If the individual seeks to satisfy his needs by recognizing that social situations are varied, that the needs of others change from situation to situation, and that the potential reinforcements in some conditions can be seriously limited, he may be far better able to deal satisfactorily with life problems.

This notion might give the impression of advocating the training of the patient to be a kind of chameleon who changes his personality for every situation, to be, in other words, a conformist or opportunist. This is not at all the intent. The therapeutic goal here is one in which the patient recognizes the real differences that exist in the purposes of people in different situations and the purposes which these situations are intended to serve. For example, it is important for some patients to discover that although competitive behavior may be admired and rewarded in academic and job conditions it is neither admired nor rewarded in many social situations. Behavior appropriate for one situation is not appropriate for another although one may maintain the same set of consistent goals in both. Although one may always choose to value achievement in any situation, there are some circumstances in which rewards for competitive achievement are not only not possible but attempts to gain such satisfactions are likely to lead to frustration of the patient's other goals. What the patient may wish to do in these different circumstances is his problem to work out, but that he realizes that there are differences and discovers what these differences actually are, is something with which the therapist can help. *It is usually believed that what the patient lacks most is insight into himself but it is likely that in general what characterizes patients even more consistently is lack of insight into the reactions and motives of others.*

Another implication of social learning theory deserves brief mention. Consistent research in human learning indicates that when the subject is set to attend to the relevant aspects of a complex problem, his problem solving is much more efficient (Johnson, 1955). It appears that there is an analogue to therapy here. Frequently much time is lost in treatment because the patient is attending to the wrong (less crucial) aspects of the situation. Uncovering unconscious repressions, dreaming more interesting dreams, achieving a less inhibited freedom of expression, which were all intended as a *means* of psychotherapy may become, for many, the *goals*. One implication of this is that therapy requires frequent and successive structuring.

The therapist's as well as the patient's role in therapy needs to be discussed many times so that the patient is fully aware of why he is doing what he is doing in therapy, what his ultimate purpose is, and that there may be alternative ways of achieving the same ends. It is important that the patient does not get fixated on the means rather than the goals of psychotherapy. Too often ex-patients appear to leave therapy with behavior and characteristics which are learned to please the psychotherapist. However, their behavior continues to lead to a baffling kind of failure to obtain satisfactions from the significant people in their own life circumstances.

Finally, it is necessary to describe a last concept, that of broad generalized expectancies, which can be likened to the idea of higher level learning skills. These are very broad expectancies for behavior-reinforcement sequences which cut across need areas. Such expectancies are partial determinants of specific behaviors in many specific situations. Some examples of some of these, of particular significance to psychotherapy, are: (1) the now popular notion of internal versus external control or the belief that reinforcement is contingent upon one's own behavior or characteristics versus the notion that reinforcement is contingent upon chance, fate, or powerful others, (2) the expectancy that people cannot be believed or trusted to fulfill promises, which will affect the learning of delay of gratification and seriously affect the efficiency of almost any type of psychotherapy, (3) the expectancy that frustration can be overcome by seeking alternative ways of achieving goals, (4) an expectancy that reinforcement will follow from a better understanding of other people's motives, (5) an expectancy that directing attention to other people in a difficult situation will suppress distressing behaviors, and (6) a belief that many negative reinforcements can be avoided by better discrimination of situations previously regarded as the same. Clearly the learning of social skills may greatly enhance the patients' potential to deal with difficult situations on their own without requiring the intervention of a therapist.

It can be seen from these illustrations of the implications of social learning theory for the practice of psychotherapy that the therapist's behavior must depend on the nature of the problem, the nature of the resources open to him outside of therapy as well as within therapy, and the kind of patient with whom he is dealing. For example, when the problem is one of reducing the patient's need for dependency and increasing the value he places on independence, the therapist's behavior would have to be considerably different from that in which the problem of the patient is one of seeking dominance satisfactions to the exclusion of almost all other needs. Similarly, a patient who seeks sympathy as an indication of social support for retreating from life's problems needs to be reacted to differently from one who is oppressed by his inability to meet successfully an unrealistic burden of responsibilities he has already accepted.

Just as highly dependent people will reject non-directive therapy—highly independent ones may reject direct reinforcement techniques. The broader needs of the patient may not be crucial in curing many cases of snake phobia, but they are in selecting a therapist and a method of treatment for a generally depressed young man who finds society a fraud, achievement meaningless, and feels that nothing is worth striving for.

It seems characteristic of this view that rather than leading to implications for a specific technique of therapist behavior, the theory itself implies that the therapist must exercise great flexibility in adjusting his own behavior to the specific needs of the patient. In fact, considering the limitations of flexibility of every therapist, there should be much more concern with matching patients and therapists and consideration of changing therapist or techniques early in therapy. Of course such a therapeutic attitude emphasizes the importance of understanding the basis for the patient's behavior as early as possible.

We have suggested five sets of content variables to provide such generalized descriptions from which gradients of generalization can be predicted. (1) Behaviors leading to the same or similar reinforcements or need potentials. (2) Expectancies for gratification for functionally related sets of reinforcements, or freedom of movement. (3) Preference value of a group of reinforcements, or need values. (4) Classes of situations functionally related on the basis of the predominant satisfaction usually obtained in them; and (5) broad generalized expectancies which cut across need areas and are related to a wide variety of behaviors and situations and have to deal with expectancies of how and under what conditions reinforcements are likely to occur. We have demonstrated in a great variety of studies that all of these variables are capable of reliable measurement.

In summary, in this view no mysterious process special to psychotherapy is assumed nor does every therapist have to discover the same special set of ideal behaviors which will maximally facilitate this mysterious process. Rather, it is assumed that psychotherapy is a social interaction which follows the same laws and principles as other social interactions, and from which many different effects can be obtained by a variety of different conditions. It is also possible that the same effects may be obtained by a variety of different methods. The effectiveness of the changes that take place and the efficiency in arriving at them are the criteria for adequacy of method rather than conformity to any doctrine.

IMPLICATIONS OF SOME RESEARCH FINDINGS

Thus far this paper discusses only some general implications of very broadly stated hypotheses regarding the nature of goal-directed behavior. One of the advantages of social learning theory is that it deals with constructs which are amenable to measurement and with hypotheses which are amenable to test. Under limited laboratory conditions exercising as much control as possible, a large number of studies testing some of the broader and some of the more specific hypotheses of the theory have been investigated. Many of these experiments deal with quite general propositions. A few of the studies, however, appear to have somewhat more direct analogical relationship to the type of social interaction involved in psychotherapy and to some of the specific problems encountered with particular kinds of patients. Primarily for purposes of illustration, it seems desirable to present briefly some of these and the implications they may have for more specific problems of psychotherapeutic practice.

In the course of psychotherapy the patient's own efforts need to be rewarded so that he maintains both involvement and expectation of success in this sometimes painful and slow process. If the patient experiences some positive change in himself this may frequently serve as a starting point for a benign cycle. Relevant to this are studies by Good (1952), Castaneda (1952), and Lasko (1952). In these studies the effects of success and failure on the expectancy for future success were studied as a function of amount of experience within a particular task. All three of these experiments demonstrate that expectancies built up on the basis of many previous trials will change least with new experience. On the other hand, expectancies based on only one or two events may change dramatically with new experience. One inference from these studies for the practice of psychotherapy is the suggestion that early in therapy the therapist might well deal with more recent and less "significant" problems which may be most amenable to change. This may have the effect of encouraging the patient and reducing his resistance to change, which is usually based on his fear that without his defenses he would have no alternate ways of dealing with his problems.

Efran and Marcia (1967) conducted a "pseudo" desensitization study of snake and spider phobias. They told subjects that their fears were based on unconscious learning. In order to eliminate them, subliminal stimuli had to be presented to the subject on a screen and the fear response had to be suppressed by an unpleasant stimulus while the subject was unconsciously reacting to the stimulus. Of course, nothing was presented on the screen, and following a signal occasional shocks were given. Fake G.S.R. improvement graphs were shown to subjects at the end of each session. Using less time than previous desensitization studies, their results compare favorably in cure and improvement measures.

What appears to have happened here is that the procedure succeeded in changing the patient's expectancies about whether or not he could be cured. Looking at fake improvement curves under convincing conditions, the subjects decided they were sufficiently cured to allow them to pick up or touch the spiders or snakes. Such an expectancy for cure may well be the basis for the start of a benign cycle allowing the patient to try, one after another, behaviors which previously have been strongly avoided. Whether conducted with relaxation or other behavior modification techniques such procedures, used as part of a more extensive psychotherapy, may serve to start a benign cycle.

A study of Rychlak (1958) pertains to the stability of freedom of movement as a function of the number of different kinds of experiences on which it is based. Varying the number of different tasks but controlling the number and kind of reinforcements, Rychlak demonstrated freedom of movement or generalized expectancies are more stable the greater the number of different but related kinds of events the expectancies were built upon. As an analogy, a male who has had several bad experiences with the same female would have his expectancies more likely to change after a new positive experience with another female than if he had had the same number of experiences of the same kind but with several different females. Like the studies of Good, Castaneda, and Lasko, Rychlak's experiment suggests another condition which may help identify the attitudes which can change most readily.

Phares (1964) and Schwarz (1966) have demonstrated that massed trials of success and failure experiences lead to quick changes in verbalized expectancies. Delay between trials, however, leads to a return to earlier levels of expectancy, presumably as previous experience is rehearsed by the subject during delay periods. There is a suggestion here that to achieve more stable changes spaced therapeutic interviews or training sessions would be more efficient for most cases.

The great quantity of work on verbal conditioning has shown both how a therapist may serve as a reinforcer unwittingly and in addition, the powerful potential the therapist has to change behavior by direct reinforcement. A study by Shaffer (1957) suggests in addition that various therapists would serve differentially as reinforcers for subjects who have identifiably different learning histories. Shaffer investigated one implication of social learning theory having to do with the potential reinforcement value of the therapist. From questionnaires given both to adjusted and maladjusted college students he determined the kind and amount of parental reinforcement during childhood. From these questionnaires he was able to predict to some extent the age and sex preferences for a therapist. Specifically, he found that female subjects who prefer a female therapist tend to have seen their mothers as more reinforcing than females who prefer a male therapist. Males almost universally state preferences for male therapists but those males who saw both parents as positively reinforcing tend to prefer an older therapist to a younger one. This study suggests that the utilization of such preferences significantly related to early learning experiences, by matching the patient to the therapist, may considerably increase the efficiency of psychotherapy.

Crandall, Good and Crandall (1964) have also studied the reinforcement effects of adults on children and found that children react to no reinforcement as either positive or negative depending on the previous history of reinforcement with these same adults in the same situation. These reactions may also be predicted from generalized expectancies for positive and negative reinforcement based on earlier childhood experiences.

A therapy investigation by Strickland and Crowne (1963) had similar implications for matching patients and techniques. They found that patients with a high need for social approval dropped out of insight type therapy prematurely. Possibly they did so because of the greater conflict engendered by the pressure to reveal their psychopathology. It is apparent that traditional insight therapy approaches would have to be modified with such patients or other techniques used.

Two other lines of research have important implications for the practice of psychotherapy. One of these deals with the specificity of behavior in various situations. Although recognizing the generality of some behaviors, one characteristic of social learning theory is the emphasis on interaction of the individual and his meaningful environment or life space (Rotter, 1955, 1960). Like the psychology of Lewin (1951) and of Brunswik (1947), emphasis is not on abstracted traits as the basic component of personality, but rather on potentials of given classes of responses in given classes of situations.

It would be impossible here to review the many studies indicating that there are strong and significant interactions between social situa-

tions and personal characteristics. A single example from the literature on internal versus external control will have to serve to illustrate
the many implications these studies have for psychotherapy practice. On separate studies, one an experimenter bias study by Gore
(1962) and a verbal conditioning study by Strickland (1962), it was
found that Internals, if they are aware of subtle attempts to influence them, are much more resistant to the influence than Externals.
However, if overt attempts at influence are made, Internals like Externals will respond positively. In general these studies simply produce additional data to support the idea that therapist, method and
patient have to be carefully matched in order to maximize the beneficial results from psychotherapy.

Another line of related research has to do with the generalization
of changes in expectancies from one task to another. Studies by
Crandall (1955), Jessor (1954) and Chance (1959) have all shown
that a gradient of generalization is present which can be predicted
on the basis of a common sense analysis of similarity along dimensions of psychological needs, goals, or reinforcements. In these
studies expectancies for reinforcement were sampled in more than
one situation or task, changes in expectancies in one task were then
effected by experimental manipulations and changes in the other
task or tasks were measured.

The implication from both of these kinds of studies is that in
many instances the therapist is counting on *more* generalization of
changes in behavior from the therapist in the therapeutic situation to
other people in other situations than is warranted by the experimental evidence. It follows that if the therapist wishes to change
attitudes and behaviors in situations outside of therapy most efficiently, then he would need to deal with these other situations, at
least on a verbal basis, as much as possible in therapy. The working
through and analysis of the relationship with the therapist has its
value. However, these studies suggest that such behavior on the part
of the therapist has its limitations in affecting changes in life situations outside of therapy or with individuals other than the therapist.
When one considers how different the therapist's behavior toward
the patient is from other people's and the therapeutic situation is
from other life situations, this limitation takes on special significance.

Perhaps the most significant research relating to psychotherapy is
the work on generalized expectancies which refer to how and under
what conditions reinforcements may be expected. Investigation of
generalized expectancies for internal-external control, looking for
alternatives, delay of gratification, and interpersonal trust have clear
implications for psychotherapy procedures.

The extensive work in internal-external control has been reviewed by Rotter (1966) and by Lefcourt (1966). It is clear that such broad generalized expectancies exist and that patients who feel that their own behavior and characteristics have little or no influence on what happens to them can learn only inefficiently from therapy. It seems evident that if significant improvement is to take place, the patient must become more internal as therapy progresses. Gillis and Jessor (1961) have shown such changes in improved versus unimproved delinquent therapy patients. In some cases this attitude itself must be dealt with prior to working on other more specific problems. One suggested technique is to have the patient, early in therapy, practice different ways of behaving in some specific situation, not merely to indicate to him that he can respond a different way, but also to show him that his behavior can, in fact, change the behavior of others toward him.

Delay of reinforcement is another more specific area in which there are investigations completed. The work of Mahrer (1956) and Mischel (1958, 1961a, 1961b) indicates that the preference for immediate over delayed gratification is directly related to the degree of expectation that the delayed rewards will actually occur. In these experiments children are offered the choice of obtaining a pre-established reward of lesser value (candy or a toy) immediately, or waiting a week or more for one of clearly greater value. To some extent such tendencies to delay or not to delay gratification are attached to specific social agents and to some extent they are generalized. Since the problem of therapy in many cases may be conceived of as one in which the patient must learn to give up some immediate gratification for delayed benefits, these studies have some possible implications for psychotherapy. One such implication is that the therapist himself is a social agent who must be careful not to make promises or unconsciously suggest to the patient that he is capable of "delivering the goods" in an effort to sell psychotherapy to the patient or encourage him to continue. Once he becomes an agent who does not keep his promises, his implicit or explicit attempts to get the patient to give up immediate gratifications for future benefits are not likely to be effective. Another inference from these studies is that in some cases the patient's generalization from specific figures in his past to others has led him to be overly distrustful, or to have low expectancies for reinforcements which are presumably likely to occur if he gives up his present defenses. Consequently, with such patients great emphasis must be placed on this overgeneralization and its negative consequences.

Recent work (Rotter, 1966) has supported the construct validity of a generalized expectancy for interpersonal trust defined as belief in the truthfulness of communications from others. Preliminary analysis of a study with Getter strongly suggests that attitudes of distrust impair therapeutic relationship and outcome.

Two investigations related to the problem of teaching patients a general skill of looking for alternative solutions in problem situations. In one such study, Schroder and Rotter (1952) trained subjects on different sequences of simple concept formation problems by varying the number of *times* they were forced to find a new type of solution but keeping constant the number and type of solutions involved. They were able to demonstrate that the behavior of looking for alternatives could be rather easily learned and generalized to new problems, resulting in what is typically called flexible or nonrigid behavior. In a more direct study of therapy, Morton (1955) trained clients in a counseling center to look for alternative solutions in TAT stories they had told. Using this procedure as the primary basis for very brief psychotherapy, he was able to demonstrate a significant improvement in adjustment in comparison to matched control cases.

The generalized expectancies discussed above are only some of the important variables which describe how a person learns from experience. To find others is a task of considerable importance so that the therapist can make maximum use of what the subject has already learned in planning a therapeutic program. It is on the learning of such skills and their application to present and future life problems that the social learning therapist places reliance rather than the automatic generalization of changes in attitude toward the therapist.

SUMMARY OF IMPLICATIONS FOR THERAPEUTIC PRACTICE

The preceding discussion provides only a sketchy picture of the possible implications of social learning theory for psychotherapy. To summarize these comments it seems useful to point up some of the major differences between social learning theory and other points of view in the kinds of techniques the therapist might use were he to accept the same set of value commitments described earlier. It should be understood that these are frequently differences of degree, rather than of kind, or differences in relative emphasis.

1. The problem of psychotherapy is seen as a learning situation in which the function of the therapist is to help the patient accomplish planned changes in his observable behavior and thinking. Since patients come into therapy with many different motives, different values placed upon particular kinds of reinforcements, different expectancies for possible sources of gratification, different limits on

skill, and different higher level learning skills, conditions for optimal learning will likewise vary considerably from patient to patient. One characteristic of therapy derived from a social learning theory point of view is that the technique must be suited to the patient. Flexibility, experimentation, marked variations in method from patient to patient might be considered characteristic of this approach. Consequently, there is no special technique which can be applied to all cases and differences in therapists must eventually be systematically related to patient differences to obtain maximally efficient results.

2. The patient's difficulties are frequently seen from a problem solving point of view. As a result, there tends to be a greater emphasis on the development of higher level problem solving skills, such as those of looking for alternative ways of reaching goals, thinking through the consequences of behavior, looking for differences or discriminations in life situations, and turning attention in social situations to the needs and attitudes of others and recognizing that one can exercise some control over one's fate by one's own efforts.

3. In most cases the therapist perceives his role partly as guiding a learning process in which there are not only inadequate behaviors and attitudes to be weakened but more satisfying and constructive alternatives to be learned. Consequently, the tendency is for a more active role in interpretation, suggestion and direct reinforcement for the therapist than would be typical of traditional analytic or Rogerian therapy. In this regard there is more awareness on the part of the therapist of his role as a direct reinforcer of behavior and presumably a more deliberate use of such direct reinforcement. While the more specific behavior modification (Ullman & Krasner, 1965) techniques are happily included in this approach, for many kinds of problems they would be used as *part* of a more comprehensive attack on the patient's problems. The therapist, however, does not consider himself merely a mechanical verbal conditioner, but rather a person whose special reinforcement value for the particular patient can be used to help the patient try out new behaviors and ways of thinking. The patient ultimately determines for himself the value of new conceptualizations and alternate ways of behaving in his experiences outside of therapy.

4. In changing unrealistic expectancies it is important to understand how particular behaviors and expectancies arose and how past experience has been misapplied or overgeneralized to present situations. Similarly, when there are conflicting goals in a situation, it is important to know how they arose and what they are. However, such insights are considered helpful but not a necessary part of change. The use of insight as a technique varies with the patient,

depending on the patient's own need and ability to use rational explanations of his current problems. Another kind of insight is of equal
importance and possibly tends to differentiate a social learning
approach from other methods to a greater extent, that is, insight
into the long term consequences of particular behaviors and of the
values placed on particular goals. This includes not only an understanding of what consequences of behavior there are in present life
situations, but also of probable consequences of current modes of
behavior for the future. An individual may mold his behavior for
many years in the expectancy of achieving some positive gratification
(e.g., a college degree) which, in fact, he has never received. He may
likewise mold his behavior considerably in expectation of a negative
reinforcement (e.g., being left alone in one's old age) which he has
not directly experienced.

5. Related to this latter point is a concern for the expectations,
feelings, motives, or needs of others. Long term psychotherapy, as
Otto Rank has observed, frequently encourages a patient to remain
or sink deeper into his egocentric predicament through continuous
emphasis on the patient's subjective reactions, past and present.
However, many of the patient's problems arise from frustrations that
are a result of misinterpretation of the behavior, reactions and
motives of others. From a social learning point of view the patient's
problem frequently requires considerable emphasis and discussion
focused on understanding the behavior and motives of others, both
past and present. In this regard learning through observation, modeling or imitation as Bandura and Walters (1963) have pointed out,
can be a source of change in expectancies for behavior-reinforcement
sequences. The use of movies, examples, books and special groups
have probably not been sufficiently exploited in psychotherapy.

6. In place of the belief that experience changes people but little
once they pass infancy and that only therapy can make major
changes, a major implication of social learning theory is that new experiences or different kinds of experience in life situations can be
far more effective in many cases than those new experiences that
occur only in the special therapy situation. While it is true that an
analysis of the patient's interaction with the therapist can be an
important source of learning, it is unsafe to overemphasize this as the
main vehicle of treatment. Many times improvements seen by the
therapist are improvements or changes which take place in relationship to the therapist or in the therapy situation but the patient dis-
criminates this situation from others and generalizes little to other
life situations.

It is in the life situation, rather than in the psychotherapy room,
that the important insights and new experiences occur. There are

two implications of this view. One implication is that there should be considerable stress in treatment discusssions of what is happening in the patient's present life circumstances. Questions such as "What are the motives of others?", "What are the motives of the patient?", "How does the situation differ from other situations past and present?" and "How may the patient deal with the same situation in a way which is more satisfying and constructive?" need to be discussed in detail.

The second implication is that wherever it is possible and judicious to control the patient's experience outside of therapy by the use of what is usually called environmental manipulation that such opportunities be used maximally. Although the principal of environmental manipulation has long been accepted in the treatment of children, it is sometimes felt that this is only because the child lacks the ability to deal with his problems on a verbal or conceptual level. Environmental therapy is frequently seen only as second best treatment. However, no such hierarchy of importance seems logical. Changes in the behavior of parents, teachers, wives or husbands and other members of a family may frequently result in far greater changes in the patient than his direct experience with the therapist. The current trend toward behavior modification of parents fits in very well with this emphasis.

Likewise the opportunity for the patient making environmental changes himself, such as changes in jobs, living circumstances, social groups, etc., should not be overlooked or discarded in favor of a belief that all his problems lie inside of himself rather than in his interactions with the meaningful environment.

Hospitalizing a patient, whether psychotic or not, thereby removing him from a destructive environment to which he must eventually return, will reinforce his avoidance symptoms. Treating him in the absence of the situations which produced his symptoms, does not make much sense. It makes much better sense to keep him in his natural environment whenever possible, but to make concerted efforts to make it a more satisfying one by changing attitudes of relatives, bosses, encouraging job changes, utilizing public agencies for relief, etc., while at the same time directly treating the patient on an outpatient basis. Similar comments can be made about the problems of delinquency.

7. At the most general level, the implications of this theory are that psychotherapy should be viewed as a social interaction. The therapist helps the patient achieve a more satisfying and constructive interrelationship with his social environment. The laws and principles which govern behavior in other interpersonal learning situations apply as well to the therapy situation. There is no process

special to psychotherapy and there is no need, even if were possible, for the therapist to be a shadowy figure or "catalyst." Rather, he is an active partner who utilizes learning principles, applied to a particular set of circumstances, to help that person achieve a better way of dealing with the problems of life.

REFERENCES

Adler, A. *Social interest: A challenge to mankind.* New York: Harper & Bros., 1939.

Bandura, A., & Walters, R. H. *Social learning and personality development.* New York: Holt, Rinehart & Winston, 1963.

Brunswik, E. *Systematic and representative design of psychological experiments.* Berkeley, Calif.: University of California Press, 1947.

Castaneda, A. A systematic investigation of the concept expectancy as conceived within Rotter's Social Learning Theory of Personality. Unpublished doctoral dissertation, The Ohio State University, 1952.

Chance, June E. Generalization of expectancies among functionally related behaviors. *Journal of Personality,* 1959, *27,* 228-238.

Crandall, V. An investigation of the specificity of reinforcement of induced frustration. *Journal of Social Psychology,* 1955, *41,* 311-318.

Crandall, V. C., Good, S., & Crandall, V. J. Reinforcement effects of adult reactions and nonreactions on children's achievement expectations; a replication study. *Child Development,* 1964, *35,* 485-497.

Dollard, J., & Miller, N. E. *Personality and psychotherapy.* New York: McGraw-Hill, 1950.

Efran, J. S., & Marcia, J. E. Treatment of fears by expectancy manipulation: An exploratory investigation. *Proceedings, 75th Annual Convention, APA,* 1967, 239.

Gillis, J., & Jessor, R. The effects of psychotherapy on internal-external control. Unpublished manuscript, 1961.

Good, R. A. The potentiality for changes of an expectancy as a function of the amount of experience. Unpublished doctoral dissertation, The Ohio State University, 1952.

Gore, Pearl Mayo. Individual differences in the prediction of subject compliance to experimental bias. Unpublished doctoral dissertation, The Ohio State University, 1962.

Jessor, R. The generalization of expectancies. *Journal of Abnormal and Social Psychology,* 1954, *49,* 196-200.

Johnson, D. M. *The psychology of thought and judgment.* New York: Harper & Bros., 1955.

Kelly, G. A. *The psychology of personal constructs.* Vols. 1 & 2. New York: W. W. Norton, 1955.

Krasner, L. Studies of the conditioning of verbal behavior. *Psychological Bulletin,* 1958, *55,* 148-170.

Lasko, A. A. The development of expectancies under conditions of patterning and differential reinforcement. Unpublished doctoral dissertation, The Ohio State University, 1952.

Lefcourt, H. M. Internal vs. external control of reinforcement: A review. *Psychological Bulletin*, 1966, *65*, 206-220.

Lewin, K. The nature of field theory. In M. H. Marx (Ed.), *Psychological theory*. New York: Macmillan, 1951.

Mahrer, A. R. The role of expectancy in delayed reinforcement. *Journal of Experimental Psychology*, 1956, *52*, 101-105.

Mischel, W. Preference for delayed reinforcement: An experimental study of a cultural observation. *Journal of Abnormal and Social Psychology*, 1958, *56*, 55-61.

Mischel, W. Preference for delayed reinforcement and social responsibility. *Journal of Abnormal and Social Psychology*,1961a, *62*, 1-7.

Mischel, W. Father absence and delay of gratification: Cross cultural comparisons. *Journal of Abnormal and Social Psychology*, 1961b, *63*, 116-124.

Morton, R. B. An experiment in brief psychotherapy. *Psychological Monographs*, 1955, *69* (Whole No. 1).

Mowrer, O. H. Leaning theory and the neurotic paradox. *American Journal of Orthopsychiatry*, 1948, *18*, 571-610.

Phares, E. J. Delay as a variable in expectancy changes. *Journal of Psychology*, 1964, *57*, 391-402.

Rogers, C. R. *Client centered therapy, its current practice, implications and theory*. Boston: Houghton Mifflin, 1951.

Rotter, J. B. *Social learning and clinical psychology*. New York: Johnson Reprint Company, 1973, 1980. (Originally published, 1954.)

Rotter, J. B. The role of the psychological situation in determining the direction of human behavior. In M. R. Jones (Ed.), *Nebraska symposium on motivation*. Lincoln, Neb.: University of Nebraska Press, 1955.

Rotter, J. B. Psychotherapy. In P. R. Farnsworth & Q. McNemar (Eds.), *Annual Review of Psychology* (Vol. 11). Palo Alto, Calif.: Annual Reviews, Inc., 1960.

Rotter, J. B. Generalized expectancies for internal versus external control of reinforcement. *Psychological* Monographs, 1966, *80*, No. 1 (Whole No. 609).

Rotter, J. B. Beliefs, social attitudes and behavior: A social learning analysis. In R. Jessor & S. Feshbach (Eds.), *Cognition, personality and clinical psychology*. San Francisco, Calif.: Jossey-Bass, 1967a.

Rotter, J. B. A new scale for the measurement of interpersonal trust. *Journal of Personality*, 1967b, *35*, 651-665.

Rychlak, J. F. Task influence and the stability of generalized expectancies. *Journal of Experimental Psychology*, 1958, *55*, 459-462.

Schroder, H. M., & Rotter, J. B. Rigidity as learned behavior. *Journal of Experimental Psychology*, 1952, *44*, 141-150.

Schwarz, J. C. Influences upon expectancy during delay. *Journal of Experimental Research in Personality*, 1966, *1*, 211--220.

Shaffer, J. A. Parental reinforcement, parental dominance and therapist preference. Unpublished doctoral dissertation, The Ohio State University, 1957.

Strickland, Bonnie R. The relationships of awareness to verbal conditioning and extinction. Unpublished doctoral dissertation, The Ohio State University, 1962.

Strickland, Bonnie R., & Crowne, D. P. Need for approval and the premature termination of psychotherapy. *Journal of Consulting Psychology,* 1963, *27,* 95–101.

Ullman, L. P., & Krasner, L. *Case studies in behavior modification.* New York: Holt, Rinehart & Winston, 1965.

Wolpe, J. *Psychotherapy by reciprocal inhibition.* Stanford, Calif.: Stanford University Press, 1958.

Commentary to Chapter 9

The popularity of the I-E Scale was a mixed blessing. Some things in the ensuing flood of literature bothered me. Number one on my irritation list was a series of articles in which the authors discovered that I-E was not a general characteristic, but one that had some specificity. They believed that their ability to demonstrate some specificity disproved the notion that it was a generalized characteristic that was being measured—this despite the fact that the monograph they all cited and presumably had read said "such generalized expectancies in combination with specific expectancies act to determine choice behavior" (p. 2), and "From social learning theory one would anticipate that the more clearly and uniformly a situation is labeled, as skill or luck determined in a given culture, the lesser the role such a generalized expectancy would play in determining individual difference in behavior" (p. 2).

A second methodological problem with some of the literature was the use of the test as a before-and-after measure following a therapeutic intervention or as a veridical report of internalized expectancies under unusual testing circumstances (for example, giving the test to drug addicts while they were on methadone treatment).

I wrote the following article in order to address some of these misuses and misunderstandings. However, its main value at this time is probably in the further explication of the idea of a generalized expectancy and/or a stable personality characteristic from a social-learning point of view. The paper also discusses some general problems of personality measurement and inference from test scores from a social-learning point of view, continuing the concern with the meaning or significance of test responses.

9

Some Problems and Misconceptions Related to the Construct of Internal Versus External Control of Reinforcement

Estimates of the number of published articles dealing with some aspect of internal versus external control of reinforcement (sometimes referred to as "locus of control") vary, but it is clear that there are well over 600 studies. The number of unpublished investigations, master's theses, and doctoral dissertations dealing with this topic are impossible to estimate. Most of these studies have been published in the last 15 years, and there seems to be still an active, if not increasing, interest in the topic. The concept deals both with situational parameters and individual differences, although the bulk of the studies have been concerned with the latter.

One can only speculate on the surprising popularity of this concept as a subject for psychological investigations. Interest in this concept surely must be related to some persistent social problems, which in turn are related to the tremendous growth in population, increasing complexity of society, and the subsequent feeling of powerlessness that seems to permeate all levels of society, at least in Western culture. The research referred to above has produced some important and some well-replicated findings. It has also produced a series of studies that appear to reflect a basic misunderstanding of the nature of the variables and measurement devices used to assess individual differences. It is hoped that this article will help to clarify some of the theoretical problems, so as to enhance either the practical or theoretical contribution of future research. It may also be helpful to try to specify some of the limitations both of the predictive power of the concept as well as of the devices used for measuring individual differences. This article is not intended to review the locus of control research. A number of reviews and bibliographies are available (Joe, 1971; Lefcourt, 1966, 1972; Phares, 1973, in press; Rotter, 1966; Throop & McDonald, 1971). The most comprehensive and recent review and analysis of the locus of control literature is in a book recently completed by Phares (in press).

The concept of internal versus external control of reinforcement developed out of social learning theory (Rotter, 1954; Rotter, Chance, & Phares, 1972). It seems to be referred to by some investigators as the major or central concept in social learning theory. It is not. Our interest in this variable developed because of the persistent observation that increments and decrements in expectancies following reinforcement appeared to vary systematically, depending on the nature of the situation and also as a consistent characteristic of the particular person who was being reinforced. We were interested, in other words, in a variable that might correct or help us to refine our prediction of how reinforcements change expectancies. The nature of the reinforcement itself, whether positive or negative; the past history, sequence, and patterning of such reinforcements; and the *value* attached to the reinforcement are obviously important and probably more crucial determinants of behavior. This concept is defined as follows:

> When a reinforcement is perceived by the subject as following some action of his own but not being entirely contingent upon his action, then, in our culture, it is typically perceived as the result of luck, chance, fate, as under the control of powerful others, or as unpredictable because of the great complexity of the forces surrounding him. When the event is interpreted in this way by an individual, we have labeled this a belief in *external control*. If the person perceives that the event is contingent upon his own behavior or his own relatively permanent characteristics, we have termed this a belief in *internal control* (Rotter, 1966, p. 1).

As a situational variable, those situations in a particular culture that produced the belief that the reinforcement was under outside control would be called external control situations, and those that produced a belief that reinforcement was under the subject's own control could be called internal control situations. Most of the research dealing with situational parameters have used chance and skill situations; such situations, though clearly external and internal, are not identical with the concept of internal and external control of reinforcement, but rather they represent an important class of internal and external situations. In neither the case of situational differences nor individual differences were we hypothesizing a typology or a bimodal distribution. Rather, we assumed that with internal-external control something approximating a normal curve described the populations that we were interested in.

INTERNAL-EXTERNAL CONTROL AND
SOCIAL LEARNING THEORY

Social learning theory is a molar theory of personality that attempts to integrate two diverse but significant trends in American psychology—the stimulus–response, or reinforcement, theories on the one hand and the cognitive, or field, theories on the other. It is a theory that attempts to deal with the complexity of human behavior without yielding the goal of utilizing operationally definable constructs and empirically testable hypotheses.

There are four classes of variables in social learning theory: behaviors, expectancies, reinforcements, and psychological situations. In its most basic form, the general formula for behavior is that the potential for a behavior to occur in any specific psychological situation is a function of the expectancy that the behavior will lead to a particular reinforcement in that situation and the value of that reinforcement.

It is hypothesized in social learning theory that whan an organism perceives two situations as similar, then his expectancies for a particular kind of reinforcement, or a class of reinforcements, will generalize from one situation to another. This does not mean that the expectancies will be the same in the two similar situations, but the changes in the expectancies in one situation will have some small effect in changing expectancies in the other. *Expectancies in each situation are determined not only by specific experiences in that situation but also, to some varying extent, by experiences in other situations that the individual perceives as similar.* One of the determinants of the relative importance of generalized expectancies versus specific expectancies developed in the same situation is the amount of experience in the particular specific situation. These relationships are expressed in the formula below (Rotter, 1954, p. 166):

$$E_{s_1} = f\left(E'_{s_1} \,\&\, \frac{GE}{N_{s_1}}\right).$$

In this formula s_1 represents the specific situation and N represents the amount of previous experience the individual has had in that situation. E represents expectancy; E' represents a specific expectancy; and GE represents generalized expectancy. Clearly, if the formula is correct, and there is considerable empirical evidence to support it, then the relative importance of generalized expectancy goes up as the situation is more novel or ambiguous and goes down as the individual's experience in that situation increases. The point is important in understanding under what conditions one might expect clear prediction from an accurate measure of a generalized expectancy.

In social learning theory we have described two kinds of generalized expectancies. One of these that is involved in the formula for need potential involves expectancies for a particular kind of reinforcement, such as achievement, dependency, conformity, social approval, etc. Perceived similarity has to do with the nature of the reinforcement. The second kind of generalized expectancy deals with expectancies that generalize from other aspects of a series of situations involving some decision or problem solving where the nature of the reinforcements themselves may vary. For example, in situations involving different kinds of reinforcements, we may be asking ourselves if we can trust this individual to tell the truth or we may ask ourselves how we are going to find the solution when our previous plan was blocked. The first kind of generalized expectancy we designate with the subscript r for reinforcement (GE_r); the second kind is designated as a problem-solving generalized expectancy (GE_{ps}). In considering the expectancy for some reinforcement to follow some behavior in a given situation, not only would a generalized expectancy reinforcement be involved, but very possibly one or more problem-solving generalized expectancies would be involved. The above discussion can be represented in the following formula (Rotter et al., 1972, p. 41):

$$E_{s_1} = f \left(E' \ \& \ \frac{GE_r \ \& \ GE_{ps_1} \ \& \ GE_{ps_2} \ \dots \ GE_{ps_n}}{f \ (N_{s_1})} \right).$$

If we could accurately calculate all of the relevant variables in determining an expectancy, we would still be a long way from the prediction of a specific behavior. Expectancy is only one of the three determinants of a behavior potential in social learning theory. The second is the value of the reinforcement. If we want to predict a specific behavior, such as studying for an exam, voting in an election, taking part in a student protest, etc., we would have to know something about the values of the available reinforcement to a particular person before anything like an accurate prediction could be made.

The third major variable is the psychological situation. Psychological situations determine both expectancies and reinforcement values; consequently, they affect behavior potential. In addition, in social learning theory, the predictions of the potential of a particular behavior occurring in some situations must involve assessment of the alternative behaviors available in the same situation. For example, it is not sufficient if we would want to predict students' participation in some all-day protest to determine whether they are internals or externals according to some test; we would also need to know something about what alternative behaviors (such as reading in the library, attending classes, or even playing tennis) are available.

It is necessary to consider one further complication before one can thoroughly understand how subjective expectancy operates in the prediction of a behavior. The generalized expectancy that one might wish to use in a predictive formula, or rely upon as a basis for prediction, is arbitrary in the breadth of situations it might include. For example, if we want to predict a particular behavior involving studying for a psychology exam, and we wish to take into account some generalized expectancy that studying would lead to a better grade, we could assess this as a generalized expectancy for studying based on the person's previous experience in psychology courses. We may wish to use an even broader expectancy including not only studying but all other forms of increased effort as a technique of obtaining achievement satisfactions. A theorist may choose to use a construct of any breadth that he wishes, as long as it meets the criterion of functionality. That is, the referents that are included within the construct have a greater than chance correlation. Not every referent must correlate greater than chance with every other, but any referent must on the *average* correlate better than chance with all of the others. This is the same criteria that should be used in developing a measure of the same construct; namely, that each item should correlate significantly with the sum of the other items, with that item removed.

Clearly, we would expect that the more narrowly we define our generalized expectancy, the higher the prediction that results. It can also be seen that the distinction between specific expectancy and generalized expectancy is also arbitrary and is only a means of clarifying the problem of arriving at an accurate estimate. If we could obtain an exact expectancy measurement, regardless of how much of it was generalized and how much was specific, we would not have to look at separate components. However, generalized expectancies are interesting in their own right, since they may be thought of (a) as important personality characteristics, (b) as defining dimensions of generalization, and (c) as allowing broad prediction from limited data. They do, however, have their limitations, since they represent only one of many variables that enter into the prediction of behavior, and their relative importance is a function of the novelty and/or ambiguity of the situation.

The implication of the above statement is that some measure of a very broad generalized expectancy allows prediction in a large number of different situations; but at a low level. A narrower or more specific generalized expectancy should allow greater prediction for a situation of the same subclass but poorer prediction for other kinds of situations that are nevertheless to some degree similar. That is, some measure of a generalized expectancy that studying leads to higher grades in psychology might produce a better predictor of studying behavior for a particular psychology exam (the same subclass) but a poor one for a prediction of how much time someone may spend studying in order to improve their grades in mathematics (similar, but a different subclass). A very broad generalized expectancy might give a significant, but lower, prediction of the studying behavior in psychology and also a significant and low prediction for studying for a mathematics exam. What kind of measure an investigator might prefer and the kind of data available to him depends on his purpose. Since development of any adequate measure includes careful test construction and discriminant validity studies, constructing a different measure for every specific purpose would be a very expensive undertaking. Nevertheless, it would be worth developing such a specific measure if one's interest is in a limited area and particularly if one is seeking some practical application where every increment in prediction is important. A very broad measure has the advantage that it can be used to explore a large variety of possible theoretical and practical problems without necessitating the years of research necessary to develop the more specific instrument for every purpose. Such a measure, however, is necessarily limited to a lower level of prediction.

With this background in mind, it should now be possible to explore a number of misconceptions or misuses of the concept of a generalized expectancy for internal versus external control of reinforcement, at least as this concept was developed and measuring devices were constructed.

INTERNAL-EXTERNAL CONTROL PROBLEMS

Problems Associated with Conceptualization

Without doubt, the most frequent conceptual problem on the part of a number of investigators is the failure to treat reinforcement value as a separate variable. To make a locus of control prediction, one must either control reinforcement value or measure it, and systematically take it into account. The problem arises particularly in studies of social action, social protest, independence, conformity, etc. As we mentioned earlier, an internal person may *not* protest, be a member of a protest group, or sign a petition, simply because he does not believe in the cause; he may feel that his best interests lie in some other kind of activity, or he may merely feel that the particular action involved is bad strategy. On the other hand, a very external person may be a member of a protest group because he likes the other people who are members of the groups, because it is less boring than studying, because it will upset his parents if they find out, because it is the conforming thing to do, etc. In some of the early studies of locus of control differences (e.g., the tubercular patients of Seeman and Evans, 1962, who differed in their efforts to find out about their disease and do something about it, or the Southern blacks in the early days of the civil rights movement, Gore & Rotter, 1963, who differed in their willingness to take part in civil rights activities), there is a strong reason to assume high motivation for all subjects toward the same goals. The same cannot be said about many recent studies attempting to evaluate the relationship between internal and external control and social action. In fact, it may very well be, and there is some evidence to support the notion, that people engage in violent demonstrations rather than take part in some kind of planned activity leading to a constructive end, because they feel unable to cope with their frustrations.

A second problem area is that of specificity–generality. This seems to be a particular problem for those people concerned with predicting achievement behavior or performance in achievement situations. There seems to be a persistent effort to obtain highly accurate and reliable predictions of achievement behavior by the use of a generalized expectancy for internal versus external control. While this appears, on the face of it, to be reasonable, it becomes *less* reasonable the more structured, the more familiar, and the more unambiguous a particular situation is. There seems to be some successful prediction, with ability controlled, of achievement in early grades as a function of attitudes toward internal versus external control. But as the child becomes older and enters college, the relationship between locus of control and grades or college entrance scores is no longer apparent. On the other hand, some studies do show relationships between locus of control scores and study habits, that is, study habits as described in questionnaires by the subject. If it is true that internals study more, then according to the myths of our society, they ought to get higher grades. Why don't they? Probably because what differs is the self-reports about studying rather than their actual studying behavior. It may well be that when two students are faced with the prospect of having to guess what to study in order to pass an exam, then such generalized expectancies as internal versus external control may play some role in their behavior. However, by the time the student is in college, he knows pretty well what the relationship is for him between effort, studying, etc., and grades. What will differentiate his behavior from that of another student with the same ability is apparently level of motivation or the value placed upon academic achievement reinforcements versus other reinforcements that are competing. A great many achievement situations may be relatively novel or ambiguous for most subjects. The ones that are least ambiguous are academic achievement situations and tasks involving motor coordination or motor skills. Unfortunately, it is the latter two kinds of achievement situations that have been used most often in investigations attempting to demonstrate the predictive utility of individual differences in internal versus external control.

It is also true that some subjects may verbally express external attitudes on locus of control measures as a defense or rationalization for expected failure but act in an internal fashion in competitive situations. These individuals have been designated as defensive externals, and the problem of identifying them is discussed in the next section.

The third problem in conceptualization is the intrusion of the "good guy–bad guy" dichotomy. In spite of fears, and even warnings to the contrary, some psychologists quickly assume that it is good to be internal and bad to be external. Of course, in some senses, this may be true, but the problem then lies in assuming that all good things are characteristic of internals and all bad things are characteristic of externals. Internals should be more liberal, more socially skilled, better adjusted, more efficient, etc. Our early studies showed no relationship between locus of control and political liberalness–conservatism. I do not think that the situation has changed, although there may be some greater tendency recently for the endorsement of some external items by people who identify themselves as political radicals. But aside from the peculiarities of one test or another, there is no logical basis to assume any relationship.

The problem of the relationship between such a generalized expectancy such as locus of control and adjustment is indeed complicated. Adjustment, after all, is only a value concept, and any relationship must depend upon the definition of adjustment. It seems clear that self-report locus of control scales correlate with self-report scales of anxiety, adjustment, or scales involving self-description of symptoms. However, there are several studies (Efran, 1963; Lipp, Kolstoe, James & Randall, 1968; Phares, 1968) that suggest that it is typical of internals to repress (forget?) failures and unpleasant experiences. Consequently, they may report (or admit) less anxiety, fewer symptoms, etc., and thereby create a positive relationship between internality and adjustment. Of course, we do not know whether people who repress a great deal are happier or better off than those who do not. Neither the Freudian hypothesis nor its opposite has been demonstrated. And what is the relationship between internality and guilt? Can one feel guilty without first feeling some responsibility for one's actions?

It may be better for people who are in obvious difficulties, who are trying to cope with failing abilities, such as the aged and those who have become victims of addictions, to have a greater feeling that they can, in fact, control what happens to them. But there must also be a limit on personal control. Many people may already feel that they have more control than is warranted by reality, and they may be subject in the future (or may have already been subjected) to strong trauma when they discover that they cannot control such things as automobile accidents, corporate failures, diseases, etc. Our early hypothesis that locus of control would have a curvilinear relationship to adjustment has not been borne out, but the fault may be in the methods of measurement of the adjustment variable. There are many interesting problems that can be investigated here, some practical and some theoretical. It would help in such investigations if the researcher had not already predetermined that internals are always "good guys" and externals are always "bad guys."

Problems Associated with the Measurement of Individual Differences

The preceding section deals with some of the limitations of prediction from a conceptual point of view. The following section deals with limitations related to the measurement problem. In discussing problems arising in the measurement of locus of control, we are concerned primarily with the adult Internal–External Locus of Control (I–E) Scale. Most of the comments, however, are appropriate for all of the children's and adults' scales that have been developed to date.

In the development of the I–E scale, it was intended to build an easily administered instrument with a low, but not zero, correlation with a social desirability scale that could be used to investigate the potential operation of the variable in a broad array of specific situations. In the process of development, various scales were built, tried out, and discarded. The Likert format, which has certain advantages, was discarded in favor of a forced-choice instrument in order to reduce correlations with the Marlowe–Crowne Social Desirability Scale. Tests of 100 items and 60 items, each including a number of subscales, were built and discarded, usually because the subscale intercorrelations were almost as high as the subscale internal reliabilities. Finally, only those items were included in the measure (a) that correlated with at least one of two criteria, (b) that had low correlations with the Marlowe-Crowne Social Desirability Scale, (c) for which both alternatives were selected by college students at least 15% of the time, and (d) that correlated with the total of the other items with that item removed. The two criterion behaviors were expectancy statements in a laboratory task (Rotter, Liverant, & Crowne, 1961) and the behavior of tubercular patients in actively trying to improve their condition (Seeman & Evans, 1962). While the criterion behaviors used were both drawn logically from the population of locus of control referents, they were obviously quite different from each other.

Many items dealing with academic achievement had to be dropped because of high correlations with social desirability. However, some items concerned with the basis for grades produced sufficient endorsement of the external alternative to be retained.

The final scale that is referred to in the literature as the Rotter I-E scale was based on the contributions of many people, including E. Jerry Phares, William James, Shepherd Liverant, Douglas Crowne, and Melvin Seeman. The late Shepherd Liverant, particularly, contributed to the development of the final forced-choice scale.

The final test used was developed on college students. It consisted of 23 items and 6 filler items that sampled widely from different life situations where locus of control attitudes might be relevant to behavior. Each item was given equal weight, and it was hoped that the content of the various items would provide an adequate sampling of situations in which internal–external attitudes might be expected to affect behavior. In other words, it was developed as a broad gauge instrument—not as an instrument to allow for very high prediction in some specific situation, such as achievement or political behavior, but rather to allow for a low degree of prediction of behavior across a wide range of potential situations.

Because additive scales (Rotter, Chance, & Phares, 1972, p. 326) such as this one sample widely from a variety of different situations, they cannot be expected to have as high internal consistency as a power scale that samples different strengths of response in a narrow area. While they may also be expected to provide some significant prediction in comparing groups, the level of that prediction in any specific situation is theoretically limited, and individual prediction for practical purposes using such a scale would not be warranted.

Even though the forced-choice method allows some control over social desirability, it is well-known that such measures change in their relationship to social desirability under different testing conditions. It may be equally socially desirable to select either alternative to a question that asks the subject to choose between the statements (a) "Success in business is a matter of luck" and (b) "Success in business is a matter of hard work and skill," when they are college students. It is obviously not equally socially desirable to choose either alternative when applying for a job. Responses to questionnaires may be consciously or unconsciously distorted regardless of format. *All questionnaires are subject to error under particular testing conditions.* They are also limited by their dependence on conscious awareness. For example, studies have shown that alcoholics (Goss & Morosko, 1970) are more internal in their test response scores than college students. It is possible that this is an accurate portrayal of alcoholics and that their alcoholism is related to their guilt over failure. However, it is more likely that they have been told so many times and by so many people that their cure is "up to them" that they have fully recognized that this is the attitude they are supposed to present to the staff when they are trying to appear cooperative in a treatment program, either in an institution or as an outpatient. Very similar statements can be made for delinquents and drug addicts. Clearly, if one wished to determine which of the two explanations described above is more applicable to these groups, a more subtle form of testing would be necessary.

A last point should be made regarding test characteristics. When the I–E scale was first developed, most of the research used a median split to obtain groups called "internals" and "externals." Since that time the mean for college students has risen from a score of 8 (*SD* = approximately 4.0) to somewhere between 10 and 12, depending upon the sample (the test is scored in the external direction). In early samples and in current samples, the distribution of scores tends to be normal. There is nothing to suggest a typology. In addition, it is clear that if median scores are now used, subjects who were considered externals in the early samples would now be considered internals. In other words, there is absolutely no justification for thinking in terms of a typology.

In summary, the I–E scale is subject, as are all personality measures, to the conditions of testing and the known or suspected purposes or nature of the examinee. For many studies, questionnaires to measure internal–external control are simply not appropriate, and either more subtle or unobtrusive behavioral measures are called for. Addams-Webber (1969) and Dies (1968) have developed projective measures of internal–external control with a reasonable correlation with the questionnaire measure.

The second important problem involves the question of unidimensionality versus multidimensionality: whether or not there are important subscales within the I–E scale or whether the concept itself should be broken down into more specific subconcepts. This issue has often been approached in an either/or manner. Either it is a unidimensional construct, or it is a multidimensional construct. Such thinking is contrary to a social learning approach to the nature of stable behavior.

The construct of dependency may be functional. That is, broad classes of dependency behaviors show something more than a chance relationship to each other. However, by demonstrating such a relationship, or asserting it, one does *not* indicate therefore that there are no subclasses of dependency behavior in which referents are more closely related to each other than to referents of other subclasses. Similarly, a broad concept of internal versus external control is viable if in most samples of subjects a better-than-chance relationship can be seen between attitudes of subjects toward fate, luck, and control of powerful others, or the belief that one can control distant political events as well as personal ones. In each case the subclasses may show interrelationships among referents that are significantly higher than those between referents for one subclass and those of another subclass. Where such functional relationships exist, it is perfectly reasonable, if one has some purpose for doing so, to develop subscales or to use clusters of items within the present scale. It would be surprising, indeed, if such clusters of items did not appear in any scale of personality, particularly when the scale attempts to sample over a broad area of behaviors or situations.

The kinds of differentiation that appear among a group of items may vary from one sex to the other, or from one population to the other, and in effect, that is what is being found by a number of investigators. Since the availability of computer programs for factor analyses, a large number of such analyses have been done, and they have produced considerable variations (MacDonald, in press; Phares, in press). If the scale had been built in some other way, or had included 40 items instead of 23, the nature of the factor analyses might well be different from the ones now obtained. In other words, such factor analyses do not reveal "the true structure of the construct"; they only reveal the kinds of similarities perceived by a particular group of subjects for a particular selection of items.

In the early development of the I–E scale, two factor analyses were done (Franklin, 1963; Rotter, 1966), both of which showed that most of the variance was accounted for by one general factor. But some factors with only a few items with significant loadings did account for a small but significant variance. Since that time there has been strong reason to feel that there has been an increased differentiation in attitudes, so that some separate factors are emerging, although these still vary from population to population and between the sexes (Gurin, Gurin, Lao, & Beattie, 1969; Mirels, 1970). It is still true, however, that each of the items correlates with the total of the other items with that item removed, and that usually when factor analyses are done and applied to a different population, the factor scores, based on specific items that load most heavily on a particular factor, intercorrelate significantly.

The point of the preceding discussion is not to discourage factor analyses, the use of subscales, or conceptualizing in terms of subconcepts. It is only to discourage the notion that the factor analysis of any particular scale reveals the "true structure of a concept." Such factor analyses are not interesting in themselves, but they may be important as a first step toward the building of new instruments. They may be useful if it can be demonstrated that reliable and logical predictions can be made from the subscales to specific behaviors and that a particular subscale score produces a *significantly higher relationship than that of the score of the total test.* It is possible, as was done in one such factor analysis, to develop subscales that do not intercorrelate by throwing out those items that load highly on more than one factor. But whether or not the resulting factors are usable can only be demonstrated by showing that they have a logical and significant prediction to a *set* of criteria.

A third problem in interpreting locus of control scores has to do with the meaning of externality on the I–E scale. It would seem that if a person felt that what happens to him is the result of forces outside his own control, then he would tend to be relatively passive, unambitious, and noncompetitive. In our early studies involving expectancy stating in laboratory motor skill tasks we found that some externals showed patterns of behavior much like the behavior of ambitious, aggressive, and competitive subjects previously identified in studies of level of aspiration. It was also surprising, but true, that externals showed a wide spread of scores on college entrance tests and with grades, often including a number of subjects with very high scores. Stated another way, particularly in competitive achievement skill situations, there were a number of externals who acted much as we expected internals to act and others who acted much as we expected externals to act. That we were not dealing with simple absence of validity of the concept but rather with two different groups was suggested by the high variability of the external as compared to internal subjects—a fact later strikingly confirmed by Hersch and Scheibe (1967).

In these early samples our competitive externals tended to show up more in male samples. Although the correlations of college entrance scores and the I–E scale are uniformly low, with large samples it is true that the correlation for males was positive (i.e., externals were slightly higher on college aptitude scores) and negative for females. While neither correlation differed from zero significantly, they differed significantly from each other. We attributed this difference to a greater number of these competitive externals among our male subjects.

It also became apparent that psychologists interpreted the meaning of the external alternatives differently (presumably depending on their own locus of control attitudes). Some felt that when an individual endorses an item which states that success is primarily a matter of luck, he is rationalizing or that when he agrees that powerful others control his life, he is blame projecting. In other words, the nature of externality was essentially defensive. Other psychologists regarded endorsement of external statements much more literally and assumed that passivity was the only logically expected outcome of external attitudes. Such passive attitudes result from direct teaching or learning, although it is contrary to the middle-class "Protestant ethic," which supposedly, but does not necessarily, typify American society. Such passive-external attitudes would clearly be the norm in more fatalistic cultures, such as Hindu and Moslem. This latter observation has been substantiated in studies involving translated versions of the I–E scale (Parsons & Schneider, 1974). In other words, it is clearly possible that we could have two kinds of "externals" in our society.

Using the more versus less ambitious patterns of expectancy statements, we tried to differentiate our two groups of externals (which we tentatively called "defensive externals" and "passsive externals") on the basis of the items they endorsed. We tried two methods: one involving the content of items and the other involving the question of whether or not they endorsed internal items when dealing with success and external items when dealing with failure. Both attempts resulted in failure. We found that if rationalization was the basis for saying that luck was important, it was also a basis for saying that powerful others and fate were important. Item content did not differentiate our groups. We also found, at least among our college students, that if the subject said luck was important for failure, he remained consistent and said luck was also important for success. More recently, Levenson (1973, in press) has developed separate scales for belief in powerful others and chance. It is still true, however, that these scales have a relatively high intercorrelation in most samples that she studies.

Using the adult I–E scale, an investigation by Hamsher, Geller, and Rotter (1968) produced some unexpected results which suggested that a differentiation between defensive and passive externals might be made by the use of the Interpersonal Trust Scale (Rotter, 1967). This notion has been followed up by Hochreich (1968, in press; Note 2) in a series of studies and in a recent dissertation by Bander (Note 1). The rationale for using trust as a moderator variable is aptly described by Hochreich (in press). In substance, these studies demonstrate that the trust scale can help select these two different kinds of externals and that differential predictions can be made regarding their behavior in a variety of situations. Phares and his students (Davis, 1970) have also used other kinds of questionnaire data to make this differentiation with some success. They used the terms "defensive" and "congruent" for the two groups. It is possible that Levenson's distinction of belief in powerful others versus belief in chance overlaps that of defensive and passive externals.

Our own early attempt to pick up defensiveness by endorsement of failure versus success items did not work for college adults who apparently felt the necessity for some consistency in their responses. However, this differentiation does appear to work for children, as demonstrated by Crandall, Katkovsky, and Crandall (1965) and later by Mischel, Zeiss, and Zeiss (1974). It may be the case that younger children are less influenced by social desirability factors, particularly in the area of academic achievement. Long experiences in our school system must increase the social desirability of internal attitudes. There is, however, some evidence that internal attitudes are seen as more socially desirable even in the early grades. The direct prediction of school achievement by locus of control scales has been consistently more successful with children than with college students (Coleman, Campbell, Hobson, McPartland, Mood, Weinfeld, & York, 1966; Crandall, Katkovsky, & Crandall, 1965; Nowicki & Strickland, 1973). It may well be that this is partly a function of the fact that only those who have achieved at a consistently high level appear in the college population, and the children samples involve a much broader range of abilities, or the difference may be related to an increased tendency toward defensive externality with increased age and time in the school system.

If it is true that those people whose achievement behavior is affected by external attitudes are less likely to go on to college, while we continue to have many college students agreeing to external items on adult scales, then it may be true that defensive externals represent a higher proportion of the college population than the population at large. However, no tests of this hypothesis have been made.

It should be mentioned here that in talking about defensive versus congruent externals we are not talking about types. For subjects who may score above the median on externality, both of these reasons for endorsing external items may exist to varying proportions in varying individuals.

The importance of this distinction between two bases for endorsing external items lies in the prediction of specific criteria. It seems clear from our present data that there is a group of defensive externals who are competitive, striving, and ambitious when placed in competitive achievement situations, although the same individuals may avoid competition when it is possible to do so without apparent loss of status. In other words, depending upon the criteria, sometimes defensive externals and congruent externals act in opposing fashions (e.g., in expectancy stating on a competitive skill task), sometimes they may act in the same fashion for different reasons, and in some instances predictions are borne out because one group of externals behaves in a manner consistent with some hypothesis and the other group behaves in a manner neutral to the hypothesis. For example, in the latter case, studies showing that externals are more maladjusted or defensive may depend mainly on the presence of defensive externals within the external group (Hochreich, in press). In order to understand or make predictions regarding the relationship of internal–external test behavior and some other criteria, it is important to make a careful theoretical analysis of the criterion behavior and its possible relationship to defensive versus congruent externality, and it may be important to use one of the methods already developed or a new method to differentiate between the two groups.

CONCLUSION

The preceding discussion permits no simple, general conclusion. It is offered in the hope that new studies involving the construct of internal versus external control of reinforcement will be carried out, taking into account the underlying theory and recognizing the limitations of this construct and its measurement so that the data obtained can be integrated into a meaningful body of knowledge. Particularly, one must guard against the assumption that expectancy regarding control of reinforcement is a behavioral trait and that the prediction of behavior can ignore the value of the reinforcement that is the expected outcome of the behavior being studied.

New methods of measurement and new scales, general or more specific, may be justified and needed, but the mere development of instruments without theoretical or practical justification based on the factor structure of old ones does not seem promising.

REFERENCE NOTES

1. K. Bander. The relationship of internal–external control and academic choice behavior. Doctoral dissertation, University of Connecticut, in preparation.
2. Also a recent study by D. J. Hochreich. Defensive externality and blame projection following failure. Unpublished manuscript, University of Connecticut, 1974.

REFERENCES

Adams-Webber, J. R. Generalized expectancies concerning the locus of control of reinforcements and the perception of moral sanctions. *British Journal of Clinical Psychology*, 1969, *8*, 340–343.

Coleman, J. S., Campbell, E. Q., Hobson, C. J., McPartland, J., Mood, A. M., Weinfeld, F. D., & York, R. L. *Equality of educational opportunity.* (Superintendent of Documents Catalog No. FS 5.238: 38001) Washington, D.C.: U.S. Government Printing Office, 1966.

Crandall, V. C., Katkovsky, W., & Crandall, V. J. Children's beliefs in their own control of reinforcement in intellectual-academic achievement situations. *Child Development*, 1965, *36*, 91–109.

Davis, D. E. *Internal-external control and defensiveness.* Unpublished doctoral dissertation, Kansas State University, 1970.

Dies, R. R. Development of a projective measure of perceived locus of control. *Journal of Projective Techniques and Personality Assessment*, 1968, *32*, 487–490.

Efran, J. *Some personality determinants of memory for success and failure.* Unpublished doctoral dissertation, Ohio State University, 1963.

Franklin, R. D. *Youth's expectancies about internal versus external control of reinforcement related to N variables.* Unpublished doctoral dissertation, Purdue University, 1963.

Gore, P. M., & Rotter, J. B. A personality correlate of social action. *Journal of Personality*, 1963, *31*, 58–64.

Goss, A., & Morosco, T. E. Relation between a dimension of internal-external control and the MMPI with an alcoholic population. *Journal of Consulting and Clinical Psychology*, 1970, *34*, 189–192.

Gurin, P., Gurin, G., Lao, R. C., & Beattie, M. Internal-external control in the motivational dynamics of Negro youth. *Journal of Social Issues*, 1969, *25*, 29–53.

Hamsher, J. H., Geller, J. D., and Rotter, J. B. Interpersonal trust, internal-external control, and the Warren Commission Report. *Journal of Personality and Social Psychology*, 1968, *9*, 210–215.

Hersch, P. D., & Scheibe, K. E. Reliability and validity of internal-external control as a personality dimension. *Journal of Consulting Psychology*, 1967, *31*, 609–613.

Hochreich, D. J. *Refined analysis of internal-external control and behavior in a laboratory situation.* Unpublished doctoral dissertation, University of Connecticut, 1968.

Hochreich, D. J. Defensive externality and attribution of responsibility. *Journal of Personality*, in press.

Joe, V. C. Review of the internal-external control construct as a personality variable. *Psychological Reports*, 1971, *28*, 619–640.

Lefcourt, H. M. Internal versus external control of reinforcement: A review. *Psychological Bulletin*, 1966, *65*, 206–220.

Lefcourt, H. M. Recent developments in the study of locus of control. In B. A. Maher (Ed.), *Progress in experimental personality research.* Vol. 6. New York: Academic Press, 1972.

Levenson, H. Multidimensional locus of control in psychiatric patients. *Journal of Consulting and Clinical Psychology*, 1973, *41*, 397–404.

Levenson, H. Activism and powerful others: Distinctions within the concept of internal-external control. *Journal of Personality Assessment*, in press.

Lipp, L., Kolstoe, R., James, W., & Randall, H. Denial of disability and internal control of reinforcement: A study using a perceptual defense paradigm. *Journal of Consulting and Clinical Psychology*, 1968, *32*, 72–75.

MacDonald, A. P. Measures of internal-external control. In J. P. Robinson & P. R. Shaver (Eds.), *Measures of social psychological attitudes* (rev. ed.) Ann Arbor: Institute for Social Research, University of Michigan, in press.

Mirels, H. L. Dimensions of internal versus external control. *Journal of Consulting and Clinical Psychology*, 1970, *34*, 226–228.

Mischel, W., Zeiss, R., & Zeiss, A. Internal-external control and persistence: Validation and implications of the Stanford Preschool Internal-External Scale. *Journal of Personality and Social Psychology*, 1974, *29*, 265–278.

Nowicki, S., & Strickland, B. R. A locus of control scale for children. *Journal of Consulting and Clinical Psychology*, 1973, *40*, 148–154.

Parsons, A., & Schneider, J. M. Locus of control in university students from eastern and western societies. *Journal of Consulting and Clinical Psychology*, 1974, *42*, 456–461.

Phares, E. J. *Locus of control: A personality determinant of behavior.* (A modular publication). Morristown, N.J.: General Learning Press, 1973.

Phares, E. J. *Locus of control in personality.* Morristown, N.J.: General Learning Press, in press.

Phares, E. J., Ritchie, D. E., & Davis, W. L. Internal-external control and reaction to threat. *Journal of Personality and Social Psychology,* 1968, *10,* 402–405.

Rotter, J. B. *Social learning and clinical psychology.* Englewood Cliffs, N.J.: Prentice-Hall, 1954.

Rotter, J. B. Generalized expectancies for internal versus external control of reinforcement. *Psychological Monographs,* 1966 *80*(1, Whole No. 609).

Rotter, J. B. A new scale for the measurement of interpersonal trust. *Journal of Personality,* 1967, *35,* 651–665.

Rotter, J. B., Chance, J., & Phares, E. J. (Eds.). *Applications of a social learning theory of personality.* New York: Holt, Rinehart & Winston, 1972.

Rotter, J. B., Liverant, S., & Crowne, D. P. The growth and extinction of expectancies in chance controlled and skilled tasks. *Journal of Psychology,* 1961, *52,* 161–177.

Seeman, M., & Evans, J. W. Alienation and learning in a hospital setting. *American Sociological Review,* 1962, *27,* 772–783.

Throop, W. F., & MacDonald, A. P. Internal-external locus of control: A bibliography. *Psychological Reports,* 1971, *28,* 175–190.

Commentary to Chapter 10

*I became interested in the construct of trust as a result of partici-
pation in a faculty seminar on disarmament at Ohio State University.
It seemed clear to me that the issue of disarmament was essentially a
problem of trust—that is, a belief in others' communications—and I
began to see that many problems—national, social, and individual—
revolved around the issue of trust. I began the process of studying
trust by seeking to understand the basis for individual differences,
and I devised a measure of interpersonal trust. The studies summarizing the construct validity of this test were reported in an earlier
article (Rotter, 1971).*

*The following article is a report of many studies done by myself,
students, and colleagues, all focusing on the consequences of trusting
and distrusting expectancies. Perhaps it is characteristic of pyscholo-
gists and other social scientists that in looking for consequences of
certain attitudes they focus their attention on negative consequences—just as we have emphasized the study of negative emotional
states over positive ones. Because trust of the stranger can have
negative consequences, we assume it is usually safer to distrust;
but we rarely assess the loss of positive satisfactions of trusting
others or the direct losses of distrust. Although this article naturally
cannot lead to a quantification of these losses for a given person or
group faced with a specific problem, it does strongly suggest that the
bad consequences of distrust need to be assessed and that our initial
reaction of distrust may need to be inhibited in many circumstances.*

*Some mention should be made of the prejudice against accepting
the null hypothesis. Although it is true that more stringent criteria
may need to be met, the article provides four criteria that, if met,
increase the probability that the null hypothesis can be accepted.*

*These criteria may have considerable generality for social science
research.*

REFERENCES

Rotter, J. B. Generalized expectancies for interpersonal trust. *American Psychologist*, 1971, *26*, 443–452.

10

Interpersonal Trust, Trustworthiness, and Gullibility

A recent *New York Times* editorial referred to the present time as "the age of suspicion." Focusing on the political costs of excessive distrust, the editors expressed the hope that Americans might return to a more trusting attitude toward their government and themselves. An equally forceful plea might be made in terms of the enormous personal costs of excessive distrust. Common sense tells us that interpersonal trust is an important variable affecting human relationships at all levels: relationships between governments, between minorities and majorities, buyers and sellers, patients and therapists, parents and children, and so on. As distrust increases, the social fabric disintegrates. Unwarranted distrust can result in serious negative consequences, but "foolish trust," or gullibility, can also lead to serious consequences. We need to ask two questions: What is unwarranted distrust? And what are the costs of trusting too much?" Although psychologists cannot be expected to provide definitive answers to such complex questions, we can address ourselves to aspects of the problem.

About 14 years ago at the University of Connecticut, a program of research dealing with interpersonal trust was begun. The present report deals with some of this research involving the personal consequences of being high or low in interpersonal trust. Most psychologists have to answer the question of how trusting they should be, not only in making decisions about their personal lives but also in deciding about their roles as teachers, therapists, and parents. How

Rotter, Julian A. Interpersonal trust, trustworthiness, and gullibility. *American Psychologist,* 1980, *35,* 1-7. Copyright 1980 by the American Psychological Association. Reprinted by permission of the publisher and author.

This article is revised from the Presidential Address to the Eastern Psychological Association, April 1977. I am indebted to Dorothy J. Hochreich, Clara B. Rotter, and David Zuroff for their helpful comments.

trusting we are is important to others as well as to ourselves, since some of our research strongly suggests that modeling and direct teaching are the most potent forces in developing high- or low-trusting beliefs in children (Into, 1969; Katz & Rotter, 1969).

In the context of social learning theory, interpersonal trust has been defined as a generalized expectancy held by an individual that the word, promise, oral or written statement of another individual or group can be relied on (Rotter, 1967). This definition differs from that of other psychologists who define trust as a belief in the goodness of others or in the benign nature of the world.

If expectancies that others' communications can be relied on are generalized from one social agent to another, then the individual will build up a generalized expectancy for trust of others that might be viewed as a relatively stable personality characteristic. In our original research we attempted to determine whether such generalized, relatively stable expectancies for trusting others exist and can be reliably measured, and we have found considerable support for the utility of such a generalized expectancy (Rotter, 1971). But it is necessary at this point to describe what is meant by a generalized expectancy and its place in social learning theory (Rotter, 1954; Rotter, Chance, & Phares, 1972).

In social learning theory *expectancies in each situation are determined not only by specific experiences in that situation but also, to some varying degree, by experiences in other situations that the individual perceives as similar. One of the determinants of the relative importance of generalized expectancies, as opposed to specific expectancies, in a given situation is the amount of experience one has had in that particular situation.* These points are emphasized because, for some people, the idea of a generalized expectancy means an assumption that there is no situational specificity. Of course there is both situational specificity and cross-situational generality determining behavior, and the relative importance of each depends on the amount of previous experience with the particular situation being considered. It also follows that if one is trying to get a good measure of a generalized expectancy, one should avoid stimuli with which the individual has had a great deal of previous, specific experience, such as father, mother, lover, and friend, and one should try instead to sample widely from a large number of social agents. So it is the trust of a generalized other—a person or group with whom one has not had a great deal of personal experience—in which we are most interested.

In order to measure such a generalized expectancy, we developed a questionnaire that has shown construct validity in prediciting attitudinal, sociometric, behavioral, and unobtrusive criteria in a variety of situations (Rotter, 1967, 1971); that is, consistent with theoretical expectations, a moderate portion of the variance was predicted by this test for these criteria. Most correlations have been in the .30s and .40s. In the great majority of these studies, the Interpersonal Trust Scale was administered by someone other than the experimenter and was separated in time from the criterion situation by periods ranging from one to four months. This temporal separation of test administration and experimental criterion situation was maintained in all the investigations discussed below, with a few specified exceptions.

Below, I first examine the positive relationships or consequences of being a high truster, and later I deal with the question of the negative relationships or consequences, particularly the issue of gullibility.

TRUST AND PROSOCIAL BEHAVIOR

Previously reported research (Rotter, 1971) has documented the strong relationship between high trust and trustworthiness. Whether the criterion is a self-report questionnaire or behavior in a controlled experiment, people who act more trusting or say they are more trusting are themselves less likely to lie.

In addition to lying, other behavioral indicators of trustworthiness have been studied. For example, it is reasonable to expect that some people are more likely than others to behave in an untrustworthy fashion in situations in which the perceived risk of being caught in the act is minimal.

In an experiment whose primary focus was the investigation of sex guilt, Boroto (1970) obtained the interesting incidental finding that subjects who did not invade the privacy of the experimenter when they did not think they were being observed were very high on interpersonal trust.

Steinke (1975) tested subjects on a task in which it was possible for the experimenter to detect cheating without directly observing the subjects. Subjects were tested in groups of four and were told that they were competing with one another and with other subjects in the experiment for a monetary prize to be awarded when the experiment was completed. When the Peer subscale of the Interpersonal Trust Scale was used to divide subjects into high and low trusters, it was found that low trusters had cheated significantly more often than had high trusters.

In another study, subjects' belief that they were being observed was experimentally manipulated. Hochreich (Note 1) asked subjects to practice on a series of boring and repetitive arithmetic problems for 10 minutes as preparation for a related test. In one condition, each subject was told that the experimenter would be in an adjacent room, behind an observation window, while the subject worked on the practice problems. In a second condition, the observation window was present but the subject was told the experimenter would wait down the hall. In the third condition, there was no observation window in the room and the subject was told the experimenter would wait down the hall. Among females, high trusters worked as hard, that is, completed the same number of problems, regardless of whether they believed that the experimenter was watching them. Low trusters, on the other hand, worked significantly less hard when they believed they were not being observed than when they believed the experimenter was behind the one-way mirror. In the surveillance condition, they worked as hard as high-trusting females; in the no-surveillance conditions, they worked less hard than did high trusters. No such pattern of differences was obtained for males for reasons that are not clear but are probably related to different attitudes of males and females toward the arithmetic task.

Wright and Kirmani (1977) surveyed a large number of high school students and had them complete an anonymous questionnaire, as well as the Interpersonal Trust Scale and items dealing with a number of social attitudes. They also included self-reports of shoplifting. Although, overall, females admitted to less shoplifting than did males, female low trusters reported significantly more shoplifting than did female high trusters. Wright and Kirmani also asked whether the subjects felt that people in the two surrounding communities distrusted students. The low trusters of both sexes showed significantly greater feelings of being distrusted, and this item was significantly related to frequency of shoplifting.

Of course, the relationship between low trust and untrustworthy behavior seems readily explainable. If low trusters truly feel that other people cannot be trusted, there is less moral pressure on them to tell the truth, and under some circumstances they may feel that lying, cheating, and similar behaviors are necessary for defensive reasons—because everybody else is doing it to them.

Most of the work reported above has been done with college students, and the generalizability of these findings to other populations is not known. It may seem that the interpretation of these studies is leading to good guy–bad guy stereotypes, but that may be due to the nature of the variable we have been investigating and to the logical criteria that variable predicts. We do have some data which suggest that high trusters may be more conventional and more moralistic than low trusters. These attributes, at least, are not necessarily positive ones.

In addtion to trustworthiness and moral behavior, there are other concomitants or consequences of trust that may be of interest, namely, personal adjustment and likability. In six of the studies we have done with college students, scores on the Incomplete Sentences Blank, a semistructured test of college student adjustment or conflict, were available. In all six studies, higher trust was significantly related to better adjustment for the total sample of the study. The correlations ranged from .20 to .44. These findings are in general agreement with those of Collins and Wrightsman (1962), who found a similar relationship between trust and adjustment with 12–15-year-old boys, using other measures of trust and adjustment.

Before describing the investigations of gullibility, I should mention one other recently completed study, which dealt with the positive consequences of being more trusting. Hochreich (Note 2) asked a large number of subjects, male and female, high and low trusters, simply to read a test protocol of the Interpersonal Trust Scale, presumably filled out by a real subject. The name at the top of the protocol indicated that the person who had taken the scale was either a male or a female, and the scale was answered either in a trusting or a distrusting direction. After reading the protocol, subjects were asked to rate the target person on a number of characteristics. Hochreich's results were surprising. Byrne (1971) and his colleagues have repeatedly demonstrated that there is a strong tendency for people to like others who are similar to themselves in attitudes, opinions, and personality characteristics, but Hochreich found that in general, everyone likes a high truster. More specifically, regardless of the sex of either the subject or the target person, the high truster was seen as being happier, more ethical, and more attractive to the opposite sex, as having had a happier childhood, and as more desirable as a close friend than the low-trust target. There was strong agreement among all subjects on many of these ratings, but some of the other findings indicated that subjects were not responding in a simple-minded, nondiscriminating fashion. For example, all subjects believed that the low-trust target was more likely than the high-trust target to have had varied and unusual experiences. Overall, too, the low-trust target, was seen as having more common sense than the high-trust target, though this difference was significant only for subjects who were themselves low in trust. There was no overall effect for ratings of academic ability, although female high trusters did rate the high-trust target as significantly higher on this variable.

TRUST AND GULLIBILITY

So much for the positive concomitants or consequences of being a high truster. What can be said about the possible negative consequences of being taken in too much, of being gullible?

Before considering the relationship of gullibility to interpersonal trust, some refinement of the concept of trust has to be made. If trust is simply believing communications, then high trust must be equated with gullibility. However, if we redefine trust as believing communications in the absence of clear or strong reasons for not believing (i.e., in ambiguous situations) and gullibility as believing when most people of the same social group would consider belief naive and foolish, then trust can be independent of gullibility. In fact, anecdotal evidence suggests that it is the low truster who is taken in by the disarming dishonesty of the con artist and is the frequent victim of con games.

It may also be true that the belief of the high truster is more a belief in the moral rightness of trust of the stranger than it is an expectancy of less risk in trusting others. The studies already reviewed clearly suggest that the high truster is more likely than the low truster to act morally.

Gullibility has been defined as naiveté or foolishness. To translate that into experimental criteria is not always easy. In the studies now to be reviewed, gullibility was defined as believing another person when there was some clear-cut evidence that the person should not be believed. Either the other person had already lied to the subject one or more times, or most people would consider that person's statement to be implausible on other grounds. To trust a stranger who had not lied to you before would not be gullibility; to believe a politician who has lied to you many times before is gullibility.

In several of our earlier investigations no evidence was found that high trusters behaved in a way that can be called, somwhat arbitrarily perhaps, more gullible than low trusters. Of course, there are problems in trying to prove the null hypothesis. However, in reviewing these studies and some others to be described, there are considerations that at any rate increase the plausibility of the idea that, overall, high trusters are no more gullible than low trusters.

It appears to me that there are four criteria that can be applied in estimating the probability that the null hypothesis can be accepted. First, is the criterion behavior measured reliably? Second, is the criterion behavior valid? That is, is there evidence that it can be predicted by or related to other variables in a logical way? Third, are there a number of investigations with different subjects and different operations that have produced similar results? And fourth, are the statistically nonsignificant differences in various studies not all in the same direction?

In other words, if one can show in a series of investigations in which two groups did not differ significantly that the criterion behaviors were reliably measured, the criterion behaviors could be logically predicted by other variables, the subject populations were varied as were the criteria, and the nonsignificant differences were not always in the same direction, then one can assert that one has produced evidence increasing the probability that the null hypothesis can be accepted.

For example, we can apply these criteria to Rotter's (1967) sociometric study. In this study of college fraternity and sorority members who had lived with each other for at least six months, the Interpersonal Trust Scale did correlate .38 with the sociometric ratings of interpersonal trust; in this case the two measures were given in the same experimental session. However, there was no significant relationship between the Interpersonal Trust Scale or the sociometric rating of trust and the sociometric ratings of gullibility, where gullibility was defined as being "naive and easily fooled." Ratings for sociometric variables were highly reliable, and the sociometric ratings of dependency were highly related to gullibility. The later relationship was significantly higher than that between gullibility and any other variable.

A study by Geller (1966) involved a faulty apparatus that had ostensibly just delivered a strong shock to the experimenter. Following his shock the experimenter took a few seconds to "fix" the apparatus and then told the subject it was all right. Geller had three conditions. In the first condition, subjects had no prior reason to be suspicious. In the second, involving a mildly suspicious group, the subjects had previously gone through an Asch conformity situation with the same experimenter. In the third condition, subjects had been told by a confederate that they had been deceived by the experimenter in the Asch situation.

The three groups differed as expected in the behavioral trust shown toward the apparatus. Trusting behavior was reliably rated by two observers behind a one-way vision screen. High-trust subjects were significantly more trusting than low-trust subjects in the first condition but were no more trusting behaviorally in the third, deception-revealed condition. In other words, the criterion behavior could be shown to be a reliable and valid measure of trust, but high-trust subjects were no more gullible than low-trust subjects, once the former had a strong reason to distrust the experimenter.

Two studies involving game behavior, by Wright (1972) and Hamsher (1968), are also relevant to the study of trust and gullibility. Both of these involved passing notes to another player; the notes were intercepted by the experimenter, who substituted his own. After being deceived once before and with no apology, high and low trusters did not differ significantly in their subsequent trust of the other subject. Both of these studies also met the criteria proposed above for a valid test of the null hypothesis. In the four studies referred to above, two of the nonsignificant differences in gullibility between high and low trusters favored high trusters, and two favored low trusters.

There are some additional data that bear, perhaps less directly, on the gullibility of high trusters. Some people, obviously low trusters, believe that high trusters are just plain dumb. We do not have individual intelligence tests on our subjects, but we do have college aptitude scores and in one study a range of educational attainment. In several of our studies, we have correlated scholastic aptitude scores with trust scores and have in each case found a nonsignificant relationship. Rotter and Stein (1971) investigated subjects' trust of a number of occupational groups, using a variety of different populations. There were no differences in the average trust assigned to the various occupations as a function of the subject' educational attainment. Educationally, the subjects ranged from high school graduates through holders of a master's degree.

Wright and Shea (Note 3) examined the acceptance of personality interpretations in a study in which all subjects were given the same stereotyped, positive, high-base-rate statements as feedback a week after taking two personality questionnaires that were not relevant to the actual statements made about them. The students rated the accuracy of the statements. As in our other studies, the Interpersonal Trust Scale had been administered earlier in the semester, along with the Internal–External Locus of Control Scale. Here again, high trusters and low trusters did not differ in their degree of acceptance of these stereotyped personality analyses, but internal subjects accepted these interpretaions significantly less than did external subjects, indicating again that the criterion was reliable and meaningful.

Rotter and Zuroff (Note 4) asked subjects to determine the guilt or innocence of a defendant by reading a typescript of a courtroom scene. The conditions that were varied were the flamboyance and sex of the defendant. There were a number of interactions involving sex of subjects, sex of defendant, style, and trust. However, most of the subjects saw the defendant as guilty, and high trusters did not differ from low trusters in the percentage who regarded the defendant as guilty. Since the overwhelming majority of the subjects regarded the defendant's explanations as weak and illogical, this research has some relevance to a discussion of gullibility. High trusters were not any more likely to be taken in than low trusters.

Finally, Lajoy (1975) investigated the effects of arrogance and expertise on subjects' trust of physicians and automobile mechanics. Lajoy used eight videotapes. In the first, a professional actor portrayed a physician giving a diagnosis to a patient and answering his questions arrogantly. In the second, the same actor gave the same diagnosis and advice, but nonarrogantly, and in the third and fourth tapes, the same actor, designated as a physician, gave advice to an acquaintance on a zoning referendum (a topic presumably outside his area of expertise), arrogantly and nonarrogantly. The other four videotapes, in which the actor portrayed an automobile mechanic, paralleled the first set in the way arrogance and expertise were varied. Different groups of subjects observed each tape, and all the subjects had been tested with the Interpersonal Trust Scale some months earlier. In addition to ratings of the trustworthiness of the central character, ratings were also made of his competence, his altruism, and whether or not the subject would take the advice given if he or she were the other person portrayed in the videotape.

Although it is not central to the purposes of this article, let me say that arrogance lowered the ratings of trustworthiness of both physicians and mechanics, and this effect was even stronger when the physician was not speaking in an area of his expertise. It is interesting that the ratings of competence did not suffer as much, but that is of little consequence because the subjects indicated they would be less likely to follow the advice of the more arrogant person.

In this study high and low trusters did not differ overall on their ratings of the trustworthiness of the main characters of the tape. However, there was a strong interaction as a function of trust of subject and arrogance of character. High trusters gave significantly lower ratings on trustworthiness to arrogant speakers than they did to nonarrogant speakers. Low trusters did not significantly differentiate the arrogant from the nonarrogant speaker, although both high trusters and low trusters tended to rate the arrogant speaker as less trustworthy. Although these results do not apparently have any direct bearing on the gullibility of high trusters, they do indicate that high trusters are differentiating whom to trust and whom not to trust on the basis of specific cues. We have no evidence that they differentiate any better or worse than do low trusters, but these results suggest that high trusters and low trusters may be using different cues in making their decisions.

To summarize the research regarding the gullibility of high and low trusters, it can be said, most conservatively, that we have failed to establish that high trusters are any more likely to be fooled than are low trusters. This conclusion seems warranted, since we have examined the issue in a wide variety of studies involving many different kinds of criteria, and the criteria themselves were reliable and could be significantly related logically to variables other than the level of generalized trust of the subject. It seems that high trusters can read the cues as well or as poorly as low trusters. They differ, however, in their willingness to trust the stranger where there are no clear-cut data. The high truster says to himself or herself, I will trust the person until I have clear evidence that he or she can't be trusted. The low truster says, I will not trust the person until there is clear evidence that he or she can be trusted. Whether what we have called high trust is a difference in the expectancy of risk or in the importance to the subject for acting trusting and verbalizing trust, or both, still needs to be determined.

Before attempting to draw conclusions from these studies, it should be noted that none of them dealt with deprived populations or groups that are subject to strong prejudice. We simply do not know whether or not these findings would hold in such populations. The notion of risk, or in social learning theory terms, the reinforcement value of the consequences of trust, has not been systematically considered in these studies. Deutsch (1960) regarded risk as an important aspect of his definition of trusting behavior. Several of the studies reported here do involve a low level of risk, such as the game situations and the apparatus that might deliver a strong shock, and others perhaps involve moderate risk, for example, the investigations of cheating and shoplifting. However, the data are insufficient to generalize our results easily to conditions of very high risk.

SUMMARY AND CONCLUSION

It is not difficult to summarize these studies, keeping in mind the limitations previously mentioned. The results are not surprising; they may not go much beyond common sense, but neither are they trivial.

First, a strong statement can be made about the consequences to the society of people being more trusting. People who trust more are less likely to lie and are possibly less likely to cheat or steal. They are more likely to give others a second chance and to respect the rights of others.

Second, the personal consequences for the high truster also seem beneficial. The high truster is less likely to be unhappy, conflicted, or maladjusted; he or she is liked more and is sought out as a friend more often, both by low-trusting and by high-trusting others.

Third, the high truster is no less capable of determining who should be trusted and who should not be trusted, although in novel situations he or she may be more likely to trust others than is the low truster. It may be true that the high truster is fooled more often by crooks, but the low truster is probably fooled equally often by distrusting honest people, thereby forfeiting the benefits that trusting others might bring.

Finally, what does this mean for us as teachers, parents, educators, psychologists? We cannot control the forces at work in society by ourselves, but within our own smaller circles of influence, we can model and encourage a little more trust. The consequences can be beneficial, the risks do not seem to be too great, and a younger generation may be a little more ready for a better world—just in case there is one coming.

REFERENCE NOTES

1. Hochreich, D. J. *Interpersonal trust and trustworthiness under conditions of surveillance and non-surveillance.* Unpublished manuscript, 1977. (Available from Dorothy J. Hochreich, Department of Psychology, University of Connecticut, Storrs, Connecticut 06268.)
2. Hochreich, D. J. *Trust and interpersonal attraction.* Unpublished manuscript, 1977.
3. Wright, T. L., & Shea, J. J. *Locus of control, interpersonal trust, expertise of diagnostician, and acceptance of personality interpretations in the Barnum effect.* Unpublished manuscript, 1976. (Available from Thomas L. Wright, Department of Psychology, Catholic University, Washington, D.C. 20013.)
4. Rotter, J. B., & Zuroff, D. C. Unpublished data, 1977. (Available from Julian B. Rotter, Department of Psychology, University of Connecticut, Storrs, Connecticut 06268.)

REFERENCES

Boroto, D. R. *The Mosher Forced Choice Inventory as a predictor of resistance to temptation.* Unpublished master's thesis, University of Connecticut, 1970.
Byrne, D. *The attraction paradigm.* New York: Academic Press, 1971.
Collins, W., & Wrightsman, L. S., Jr. Indicators of maladjustment in preadolescent and adolescent boys. *American Psychologist,* 1962, *17,* 318. (Abstract)
Deutsch, M. Trust, trustworthiness and the F scale. *Journal of Abnormal and Social Psychology,* 1960, *61,* 138–140.

Geller, J. D. *Some personal and situational determinants of interpersonal trust.* Unpublished doctoral dissertation, University of Connecticut, 1966.

Hamsher, J. H., Jr. *Validity of personality inventories as a function of disguise of purpose.* Unpublished doctoral dissertation, University of Connecticut, 1968.

Into, E. C. *Some possible childrearing antecedents of interpersonal trust.* Unpublished master's thesis, University of Connecticut, 1969.

Katz, H. A., & Rotter, J. B. Interpersonal trust scores of college students and their parents. *Child Development,* 1969, *40,* 657–661.

Lajoy, R. J. *The effects of arrogance and expertise on the communications of physicians and auto repairmen.* Unpublished doctoral dissertation, University of Connecticut, 1975.

Rotter, J. B. *Social learning and clinical psychology.* Englewood Cliffs, N.J.: Prentice-Hall, 1954. (Reprinted by Johnson Reprint Co., New York.)

Rotter, J. B. A new scale for the measurement of interpersonal trust. *Journal of Personality,* 1967, *35,* 651–665.

Rotter, J. B. Generalized expectancies for interpersonal trust. *American Psychologist,* 1971, *26,* 443–452.

Rotter, J. B., Chance, J., & Phares, E. J. *Applications of a social learning theory of personality.* New York: Holt, Rinehart & Winston, 1972.

Rotter, J. B., & Stein, D. K. Public attitudes toward the trustworthiness, competence, and altruism of twenty selected occupations. *Journal of Applied Social Psychology,* 1971, *1,* 334–343.

Steinke, G. D. *The prediction of untrustworthy behavior and the Interpersonal Trust Scale.* Unpublished doctoral dissertation, University of Connecticut, 1975.

Wright, T. L. *Situational and personality parameters of interpersonal trust in a modified Prisoner's Dilemma Game.* Unpublished doctoral dissertation, University of Connecticut, 1972.

Wright, T. L., & Kirmani, A. Interpersonal trust, trustworthiness and shoplifting in high school. *Psychological Reports,* 1977, *41,* 1165–1166.

Commentary to Chapter 11

This last selection is a brief chapter from a recent book edited by N. Feather. The book is concerned primarily with expectancy-value approaches to social psychology, and the description of SLT provided in this chapter is a selective series of comments on some issues that are or have been important to social psychologists in recent years. Some of the first part of the paper covers material that has appeared earlier in this book. However, it is applied here to specific issues that may help to illuminate the principles expressed.

Although most theories of motivation, such as those of need achievement and aggression, now recognize that the relationship of motive and behavior must be mediated by an expectancy construct, this has not always been the case. SLT can take some credit for its influence on the more sophisticated recent theories. It is still true, however, that the related areas of research, motivation, emotions, and reinforcement are not treated as related or overlapping by the majority of writers. Theorists working in one area ignore important data collected by scientists working in another. In this paper I have tried again to bring them together.

At one time the measurement of social attitudes and the prediction of behavior from such measurements were the central concerns of social psychologists. Part of the reason for the current marked drop in interest was the failure to make consistent *behavioral prediction from these attitude measurements. A section of this paper deals with this problem and analyzes the complexity of the relationship between attitude and observable behavior. I am sure that reasonable predictions of social behavior can be made, but it requires an understanding of many variables and much more sophisticated measurement techniques than have been used in the past.*

Finally, a comment is needed regarding the section on the psychological situation. I have attempted here a much more specific definition, one that confronts some important problems in defining the environment in psychological or subjective terms but that still allows for objective prediction. I have also attempted to deal more realistically with the problem of a taxonomy of situations. At one time I believed a useful general taxonomy of all meaningful situations might be achievable, at least for a relatively homogeneous culture. *However, the situational variables relevant to a specific problem in prediction vary so much from problem to problem, are so numerous, and interact so much that we evidently need to develop analyses of situational differences and variables for each problem of prediction. It will be a long time before a taxonomy of situations relevant for all problems can be regarded as a meaningful goal.*

11

Social Learning Theory

In 1954 the author published a social learning theory of personality (SLT) which represented an attempt to integrate reinforcement theories and cognitive or field theories of behavior. As a personality theory, it included both a theory of how individual differences in stable behavior are acquired, generalized and changed (i.e., a process theory) and a descriptive system of individual differences, focusing on some of the dimensions on which individuals may differ.

The range of convenience of such a theory clearly goes beyond problems traditionally considered personality problems and applies to some of the problems presented in fields such as human learning and performance, development, social psychology and the social sciences, psychopathology, and psychotherapy. A description of such applications has been presented by Rotter, Chance, and Phares (1972).

In this chapter I shall attempt to describe briefly some of the basic principles of this theory and then to elaborate by applying them to four problem areas of special significance to this book. The four areas to be discussed are: 1) motivation, incentive and emotion, 2) beliefs, expressed social attitudes and social action, 3) attribution theory and defensive behavior, and 4) the psychological situation and interactionism.

Rotter, Julian B. Social learning theory. In N. T. Feather (Ed.), *Expectations and actions: Expectancy-Value models in psychology.* Hillsdale, N.J.: Lawrence Erlbaum Associates, 1982. Reprinted by permission.

SOME BASIC PRINCIPLES OF
SOCIAL LEARNING THEORY

In SLT, four basic concepts are used in the prediction of behavior. These concepts are: behavior potential, expectancy, reinforcement value, and the psychological situation. In addition, somewhat broader concepts are utilized for problems involving more general behavioral predictions; i.e., those dealing with behavior over a period of time and those including a number of specific situations. These variables and their relationships may be conveniently stated in the formulas which follow. It should be remembered, however, that these formulas do not at this time imply any precise mathematical relationships. Indeed, although the relationship between expectancy and reinforcement value is probably a multiplicative one, there is insufficient systematic data at this point which would allow one to evolve any precise mathematical statement.

The basic formula is stated thus:

$$1. \quad BP_{x_1, s_1, r_a} = f(E_{x_1, r_a, s_1} \ \& \ RV_{a, s_1})$$

This formula is read: the potential for behavior x to occur, in situation 1 in relation to reinforcement a, is a function of the expectancy of the occurrence of reinforcement a, following behavior x in situation 1, and the value of reinforcement a in situation 1.

The above formula is obviously limited, inasmuch as it deals only with the potential for a given behavior to occur in relation to a single reinforcement. As noted earlier, description at the level of personality constructs usually demands a broader, more generalized concept of behavior reflected in the following formula:

$$2. \quad BP_{(x-n), s_{(1-n)}, R_{(a-n)}} = f(E_{(x-n), s_{(1-n)}, R_{(a-n)}} \ \& \ RV_{(a-n), s_{(1-n)}})$$

The formula is read: the potentiality of functionally related behaviors x to n to occur, in specified situations 1 to n in relation to potential reinforcements a to n, is a function of the expectancies of these behaviors leading to these reinforcements in these situations and the values of these reinforcements in these situations. To simplify communication, this second formula can be restated by introducing three terms—*need potential, freedom of movement,* and *need value*—to represent the three terms in Formula 2.

$$3. \quad NP = f(FM \ \& \ NV)$$

Thus, need potential is a function of freedom of movement and need value. In broader predictive or clinical situations, the latter formula would more likely be used, while the first formula would be appropriate in testing more specific, experimental hypotheses. A special significance of this formula is that when freedom of movement is low and need value is high, then the probability of defensive behavior increases. Such defensive behavior would include avoidance behaviors and attempts to attain the desired goal by irreal (Lewin) or symbolic means.

The fourth variable, *the psychological situation,* is implicit in Formula 3. In SLT the psychological situation is considered to be of considerable importance. It is emphasized that behavior varies as the situation does. But, obviously, there is also transituational generality in behavior. If there were not, there would be no point in discussing "personality" as a construct or as a field of study. However, along with generality there is also situational specificity. While it may be true that person A is generally more aggressive than person B, nonetheless, there may be certain situations in which person B behaves more aggressively than does person A. Predictions based solely on internal characteristics of the individual are not sufficient to account for the complexities of human behavior.

Our definition of *behavior* is a broad-gauged one. Any response to a meaningful stimulus (one that has acquired meaning as a result of previous experience) which can be *measured* either directly or indirectly would qualify. Behavior usually labelled as "cognitive" or "implicit" is included in this definition. Such behavior is not observed directly—it must be inferred from the presence of other behaviors. For example, the behavior of looking for alternative solutions, studied by Schroder and Rotter (1952), is a case in point. Looking for alternative solutions to problems was inferred to be present when the test for its occurrence—longer time taken by a subject for solution of a previously solved task and shorter time for the solution of a new task requiring an alternative solution as compared to other subjects—took place. Likewise, rehearsal of thoughts about failure and its consequences may be measured, inferentially, by assessing subjects' performance on a difficult task where concentrated attention is necessary for problem solution.

Three different kinds of expectancies are postulated in social learning theory. 1. Simple cognitions or labeling of stimuli; such as, "that's a chair," "I am warm," etc. 2. Expectancies for behavior-reinforcement sequences; such as, "If I cough, she will notice me," and 3. Expectancies for reinforcement-reinforcement sequences;

such as, "when I get my Ph.D., I will become rich and respected," "if my mother praises me now, the other boys will tease me later."

It is hypothesized in social learning theory that when a person perceives two situations as similar, then his or her expectancies for a particular kind of reinforcement, or class of reinforcements, will generalize from one situation to another. This does not mean that the expectancies will be the same in the two situations, but that the changes in expectancies in one situation will have some small effect in changing expectancies in the other. *Expectancies in each situation are determined not only by specific experiences in that situation, but also, to some varying extent, by experiences in other situations which the individual perceives as similar.* One of the determinants of the relative importance of generalized expectancies versus specific expectancies developed in the same situation is the amount of experience in the particular specific situation. These relationships are expressed in the formula below (Rotter, 1954, p. 166):

$$4. \ E_{s_1} = f\left(E'_{s_1} \ \& \ \frac{GE}{f(N_{s_1})}\right)$$

In this formula s_1 represents the specific situation and N is a function of the amount of previous experience the individual has had in that situation. E represents expectancy, E' represents a specific expectancy, and GE represents generalized expectancy. Clearly, if the formula is correct (and there is considerable empirical evidence to support it), then the relative importance of generalized expectancy increases as the situation becomes more novel or ambiguous and decreases as the individual's experience in that situation increases. This point is important in understanding under what conditions one might expect clear prediction from an accurate measure of generalized expectancy.

In social learning theory we have described two kinds of generalized expectancies. One of these, the generalized expectancy referred to in the formula for need potential, involves expectancies for a particular kind of reinforcement; e.g., achievement, dependency, conformity, social approval, etc. In this case it is the similarity of the reinforcement that provides the dimension for the generalization of expectancies. The second kind of generalized expectancy deals with expectancies that generalize from other aspects of a series of situations involving some decision or problem solving. In this case the nature of the reinforcements themselves may vary, but the similarity of the problem provides the dimension for the generalization of expectancies. For example, in situations involving different kinds of reinforcements, we may be asking ourselves if we can trust this individual to tell the truth or we may ask ourselves how we are going to find the solution when our previous attempt was blocked. The first kind of generalized expectancy we designate with the subscript r for reinforcement (GE_r); the second kind is designated as a problem-solving generalized expectancy (GE_{ps}). In considering the expectancy for some reinforcement to follow some behavior in a given situation, both kinds of generalized expectancies might be involved. The above discussion can be represented in the following formula (Rotter, Chance, & Phares, 1972, p. 41):

$$5. \ E_{s_1} = \frac{f(E' \ \& \ GE_r \ \& \ GE_{ps_1} \ \& \ GE_{ps_2} \ \ldots GE_{ps_n})}{f(N_{s_1})}$$

If we could accurately calculate all of the relevant variables in determining an expectancy, we would still be a long way from the prediction of a specific behavior. Expectancy is only one of the three major determinants of a behavior potential in social learning theory. The second is the value of the reinforcement. (The third, the psychological situation, will be discussed in detail later in this paper.) If we want to predict a specific behavior, such as studying for an exam, voting in an election, taking part in a student protest, etc., we would have to be able to assess the values of the available reinforcements to a particular person in that situation before anything resembling an accurate prediction could be made.

At this point, it would be useful to introduce a discussion of the determinants of the value of reinforcements generally. The notion that psychological goals depend for their current value upon primary drive reduction is rejected, although for some goals drive reduction may have been important in their initial acquisition of reinforcement value. Instead, it is argued that psychological goals, needs, or reinforcements acquired during the individual's life depend upon other psychological reinforcements for their value. The value of any given reinforcement depends upon its association or pairing with other reinforcements. The value of a reinforcement is determined by the value of reinforcements with which it has been associated and by the expectancy that its occurrence leads to the subsequent occurrence of the associated or related reinforcements. A generalized formula from which the value of a reinforcement may be predicted is:

$$6. \ RV_{a,s_1} = f(E_{Ra \rightarrow R(b-n),s_1} \ \& \ RV_{(b-n)s_1})$$

The formula reads: the value of reinforcement a in situation 1 is a function of expectancies that this reinforcement will lead to the other reinforcements b to n in situation 1, and of the values of these other reinforcements b to n in situation 1. To some extent, reinforcements may be expected to change value in different situations and under differing conditions. This formula provides a basis for determining these values given a variety of conditions. However, it should be recognized that quite often reinforcement values have considerable stability across both situations and time.

Once the value of reinforcement a has been firmly established through its relationship with reinforcement b, it is not necessarily true that subsequent failure of reinforcement b to occur with reinforcement a will lower the value of the latter. There are specific conditions under which lowering the value of a will be more likely. Extinction is more likely under conditions of massed trials, where the original learning was not partially reinforced, or when the relationship between the two goals has been verbalized by the person. To a great extent, however, a reinforcement will maintain its value until new associations or pairings with other reinforcements of different values (more positive or more negative) occur. Since most goals acquire their value under spaced rather than massed conditions of training, under partial rather than 100% reinforcement, and since the relationships are frequently not verbalized, most reinforcements maintain their value except as they change on the basis of new pairings with other reinforcements.

Reinforcements may also become functionally related to other reinforcements, and be changed in value, on the basis of cognitive activities. Either by means of symbolic manipulations or by attending to the behavior of another person and its consequences for him or her, an individual's reinforcement values are altered. By cognitive means, human beings are not only able to learn extremely complex methods of solving contemporary problems, but also to recreate the past and to create, through imagination, events which have not actually occurred. Imaginative rehearsal of events can affect reinforcement value. For example, in a choice situation in which the individual has to select only one of two possible alternative reinforcements, the reinforcement which is not chosen does not occur. However, in the process of deciding and imaginatively rehearsing its occurrence, its reinforcement value may change through pairings with other events that also take place in thought or imagination. In most cases, such changes may be small and subtle, but they must certainly exist, and, in some instances, they may be very great indeed.

Similarly, when we attempt to obtain a reinforcement and fail to do so, not only is our expectancy for obtaining it reduced in future circumstances, but the reinforcement itself may become associated with the unpleasantness of failure and thereby decrease in value. It is equally possible that as a result of imaginative rehearsal of additional reinforcements obtainable through later success, the value of the "lost" reinforcement could actually increase. The central point here is that both expectancies and reinforcement values may change as a result of thinking. Description and prediction of the many cognitive processes subsumed under the term *thinking* is a great challenge.

More extensive definitions of these concepts, their assumptions, justifications, and elaborations are presented in Rotter (1954), Rotter, Chance, and Phares (1972), and Rotter (1975). Further discussion of the psychological situation is reserved for the last section of this chapter.

MOTIVATION, INCENTIVE AND EMOTION

This social learning theory adopts an empirical law of effect rather than a drive reduction theory to explain motivation. This does not negate cyclical physiological drives nor ignore their possible effects on the value of reinforcements.

A theory of motivation usually attempts to explain two aspects of behavior. One aspect deals with the directionality of behavior—the selection of one kind of reinforcement over another. The other aspect deals with the "energizing" of behavior, the "strength," or "force" of the behavior.

Social learning theory takes the position that both of these aspects can be understood and predicted from the concept of reinforcement value and that notions of "strength," "force," or "energy" are hangovers from a dualistic view of psychology. While it is easy to provide examples of literal energy being expended in studies of lower organisms, there seems to be no reasonable analogue of motive strength and energy expenditure in humans. Everyone would argue that it takes high "motivation" to shoot someone, but squeezing a trigger requires very little energy. The concept of energizing applied to human motivation is merely a bad analogue.

Can physiological cyclical drives affect the value of a reinforcement? Of course they can, since they produce internal cues which, along with external cues, determine not only expectancies for behavior-reinforcement sequences but also for reinforcement-reinforcement sequences (see Formula 6); hence, they affect the value of the reinforcement in that situation. The value of a glass of water increases when one's throat is dry, whether or not the dry throat is the result of true water deprivation or a "nervous" reaction to public speaking. For most human behavior beyond infancy and early childhood, however, the role of such internal stimuli is of lesser and lesser importance in contrast to that of social motives. Social values are learned through association with unlearned values but it is not necessary for social drives to lead to physiological drive reduction in order to be maintained (Rotter, 1954). In any case, it is the perceived stimuli we have to deal with and not the presumed physiological processes.

To regard the external reward as separate from the internal state makes a distinction similar to the one between drive as an energizing property and drive as a directional property of motivation. The concept of reinforcement value includes both of these. It is the *subjective* value placed on the external reward or incentive that is important and this is determined by past experience and present cues, whether they arise outside or inside the organism.

For example, "strength" of one's motivation for achievement, for some class of reinforcements and across some class of situations, can be stated as the need value (see Formula 3) of these reinforcements relative to the values of other reinforcements available in the same set of situations. Behavioral prediction (need potential) would require knowing the expectancies for obtaining these reinforcements (freedom of movement) as well as the relative values placed on them. The notion that low freedom of movement and high need value leads to defensive behavior increases the potential for prediction over that of approaches which postulate only direct relationships. A person with a high need value for academic achievement and low freedom of movement may not simply show a moderate response in an achievement situation but one which announces to others that he or she does not care about academic achievement at all.

It is clear that strong reinforcements—positive or negative—or the anticipation that such a reinforcement will take place shortly is accompanied by changes in autonomic nervous system activity. Such changes which can be thought of as resulting in changes in the state of the organism are what some psychologists refer to as emotions. In spite of its obvious relationship the close connection between reinforcement and emotional state or emotional behavior has been ignored by most writers. Theorists of emotional behavior and reinforcement theorists tend to regard problems only from the perspective of their own tradition and ignore other approaches. In social learning theory we recognize that such automatic changes can serve as cues and that, along with situational cues, they can affect learned behavior (Schachter, 1966; Lazarus, 1968). Clearly, individuals differ in the kinds of bodily changes that follow from the same reinforcement (Lacey, 1959); and some individuals are more aware of these bodily changes than others (Lazarus, 1968). Emotions have been a troublesome area for psychologists. To some extent this is the result of failure to separate behaviors from expectancies, and failure to separate bodily changes from the learned psychological patterns of response. Both physiological changes and learned response patterns have either strong reinforcement or its anticipation as a common antecedent. However, while strong reinforcement may be a common antecedent to both autonomic changes and learned behavioral responses, these two need not be highly correlated.

Occurrence of a negative reinforcement, or its anticipation, as already indicated, may lead to defensive or avoidant behaviors; and such behaviors can be understood as having a potential for a particular class of reinforcements. It may be characteristic of some people, however, to respond with aggression, repression, withdrawal, projection, depression, etc. somewhat independently of the kind (need category) of reinforcement. These responses may be a function of the sign or strength of the reinforcement rather than its particular form. In other words, we can talk not only about a behavior potential to repress competitive failures but a behavior potential to repress all strong negative reinforcements. How functional or general such potentials are across need areas is an empirical question. Mild failure in an achievement related task may increase the potential for some individuals to narrow their attention, increase concentration, etc. However, mild failure might not have the same effect should it occur in the process of initiating a social relationship.

The understanding and providing of an orderly description of this area is a current challenge to social learning theorists. In the meantime, it may be hypothesized that these psychological responses generally referred to as emotional behavior may be regarded as similar to other learned behaviors in which functional categories are related to the sign, strength, and nature of the reinforcements.

Anxiety (or certain behavioral referents for anxiety), aggression, repression, cautiousness, and rigidity are some of the characteristics that have been thought of by many investigators as consequences of "emotional" states. However, it has always been difficult to demonstrate the generality of these behaviors across different situations, at least in "normal" populations. Such behavioral characteristics appear to be more general among certain pathological groups and less general in the "normal" population. Behaviors elicited by strong positive reinforcements like elation or associated with mild positive reinforcements like relaxation have been investigated much less than those associated with negative reinforcements, but they are equally important for a comprehensive account of human behavior.

The description of states of the organism, the nature of reinforcement, and motivational states are intertwined problems. It is not necessary to explain all of these abstractions as if they were true facts of nature. From a social learning theory point of view, it is only necessary to have an integrated and efficient set of constructs to explain and/or predict complex human behavior.

BELIEFS, EXPRESSED SOCIAL ATTITUDES AND SOCIAL ACTION

Simple expectancies or cognitions were briefly mentioned earlier in this chapter. In social learning theory such expectancies about the properties of some object(s) or event(s) may also be called a belief. A belief about a class of social objects is referred to here as a social attitude. Simple cognitions, expectancies or beliefs may appear phenomenally to have an all-or-none quality, but in fact they may vary in magnitude between zero and one, and they are subject to change. The child looking at the adult may believe that he *is* smiling or that he *may* be smiling. The four-legged creature *is* a dog or *may* be a dog. Additional experience may teach the child that it is a cat. Cats are likely to scratch; dogs are not likely to scratch, etc. In other words, simple expectancies, beliefs, or cognitions may be regarded as having the properties of subjective probabilities varying in magnitude from zero to one and constantly subject to change with new experience.

No *necessary* awareness; that is, ability to verbalize, is implied by the term simple expectancy. In casting the concept of cognition into the language of an expectancy-reinforcement social learning theory, I am implicitly hypothesizing that the laws governing the growth and change of expectancies as well as those governing the relationship of expectancies to observable behaviors will also apply to simple cognition.

The simple cognitions regarding the properties of objects determine, in part, expectancies for behavior-reinforcement sequences by defining the gradients along which generalization takes place. As a consequence they determine, in part, which kinds of behaviors are likely to be tried out for novel objects and consequently, which behavior-reinforcement sequences are likely to be experienced. In the prediction of stable behavior it is the expectancies for behavior-reinforcement sequences, however, which play the major role. Behavior-reinforcement sequences in which expectancies for reinforcement are concerned solely with the characteristics of the object alone or with its potential as a source of reinforcement are only one determinant of a specific behavior choice in a given situation (e.g., "Don't sit on the radiator . . . you may get burned"). In social situations particularly, a specific behavioral choice may involve a number of reinforcements which are relatively independent of the properties of the object but which are, in fact, dependent upon other social agents present in the situation (e.g., "Don't sit on the radiator . . . it's not polite").

The formula for behavior potential, however, is limited for predictive purposes. That is, it deals only with the relationship between the potential of a single behavior and the expectancy for a specific reinforcement while in fact there is always a variety of potential reinforcements which follow from any given behavior. So, in order to make an actual prediction, it is necessary to measure not only the expectancy for one reinforcement and the value of that reinforcement but to measure the expectancy for many reinforcements and the values of all of the reinforcements. For example, the decision to study for an examination not only involves a potential grade and its value but also involves the loss of other satisfactions and the potential reactions of parents, teachers, and schoolmates. Were we, in fact, able to measure most of the important variance involved in such a behavioral choice, we still would not know whether or not the individual would choose such a behavior until we knew the relative value of other behavioral choices in that situation. These points can be illustrated by examining some of the individual difference variables involved in predicting some kinds of social action-taking behaviors.

Let us assume that an individual is approached with a request to take part in some form of civil disobedience, a disapproved march on the Capitol or a sit-in strike aimed at doing away with black-white segregation in some locality.

In Figure 11.1 potential determinants have been arranged in an hypothesized order of importance. Social approval has been placed at the top of the list. Situationally determined expectancies here would involve the nature of the person requesting participation and the degree to which the individual feels the *specific* action contemplated would or would not meet with social approval from significant others. Differences between E' and generalized expectancies could also account for those people who are in empathy with the action but somehow manage not to actually carry through with their commitment. The generalized expectancies would involve expectancies

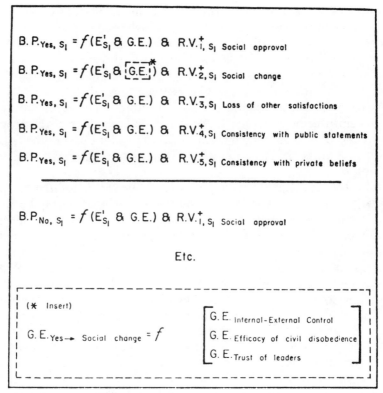

Figure 11.1 Some major sources of variance in the determination of the decision to take part in social action.

for the general class of actions for a variety of social agents and would be relatively independent of specific circumstances. Reinforcement values might differ in sign for different social agents, and the overall strength of a need value for social approval would, of course, differ among individuals.

The overall strength for such a need value as social approval in our culture is reflected in the actions of millions of people during time of war. Although thousands of persons, possibly millions, have no desire to endanger themselves, have no strong interests in the causes involved, and do not wish to interrupt the normal course of their lives, they nevertheless allow themselves to be drafted or may, in fact, enlist largely because of the fear of social disapproval for any other action. Similarly, people will go into battle in spite of strong motives to the contrary partly because of the strong social disapproval involved in taking one of various other alternatives, such as "feigning illness." Where feelings are intense, as in the taking of social action in regard to segregation in the South, expectancies for strong social disapproval can be very high and extremely important in determining behavioral choice.

In addition to different beliefs regarding the nature of blacks or of the injustice of present social conditions, people will still differ considerably in the degree to which they place value on effecting a social change. The strength of their belief in the injustice of present conditions may bear some relationship to the value they would place on social change, but it is probably far from a perfect relationship. Situational factors may again play a role in the expectancy that the behavior involved will lead to social change. The individual involved might consider it the wrong place, the wrong time, or the wrong leader. Generalized expectancies that this type of social action (i.e., civil disobedience) will lead to social change may also play a significant cross-situational role.

These generalized expectancies are illustrated at the bottom of Figure 11.1. The first, internal versus external control, is a variable with which we have done considerable research (Rotter, 1966, 1975; Phares, 1976; Lefcourt, 1976. In general, internal-external control refers to the degree to which the individual believes that what happens to him or her results from his or her own behavior versus the degree to which the individual believes that what happens to him or her is the result of luck, chance, fate, or forces beyond his or her control.

The second generalized expectancy is related to civil disobedience of many kinds. The individual may have developed, on the basis of previous experience, his or her own or that of others, an expectancy that such efforts do a great deal of good or none at all; the person may, in fact, believe that such behaviors actually delay rather than speed up social change.

The third generalized expectancy listed is one of trust of leaders for the civil rights movements. It is a more specific generalized expectancy than trust of other people, in general (Rotter, 1971, 1975), which might have been substituted in the figure for trust of leaders. Some individuals, although genuinely desiring social change and accepting the principle of civil disobedience, may expect that the leaders in the movement are dominated by Communists, are self-seeking, have ulterior motives, or cannot be relied upon to carry through. All such generalized expectancies will be partial determinants of agreeing to take part in the social action.

The third formula, dealing with loss of other satisfactions, might well be placed second, depending again upon the specific issue and place. Perhaps far more important than is the case in responses to attitude questionnaires, this behavior potential will play a significant role in the determination of social action. Even the relatively mild behavior of signing a petition may involve specific and generalized expectancies for loss of business, physical harm, persecution via the telephone, and other significant negative reinforcements. It may in fact involve only an interruption of one's other activities, but there are undoubtedly thousands of individuals who would join various protest activities were it not for the loss of other satisfactions.

The fourth formula deals with the values involved in consistency with other public statements. Obviously, the specific situation will play a role, particularly with regard to whether the individuals present have also been present when the other public statements have been made.

Our fourth formula deals with the need to maintain consistency among public statements and has been studied experimentally by focusing on the effects of commitment. Mischel (1958) and Watt (1965) have demonstrated strong effects of public commitment on resistance to changing publicly expressed expectancies for reinforcement in task situations; and Hobart and Hovland (1954) have demonstrated that public commitment leads to more resistance to attitude change.

Consistency between two public statements may not be of as great importance to some people as consistency between public statement and public action. Inconsistency here is not an intellectual matter, but rather a fear of being viewed as a "hypocrite," of not having "the courage of one's convictions." This could play an important role for many individuals who would have relatively little concern about consistency with private beliefs. The generalized expectancies in this formula would involve expectancies that lack of consistency would lead others to perceive the individual as a phony, hypocrite, or "fourflusher." What one has said on an attitude questionnaire might in fact play some role here, but far more important are public statements made under other circumstances.

Finally, we come to consistency with private beliefs. Does the action involved represent what we truly believe to be right or proper? Our simple beliefs or cognitions regarding blacks and the issues involved play a more direct role here in affecting E's and generalized expectancies. The reinforcement value of such consistency will vary greatly within our culture. For a few individuals, it may, in fact, be the strongest motive of any we have described in Figure 11.1. With the great majority of people in our society it appears that it plays a lesser role in determining social action behavior, however, than do the motives or reinforcement values we have previously discussed.

If we use Benedict's (1946) distinction between shame and guilt, we can say that consistency with public beliefs avoids shame and consistency with private beliefs avoids guilt. For most Americans I believe that, in this situation at least, the avoidance of shame is probably the stronger motive.

One implication of this analysis is that while social psychologists are generally aware of the many sources of variance, they appear in their research to have overemphasized the significance of simple beliefs about specific social groups in determining answers to questionnaires. To an even greater degree, they have exaggerated the significance both of beliefs about social objects and of responses to attitude questionnaires in determining the behavior of a person when faced with the alternative of some kind of social action.

This model does not explain how change in behavior is effected. Previous publications (Rotter, 1954; Rotter, Chance & Phares, 1972) have dealt with principles of changing expectancies and reinforcement values. By changing any of the variables in Figure 11.1 sufficiently, we can achieve behavior changes. The model in fact broadens considerably the conventional approach to behavior change in providing many more variables that can be manipulated in order to achieve such change.

There are many possible additional variables and reinforcements which have not been included in this illustration. The *behavior* of responding to a social attitude questionnaire could be analyzed similarly. In the latter case the value of consistency with private beliefs might be of much greater significance depending on the circumstances of testing and the controls for social approval exercised in the selection of items. Still it might not be the largest factor in determining a response in most circumstances.

This model does illustrate a method of analysis of a general problem and it presents a crude attempt to indicate the relationship of simple cognitions, expressed attitudes and behavior. While all these are related, the relationships are more complex than, perhaps, was originally thought. They are nevertheless amenable to systematic study.

SOCIAL LEARNING THEORY AND ATTRIBUTION THEORY

The purpose of this brief section is not to subsume attribution theory or to critically evaluate it, but rather merely to offer some comments on attribution theory from a social learning perspective.

At the outset, it should be made clear that expectations regarding causality before an event differ from beliefs after the event. Similarly, *expressed* beliefs after an event are not necessarily the same as implicit beliefs, but such verbal behaviors are subject to all the same kinds of determinants as those described in the section on social attitudes.

In the case of competitive activities it is clear that defensive behaviors are of extreme importance in failure situations; and these defenses are essentially a problem in individual differences as well evidenced by studies of level of aspiration techniques (Rotter, 1954, pp. 313–326). Even in dealing with attributions of causality for success a desire to be polite or socially acceptable may be reflected. Statements of expectancies for future success are influenced by ideas about negative sanctions for boasting, desire for conformity, etc., again, a function of individual differences. Of course, within a fairly homogeneous subculture, differences between groups subject to different conditions of success and failure will be statistically significant.

Attribution theorists also study the effect of attributions for one behavioral outcome on subsequent behaviors. Here, also, there is a tendency to accept the attributions literally (and naively). Do people really believe their own expressed attributions? Surely not always. The polite response, "it was luck," is not really believed by the tennis player who catches the edge of the line on a tennis ace and the same defensive attribution of a loser ("it was the other player's luck") does little to dispel his or her gloom.

One contribution of social learning theory to attribution theory is the concept of generalized expectancies for problem solving. Perhaps the generalized expectancy most studied in this regard is internal versus external control of reinforcement. However, it is clear from several studies that the prediction of certain behaviors may require an individual difference distinction between passive or congruent externals and defensive externals (Hochreich, 1974, 1975; Davis and Davis, 1972). Generalized expectancies such as trusting others, looking for alternatives, etc. must also affect the nature of post-hoc attributions, whether one is dealing with competitive tasks or other events. Such expectancies may also account in part for differences in the kind of attribution made for one's self versus the kind of attributions made for others, as well as other variables such as characteristic defenses.

When and why do people make attributions of causality at all? Although there is little or no research describing the conditions under which people do make attributions of causality, it seems intuitively clear that usually people do not make post-hoc attributions. In social learning theory increments and decrements in expectancies are hypothesized to be a function of differences between expected and actual outcomes and the relative novelty of the situation (Rotter, 1954, pp. 176–177). It seems that a reasonable hypothesis would be that two factors determining the spontaneous occurrence of attributions would be the unexpected nature of the event—when it does not fit previous experience, we are more likely to look for reasons. When previous experience is lacking, we are perhaps also more likely to look for causal relationships than when we are experiencing a familiar event.

The second factor would be the occurrence of strong reinforcements, particularly negative ones. "Why is God punishing me!" occurs as a spontaneous thought much more frequently than "Why is God rewarding me!" In any case, when there is both a strong reinforcement and an unexpected one, most people are more likely to make spontaneous attributions of causality.

If individual differences are an important aspect of attributions of causality then cultural differences would also account for considerable variance. Cultural differences in accepted defensive behavior, in concepts of reasonable causes, etc. should help us to understand both implicit beliefs and expressed attributions. The study of such cultural differences could reveal much about how attributions are learned and what variables control the expression of attributions.

THE PSYCHOLOGICAL SITUATION AND INTERACTIONISM

The first basic postulate of social learning theory is: "The unit of investigation for the study of personality is the interaction of the individual and his/her meaningful environment" (Rotter, 1954). This is clearly an interactionist position. It was stated earlier by Lewin (1935), Kantor (1924), and Murray (1938). Coutu (1949) in the field of sociology and Brunswik (1943) in his analysis of the field of perception expressed a similar principle. It should be noted, however, that all of these theorists have had great difficulty in using the concept of the psychological situation, meaningful environment, life space, etc., systematically in a *predictive* fashion, because they have stressed the subjective or learned nature of the environment. The term "meaningful environment" as used here refers to the acquired significance or meaning of the environment to the individual. It is the psychological, not the physical, description of the environment that is important.

In social learning theory we define the psychological situation as a complex set of interacting cues acting upon an individual for any specific time period. *These cues determine, for the individual, expectancies for behavior-reinforcement sequences and also for reinforcement-reinforcement sequences.* Such cues may be implicit as well as explicit; that is, they may be thoughts, ideas, or internal stimuli such as pain, pleasure, excitement, or fear. Implicit responses may be carried over from a prior experience and may not be related to what are considered present external cues. It is *not* necessary that the person be able to verbally express conscious awareness of these cues, but only that it can be demonstrated that he/she was reacting to them. In order to make the concept of the psychological situation operational implicit cues must be identified by inference from immediately prior events or by inference from behaviors in the situation other than the one we are predicting, including physiological observations which serve as indirect measures of the psychological state of the organism.

We define the psychological situation as the interacting cues perceived by the individual over any defined time unit; thus, we may be interested in cues over a period of a moment, an experimental hour, or over much longer periods of time, as when we talk about a person's job situation or marriage situation. The definition, then, is not precise. What we call personal variables and what we call situational variables can extend over long periods of time. The overall definition has to be in part arbitrary and relativistic, but it can be made workable and useful. The alternatives of either trying to predict behavior without paying attention to the present cues to which the individual is responding or of trying to predict behavior without taking into account what the individual brings into a situation in terms of relatively stable characteristics, limits one to extremely low levels of prediction. In other words, a useful distinction between person and situation is one which defines personal variables as a set of relatively stable characteristics and defines the other as the set of meaningful cues to which he or she is reacting at the present. Both sets of variables are presumed to be determined by past learning.

Problems Inherent in the Treatment of the Psychological Situation as a Systematic Variable

How can the psychological situation be defined independently of the person? If one defines the psychological situation as meaningful, or as truly psychological, rather than physical, or as subjective rather than objective, then the situation is a function of the person. We have already indicated that this is not a necessary barrier to problems of analysis, since we can treat situational variables as one aspect of the person and stable accumulated effects of experience, or person-ality variables, as a different aspect of the person. However, this does not tell us how to use the situation predictively.

In social learning theory this problem is treated by identifying the situation in the common sense terms of the social group, sub-culture, or culture. In other words, we can make clear the objective referent for what we are talking about and still treat the environment as a psychologically meaningful, or subjective environment. The sub-ject's reactions to the environment and the scientist's descriptions of the environment need not be identical. In fact, the social scientist is often busily engaged in using the latter in order to better understand the former. In this way, we can talk not only about differences among situations but about individual differences in response to the same objective situation. For example, we can generally obtain high agreement when we identify a situation as a classroom situation, a party, an authority situation, a frustration situation, etc. These are in themselves abstractions of a variety of cues, but at the common sense level. Note that we are not referring to an average of interpre-tations but to a descriptive level that will allow for high agreement among observers. If necessary or desirable, much more elaborate and detailed descriptions of the situation can be made, but always in the common sense terms of the subculture. Once we have identified a given situation, we can then make predictions about differences in behavior of individuals within that situation, differences of behavior of a group of individuals in one situation versus another, and inter-actions of the two. This is, of course, what social, clinical and per-sonality psychologists have been doing for a long time. We are stating here explicitly what others have done implicitly over many years. By describing how situations can be identified objectively we have opened the way, but have not solved the problem of identifying or discovering the important dimensions of situations which can be used in defining classes of situations.

How Much Variance in a Person-Situation Interaction is Due to Personality Variables and How Much Variance is due to Situational Variables?

From the point of view of social learning theory, the above question has to be regarded as a pseudo-problem. Although in the recent past, many investigators have been interested in this issue, most now recognize that the question is essentially meaningless, since both the personality variables and the situational variables de-pend on the person's previous experience. If we seek the answer to some specific, practical problem, the question may have some significance. For example, we may wish to know how much effect may be expected in measuring intelligence or school achievement when the examiner is black or white and the subjects are all black.

If one does ask the general question, there are at least seven aspects of the experimental design which will affect the answer.

The first of these is the homogeneity of subjects. If we are studying adjustment under conditions of mild and no stress, then an unselected group of college freshmen represent a much more homogeneous sample than would a group of subjects who range from hospitalized psychotic patients through the professional personnel who work at the institution. In the latter case, it is obvious that more variance will be attributable to people than to situations.

The second aspect is the question of what is being measured, or the criterion behavior being studied. That is, if we want to see how Moslem and Protestant Americans respond to success and failure situations, a measure of attributions to fate will probably show stronger between-group (person) differences than will a measure of perseverance.

The third experimental consideration which affects the relative importance of situational and individual differences is the degree of situational homogeneity. If we are examining the effects of success and failure on behavior, and we design our experiment to include passing or failing on a test of arithmetic reasoning given to high school subjects for "research purposes," with confidentiality of test scores assured, the situational variable will not account for as much variance as when we are studying the effects on behavior of passing or failing an examination in which failure would lead to the exclusion of any further educational goals.

The fourth variable affecting the relative variance attributed to behavior by situational and personality variables is the nature of the culture or subculture. This may be regarded as a special case of the first variable; namely, homogeneity of subjects. For example, consider a study of attitudes towards big-time athletics in college in which individual differences were predicted from a measure of need for achievement. The study is done in two colleges, one in which the football team has just won a national championship and the other in which they have just lost the national championship. With these situational and personality measures we might expect the degree of variance contributed by the individual difference variable to be much higher for females (who may vary more in their interest and involvement) than it is for males and for seniors (some of whom may become more cynical with longer time exposure) than it is for freshmen. In relationship to specific situations and when studying particular behaviors, one subculture may be much more homogeneous than another.

Many studies usually done by social psychologists with a secondary interest in individual differences often show little or no contribution of these individual differences to the prediction of criterion behavior. In many studies of person-situation interactions the individual differences measures employed by the investigator are invalid or irrelevant. In part, this is the result of the lack of good measures developed for specific purposes. The development of such measures requires years of careful work and modern test construction theory and technology. It is relatively easy to construct two situations which differ clearly and markedly in the degree of threat they present or in the kinds of reinforcements which it is possible to obtain. It is not nearly so easy to find a good measure of individual differences relevant to the criterion behavior being studied. And it is both difficult and time-consuming to construct such a measure and to validate it carefully. Literally hundreds of studies have thrown in a scale for measuring attitudes towards internal versus external control of reinforcement, as an afterthought in a study whose main focus is situational differences. However, it seems clear that in a significant proportion of such studies, it can be reliably established that the measure was in fact irrelevant to the behavior being studied.

The sixth variable, similar to the one just discussed, is the relevance of the situational variable which is being manipulated to the criterion behavior. If we are studying the interaction of academic aptitude and sex of the examiner during the giving of final examinations in a math course, then it is common sense that the situational variable—sex of the examiner—will have little or no effect on the criterion behavior—grade on the examination. It is not a relevant dimension for the criterion of examination grade in a math course, although it would be a relevant dimension if the test were a Rorschach test being given to college students for research purposes.

Finally, the seventh dimension is the degree of familiarity or novelty of the situation used in the experiment. For example, Schwarz (1969) has shown that several measures of a generalized expectancy for success on a relatively novel motor skill task correlated significantly with the first trial on the task. The correlation was lowered eventually to zero with increased massed trials. In social learning theory this follows from our formula that an expectancy is a function of a specific expectancy learned in that situation and related generalized expectancies. The generalized expectancies have less influence on the situation as the number of trials increase.

It is clear from the above analysis that one can easily design an experiment to either maximize variance accounted for by personality measures or by situational differences in some specific person-situation interaction.

To make use of the psychological situation for predictive purposes it is necessary to identify functional dimensions of situational similarity. Methods for doing this have been described by Rotter (1981) in another source.

REFERENCES

Benedict, Ruth F. *The crysanthemum and the sword.* Boston: Houghton Mifflin, 1946.

Brunswik, E. Organismic achievement and environmental probability. *Psychological Review,* 1943, *40,* 255-272.

Coutu, W. *Emergent human nature.* New York: Knopf, 1949.

Davis, W. L., & Davis, D. E. Internal-external control and attribution of responsibility for success and failure. *Journal of Personality,* 1972, *40,* 123-136.

Hobart, Enid M., & Hovland, C. I. The effect of "commitment" on opinion change following communication. *American Psychologist,* 1954, *9,* 394. (Abstract)

Hochreich, D. J. Defensive externality and attribution of responsibility. *Journal of Personality,* 1974, *42,* 543-557.

Hochreich, D. J. Defensive externality and blame projection following failure. *Journal of Personality and Social Psychology,* 1975, *32,* 540-546.

Kantor, J. R. *Principles of psychology.* Vols 1 & 2. New York: Knopf, 1924.

Lacey, J. I. Psychophysiological approaches to the evaluation of psychotherapeutic process and outcome. In E. A. Rubinstein and M. B. Parloff (Eds.), *Research in psychotherapy,* 1959. Washington, D.C.: American Psychological Association, pp. 160-208.

Lazarus, R. S. Emotions and adaptation: Conceptual and empirical relations. In W. J. Arnold (Ed.), *Nebraska symposium on motivation.* Lincoln, Nebraska: University of Nebraska Press, 1968.

Lefcourt, H. M. *Locus of Control: Current trends in theory and research.* Hillsdale, N.J.: Lawrence Erlbaum Associates, 1976.

Lewin, K. *A dynamic theory of personality.* New York, London: McGraw-Hill, 1935.

Mischel, W. The effect of the commitment situation on the generalization of expectancies. *Journal of Personality,* 1958, *26,* 508-516.

Murray, H. A. *Explorations in personality: A clinical and experimental study of fifty men of college age, by the workers at the Harvard psychological clinic.* New York, London: Oxford University Press, 1938.

Phares, E. J. *Locus of control in personality.* Morristown, N.J.: General Learning Press, 1976.

Rotter, J. B. *Social learning and clinical psychology.* New York: Johnson Reprint Company, 1973, 1980. (Originally published, 1954).

Rotter, J. B. Generalized expectancies for internal versus external control of reinforcement. *Psychological Monographs*, 1966, *80* (Whole No. 609), 1-28.

Rotter, J. B. Generalized expectancies for interpersonal trust. *American Psychologist*, 1971, *26*, 443-452.

Rotter, J. B. Some problems and misconceptions related to the construct of internal versus external control of reinforcement. *Journal of Consulting and Clinical Psychology*, 1975, *43*, 56-67.

Rotter, J. B. The psychological situation in social learning theory. In D. Magnusson (Ed.), *Toward a psychology of situations: An interactional perspective*. Hillsdale, N.J.: Lawrence Erlbaum Associates, 1981.

Rotter, J. B., Chance, J. E., & Phares, E. J. *Applications of a social learning theory of personality*. New York: Holt, Rinehart & Winston, 1972.

Schachter, S. The interaction of cognitive and physiological determinants of emotional state. In C. D. Spielberger (Ed.), *Anxiety and behavior*. New York: Academic Press, 1966, pp. 193-224.

Schroder, H. M., and Rotter, J. B. Rigidity as learned behavior. *Journal of Experimental Psychology*, 1952, *44*, 141-150.

Schwarz, J. C. Contributions of generalized expectancy to stated expectancy under conditions of success and failure. *Journal of Personality and Social Psychology*, 1969, *11*, 157-164.

Watt, N. F. The relation of public commitment, delay after commitment, and some individual differences to changes in verbalized expectancies. *Journal of Personality*, 1965, *33*, 284-299.

12
Summary

The preceding selections are representative of three major interests in my professional career. The first of these is the development of social learning theory, the second is a concern with the theory and methodology of personality measurement, and the third is a concern with the application of social learning theory to problems of social importance. I will discuss these in turn, including my estimate of what has been accomplished and, finally, what would be promising next steps.

THE DEVELOPMENT OF SOCIAL LEARNING THEORY

At present, social learning theory has demonstrated a strong heuristic potential. Both in its testing and in its application to a wide variety of problems, the theory has led to a substantial accumulation of research findings.

Verbalized expectancies, increments and decrements in expectancies, and the generalization of expectancies behave in lawful and predictive fashion, as do reinforcement values and their changes. Specific expectancies determine increasing variance, and generalized expectancies determine decreasing variance as experience with a task or psychological situation increases.

From its inception, the theory has proved useful as a way of *analyzing* problems. Constructs have been added only as satisfactory ways of measuring them have been developed, and the logical consistency of the operational definitions with theoretical and ideal definitions has been strong.

The process theory described here is sufficiently complex to deal

325

with a variety of psychological problems, as attested to by the great
variety of topics that have been studied from a SLT point of view
and have added some increment of knowledge to these areas. Research topics that have been attacked have dealt primarily with process variables; these include studies of increments and decrements
of expectancy and reinforcement value under a variety of conditions,
generality-specificity, situational effects on behavior, the generalization of expectancies, antecedents of and changes in minimal goal
levels, freedom of movement, and psychological defense. Thus the
contents of this book are evidence that the process theory described
here is sufficiently complex to deal with a variety of problems.

The formula on page 268 in Chapter 9 on problems and misconceptions, which includes generalized expectancies for problem solving, undoubtedly complicates the problem of accurate prediction;
at the same time, however, it provides a new and promising approach
to a vast number of problems. The consistent and replicated findings
described in Chapter 6 on internal-external control reflect this. The
section on attitude measurement in Chapter 11 illustrates the intri-
cacy and complexity of the problem of prediction when one considers the great variety of generalized expectancies that may be
involved in a single choice situation. The strategy of theory development followed here involved starting with the fewest and broadest
classes of variables and adding other variables as the necessity appeared and as it became clear that the existing constructs did not
allow for efficient prediction. The strategy was to add new classes
of variables only after it was clear how they could be measured and
how they would fit systematically into the theory. The work reported here on internal-external control of reinforcement and interpersonal trust includes only a small portion of the studies illustrating
how the addition of generalized expectancies for problem solving
allows for increased prediction in problems involving learning, perception, social action, psychopathology, cognitive development,
achievement, moral behavior, psychotherapy, and so on.

The theory is so intricate, in fact, that mathematical prediction
seems further away now than it did before the addition of generalized expectancies for problem solving as a major class of constructs.
*It has become increasingly clear that the accuracy of prediction of
choice behavior of human beings depends not only on the variables
that one uses to abstract but also on the adequacy of the selection
within a group of variables of those that are most relevant for a particular problem.*

Any theory of personality must deal with the problem of generality-specificity. In SLT we consider this an empirical problem. We

have demonstrated repeatedly that generalization of expectancies for behavior-reinforcement sequences is a regular and inevitable process. The invariable consequence is that there must be some generality to behavior. The question is not whether some characteristics are general and some specific but, rather, in a given predictive situation, how much variance is accounted for by generalization from other situations perceived as *similar* and how much from previous experience in situations perceived as the *same*. Clearly the words *same* and *similar* should be regarded as referring to relative degrees of similarity. To predict in situations that could be considered novel, measures of generalized characteristics would account for the most variance. In highly familiar situations, measures of previous behavior in the same situation would carry the most variance. However, there are always some generalized expectancies that play a role in behavior, as attested to by consistent individual differences in verbalized expectancies after a group of subjects has gone through an identical long sequence of successes and failures on some task. As expressed in our expanded formula for E (see page 268), the relative importance of generality and specificity for prediction will vary from situation to situation; but they will vary in a systematic, lawful fashion.

The content classes of social learning theory are derived from the process theory. When the members of a group generalize their experiences, and, consequently, develop a more or less similar way of reacting to a class of events, there is a potential basis for abstracting a variable describing individual differences that will be functional in nature—functional, that is, in that the observation of one or more instances of behavior will allow for the better-than-chance prediction of others in specified situations or under specified conditions. Humans, however, are capable of perceiving similarity along a vast number of dimensions and at many levels of generality. One characteristic that may be unique to social learning theory is the emphasis on the process theory determining how one selects classes of content variables. The advantages are obvious since the process theory immediately points to hypotheses regarding how the individual differences in the content variable were developed or maintained and how they are changed. Second, we have avoided the use of terms, no matter how widely used or how long their history, unless there is a genuine basis for assuming the generalization process, or functionality, although we may often deal with the same behavioral characteristics of individuals as other approaches. For this reason we have avoided content categories in terms of psychopathological diseases or disease entities, as well as broad but poorly defined concepts such as anxiety and emotions.

The content categories that were most emphasized in early research were psychological needs. Needs, characterized by perceived similarity of the reinforcement, include as subclasses (1) behaviors leading to the same or similar reinforcements (*need potential*), (2) expectancies for the attainment of these similar reinforcements (*freedom of movement*), and (3) the preference or desirability attached to these reinforcements (*need value*). In addition to the broad needs that may characterize everyone in a culture and include large numbers of reinforcements, the concept of needs includes any group of reinforcements that are perceived as similar. As pointed out in the article on social-learning-theory implications for testing, there are several advantages to this view of motivated or goal-directed behavior. For one thing, it does not emphasize only the objective behaviors, or the implicit goal strengths, or the cognitive perceptions of a situation; it includes all three. Enhanced prediction results in the consideration of all three as important and necessary aspects of goal-directed behavior.

Much of the research on social learning theory dealt with relatively broad needs and some of the more specific needs that are clearly subclasses of one of the broader needs, such as academic recognition, dependency on peers, physical skills recognition, and love and affection from opposite sex peers. There are many other concepts that cut across the broad needs described in Chapter Five. Crowne and Liverant (1963) have dealt in this way with conformity. Crowne and Marlowe (1964) describe an impressive series of studies on social approval conceived of as a need; likewise, Mosher, Mortimer, and Grebel (1968) have approached the concept of aggression as a behavior directed toward the goal of inflicting pain on others. When aggression is regarded as a need, it then includes a series of related behaviors (need potential) and of expectancies (freedom of movement) that those behaviors will lead to a differentially valued set of reinforcements (need value) contingent on the situation. Such a view contrasts with those that regard aggression either as an instinctual response to frustration or as part of an instinctual reservoir inherent in all humans. Altruistic behavior has been similarly analyzed and studied by Rettig (1956).

Just as perceived similarities of reinforcements will lead to generalization and the building up of stable modes of response, so will certain other aspects of the situation lead to similar generalizations and classes of stable behavior. One of these is the kind of problem presented in the situation; that is, the nature of the kinds of alternatives that are open for obtaining satisfactions. Internal versus external control of reinforcement appears to be a basic generalized expectancy that may have effects on a great variety of behaviors.

Mosher (1968) and his students have completed a series of investigations studying guilt, conceptualized as a generalized expectancy for self-mediated punishment following moral transgression. Much of his work to date has been in studying the functionality of the concept and in assessing construct validity of a series of measures of guilt.

Another generalized expectancy, perhaps of great potential importance in understanding broad trends in our society, is that of interpersonal trust, a generalized expectancy that others can be believed. Moss (1961) and Efran and Korn (1969) have worked with a generalized expectancy that might be called cautiousness or a belief that one must be careful and avoid risks, particularly in ambiguous situations. Such a concept certainly overlaps heavily the notions of success strivers versus failure avoiders in social-psychological problems of conformity and in studies of achievement and risk-taking behavior (Feather, 1968; Birney, Burdick, & Teevan, 1969). Other generalized expectancies for problem solving with which we have been concerned include looking for alternatives, long-term planning, seeking out the motives of others, and discriminating among situations.

These content variables differ from those of needs in that what is generalized from one situation to another is the similarity of the *problem of obtaining satisfaction or avoiding punishment* in different situations, rather than the similarity in the nature of the ultimate reinforcement. Trust may be involved in situations in which the ultimate reinforcement might be love, achievement, or physical safety. It is not the nature of the reinforcement that leads to a common expectancy; rather, in all these situations, the common or similar element is whether some other person can be believed in his communications.

Another class of content variables for the description of individual differences may be characterized as defense and enhancement behavior in which the common elements of a series of events are the sign and strength of the reinforcement. Some individuals characteristically may not only generalize the nature of the reinforcement but also perceive as similar different situations involving different reinforcements, all of which are nevertheless strongly positive or strongly negative. In such situations they may develop techniques of enhancement or defense to maintain positive reinforcement or minimize negative reinforcement. For example, one person *may* react to all strong threats by withdrawal, regardless of what goal is being blocked; another may respond to the same strong negative reinforcements with perceptual distortions. This area is not an easy one to investigate and historically has led to a variety of partially overlapping concepts such as emotions, anxiety, emotional behavior, affective responses, defensive behavior, frustration, and so forth. In many instances behavior that has been considered under these latter categories may be better thought of as instrumental behavior or goal-directed behavior, perhaps learned early in life but nevertheless predictable on the basis of expectancies and reinforcement values. The question still to be resolved is whether the generality of behavior is determined by the nature of the reinforcement, the sign and strength (positive or negative) of the reinforcement, or both. In any case there is clear indication that individuals will differ consistently in immediate responses to strong positive or negative reinforcement or the anticipation of either of these in the immediate situation. We have begun to investigate these reactions as a separate content class for the study of individual differences. Studies of some short-term effects of negative reinforcement have been published by Ford (1963) and by Mischel and Masters (1966). Ford's study suggests that overt aggression appears only when the subject feels that the frustration is unfair and not the result of his own lack of skill. Mischel and Masters's investigation supported the hypothesis that the arbitrary nonavailability of an expected reinforcement increased the value of the reinforcement. A distinction between defensive and passive externality (Davis, 1970; Hochreich, 1974, 1975, 1978) is another approach to defensive behavior; Krugman is studying the generality of ambivalence as a defense against expected failure.[1]

In order to obtain a maximum predictive efficiency or, if one prefers, to understand the determinants of behavior, it is necessary not only to characterize generality in terms of individual characteristics but also to determine the generality of situations. Implicitly, in fact, we have been discussing such generality or situational categorization throughout this section. If expectancies for reinforcement are determined by the situation, then it is clear that situations may be described as similar in that they are characteristically perceived as leading to one kind of reinforcement rather than another. In this sense we may talk about achievement situations, love and affection situations, social acceptance situations, or ambiguous or novel situations. In the literature, in fact, this problem is sometime dealt with by concepts such as arousal, instigation, press, threat, and the like.

People differ in the degree to which they perceive the world as controlled by their own efforts, skills, and characteristics, as opposed to chance, luck, fate, or powerful others; situations, too, will differ for the subculture as a whole in the degree to which they are perceived as being controlled by skill or by chance. In other words, generalized expectancies for problem solving carry with them the potential classifications of situations based on the nature of the problem to be solved, or the characteristics of the situation that determine how the individual is likely to obtain satisfaction. Similarly, strong positive or negative reinforcement or the anticipation of either also suggests a situational characteristic that for a given subculture may provide a basis for describing similarity in situations. Halpin and Winer (1952), studying leadership and the characteristics of desirable leaders, have found great utility and enhanced predictiveness in discriminating among situations with respect to the degree of outside threat to which the group is exposed. There are many other ways in which situations can be characterized as similar, depending, of course, on the problem being investigated. Social attitudes provide another class of content variables in which the principle of generalization is applied to social objects as part of the situation.

What we have contributed to the study of content of personality is not a new taxonomy of traits, or a new taxonomy of situations, or a new typology of people, but rather classes of content variables all of which are integrated with the same process theory, which provides leads to their development and change. We have provided a method of analyzing problems but not a series of answers. The answers must come from empirical study and undoubtedly will be constantly revised with the acquisition of new knowledge. The problem of the investigator—whether his or her concern is to help a particular person clinically, to do an exploratory study, or to test a theoretical hypothesis—is to *select* from among the several classes of content variables those variables that seem the most promising on the basis of knowledge already accumulated. Once these are selected, the process theory provides the basis for hypotheses, directs attention to the most likely antecedents and consequences, and indicates the empirical data needed to test hypotheses.

THE MEASUREMENT OF
PERSONALITY CONSTRUCTS

Perhaps it is in the area of personality measurement that SLT has made its most substantial and systematic contributions. Although new statistical techniques for analysis of test responses have flourished, it is still impossible to devise a useful test without an adequate theory of the nature of the characteristic that is being measured and an analysis of the determinants of test-taking behavior. The same is true of validation procedures. What a test can and cannot predict should be determined according to some laws, not be merely a matter of luck or trial and error.

I have believed for many years that the inconsistency and lack of predictiveness of so many personality measures is the result of avoidable conceptual errors in test construction and validation. Some examples of such errors are as follows:

1. A thematic apperception test that probably measures need values fails to predict choice behavior (need potential).
2. A questionnaire containing some behavior potential, some expectancy, and some reinforcement value items provides a mixed and low set of predictors for a variety of criteria.
3. A questionnaire measuring frequency of behaviors but paying no attention to situation sampling predicts some behavioral criteria but not others perceived as equally logical.
4. An atheoretical or "empirical" test that keys items to a single criterion but makes no analysis of the situational variables influencing the criterion behavior provides little or no consistent prediction to other *apparently* similar criteria.

The strength of SLT lies in the fact that it regards the test-taking behavior; the format, instructions, and test items; and the criterion all from the same theoretical perspective.

A tendency to respond to test items with a response that one thinks will elicit social approval from the examiner or people in general is not error to be controlled but, rather, information that will provide a basis for determining the conditions under which the test scores will predict behavior. Conceiving of social approval as one of many reinforcements in the situation changes our conception of the variables to be measured. The variable to be measured may bear a strong relationship to social approval as a motive; therefore, attempts to exclude social approval or reduce its influence to zero may actually eliminate powerful referents needed to make an adequate test in the first place. Finally, if we do eliminate social approval from the items or from the test procedure, then it should be eliminated also from the situations for which we wish to predict. For example, if people are likely to make a more trusting verbal response because they believe that social approval calls for them to be more trusting, then in some behavioral-criterion situation they also will make a more trusting response if they believe that social approval requires that response in that situation.

Another contribution of social learning theory to understanding the principles involved in test construction lies in the concept of the *additive* test in contrast to the *power* test. Although additive tests have been constructed, often they have lacked any clear or explicit theoretical justification. Often the purpose of a test is to provide cross-situational generality or to make predictions in a variety of different situations. The notion of a population of referents for a construct leads naturally to sampling of referents in order to obtain a general measure. The I-E Control Scale and the Interpersonal Trust Scale were constructed on this principle. Rather than working on a narrow or highly specific variable in which the items differ in degree or power, the attempt is to make the items of more or less equivalent power and to sample a broad variety of different kinds of situations. Such tests are useful for particular kinds of applications, as well as for measures of theoretical variables in order to test a series of hypotheses. Additive tests also have different characteristics than do power tests. It may be expected that the intercorrelation among items, though positive, would be low and that, consequently, measures of internal consistency would also be relatively lower than power tests.

Another logical inference from social learning theory is that what can be predicted from a test becomes a hit-or-miss proposition if one does not construct the test to measure either behavior, expectancies, or reinforcement values, rather than mixing them in unknown proportions. Goal preferences alone or expectancies alone cannot predict choice behavior efficiently. However, we may wish to measure need values to make some tests of theoretical hypotheses, or to measure generalized expectancies such as trust or internal-external control because such expectancies can lead to behavioral predictions in specific situations when additional knowledge of that situation is taken into account. Nevertheless, it does follow from social learning theory that the best predictor of a class of behaviors is behavior. The theory does lead to an implication that those tests that are likely to give the highest prediction of observed behavior are essentially work-sample tests. However, work sample tests involve only one or a few limited situations; although they may have predictive power for very similar situations, they may give lower prediction for dissimilar situations than would a very generalized test that has sampled a variety of situations. The generalized test may predict at a lower level in some situations, but it can predict for significantly more situations than can a very specific test. For example, a measure of trustworthiness based on whether or not people returned extra change they were not entitled to in a supermarket might predict with reasonable accuracy whether or not they would be honest in leaving money for newspapers on a newstand run on an "honor system." However, such a test might bear no relationship to their trustworthiness in telling their own child about their sexual behavior prior to marriage or to their willingness to cheat on an examination.

It follows from the formula for expectancy that the more novel the situation or test stimulus, the more, in relative terms, the response is determined by generalized expectancies. Therefore, if one wanted a broad measure of a generalized expectancy, more novel stimuli would provide a better measure. A college student may not have a lot of experience with Supreme Court justices, but he does have a lot of experience with his father. A questionnaire item about the truthfulness of Supreme Court justices, then, should be a more predictive item in a questionnaire designed to measure trust of people in general than would an item concerning the truthfulness of one's father. However, a more general item, such as "Most people can be relied on to tell the truth," would be better than one dealing with Supreme Court justices.

One effect of SLT has been to direct increasing attention to the importance of the psychological situation in understanding the significance of test responses. In SLT the situation provides cues for expectancies for behavior-reinforcement sequences; as the cues change, so does behavior. From a SLT point of view, not only are the examiner and place or purpose of testing situational cues; so are the instructions and the items or test stimuli. Even slight differences in instructions can produce profound effects.

A subtle and interesting implication here has to do with the utilization of projective tests (particularly those involving "novel" tasks and "unstructured" instructions) for personality measurement. It follows from the theory that when the situation is ambiguous and there are few cues to determine what behavior will be most satisfying, the subject will seek cues to provide additional information or will respond to cues that might otherwise be ignored as not significant. One would expect, therefore—and the evidence seems to bear this out (Henry & Rotter, 1956; Rotter, 1960; Masling, 1960)—that such tests would be maximally subject to slight differences in instructions, examiner characteristics, influences of the physical place of testing, and so forth. Such tests may in fact be more suitable for studying the effects of subtle cues or for studying person-situation interactions than for investigating traits or transsituational ways of responding.

The problem of generality-specificity is related to this discussion of test construction and validation. At what levels of generality should the student, clinician, or applied social scientist work or think about his or her problem? It has been demonstrated that the more specific the categories one works with, the higher the degree of prediction one can generate from one situation to another. To predict whether or not an individual will study for a particular examination in a psychology class, a general measure of "achievement need" based on the evaluation of the content of stories he or she tells to a set of pictures could not possibly achieve the same level of prediction as could a measure based on a concept of need to obtain a high grade in psychology and measuring how much the student studied for the previous examination. *The broader the concepts we work with, the*

less predictability from one randomly selected referent to another.
The same is true if we are speaking of situation similarity or situational categories. Attempts to predict defensive behavior using a broad classification of "frustration situations" will produce much less accuracy in predicting from one randomly selected referent to another than the use of more specific categories such as "love rejection" or "arbitrary failure" as the basis for assuming a constancy of behavioral response.

It must be clear that there is no single answer to the question of how specific our descriptive variables should be. A theoretical approach that is highly general in its description of individual differences will fail to make many important discriminations among individuals (Will this individual benefit more from a male than a female therapist? Will the person show hostility to everyone or only to authority figures? Will he or she show hostility to all authority figures or only to those who use overt dominance behaviors? On the other hand, if we wish to study interpersonal trust, do we need one measure for interpersonal trust of doctors, another for interpersonal trust of lawyers, another for interpersonal trust of high school teachers, and still another for interpersonal trust of college teachers? Obviously, this depends on the scientist's purposes. Not only must he or she choose the variables that are most relevant to study the problem of interest, but the psychologist must also choose a level of generality that is most efficient for his or her purposes. The theory must provide potential classes of content variables and the alternative of selecting specific variables at any level of generality, provided functional utility can be demonstrated. The same rules that apply to the selection of any broad or highly general variable apply to the selection of much more specific variables.

APPLICATIONS OF SOCIAL LEARNING THEORY
TO PROBLEMS OF SOCIAL SIGNIFICANCE

What constitutes an application and what a pure or theoretical contribution? As with many other attempts to classify, there are no clear-cut categories, only points along a continuum that can be identified. Differences are relative. However, in this section I shall try to review direct applications to problems considered important by nonpsychologists. These areas include general contributions to the practice of psychotherapy; specific contributions to the understanding and treatment of problems such as depression and deviant behavior—alcoholism, drug addiction, and delinquency—of adolescents and adults; and contributions to increasing the potential to acquire skills and better one's life by changing attitudes toward internal versus external control in education, counseling, job retraining, and medical rehabilitation. Another example would be sensitizing people to the importance of increasing interpersonal trust if our society is to remain healthy or (depending on one's current assessment of our society) become healthy.

I do not intend to repeat here the material already included in the articles presented earlier on I-E control, psychotherapy, and trust, but only to mention some applications not covered in those articles.

In the area of psychotherapy the contributions to practice are of two kinds. The first of these was the early description of psychotherapy as a cognitive learning process with an emphasis on the importance of changing expectancies. Later developments in behavior modification derived from Hull and Skinner were partly influenced by the SLT attempt to use learning theory systematically in accomplishing therapeutic change. Still later developments in behavior-modification methods that recognized expectancy effects on outcome and the importance of self-control were more directly affected by this social learning theory, as was the present interest in cognitive behavior modification. Of particular importance here was the early work of Efran and Marcia (1972), which dramatically showed the importance of expectancy effects in what was regarded as a simple conditioning phenomenon of "curing" snake phobias. Following SLT clinical hypotheses, Strickland and Crowne (1963) and Piper, Wogan, and Getter (1972) have done studies that lead to very clear suggestions for avoiding the problems of early termination in psychotherapy.

There are more specific techniques in the area of psychotherapy that, at least when they were first described, were uniquely emphasized in social learning theory (that is, as uniquely as is possible in psychology). These include successive structuring; lowering of minimal goals; insight into the long-term consequences of defensive behavior; and, most important, the teaching of interpersonal problem-solving techniques. Attempts to increase generalized expectancies for constructive problem solving are described in an article (Rotter, 1978) not included in this book.

Allen et al. (1976) have applied one of these generalized expectancies for problem solving, namely "looking for alternatives," very successfully to a large-scale intervention in the school system. Rappaport (1977) has made extensive use of SLT in a comprehensive approach to problems in community psychology. Attempts at increasing internal control have been taken up extensively by national governments, education systems, and psychotherapists for a host of specific problems.

Several of my former students have made important contributions to the area of child development. Their studies have great practical significance in identifying parental behavior as it relates to the development of need values and need potential in their children (Tyler, Rafferty, & Tyler, 1962; Tyler, Tyler, & Rafferty, 1961), especially in the area of achievement (Battle, 1965, 1966; Chance, 1961; Crandall & Battle, 1970; Crandall, 1963; Crandall et al., 1964).

Of course, the greatest number of applications of SLT concern the work in internal versus external control. Some articles provide psychotherapists with specific suggestions for increasing clients' sense of being able to control their own destiny, at least in part. Another series of studies has shown that individuals with a stronger sense of their own control do better in psychotherapeutic approaches that involve more active participation on their own parts, whereas externals do better with approaches in which they are more passive. Other investigations have indicated that increased internality is related to positive outcome in psychotherapy, and still others have shown that elderly people with more internal attitudes are better able to cope with the problems of aging. Usually these studies deal with populations that are, on the whole, external in their beliefs; the dangers of too much internality have not really been investigated.

Perhaps the most useful and well-replicated application of this work has been in the field of medical rehabilitation (Strickland, 1978; Wallston, Maider & Wallston, 1976). A surprising number of such studies have been reported, from Seeman and Evans's (1962) early work on tuberculosis to recent studies on surgical patients, post–heart attack patients, dialysis patients, cancer victims, and people with high blood pressure. All these studies indicate that patients with more internal attitudes do more to aid their own recovery and recover faster or function better. Many of these studies are being conducted by graduate nurses, and the importance of working on I-E control attitudes is now well established in nursing training.

Applications of the work on interpersonal trust are less obvious. An article on the perceived trustworthiness of twenty selected occupations (Rotter & Stein, 1971), prior to Watergate, received considerable publicity in all the news media because it indicated clearly that politicians were second only to used car salesmen in being distrusted by the general public. It may have been a coincidence that trust appeared to become a more frequent theme in political speeches. Whether or not politicians' awareness of public distrust has made them any more trustworthy is an open question.

With the exception of my early work on stuttering, it is my students rather than myself who have tried to apply SLT to problems of deviance and psychopathology. Some outstanding examples include Jessor and Jessor's (1977) work on alcohol and drug usage of adolescents and young adults, Phares's (1972) general analysis of psychopathological syndromes, Cromwell's (1963) analysis of the problems of the mentally retarded, and Zuroff's (1980) analysis of the nature of depression.

FUTURE DEVELOPMENTS IN SOCIAL LEARNING THEORY

I hope that both the theory and the applications of this social learning theory will continue to grow. There are several areas of research and application that I see as necessary for increasing the predictive value of the theory and as having a strong potential for useful application. I would like to mention briefly five areas that currently interest me.

The first of these is the study of defensive behavior. Although it is abundantly clear that people repress many things, it is equally clear that some people repress their failures and traumas to a much lesser degree than others do. It is doubtful that there are genes for repression, withdrawal, rationalization, obsessive thinking, reaction formation, excessive fantasy, and the like. What are the antecedents for acquiring such cognitive behaviors? How generalized is projection as an individual characteristic? A broadly useful approach to psychotherapy has to provide the answers to these questions. Such defensive behaviors are the "symptoms" of the presumed psychopathological syndromes many clinicians deal with. Understanding the antecedents and generality of defensive behavior would lead to newer and better ways of understanding and dealing with psychopathology.

The issues surrounding negative and positive states of the organism also require more empirical and theoretical development in social learning theory. There are, of course, many theories and many studies of emotions and emotional behavior; but the concept is so badly mired in dualism, disagreement, and confusion that I prefer to deal with the *psychological* concept of pleasurable and painful states of the organism that follow from or are associated with strong positive or negative reinforcement or their anticipation. The work of Lazarus (1968) and Schachter (1966) strongly suggest that emotional behavior is determined in part by labeling, which in turn is determined at least in part by situational cues. A host of individual difference variables need to be investigated here, and important studies remain to be done of the antecedents of stable individual differences in behavior associated with such states of the organism.

An area that has been neglected is the other side of the coin from defensive behavior and negative emotional states. Whereas expectations of negative reinforcement are cues for defensive behaviors for many people, expectations of positive reinforcement may be cues for enhancement behavior. It seems reasonable, both intuitively and clinically, that there are people who are happy, content, and in a good mood much of the time, and that the objective circumstances of such people may not differ markedly from those of others who are mildly unhappy, discontent, or worried about bad things that might happen. Although these differences may be accounted for in part by past history of reinforcements and minimal goal levels, it seems likely that there are specific cognitive activities that are used to enhance and maintain a good feeling. Such behaviors might include imaginative rehearsal of good outcomes, conscious resistance to the raising of minimal goals, and a search for long-term positive effects of currently difficult or uncomfortable conditions. In many situations that are mixed, in that they provide both negative and positive reinforcements, individuals may attend to the positive aspects and perhaps suppress the negative ones; they may search the negative aspects for positive outcomes (for example, a frustration may provide good experience for future decisions); and they may consciously increase their assessment (expectation) of long-term positive outcomes and reduce their assessment of long-term negative outcomes. I am aware that some of the behaviors listed here are often regarded as defenses and distortions that are "unhealthy," but they may not be. Even repression, if it is successful and if one discounts the psychoanalytic hypothesis of stored energy, may be an adjustive device necessary to deal with conflicts and problems of living in a complex and conflict-ridden society.

Since I have abandoned as nonproductive the search for some omnibus classification of all psychological situations, the problem that remains is to identify situational variables in order to predict behavior across situations with practically significant levels of accuracy. This requires the systematic analysis of dimensions of similarity for some limited class of situations when one is studying a particular set of behaviors for a particular purpose. Jessor and Jessor (1977) have done this for drinking and drug-taking behavior. Although there has been much research on situational factors in personality testing, most studies either were designed only to show the importance of situational factors or have dealt with only a single dimension. A systematic analysis of the psychological-testing situation is still needed, as are studies of the interactions of the many variables involved.

The same can be said for the psychotherapy situation or situations involving trust, internal-external control, and so forth. The significance of situational variables has been demonstrated; we have reached a point at which long-term programmatic research on situational variables for practically important problems is badly needed.

Finally, an area of research that seems important is the study of the efficacy of the problem-solving approach to psychotherapy. Such studies are difficult but not impossible. The method advocated of strengthening, teaching, or correcting generalized expectancies for problem solving (Rotter, 1978) does not lend itself to simple cookbook formulas. To apply this approach requires flexibility and problem-solving strategies on the part of the therapist. Some beginnings have been made, but much more remains to be done.

NOTE

1. M. Krugman. The generality of ambivalence as a psychological defense mechanism. Masters Thesis, University of Connecticut, in progress.

REFERENCES

Allen, G. J., Chinsky, J. M., Larcen, S. W., Lochman, J. E., & Selinger, H. V. *Community psychology and the schools.* Hillsdale, N.J.: Lawrence Erlbaum Associates, 1976.

Battle, E. S. Motivational determinants of academic task persistence. *Journal of Personality and Social Psychology,* 1965, *2,* 209–218.

Battle, E. S. Motivational determinants of academic competence. *Journal of Personality and Social Psychology,* 1966, *4,* 634–642.

Birney, R. C., Burdick, H., & Teevan, R. C. *Fear of failure motivation.* New York: Wiley, 1969.

Chance, J. E. Independence training and first graders' achievement. *Journal of Consulting Psychology,* 1961, *25,* 149–154.

Crandall, V. C., & Battle, E. S. The antecedents and adult correlates of academic and intellectual achievement efforts. In J. P. Hill (Ed.), *Minnesota Symposia on Child Psychology.* Vol. 4. Minneapolis: University of Minnesota Press, 1970.

Crandall, V. C., Dewey, R., Katkovsky, W., & Preston, A. Parents' attitudes and behaviors and grade-school children's academic achievement. *Journal of Genetic Psychology,* 1964, *104,* 53–66.

Crandall, V. J. Achievement. In H. W. Stenson, J. Kagan, and C. Spiker (Eds.), *Child psychology.* The 62nd yearbook of the National Society for the Study of Education. Chicago: University of Chicago Press, 1963.

Cromwell, R. L. A social learning approach to mental retardation. In N. R. Ellis (Ed.), *Handbook of mental deficiency*. New York: McGraw-Hill, 1963.

Crowne, D. P., & Liverant, S. Conformity under varying conditions of personal commitment. *Journal of Abnormal and Social Psychology*, 1963, *66*, 547–555.

Crowne, D. P., & Marlowe, D. A. *The approval motive*. New York: Wiley, 1964.

Davis, D. E. Internal-external control and defensiveness. Unpublished doctoral dissertation, Kansas State University, 1970.

Efran, J. S., & Korn, P. R. Measurement of social caution: Self-appraisal, role playing, and discussion of behavior. *Journal of Consulting and Clinical Psychology*, 1969, *33*, 78–83.

Efran, J. S., & Marcia, J. E. Systematic desensitization and social learning. In J. B. Rotter, J. E. Chance, & E. J. Phares (Eds.), *Applications of a social learning theory of personality*. New York: Holt, Rinehart and Winston, 1972.

Feather, N. T. Valence of success and failure in relation to task difficulty: Past research and recent progress. *Australian Journal of Psychology*, 1968, *20*, 111–122.

Ford, L. H., Jr. Reaction to failure as a function of expectancy for success. *Journal of Abnormal and Social Psychology*, 1963, *67*, 340–348.

Halpin, A. W., & Winer, B. J. Studies in aircrew composition: The leadership behavior of the airplane commander. Technical Report No. 3, Columbus: Personnel Research Board, Ohio State University, 1952.

Henry, E. M., & Rotter, J. B. Situational influences on Rorschach responses. *Journal of Consulting Psychology*, 1956, *20*, 457–462.

Hochreich, D. J. Defensive externality and attribution of responsibility. *Journal of Personality*, 1974, *42*, 543–557.

Hochreich, D. J. Defensive externality and blame projection following failure. *Journal of Personality and Social Psychology*, 1975, *32*, 540–546.

Hochreich, D. J. Defensive externality and level of aspiration. *Journal of Consulting and Clinical Psychology*, 1978, *46*, 177–178.

Jessor, R., & Jessor, S. L. *Problem behavior and psychosocial development: A longitudinal study of youth*. New York: Academic Press, 1977.

Lazarus, R. S. Emotions and adaptation: Conceptual and empirical relations. In W. J. Arnold (Ed.), *Nebraska symposium on motivation*. Lincoln: University of Nebraska Press, 1968.

Masling, J. The influence of situational and interpersonal variables in projective testing, *Psychological Bulletin*, 1960, *57*, 65–85.

Mischel, W., & Masters, J. C. Effects of probability of reward attainment on responses to frustration. *Journal of Personality and Social Psychology*, 1966, *3*, 390–396.

Mosher, D. L. Measurement of guilt in females in self-report inventories. *Journal of Consulting and Clinical Psychology*, 1968, *32*, 690–695.

Mosher, D. L., Mortimer, R. L., & Grebel, M. Verbal aggressive behavior in delinquent boys. *Journal of Abnormal Psychology*, 1968, *73*, 454–460.

Moss, H. A. The influence of personality and situational cautiousness on conceptual behavior. *Journal of Abnormal and Social Psychology*, 1961, *63*, 629–635.

Phares, E. J. A social learning theory approach to psychopathology. In J. B. Rotter, J. E. Chance, & E. J. Phares (Eds.), *Applications of a social learning theory of personality*. New York: Holt, Rinehart and Winston, 1972.

Piper, W. E., Wogan, W., & Getter, H. Social learning theory predictors of termination in psychotherapy. In J. B. Rotter, J. E. Chance, & E. J. Phares (Eds.), *Applications of a social learning theory of personality*. New York: Holt, Rinehart and Winston, 1972.

Rappaport, J. *Community psychology: Values, research and action*. New York: Holt, Rinehart and Winston, 1977.

Rettig, S. An exploratory study of altruism. Unpublished doctoral dissertation, Ohio State University, 1956.

Rotter, J. B. Some implications of a social learning theory for the prediction of goal directed behavior from testing procedures. *Psychological Review*, 1960, *67*, 301–316.

Rotter, J. R. Generalized expectancies for problem solving and psychotherapy. *Cognitive Therapy and Research*, 1978, *2*, 1–10.

Rotter, J. B., & Stein, D. K. Public attitudes toward the trustworthiness, competence, and altruism of twenty selected occupations. *Journal of Applied Social Psychology*, 1971, *1*, 334–343.

Schachter, S. The interaction of cognitive and physiological determinants of emotional state. In C. D. Spielberger (Ed.), *Anxiety and behavior*. New York: Academic Press, 1966.

Seeman, M., & Evans, J. W. Alienation and learning in a hospital setting. *American Sociological Review*, 1962, *27*, 772–783.

Strickland, B. R. Internal-external expectancies and health-related behaviors. *Journal of Consulting and Clinical Psychology*, 1978, *46*, 1192–1211.

Strickland, B. R., & Crowne, D. P. Need for approval and the premature termination of psychotherapy. *Journal of Consulting Psychology*, 1963, *27*, 95–101.

Tyler, F. B., Rafferty, J. E., & Tyler, B. B. Relationships among motivations of parents and their children. *Journal of Genetic Psychology*, 1962, *101*, 69–81.

Tyler, F. B., Tyler, B. B., & Rafferty, J. E. Need value and expectancy interrelations as assessed from motivational patterns of parents and their children. *Journal of Consulting Psychology*, 1961, *25*, 304–311.

Wallston, K. A., Maides, S., & Wallston, B. S. Health-related information seeking as a function of health-related locus of control and health value. *Journal of Research in Personality*, 1976, *10*, 215–222.

Zuroff, D. C. Learned helplessness in humans: An analysis of learning processes and the roles of individual and situational differences. *Journal of Personality and Social Psychology*, 1980, *39*, 130–146.

13
Brief Biography of the Author

Many professional biographies of scientists begin with an acknowledgment to an outstanding teacher who first interested and excited the writer in a field of intellectual inquiry. In my own case I have to make that acknowledgment to the Avenue J Library in Brooklyn, New York. In both grade school and high school I was an omnivorous and not too discriminating reader. One day during my junior year in high school, when I could find no new fiction to read, I wandered over to the shelf labeled "Philosophy and Psychology." There weren't too many books there, but some of the titles seemed interesting.

I do not remember the order in which I read them, but the first three books I took out were Adler's *Understanding Human Nature,* Freud's *Psychopathology of Everyday Life,* and Menninger's *Human Mind.* The first two impressed me clearly, and I followed these with Adler's *Practice and Theory of Individual Psychology* and Freud's *Interpretation of Dreams.* In my senior year in high school I was interpreting other people's dreams and wrote a senior thesis entitled "Why We Make Mistakes."

By the time I entered Brooklyn College, I was seriously interested in psychology. I found that Adler's insights into human nature made a great deal of sense in my efforts to understand myself and the people around me. But there was no profession of psychology that I knew of; and in 1933, the depths of the Great Depression, one majored in a subject one could use to make a living. In general, I was a good student in science and math, and I had earned some honors in biology and chemistry. Chemistry seemed my best bet for earning a living, so I chose that as my major. My primary interest, however, remained in psychology and philosophy; I took all my electives in these two subjects, completing my B.A. with more credits in psychology than in chemistry. In retrospect, however, the hard science background, along with courses in vertebrate biology, logic, epistemology, and math, were an excellent preparation for graduate training in psychology.

At Brooklyn College the staff in psychology was young and enthusiastic. Two teachers in particular influenced my development as a psychologist. Austin B. Wood's lectures on the scientific method were inspiring, and Solomon Asch introduced me to the fascinating controversy between Gestalt and Thorndikian approaches to learning theory. It was Asch, also, who got me interested in the work of Kurt Lewin. The honesty and involvement of both of these teachers made me consider a possible career in teaching psychology.

When I began my junior year in college, I discovered that Alfred Adler had come to the United States and had accepted a chair in medical psychology at Long Island School of Medicine, whose campus was in downtown Brooklyn. Adler, a socialist, left Vienna on short notice after the socialist government fell, when Vienna was no longer a healthy place for socialists to work and thrive. Adler taught his course to medical students at the third-year level; but at the request of fourth-year students, he gave a similar course to seniors and faculty at night. I began to attend these lectures. Once, when I stayed after the lecture to ask a question, he invited me to attend the clinic demonstration he gave each week at the medical school. I explained that I was not a medical student, which did not seem to bother Adler. Eventually this led to invitations to attend his child and family clinic in uptown Manhattan and monthly meetings of the Society of Individual Psychology in his home. Unfortunately, Adler died in the summer of 1937, the year that I was graduated from college. With no money and no job, I planned to stay in New York, try to find a job, and continue my studies at night wherever I could. Adler's death, talks with Asch and Wood, and the presence of Kurt Lewin at the University of Iowa convinced me at least to attempt to go there and see if I could survive financially. With round-trip railroad coach fare of about $25.00 and tuition of about $35.00, I could survive two or three weeks on the money left over from a summer job as a camp counselor.

Lee Travis, chairman of the psychology department, told me sympathetically but definitely that all psychology department funds were gone, and I soon learned that no other job was available in Iowa City. Nevertheless, I decided to stay there until my money ran out. I did get to know Travis better—mainly on the tennis court—and after two weeks he managed to find $200 for a part-time research assistantship. So began my graduate career as a psychologist.

The year at Iowa was profitable in many ways. Kurt Lewin's course, which focused on his theory, and his weekly seminar dealing with current research generated excitement and controversy. His basic interactionism and purely psychological approach influenced me greatly, although I was somewhat surprised at the scant attention Lewin and his students paid to individual differences. I also came to disagree with his belief that psychology was or could be an ahistorical science.

Wendell Johnson, whose main interest was in stuttering, was a general semanticist, a follower of Korzybski. Johnson viewed stuttering as a semantic problem; from him I learned about abstractions, referents, and the problems that arise when two or more people use the same words but have different meanings in mind. Herbert Feigl's excellent and exciting seminar on the philosophy of science consolidated my interest in theory building in psychology.

My own first research study (Rotter, 1938) was an investigation of stuttering and position in the family, undertaken from an Adlerian point of view. My master's thesis, with Lee Travis as my advisor and Wendell Johnson as a committee member, was undertaken as a test of Travis's theory of lack of cerebral dominance as the main cause of stuttering. It was not surprising that, with Travis committed to an organic theory and Johnson to a psychological theory of etiology, the results of this study of the motor integration of young adult stutterers were ultimately interpreted as equivocal.

Toward the end of the year at Iowa I learned that applications were being accepted for an internship in clinical psychology at Worcester State Hospital. The notion of an internship in clinical psychology was a new one at that time. Lee Travis was leaving Iowa, and, although I could have had a full assistantship with Wendell Johnson, the internship opportunity seemed too intriguing to pass up.

I knew nothing about Worcester State Hospital when I arrived there in the fall of 1938. As far as I knew, no other institution in the country offered a formal internship, and very few universities offered the Ph.D. degree with a major in clinical psychology. David Shakow was chief psychologist at Worcester, and the staff included Eliot Rodnick and Saul Rosensweig. It was an important center of research and training in both psychology and psychiatry.

At Worcester I began my work on level of aspiration, which later evolved into my dissertation. I also began research with the TAT, using an early experimental set of pictures of H. A. Murray's that Saul Rosensweig had shown me. Within psychiatry, psychoanalytic, disease entity, and organic approaches to psychopathology battled for dominance as explanations of etiology. Although none of these approaches satisfied me, the controversy was exciting. To my good fortune I met at Worcester and later married Clara Barnes, one of the other interns.

In 1936 C. M. Louttit, a professor at Indiana University, had written a textbook entitled *Clinical Psychology* that identified a field of application involving the diagnosis and treatment of psychological disorders of all kinds in children and adults. The book summarized existing data and attempted a kind of integrated approach to topics ranging from speech problems in children to adult psychoses. Because of this book, I applied to Indiana for my Ph.D. work and in 1939 was given an assistantship with Louttit, working in the university's psychological clinic.

C. M. Louttit was my dissertation advisor. His method of teaching was essentially a willingness to discuss anything at any time in an open and egalitarian manner. Although he contributed much to my intellectual growth, as friend and advisor he contributed even more to my personal growth. At this time J. R. Kantor was very influential at Indiana on both staff and students. Courses with Kantor furthered my education in philosophy of science and the nature of theory in psychology. My dissertation was on level of aspiration; it included a series of studies begun at Worcester State Hospital and continued throughout my two years at Indiana, where I completed my work in 1941.

At Brooklyn College and again in graduate school, I had been warned that Jews simply could not get academic jobs, regardless of their credentials. The warnings seemed justified. There were few academic positions open in 1941; except for one job, teaching at a branch of a midwestern university, I was unable to obtain a position. However, I was interested in clinical work as well as in research and teaching, and I was hired as a clinical psychologist at Norwich State Hospital, where I remained for thirteen months before going into the Army. At that time the University of Connecticut and Wesleyan University both had M.A. programs that included a year's internship at Norwich State Hospital, and my job included the training of the interns and assistants. Although I had taught a course on personality at Indiana University, this was my first experience in one-to-one, long-term teaching. I found it very satisfying. For me, it is still the most rewarding part of my professional experience.

I entered the army as a private (having failed a year earlier to obtain a commission in the navy because of partial red-green color blindness). However, after a month I was transferred to the Armored School at Fort Knox to work in the "Office of the Military Psychologist." Except for seventeen weeks of training in Officer Candidate School as an armored officer, I spent the rest of my three and a quarter years in the army and air force working as a psychologist. The military psychologist at Fort Knox was Milton B. Jensen, a Stanford Ph.D. who had worked with Terman and who had the complete confidence of the commanding general of the Armored School. Our job was to see every individual who had charges preferred against him or who was being considered for discharge for psychological reasons, and to make recommendations regarding overall problems of the school and officer candidate selection.

Since our recommendations were almost always carried out, it was a remarkable, informal field study of the value of environmental treatment of young adults. I found the results astonishing. A set of recommendations for reducing AWOL—a serious problem among base personnel—were followed to the letter and succeeded in reducing AWOL to less than 25 percent of its former rate in a two-month period. Students failing in their courses could show remarkable changes as a result of simply being allowed a three-day pass to go home to settle a personal problem not officially recognized by the army as meriting special consideration. Drunkenness and AWOL by soldiers on permanent kitchen duty was reduced remarkably when the status of their jobs was increased and their working conditions improved. The range of problems that could be dealt with by environmental manipulation was extensive, and I learned the lesson well.

In true army fashion, after long and expensive training as a tank officer, I was transferred to the air force, where I again was involved in diagnostic and selection work in Air Force convalescent hospitals. It was in this capacity that I developed the Incomplete Sentences Blank as a selection and clinical test.

World War II produced many psychological casualties but had few trained people to deal with them. Psychologists in the armed forces apparently proved their usefulness to the medical profession. Consequently, shortly after the war, first the Veterans' Administration and then the U.S. Public Health Service began to support Ph.D. training in clinical psychology. The result was a rapid expansion of academic positions in clinical psychology, often accompanied by much internal stress within university psychology departments as the dominant experimental psychologists clashed with the upstart clinicians.

As one of the relatively few Ph.D. psychologists trained as a clinical psychologist in 1946, I found myself sought after for academic positions. After a brief return to Norwich State Hospital in

Connecticut, I went to Ohio State University as an assistant professor. It was a happy, productive, and rewarding situation for me. I was soon heavily involved in teaching, research, regional and national psychological organizations, and consultation with government agencies.

During my army days I had been attempting to integrate current learning theory and personality theory in my spare time, and at Ohio State I set to work more systematically to construct a social learning theory of personality. Weekly meetings with a group of bright, dedicated, and otherwise marvelous graduate students were an important part of the process. Also of great help was my friend and colleague Delos D. Wickens, from whom I continued to learn about the data and current thinking of learning theorists. On the "softer" side, a close association with Melvin Seeman, a sociologist, kept me involved in broader social constructs and social issues.

C. M. Louttit had gone into the navy and from there to Ohio State University as director of their psychological clinic and training program. When he left after one year, George A. Kelly came in to replace him. Along with Victor Raimy, we developed a training program based on the Boulder model. If success of an educational program can be measured by the prominence of its graduates, it was a highly successful program. Our philosophy was to provide the student with as many different theoretical approaches as possible in an atmosphere of friendly controversy. We paid more than lip service to the notion that a clinical psychologist was first a psychologist and then a clinician; we placed a heavy emphasis on understanding theory and research methods as well as clinical practice.

When George Kelly gave up the clinical directorship in 1951, I took it on. This made little difference in the program, however, since we continued to work in reasonable harmony as a congenial committee of all the clinical faculty, including at different times my valued colleagues and friends Boyd McCandless, Paul Mussen, Alvin Scodel, and Shepherd Liverant. The usual conflict between clinical psychology and experimental or general psychology did not develop at Ohio State, partly because we insisted that clinical students be broadly trained; and no time or effort was wasted in fighting with one's colleagues. Most of my own time was spent in directing dissertations and masters theses, and it was primarily through this research that social learning theory was tested and modified.

Ohio State did not provide sabbaticals, but several times I took leave to teach elsewhere as a visiting professor, sometimes for a summer and sometimes for the full academic year. In this way I continued to interact with and learn from colleagues in many institutions, including the University of Minnesota, the University of Colorado, the University of California at Berkeley, UCLA, and the University of Pennsylvania.

McCarthyism found fertile soil in central Ohio; although it did not affect the day-to-day work of the psychology department, both in the city of Columbus and in the university administration the attempts to suppress radical ideas were a constant irritation. Partly because of this and partly because of a desire to return to New England, I left Ohio State in 1963 to come to the University of Connecticut to direct the clinical training program they were in the process of rebuilding.

With the move to Connecticut, the emphasis of my writing and research changed in some subtle way. It has been a period devoted mostly to consolidation of previous ideas and application. The earlier work on I-E was consolidated into a monograph, and I began work on interpersonal trust more with a view toward application than toward new theoretical development. Nevertheless, I have continued to expand on and revise previous theoretical conceptions. I have also become more involved in national and regional organizations.

I continued my work in selection with the Peace Corps. During these years I served a second term on the APA Education and Training Board and APA Council, as well as a term on the psychology training committees of the United States Public Health Service. I also served terms as president of the APA Division of Social and Personality Psychology, the APA Division of Clinical Psychology, and the Eastern Psychological Association.

The clinical program developed at the University of Connecticut continued the Boulder Model and still does, although many schools have opted for programs and degrees emphasizing the practitioner role at the expense of the scholar and scientist role, a development I consider premature and mistaken. Like Ohio State, Connecticut has provided a congenial and productive atmosphere, where students and colleagues have been helpful and stimulating.

Since this book is dedicated to my students, it is appropriate that this professional biography should end with a further acknowledgment of them. It is not my intention here to list the names of the over one hundred students whose master's theses and/or doctoral dissertations I have directed, or to mention some and slight others. They all provided stimulation, criticism, enthusiasm, and friendship throughout my career. I can only hope that they obtained from me as much as I have obtained from them.

Publications:
A Comprehensive Bibliography

1938

Studies in the psychology of stuttering XI. Stuttering in relation to position in the family. *Journal of Speech Disorders, 3,* 143–148.

1940

1. Studies in the use and validity of the Thematic Apperception Test with mentally disordered patients. I. Method of analysis and clinical problems. *Character and Personality, 9,* 118–134.
2. With E. H. Rodnick. A study of the reactions to experimentally induced frustration (Abstract). *Psychological Bulletin, 37,* 577.

1942

1. Level of aspiration as a method of studying personality. I. A critical review of metholdology. *Psychological Review, 49,* 463–474.
2. Level of aspiration as a method of studying personality. II. Development and evaluation of a controlled method. *Journal of Experimental Psychology, 31,* 410–422.

1943

Level of aspiration as a method of studying personality. III. Group validity studies. *Character and Personality, 11,* 254–274.

1944

The nature and treatment of stuttering: A clinical approach. *Journal of Abnormal and Social Psychology, 39,* 150–173.

1945

1. Level of aspiration as a method of studying personality. IV. Patterns of responses. *Journal of Social Psychology, 21,* 159–177.
2. With R. Harrison. A note on the reliability of the Thematic Apperception Test. *Journal of Abnormal and Social Psychology, 40,* 97–99.
3. With M. B. Jensen. The validity of the Multiple Choice Rorschach Test in officer candidate selection. *Psychological Bulletin, 42,* 192–193.
4. With M. B. Jensen & R. Harrison. Military psychology in the Armored School. *Psychological Bulletin, 42,* 91–97.

1946

Thematic Apperception Tests: Suggestions for administration and interpretation. *Journal of Personality, 15,* 70–92.

1947

1. With M. B. Jensen. The value of thirteen psychological tests in officer candidate screening. *Journal of Applied Psychology, 31,* 312–322.
2. With B. Willerman. The Incomplete Sentence Test as a method of studying personality. *Journal of Consulting Psychology, 11,* 43–48.

1948

1. The present status of the Rorschach in clinical and experimental procedures. *Journal of Personality, 16,* 304–311.
2. With D. D. Wickens. The consistency and generality of ratings of "social aggressiveness" made from observation of role playing situations. *Journal of Consulting Psychology, 12,* 234–239.

1949

With J. E. Rafferty & B. Schachtitz. Validation of the Rotter Incomplete Sentences Blank for college screening. *Journal of Consulting Psychology, 13*(5), 348–356.

1950

With J. E. Rafferty. *The Rotter Incomplete Sentences Blank Manual: College form.* New York: Psychological Corporation.

1951

1. Word association and sentence completion methods. In H. H. Anderson & G. L. Anderson (Eds.), *An introduction to projective techniques.* New York: Prentice-Hall.
2. With S. Jessor. The TAT of John Doe. In H. S. Schneidman (Ed.), *Thematic test analysis.* New York: Grune and Stratton.

1952

With H. M. Schroder. Rigidity as learned behavior. *Journal of Experimental Psychology, 44,* 141–150.

1953

1. Clinical methods: Psychodiagnostics. In C. Stone (Ed.), *Annual review of psychology.* (Vol. 4) Stanford, Calif.: Annual Reviews, Inc.
2. With E. M. Bruner. A level of aspiration study among the Ramah Navaho. *Journal of Personality, 21,* 375–385.

1954

1. *Social learning and clinical psychology.* New York: Johnson Reprint Company, 1973, 1980. (Originally published, 1954).
2. With B. J. Fitzgerald & J. N. Joyce. A comparison of some objective measures of expectancy. *Journal of Abnormal and Social Psychology, 49,* 111–114.
3. With J. E. Rafferty & A. B. Lotsof. The validity of the Rotter Incomplete Sentences Blank: High School Form. *Journal of Consulting Psychology, 18,* 105–111.
4. With H. M. Schroder. Generalization of expectancy changes as a function of the nature of reinforcement. *Journal of Experimental Psychology, 48,* 343–348.

1955

1. The role of the psychological situation in determining the direction of human behavior. In M. R. Jones (Ed.), *Nebraska Symposium on Motivation,* vol. 3. Lincoln: University of Nebraska Press. Pp. 254–269.
2. A study of the motor integration of stutterers and non-stutterers. In W. Johnson (Ed.), *Stuttering in children and adults.* Minneapolis: University of Minnesota Press.

1956

1. With E. M. Henry. Situational influences on Rorschach responses. *Journal of Consulting Psychology, 20,* 457–462.
2. With E. J. Phares. An effect of the situation on psychological testing. *Journal of Consulting Psychology, 20,* 291–293.

1958

With W. James. Partial and one hundred percent reinforcement under chance and skill conditions. *Journal of Experimental Psychology, 55,* 397–403.

1960

1. Psychotherapy. In P. R. Farnsworth and Q. McNemar (Eds.), *Annual Review of Psychology* (Vol. 11) Palo Alto, Calif.: Annual Reviews, Inc.
2. Some implications of a social learning theory for the prediction of goal direcrected behavior from testing procedures. *Psychological Review, 67,* 301–316.

1961

With S. Liverant & D. P. Crowne. The growth and extinction of expectancies in chance controlled and skilled tasks. *Journal of Psychology, 52,* 161–177.

1962

1. An analysis of Adlerian Psychology from a research orientation. *Journal of Individual Psychology, 8,* 3–11.

2. With K. B. Holden. A nonverbal measure of extinction in skill and chance situations. *Journal of Experimental Psychology, 63,* 519–520.
3. With M. R. Seeman & S. Liverant. Internal versus external control of reinforcement: A major variable in behavior theory. In N. F. Washburne (Ed.), *Decisions, values and groups.* Vol. 2. London: Pergamon Press.

1963

1. An historical and theoretical analysis of broad trends in clinical psychology. In S. Koch (Ed.), *Psychology: A study of a science,* V. 5. New York: McGraw-Hill.
2. With E. S. Battle. Children's feelings of personal control as related to social class and ethnic group. *Journal of Personality, 31,* 482–490.
3. With P. M. Gore. A personality correlate of social action. *Journal of Personality, 31,* 58–64.

1964

Clinical psychology. Englewood Cliffs, N.J.: Prentice-Hall. (Rev. ed., 1971.)

1965

With R. C. Mulry. Internal versus external control of reinforcement and decision time. *Journal of Personality and Social Psychology, 2,* 598–604.

1966

Generalized expectancies for internal versus external control of reinforcement. *Psychological Monographs, 80.* (Whole No. 609).

1967

1. Beliefs, social attitudes and behavior: A social learning analysis. In R. Jessor & S. Feshbach (Eds.), *Cognition, personality and clinical psychology.* San Francisco: Jossey-Bass.
2. Can the clinician learn from experience? *Journal of Consulting Psychology, 31,* 12–15.
3. A new scale for the measurement of interpersonal trust. *Journal of Personality, 35,* 651–665.
4. Personality theory. In H. Helson and W. Bevan (Eds.), *Theories and data in psychology.* New York: VanNostrand.

1968

1. With J. H. Hamsher & J. D. Geller. Interpersonal trust, internal-external control, and the Warren Commission Report. *Journal of Personality and Social Psychology, 9,* 210–215.
2. With B. A. Henker. Effect of model characterization on children's play and task imitation. Proceedings of the 76th Annual Convention of the American Psychological Association. *American Psychologist, 23,* 341–342.

1969

With H. A. Katz. Interpersonal trust scores of college students and their parents. *Child Development, 40,* 657–661.

1970

1. Comments on Fitzgerald, Pasewark and Noah's study of the validity of the Interpersonal Trust Scale. *Psychological Reports, 26,* 517–518.
2. Report from Miami. *Clinical Psychologist, 24,* 1.
3. Some implications of a social learning theory for the practice of psycho-therapy. In D. Levis (Ed.), *Learning approaches to therapeutic behavior change.* Chicago: Aldine Press.
4. With D. J. Hochreich. Have college students become less trusting? *Journal of Personality and Social Psychology, 15,* 211–214.

1971

1. Generalized expectancies for interpersonal trust. *American Psychologist, 26,* 443–452.
2. On the evaluation of methods of intervening in other people's lives. *Clinical Psychologist, 24,* 1.
3. With D. K. Stein. Public attitudes toward the trustworthiness, competence, and altruism of twenty selected occupations. *Journal of Applied Social Psychology, 1,* 334–343.

1972

With J. E. Chance & E. J. Phares. *Applications of a social learning theory of personality.* New York: Holt, Rinehart and Winston.

1973

The future of clinical psychology. *Journal of Consulting and Clinical Psychology, 40,* 313–321.

1975

1. Some problems and misconceptions related to the construct of internal versus external control of reinforcement. *Journal of Consulting and Clinical Psychology, 43,* 56–67.
2. With D. J. Hochreich. *Personality.* Glenview, Ill.: Scott, Foresman.

1978

Generalized expectancies for problem solving and psychotherapy. *Cognitive Therapy and Research, 2,* 1–10.

1979

Individual differences in perceived control. In L. C. Perlmuter & R. A. Monty

(Eds.), *Choice and perceived control.* Hillsdale, N.J.: Lawrence Erlbaum Associates.

1980

1. Some views on effective principles of psychotherapy. In M. R. Goldfried (Ed.), Special issue: Psychotherapy process. *Cognitive Therapy and Research, 4,* 271–306.
2. Trust, trustworthiness, and gullibility. *American Psychologist, 35,* 1–7.

1981

1. The psychological situation in social learning theory. In D. Magnusson (Ed.), *Toward a psychology of situations: An interactional perspective.* Hillsdale, N.J.: Lawrence Erlbaum Associates.
2. With M. Lah. Changing college student norms on the Rotter Incomplete Sentences Blank. *Journal of Consulting and Clinical Psychology, 49,* 985.

1982

Social learning theory. In N. T. Feather (Ed.), *Expectations and actions: Expectancy-value models in psychology.* Hillsdale, N.J.: Lawrence Erlbaum Associates.

Indexes

Author Index

Subject Index